"[*Lingua Franca*] finds the life in the driest of academic precincts . . .
An insider's guide to the groves of academe, affectionate but
probing, serious but humorous, a hip trade journal for the cerebral
set."

—JANNY SCOTT, *The New York Times*

"It was a magazine that invented a new way of writing about ideas—a
new kind of journalism, really—[by] searching out the genuinely
important controversies over ideas emerging from the academic
world. Searching through the vast torrents of jargon-addled dross to
find and convey the rare excitement of real thinkers grappling with
original ideas. And exposing the sad comedy of pretentious sophists
confecting academic simulacra of real thinking."

—RON ROSENBAUM, *The New York Observer*

"The liveliest magazine in higher education."

—LOUIS FREEDBERG, *San Francisco Chronicle*

"This feisty little intellectual weathervane . . . had the rare distinction
of penetrating the American academic world and subjecting it to
criticism, satire, humour, scrutiny—to journalism . . . By recruiting
edgy young writers just out of university (and not necessarily
graduates) and asking them to tackle the academic intellectual world
with dog-with-a-bone tenacity, *Lingua Franca* proved that high ideas
are just as worthy of public scrutiny as high finance. And (big
surprise, this) more fun. *Lingua Franca* shook the professors' cage
and it made them sing."

—LUKE SLATTERY, *The Australian*

"*Lingua Franca* is that rare thing: a publication that earned its
intellectual chops with knowledgeable pieces on hot-button issues . . .
yet remained accessible to the general reader by eschewing jargon

and gratuitously polysyllabic words [and] reported on academic and cultural issues with depth and flair."

—JULIA KELLER, *Chicago Tribune*

"The most sophisticated 'in' journal of academia."

—GERTRUDE HIMMELFARB, *Commentary*

"Required reading . . . Anyone who has slogged through turgid academic pontification will find this hard to believe, but *Lingua Franca* . . . is among the liveliest journals on the shelves."

—BOB SIPCHEN, *Los Angeles Times*

"If you think hipness stops with *Vanity Fair*, *Details* and some of those unintelligible fanzines, then you haven't found *Lingua Franca*, a witty bimonthly that has been turning new readers into admirers."

—DEIRDRE DONAHUE, *USA Today*

"The self-billed 'review of academic life,' now celebrating its 10th anniversary, is respected by almost everyone who knows about it . . . *Lingua Franca*'s influence on '90s magazine culture has been so strong, it's sometimes hard to remember that it was unique in academia when it began."

—NORAH VINCENT, *The Village Voice*

"Aims its cheerfully remorseless gaze at the heretofore unpublicized workings of American universities. The magazine—irreverent, intelligent and a bit of a muckraker—regularly makes the academic establishment uncomfortable by publishing stuff that otherwise might not see the light of day."

—VINCE PASSARO, *Mirabella*

"The United States's hottest and hippest academic publication . . . With its raffish, often irreverent tone, tidbits of professional gossip and muckraking articles, *Lingua Franca* has an appeal that extends beyond the groves of the academy."

—SHIRA DICKER, *The International Herald Tribune*

Quick Studies

Quick Studies

THE BEST OF *LINGUA FRANCA*

EDITED AND INTRODUCED BY

Alexander Star

FARRAR, STRAUS AND GIROUX
NEW YORK

Farrar, Straus and Giroux
19 Union Square West, New York 10003

Distributed in Canada by Douglas & McIntyre Ltd.
Printed in the United States of America
First edition, 2002

Library of Congress Cataloging-in-Publication Data
Quick studies : the best of *Lingua Franca* / edited and introduced
   by Alexander Star.
      p. cm.
   Includes index.
   ISBN 0-374-52863-2 (pb : alk. paper)
   1. United States—Intellectual life—20th century—Sources.   2. Learning
and scholarship—United States—History—20th century—Sources.
   I. Star, Alexander, 1967–   II. Lingua Franca.

E169.12 .Q34 2002
001'.0973'0904—dc21

                                                          2002023061

Designed by Alissa Levin, Point Five Design

www.fsgbooks.com

10 9 8 7 6 5 4 3 2 1

Contents

PART VI

ARTS AND LETTERS

Introduction

ALEXANDER STAR

FOR ELEVEN YEARS, from 1990 to 2001, the editors of *Lingua Franca*
sought to put out the liveliest intellectual publication in America with
the least possible expenditure of resources. The magazine's articles
were printed on thin paper in smudgeable ink and illustrated with engravings lifted from old books. The writers were young and often inexperienced in the arts of journalism. And the quarters were always
modest. *Lingua Franca* was originally housed above a travel agency in
Mamaroneck, New York. Later it moved to a cubicle in SoHo, then
to a dusty office on the fringes of Manhattan's Garment District,
where the neighbors specialized in the sale of beads, buttons, and
feathers. A sign in the wig shop next door read, WE SELL HEADS. Unbeknownst to us, we shared the block with a brothel that catered to
police officers and a store whose basement was so full of shoes that
firemen would be unable to reach an electrical blaze that brought
down two buildings. Our doorman, a former policeman from Communist Poland, spent most of his days thinking up obscene slogans to
submit to T-shirt contests. It felt a long way from the seminar rooms
and the library stacks.

And yet those were our beat. *Lingua Franca* was the invention of
Jeffrey Kittay, a former Yale professor (and jazz pianist) with a consuming interest in the aspects of academia that get left out of its
official proceedings. Kittay had spent many years in the crowded cor-
ridors of academic conferences, and he was struck by how little of

their spirited conversation and informal intellectual discourse made it into print. In the late 1980s, he conceived of a new magazine devoted to those overlooked ephemera. Just as *The American Lawyer* had shaken up the legal profession with its frank reporting about overrated defense attorneys and overpaid partners, *Lingua Franca*—Kittay hoped—would disturb the professors by amplifying their everyday shoptalk: the catty remarks about colleagues, the tenure-committee intrigues, the confessions of bafflement over a new book or bureaucratic rule. Here one could refer to Jacques Derrida on a first-name basis and worry about one's retirement portfolio without shame. To the delight of gossips everywhere, comprehensive listings would detail who had been tenured and hired in departments around the country.

At the same time, the magazine had loftier ambitions. Its name referred to the mixed language spoken by sailors in Mediterranean ports, and Kittay hoped that the magazine would prove readily comprehensible to a similarly diverse constituency. He wanted it to speak to academics of all allegiances—as well as to former academics such as himself, to the quasi academics working at university presses, libraries, or think tanks, and to the nonacademics who wanted to know about the exciting and unseemly things being done to the great ideas and the great books behind ivy-covered walls. In *Lingua Franca*, professors could follow the infighting and negotiations that were scrubbed from the prim pages of their professional journals, and nonacademics could find a far more sophisticated treatment of ideas in the making than they typically got from their daily newspaper.

Of course, not everyone agreed that the magazine lived up to its missions. When one early article chastised the editors of *The New Criterion* for failing their own standards of literary quality and "fellating heroes of the right," a letter writer complained about *Lingua Franca*'s "gutter words": "Even in the Levant, where a mixed language is spoken, there are some things that are just not tolerated." Another writer charged that the magazine had quickly matured from "plain irreverence to Arch, Snide, and Coy." Criticism arose from the academic left as well as the right. Larissa MacFarquhar's humorous portrait of a fanzine devoted to the queer theorist Judith Butler earned an angry response from Butler herself: "*Lingua Franca* reengages that anti-intellectual aggression whereby scholars are reduced to occasions for salacious conjecture . . . rather than as writers of texts to be read and seriously debated."

Even so, the magazine quickly won a place for itself—if only because it handled topics that few editors elsewhere wanted to touch. Articles about Michel Foucault's climactic acid trip in the California desert and the sudden rise of first-person "moi criticism" at Duke attracted a certain core readership. When a prominent literary critic suggested that the "pair of ragged claws" in T. S. Eliot's "Love Song of J. Alfred Prufrock" belonged to a lobster, not a crab, *Lingua Franca* treated the story as news—which it was, at least to us. It was also news when the philosopher Roger Scruton accused the British duo the Pet Shop Boys of not playing their own instruments and was promptly sued for libel or when the editorial board of an engineering journal questioned a female scholar's credentials after she submitted a detailed article on the history of the vibrator. In the early 1990s, the news on campus revolved most often around the polarizing intellectual and political debates known as the Culture Wars. Rather than polemicize about these struggles, *Lingua Franca* looked directly at the people who were bringing them about. As a matter of journalistic principle, it focused on the means of intellectual production as well as the ends.

WHEN IT FIRST SET UP SHOP as a "review of academic life," *Lingua Franca* faced little direct competition. *The Chronicle of Higher Education* reported exhaustively on campus politics and administrative policy but displayed little interest in storytelling or explaining ideas. For the most part, journalists and academics regarded each other warily across a wide gap. Journalists were frustrated by the academic taste for abstruse terminologies, elaborately qualified arguments, and outlandish subjects. Psychologists who championed the claims of UFO abductees or literary critics who studied Jane Austen and masturbation might make for good copy, but who could take them seriously or hope to maintain a reader's interest for very long? Academics, in return, filled out a bill of complaint: Journalists had no patience for complexity. They mocked what they didn't understand. They reduced ineffable mysteries to moralistic soap opera. Even the most literate and liberal-minded reporters were hardly immune to the anti-intellectualism of American life. Refusing the terms of this standoff, *Lingua Franca* sought to occupy the no-man's-land between the tabloid and the treatise.

The time was certainly ripe. Throughout the 1980s, conservative pundits warned of a multiculturalist crusade to reshape the campus. According to their well-publicized reports, "diversity" had become the mantra of the liberal administrators and radical professors who were putting the academy in danger. The university's newest mandarins had a number of tools at their disposal: Affirmative action policies attracted unqualified students and undermined the very possibility of making impartial judgments. Questionable new courses and fields of study—women's studies, labor history, queer theory—buried the great monuments of the past. Speech codes and sexual-harassment policies targeted those who did not display the proper sensitivities to minorities and women. The professors of the academic left underwrote these developments by unmasking the ideal of objectivity, erasing the distinction between language and the realities it described, and communicating in an opaque jargon that deflected criticism from the outside.

The professors themselves saw it differently. For them, the late 1980s and early 1990s were a time of heightened intellectual activity. In the humanities and social sciences, the boundaries between disciplines were breaking down, and new theories were multiplying. The social constructionists maintained that if you thought something was natural, inevitable, or universal, it probably wasn't. Influenced by imported French theory and by the homegrown social movements of the 1960s and 1970s, post-structuralists and multiculturalists engaged in a particularly tangled dance of conflict and collaboration. Post-structuralists poked holes in the fabric of individual identity, group identity, and national identity. The self had no definite substance—it was merely a phantasm created by power struggles among competing discourses. Group membership was also an artifact of language, and an unstable artifact at that. Multiculturalists applauded the post-structuralists for their dismantling of white-supremacist fictions and male-chauvinist myths. And yet they needed their own robust notions of group identity in order to argue for the enfranchisement of the excluded and the recognition of those whom history had unfairly ignored for so long. Just as medieval Schoolmen sought to reconcile Aristotle's logic and the prophecies of Scripture, 1990s academics sought to yoke the deconstruction of identity and its redemption.

If the logic was more rigorous, and the political grievances more justified, than critics allowed, the result was nonetheless a thick ooze of theoretical murk. Throughout the decade, debates over objectivity, aesthetics, and group identity tended to go around in circles, with no end in sight. Does human inquiry presuppose standards of truth and objectivity, or does it create them? If artistic taste is mutable, is aesthetic value an illusion? Will group membership enable individuals to achieve a measure of autonomy or erase their vital differences? Pools of ink were spilled on variants of these questions, and others like them, and the injustices of the world went on as before. Postmodern academics prided themselves on the strategic cunning of their challenge to the establishment, but outside the university they made few alliances and won fewer friends.

At the time of *Lingua Franca*'s debut, a backlash against the academic left was in full swing. Only a few months after the first issue appeared in the summer of 1990, *Newsweek* published a lurid cover story alleging that political correctness was the "new McCarthyism." Shortly thereafter, President George Herbert Walker Bush assailed campus speech codes in an address at the University of Michigan, and Dinesh D'Souza published his best-selling polemic against multiculturalism, *Illiberal Education*. At the National Endowment for the Humanities, Lynne Cheney escalated her attacks on the radicals and relativists who were disgracing the academic profession. George F. Will went so far as to hail her as a "secretary of domestic defense" whose duties were ultimately of more importance to the country's security than her husband's work as secretary of defense during the Gulf

War. Across the country, a vast army of alumni and parents, aroused by tales of postmodern decadence, was preparing to storm the ivory tower.

From the beginning, *Lingua Franca* refused to take sides in these Culture Wars. Under Kittay's direction, the original editors—Peter Edidin, followed by Margaret Talbot, then Judith Shulevitz—insisted on displaying the workings of the academy from the inside. They covered both sides of an argument, and any other sides they could find as well. When it came to a volatile issue such as affirmative action, the magazine did not discourse from a lofty height about the durability of racism or the danger to meritocracy. Rather, it printed "The Candidate," in which a pseudonymous professor recounted his participation in an affirmative action job search at a major university. The article was neither a defense of racial preferences nor a diatribe against them. Instead, it recounted the disturbing dilemmas faced by a search committee charged with a vague mandate to make a minority hire. The search was a success: It demonstrated that it was possible to give both scholarly merit and group membership their due. Yet it also showed that even vague affirmative action policies can have real costs, not least for the nonminority candidates who are invited to apply for a job that they have little chance of getting. Not long after "The Candidate" appeared in print, the candidate himself came across the article. He promptly composed an essay of his own in which he questioned his colleagues' biases; it appeared two issues later.

Margaret Talbot's "A Most Dangerous Method" translated the intimate approach to the Culture Wars evident in "The Candidate" into a full-fledged literary genre. In copious detail, Talbot related the story of Jane Gallop, a psychoanalytic theorist and feminist who made the eroticism of the classroom her central concern—only to be accused of sexual harassment by two of her female graduate students. Together, Talbot and the article's editor, Judith Shulevitz, combined the exposition of Gallop's challenging ideas with a vivid portrait of a world in which the personal and the professional were completely intermingled. The results were remarkably fresh. Unlike most reporters, Talbot was willing to treat a high-flying theorist with respect rather than condescension and ridicule; unlike most academics, she was willing to raise skeptical questions about that theorist's behavior. In the end, the profile did not lend itself to an easy moral. Talbot did not force Gallop into any of the available stereotypes: naive professor startled by reality; radical transgressor getting a taste of her own medicine; innocent victim of campus puritanism. Jane Gallop had, undoubtedly, acted unwisely and perhaps unforgivably. But her incisive mind and frank acknowledgment of the emotional connections between teacher and student made her critics seem incurious and unthinking.

Jeffrey Kittay hired me to edit *Lingua Franca* in December 1994; by the time I arrived, the magazine had taken Talbot's approach and turned it into a model. Our writers frequently combined vivacious reporting with excursions into the history of ideas. Quite often these stories focused on professors whose lives had come to echo—predictably or perversely—their own intellectual preoccupations. In "The Man Who Knew Too Much," Ruth Shalit investigated the case of Adam Weisberger, a young sociologist who asked his students to approach the work of Hegel, Marx, Durkheim, and Weber "by means of analyzing an important part of your lives—namely, your family." An inventive teacher, Weisberger instructed his students to relate the big concepts of social theory—power, status, charisma—to the most intimate details of their personal lives. But once the students did so, they began to fear that their professor was prying too far. Administrators compiled a dossier of their complaints and placed it in Weisberger's personnel file, where it would wreak havoc on his academic future. Had he recklessly invaded the privacy of his students? Or was he the victim of an overheated campus culture that conflated the experience of feeling "intellectually and emotionally uncomfortable" with sexual harassment?

In "The Stand," Daniel Mendelsohn pursued a similarly ambiguous story. Called into a Colorado courtroom to testify about antidiscrimination laws and homosexuality, the distinguished classicist Martha Nussbaum contemplated an ancient Greek word that was often associated with homosexual acts. A standard Greek-English dictionary defined *tolmêma* as "an act of outrageous effrontery," but

Nussbaum argued that Plato did not necessarily use it in a pejorative manner. A suspicious drop of Liquid Paper on one of her affidavits indicated that she might have covered up an inconvenient reference—an offense that so infuriated her critics that they nearly accused her of perjury. Was this the case of a well-meaning liberal distorting the scholarly record to suit her political ends? Or of prosecutorial bullies attempting to stigmatize—even criminalize—honest differences of opinion? Here the Culture Wars contracted into a scholarly skirmish over a dictionary entry, and expanded into the noisy public realms of law and politics.

In its many profiles, the magazine concentrated on scholars who enjoyed wide influence in the academy without quite fitting into its ranks. The historian of slavery Eugene Genovese transformed himself from a Vietcong supporter into a southern conservative while remaining true to his antiliberal Catholic roots. Richard Rorty decried the moral blindness of the academic left even as his former colleagues in philosophy departments attacked him as the arch nihilist of the age. In her work as a philosopher and as a conceptual artist, Adrian Piper sought to extinguish the cognitive errors of racism by employing the universalist ideas of Immanuel Kant. The Slovenian theorist Slavoj Žižek entertained Americans with his wicked analyses of popular culture while calling for a new politics that would somehow combine the best of Saint Paul and Karl Marx.

Though the magazine strove for balance, it did have a point of view. In the early issues, it ran hard-hitting articles that questioned Lynne Cheney's choice of a conservative polemicist for an NEH panel and challenged *The Dartmouth Review* for intimidating faculty members. Right-wing critics of the academy such as Allan Bloom and William Bennett were subjected to ritual abuse. The magazine also directed a considerable amount of criticism at the radical heroes and heroines of high theory, but this criticism was typically leavened with affection or at least familiarity. In general, the magazine's implied reader appeared to be a graduate student who was well versed in the cutting-edge theorists but also eager for some relief from their portentous obscurities. This reader wondered if just maybe the theorist du jour wore no clothes, and worried about his professional future in a world where "tenure track" and "adjunct" made up one hierarchically structured binary opposition that could not be deconstructed away.

Such a reader would have noted that the magazine frequently raised doubts about postmodernism and cultural studies. In a passionate essay, Daniel Harris accused the academics who joined the AIDS activist group ACT UP of putting their theoretical interests ahead of urgent medical necessities. Greil Marcus told an interviewer that he wondered why cultural studies scholars were so eager to read "resistance" into their favorite TV shows and pop songs. "A lot of the people in cultural studies these days kind of remind me of the FBI in the fifties: They find subversion everywhere. (The difference is that they like it, or at least claim to.)" But Harris's and Marcus's complaints were mild in comparison to what was to come.

WHEN ALAN SOKAL'S "A Physicist Experiments With Cultural Studies" appeared in 1996, it brought about the bizarre international event known as the Sokal hoax, which gave *Lingua Franca* its brief moment of fame and firmly identified the magazine in many people's minds with the attack on postmodern theory. Sokal, a physics professor at New York University, had laboriously composed an elaborate parody of postmodern writing about science. He generously stocked the parody with ideological grandstanding and dubious, even nonsensical, claims calculated to appeal to the knee-jerk social constructionist ("the π of Euclid and the G of Newton, formerly thought to be constant and universal, are now perceived in their ineluctable historicity"). Attempting to pass his essay off as the genuine article, he submitted it to *Social Text*, a journal of cultural studies whose co-editor Andrew Ross was as well known for his flashy wardrobe and nose-thumbing intellectual provocations as for his writings on popular culture and politics. After a period of indecision, the *Social Text* editors took the bait: they decided to publish Sokal's piece in a special issue devoted to the "science wars."

Not long afterward, we heard a rumor that something was awry in the forthcoming issue of *Social Text*. We examined an advance proof of the journal for about ten minutes, and then dispatched a reporter to meet Sokal for lunch. Following their meal, the reporter and Sokal burst into our offices. Sokal was nearly giddy with triumph. After some discussion, we agreed to publish an article he had written unveiling the hoax. In it, Sokal gloated freely over his accomplishment: "Would a leading North American journal of cultural studies—whose editorial collective includes such luminaries as Fredric Jameson and Andrew Ross—publish an article liberally salted with nonsense if (*a*) it sounded good and (*b*) it flattered the editors' ideological preconceptions? The answer, unfortunately, is yes." He taunted his foes: "[A]nyone who believes that the laws of physics are mere social conventions is invited to try transgressing those conventions from the windows of my apartment. (I live on the twenty-first floor.)" Like the editors of *Social Text*, Sokal hailed from the radical left, but he maintained that he was a radical "*because* of evidence and logic, not in spite of it."

The results were dramatic. The embarrassment of *Social Text*, and by extension an entire academic elite, proved to be an irresistible story line. Sokal's hoax reached the front page of *The New York Times*; columnists from George F. Will to Katha Pollitt summed up its implications. Italy's *Il Manifesto* ridiculed the assumption of so many American academics that "if some piece of nonsense has a Derrida logo, it's a deep concept." France's *Le Monde* protested that *Social Text*'s blunder must not be blamed on Jacques Lacan, "who was a great thinker in the natural sciences, an introducer of Anglo-Saxon thought, and a tenacious debater with the best logicians."

Even today, this physics scandal has yet to reach its half-life. But what were its lessons? Contrary to some reports, the debate was not exactly about whether "the world exists"; neither Sokal's allusions to the immutable laws of physics nor Ross's blithe call for the democratization of scientific method did much to clarify the vexed arguments between realists and antirealists in the philosophy of science. The hoax succeeded, and had a salutary effect, because it gave dramatic form to a number of valid and widespread concerns: academics of all faiths worried about the reflexive appeal to authority figures and political orthodoxies, the abuse of jargon, and the perils of doing interdisciplinary work when you don't know much about the other fellow's discipline. These feelings reached a strong pitch in 1996, both inside and outside the pages of *Lingua Franca*.

Shortly after the revelation of the Sokal hoax, *Lingua Franca* published another professor's confession. Frank Lentricchia's "Last Will and Testament of an Ex–Literary Critic" was a stinging repudiation of the politicized literary theory that Lentricchia himself had helped to foist upon a generation of students. His sarcastic account of his profession was tart and pointed: "Tell me your theory and I'll tell you in advance what you'll say about any work of literature, especially those you haven't read. Texts are not read; they are pre-read." But his antidote to theory could not have been more different from Sokal's; whereas Sokal recommended a thin diet of rigor, reason, and radicalism, Lentricchia rhapsodized about the flights of the soul in the presence of great literature.

Even as Sokal and Lentricchia launched their decisive sallies in the Culture Wars, those conflicts were losing some of their intensity. Debates about scientific objectivity, aesthetic value, and group identity made fitful progress. Here and there a useful idea appeared in print. The philosopher Ian Hacking insisted that a term like "social construction" needs to be used with great discrimination. It is one thing to refer to the social construction of a thing, such as a quark; it is quite another to refer to the social construction of a label, such as "the woman refugee." Meanwhile, John Guillory, a radical literary critic, spoke up for the "relative autonomy" of art. He acknowledged that the pleasures of visiting a museum or reading a novel had something to do with a feeling of social superiority. But even if "there is no realm of pure aesthetic experience," he argued, one can recognize that "the specificity of aesthetic experience is not contingent upon its 'purity.' " In a very different vein, the American-literature scholar Walter Benn Michaels sought to untie the knotted debates over multiculturalism.

Even the post-structuralists who described cultures as "complex, contradictory, discontinuous" were still committed to the idea that people fulfill or betray their cultural identities. But what if cultural identities can never be fulfilled or betrayed? Michaels suggested that in order to transcend the logic of identity politics, one must stop explaining "what people should do by reference to who they are and/or what culture they belong to." Together, these disparate thinkers suggested that the old battles did not have to end in the same stalemates.

In 1998, *The Chronicle of Higher Education* ran a symposium called "Have the Culture Wars Ended?" Of course, no one could agree on the terms of the supposed truce. According to some, the dire hegemony of the academic left was now absolute and unquestioned. Others expressed their strong satisfaction that the excesses of political correctness and theoretical obscurantism had at last been curbed. Perhaps a reasonable new center had emerged, or perhaps the antagonists were now so tired of arguing with each other that they no longer even bothered. While speech codes and sexual-harassment cases continued to raise passions, both the anti-P.C. National Association of Scholars and its foe, Teachers for a Democratic Culture, faded from view. The Association of Literary Scholars and Critics concentrated less on polemics than on actual literary criticism.

In some respects, the Culture Wars had always been a diversion. As Guillory pointed out, the arguments over the composition of the literary canon disguised the diminishing significance of the canon itself. The entrepreneurs of the computer age had little need to wrap themselves in the mantle of high art. Under these circumstances of "cultural capital flight," the enrollment in humanities courses contracted. All of the "participants in the canon debate" were stranded "on an ever shrinking island within the university itself."

Meanwhile, a great deal of the intellectual action was elsewhere. If the 1950s were the age of criticism, the 1990s were the age of biotechnology. Under the lengthening shadow of the genome, old and new ideas rapidly developed, sometimes in total defiance of the supposedly hegemonic academic left. Evolutionary psychology proposed a large-scale theory of human nature that infuriated feminists and cultural anthropologists, excited some scientists and angered others, and threatened an explanation of human behavior that was every bit as reductive in its genetic determinism as anything a theorist of power relations could devise. (After all, the notion of a responsible, coherent self could not be derived from Richard Dawkins's selfish gene any better than it could be derived from Michel Foucault's impersonal networks of power and discourse.) At the same time, the practitioners of rational-choice theory modeled every aspect of human behavior on the calculation of optimal courses of action. They spread out of economics departments into law schools, political science programs, and the social sciences more generally. While the academic left doubted that any conception of rationality is applicable to all people in all places, the rational-choice theorists imposed their own very particular system of rationality on everyone they could.

As the Culture Wars receded, *Lingua Franca* covered the sciences more frequently; most often its articles took note of the collision of scientific ideas with one another, or with interloping ideas from other disciplines. In "Oh My Darwin!" James Schwartz described the curious competition between evolutionary psychologists and their critics to define Darwinism. Helen Epstein's "Bonobos in Paradise" revealed the large hopes that feminists and primatologists pinned on the smallest chimpanzee. In his regular Hypotheses column, Jim Holt teased the reader with unlikely thoughts from the worlds of science, mathematics, and philosophy. His investigation into why mirrors reverse left and right but not up and down brought in an unprecedented amount of mail.

THE QUIETING OF THE CULTURE WARS also coincided with an escalating debate over the material conditions of life inside the university. Nineteen ninety-six, the year of the Sokal hoax, was also the year of the infamous Yale grade strike, when graduate student teaching assistants withheld marks from their undergraduates in a failed bid for union recognition. The resulting fracas, covered by Emily Eakin at the time, created some of the deepest campus divides since the Vietnam War. Nearly all of the Yale faculty opposed the strike, often passionately. In their view, it was a disturbance of the sacrosanct relationship between teacher and student. According to the literature professor Peter Brooks, Yale's graduate students were "among the blessed of the earth." But many of the local Ph.D. candidates believed that the student-mentor relationship had already been sundered. They performed much of the undergraduate teaching while receiving a stipend that, by the university's own admission, did not match the cost of living in New Haven. Incredibly, Yale's English department, one of the best in the country, placed only two of its fifteen students in tenure-track jobs in 1995. In these quarters, the Culture Wars were of little relevance: students felt more like exploited adjuncts than privileged apprentices, whatever their views about Yale's controversial deconstructionist Paul de Man.

In Margaret Talbot's article on Jane Gallop, a professor had identified the academy's "last taboo": the "unhappiness of grad students, their feelings of powerlessness, of abjectness." The taboo did not survive the mid-1990s. As a boom-time economy approached full employment, young humanists looked upon a dismal job market and despaired. The result was a riot of professional angst and self-examination. Meanwhile, university administrators were setting up elaborate Internet ventures and reading up on the principles of corporate management. In 1998, they were intrigued to learn that the for-profit University of Phoenix had become the largest private university in the country, offering preprofessional classes to busy adults in rented strip-mall offices and dispensing with a permanent faculty (and traditional library) altogether. Its brash CEO, John Sperling, became an entrepreneurial hero in the business press. (That year, *Lingua Franca* reported that he had also donated two million dollars to Texas A&M on the condition that the university attempt to clone his dog, Missy.)

Even as humanists contemplated their possible obsolescence, one aspect of their existence—the academic star system—remained firmly in place. In 1918, Thorstein Veblen had described the professor as a preternaturally conservative creature who managed the disparity between his low pay and his bourgeois aspirations by eschewing original research. He kept his superiors happy by performing administrative drudge work and by making conspicuous appearances at sporting events and gown-wearing ceremonies. Years later, the image of the cautious and ineffectual egghead had changed. The newly ambitious professor invented flashy paradigms and lobbied for the creation of interdisciplinary research centers to implement them. Readers of campus novels duly turned from the bitchily parochial small-town culture of Randall Jarrell's *Pictures From an Institution* to the bitchily cosmopolitan international conference circuit chronicled by David Lodge in his *Small World* series.

In a series of essays in *PMLA* and *the minnesota review*, the American-literature scholar David Shumway linked the academic star system to a sensationalized tabloid culture. Professors were no longer esteemed for the supposed "soundness" of their work; rather, they were applauded for their "visibility." Their function was not to persuade but to entertain, and their success became the subject of voyeuristic fantasies among the hopeless majority of the profession. In Shumway's estimation, the appearance of *Lingua Franca* and the subsequent creation of the *New York Times*'s Arts and Ideas section were both symptom and source of this transformation. As an antidote, Shumway called for a return to straightforward critical thinking: "Instead of assuming that, say, Lacan's theory tells us something about film or literature, we need to investigate whether we ought to accept that theory in the first place." When *the minnesota review* devoted a special issue to Shumway's thesis, leading academic radicals indignantly defended the star system that they knew so well. Bruce Robbins suggested that this new arrangement was far more open to women and minorities than the old-boy network it replaced; Jeffrey Williams insisted that the satisfactions of celebrity were entirely legitimate. A professor's job doesn't pay very well; fame and renown in the eyes of one's colleagues (or what Veblen called "increased creditable notoriety") are compensation well deserved.

Much of this debate took place inside a curious vacuum. The academic star could command a large salary and achieve celebrity status among graduate students without winning a single reader outside the academy. Indeed, in most precincts of the university, "public intellectual" was a term of abuse. When Russell Jacoby published *The Last Intellectuals* in 1987, he was widely scorned on campus as a sentimental nostalgist whose criticisms of academic insularity coincided with a refusal of critical thinking.

By the late 1990s, however, scholars were behaving more and more like the pundits they had once condemned. The common reader was acquiring a certain allure in the academic mind; Florida Atlantic University even inaugurated a Ph.D. program for fledgling public intellectuals. This yearning for recognition from a lay audience was the result of both academic failure and academic success. Uncertain of their employment prospects, young scholars realized they had better retain some ability to write clearly and accessibly for the world at large. At the same time, renowned professors who had won every conceivable honor within their profession were inevitably tempted to look beyond it. The celebrated English professors of past generations—the Trillings and Van Dorens—had addressed a wide audience of nonspecialists; why couldn't they? In the 1990s, Harvard's Marjorie Garber began to write about dogs, cross-dressing, and real estate, while her colleague Stephen Greenblatt set out to write a trade book on Shakespeare. Were their efforts defensible? Was this a democratic quest for a broader readership or an abject surrender to the mediocre standards of the market?

Whatever one made of the term "public intellectuals," *Lingua Franca* was a journal for and about the species. When it wasn't covering the work of academia's unsung heroes, it lavished attention on those professors who entered the rough-and-tumble world of politics and put their ideas on the line. Among graduate students, Benedict Anderson was best known for his theoretical study of nationalism, *Imagined Communities.* But in "A Return to Java," Scott Sherman described Anderson's lifelong involvement with the turbulent politics of Indonesia: banned from the country in 1972, Anderson returned in 1999 to launch a pointed attack on the new post-Suharto regime. In "The Color Test," Eyal Press studied the relationship between two liberal law professors who argued about race and crime on a public stage. And in "Testaments Betrayed," Laura Secor followed the breakup of a close-knit group of Yugoslavian intellectuals whose internal schisms prefigured, and even hastened, the breakup of Yugoslavia itself. Secor combined a detailed analysis of Tito's Yugoslavia with a startling look at how the country's most humane and cosmopolitan intellectuals became ideological apologists for the murderous Milošević regime. Amid all the newsprint on the Yugoslavian wars, Secor's article stood out because it provided an *intellectual* history of the conflict. (The article proved newsworthy even in Serbia: it was translated into Serbo-Croatian and serialized in a Belgrade paper.)

OVER THE COURSE OF THE DECADE, the magazine gained increased recognition outside the academy and greater acceptance (or at least toleration) within it. *Lingua Franca* won the National Magazine Award for General Excellence in 1993, and it would be a finalist for the same prize in four of the following six years. Lingua Franca Books created a guide to graduate schools and co-published a collection of essays with the University of Nebraska Press titled *The Sokal Hoax: The Sham That Shook the Academy*. Most dramatic, Kittay started a new magazine aimed at administrators called *University Business* and purchased the New Zealand–based Web site Arts and Letters Daily. A small academic empire was taking shape, or so it seemed as we left the wig stores and brothels of the Garment District for airier quarters farther downtown. We shared the new site with a dealer in rare Oriental rugs and an armed import-export firm; we began to receive mail addressed to a company called Lingerie France. We had, we felt, arrived.

No matter how notable we became, the editors still scrambled to find stories, and no source was ever overlooked: an e-mail from a graduate student, a professor's late-night voice-mail message, a curious item in a British newspaper. Readers themselves sent in scores of submissions: epic poems about their tenure bids; short stories about sleeping with students. Most satisfying, a group of regular writers formed around the magazine and brought us their best ideas. Some of them were professors; some of them were experienced journalists. But most of them were lapsed graduate students with a passionate interest in writing about culture and politics.

Often the writers looked into the quietist corners of the academy, where the din of the Culture Wars could barely be heard and the deeds of a Sokal or a Cheney were but a distant rumor. For "In the Franklin Factory," Jack Hitt visited the editors of the Benjamin Franklin Papers, who toil away for years on end to produce meticulously prepared scholarly editions. These conscientious scholars do not climb the usual ladder of academic prestige; engaged in "slow-motion scholarship," they relive the eighteenth century in real time, journeying through Franklin's days at the same pace that he lived them. A 1993 article by Warren St. John exposed the dubious methods of a little-known religion professor who hid his vanity press behind the prestigious facade of the scholarly monograph. After the article appeared, the professor, Herbert Richardson, filed a libel suit against the magazine that dragged on for several years. Eventually the case was dismissed; by that time, Richardson had been fired from his teaching post.

The shorter pieces that appeared in the front of the magazine were often intended as amusements and could be about nearly anything: the Mafia's efforts to control the videotaping of dissertation defenses in an Italian city or the revelation that a much-admired photograph of Oscar Wilde in drag actually depicted a female opera singer from Hungary. The November 1998 issue was typical. "Fungus Among Us" examined a new book on the world-historical influence of "mischievous molds"; "Critical Theory at the Barricades" detailed the infamous 1969 "breast-action," in which topless German student radicals rushed a podium where Theodor Adorno was speaking; and "Breaking Away" solicited commentary on an unusual advertising campaign sponsored by Indiana University: it implored students to major in the liberal arts so that they could reject the dull lives of their parents and learn to "think for a living" instead.

To our considerable frustration, the magazine's circulation refused to rise much above fifteen thousand. Why weren't there more readers? Perhaps it was because graduate students were too poor to take out subscriptions and professors were too proud. In any case, *Lingua*

Franca's small audience didn't keep it from achieving a distinctive presence in the world of journalism. We got used to hearing stories of editors around town who asked their writers to produce a "*Lingua Franca* piece." Meanwhile, our own staff members went on to successful careers at *The New Yorker*, *The New York Times*, and other highly conspicuous publications.

In October 2001, an investor suddenly pulled out his funds, and Kittay was forced—at least temporarily—to cease publication. Many magazines shut down in that dismal recessionary fall. But *Lingua Franca*'s closing inspired particularly loud songs of sorrow from across the ideological spectrum. Comparing *Lingua Franca* with its peers, *The Nation*'s Eric Alterman claimed that the magazine had done a better job "than almost anything else." Writing in *Commentary*, Gertrude Himmelfarb noted that "the most sophisticated 'in' journal of academia" was "now, unhappily, defunct." In *The New York Observer*, Ron Rosenbaum used his column to salute the magazine's twin commitments to "searching through the vast torrents of jargon-addled dross to find and convey the rare excitement of real thinkers grappling with original ideas" and "exposing the sad comedy of pretentious sophists confecting academic simulacra of real thinking."

The months that followed *Lingua Franca*'s passing were filled with the sort of high-profile academic conflict that gave the magazine so much of its raison d'être. The Middle Eastern Studies Association was excoriated for its failure to raise an alarm about Islamic fundamentalism. Harvard president Lawrence Summers rebuked his faculty for its lack of patriotism, and then feuded with star professor Cornel West over grade inflation and the scholarly standing of hip-hop. Lynne Cheney warned that the war on terrorism should not be used to justify multicultural education. These were the sorts of stories that *Lingua Franca*'s writers covered with relish. If nothing else, their example demonstrated that intellectual journalism is far from obsolete. The magazine was committed to the belief that even the most esoteric subjects can be communicated with journalistic flair—and thank heaven for that. After all, thinking is too important to be left to the professors.

center
PART I

The Reaction to Theory

A PHYSICIST EXPERIMENTS WITH CULTURAL STUDIES
A Confession
ALAN SOKAL

> *The displacement of the idea that facts and evidence matter by the idea that everything boils down to subjective interests and perspectives is—second only to American political campaigns—the most prominent and pernicious manifestation of anti-intellectualism in our time.*
> —LARRY LAUDAN, *Science and Relativism* (1990)

FOR SOME YEARS, I've been troubled by an apparent decline in the standards of rigor in certain precincts of the academic humanities. But I'm a mere physicist: if I find myself unable to make heads or tails of *jouissance* and *différance*, perhaps that just reflects my own inadequacy.

So, to test the prevailing intellectual standards, I decided to try a modest (though admittedly uncontrolled) experiment: Would a leading North American journal of cultural studies—whose editorial collective includes such luminaries as Fredric Jameson and Andrew Ross—publish an article liberally salted with nonsense if (*a*) it sounded good and (*b*) it flattered the editors' ideological preconceptions?

The answer, unfortunately, is yes. Interested readers can find my article, "Transgressing the Boundaries: Toward a Transformative

Hermeneutics of Quantum Gravity," in the Spring/Summer 1996 issue of *Social Text*. It appears in a special number of the magazine devoted to the "Science Wars."

What's going on here? Could the editors really not have realized that my article was written as a parody?

In the first paragraph, I deride "the dogma imposed by the long post-Enlightenment hegemony over the Western intellectual outlook":

> that there exists an external world, whose properties are independent of any individual human being and indeed of humanity as a whole; that these properties are encoded in "eternal" physical laws; and that human beings can obtain reliable, albeit imperfect and tentative, knowledge of these laws by hewing to the "objective" procedures and epistemological strictures prescribed by the (so-called) scientific method.

Is it now dogma in cultural studies that there exists no external world? Or that there exists an external world but science obtains no knowledge of it?

In the second paragraph, I declare, without the slightest evidence or argument, that "physical 'reality' [note the scare quotes] . . . is at bottom a social and linguistic construct." Not our *theories* of physical reality, mind you, but the reality itself. Fair enough: anyone who believes that the laws of physics are mere social conventions is invited to try transgressing those conventions from the windows of my apartment. (I live on the twenty-first floor.)

Throughout the article, I employ scientific and mathematical concepts in ways that few scientists or mathematicians could possibly take seriously. For example, I suggest that the "morphogenetic field"—a bizarre New Age idea proposed by Rupert Sheldrake—constitutes a cutting-edge theory of quantum gravity. This connection is pure invention; even Sheldrake makes no such claim. I assert that Lacan's psychoanalytic speculations have been confirmed by recent work in quantum field theory. Even nonscientist readers might well wonder what in heaven's name quantum field theory has to do with psychoanalysis; certainly my article gives no reasoned argument to support such a link.

Later in the article, I propose that the axiom of equality in mathematical set theory is somehow analogous to the homonymous concept in feminist politics. In reality, all the axiom of equality states is that two sets are identical if and only if they have the same elements. Even readers without mathematical training might well be suspicious of the claim that the axiom of equality reflects set theory's "nineteenth-century liberal origins."

In sum, I intentionally wrote the article so that any competent physicist or mathematician (or undergraduate physics or math major) would realize that it is a spoof. Evidently, the editors of *Social Text* felt comfortable publishing an article on quantum physics without bothering to consult anyone knowledgeable in the subject.

THE FUNDAMENTAL SILLINESS of my article lies, however, not in its numerous solecisms but in the dubiousness of its central thesis and of the "reasoning" adduced to support it. Basically, I claim that quantum gravity—the still-speculative theory of space and time on scales of a millionth of a billionth of a billionth of a billionth of a centimeter—has profound political implications (which, of course, are "progressive"). In support of this improbable proposition, I proceed as follows: First, I quote some controversial philosophical pronouncements of Heisenberg and Bohr and assert (without argument) that quantum physics is profoundly consonant with "postmodernist epistemology." Next, I assemble a pastiche—Derrida and general relativity, Lacan and topology, Irigaray and quantum gravity—held together by vague references to "nonlinearity," "flux," and "interconnectedness." Finally, I jump (again without argument) to the assertion that "postmodern science" has abolished the concept of objective reality. Nowhere in all of this is there anything resembling a logical sequence of thought; one finds only citations of authority, plays on words, strained analogies, and bald assertions.

In its concluding passages, my article becomes especially egregious.

Having abolished reality as a constraint on science, I go on to suggest (once again without argument) that science, in order to be "liberatory," must be subordinated to political strategies. I finish the article by observing that "a liberatory science cannot be complete without a profound revision of the canon of mathematics." We can see hints of an "emancipatory mathematics," I suggest, "in the multidimensional and nonlinear logic of fuzzy systems theory; but this approach is still heavily marked by its origins in the crisis of late-capitalist production relations." I add that "catastrophe theory, with its dialectical emphases on smoothness/discontinuity and metamorphosis/unfolding, will indubitably play a major role in the future of mathematics; but much theoretical work remains to be done before this approach can become a concrete tool of progressive political praxis."

It's understandable that the editors of *Social Text* were unable to evaluate critically the technical aspects of my article (which is exactly why they should have consulted a scientist). What's more surprising is how readily they accepted my implication that the search for truth in science must be subordinated to a political agenda, and how oblivious they were to the article's overall illogic.

WHY DID I DO IT? While my method was satirical, my motivation is utterly serious. What concerns me is the proliferation not just of nonsense and sloppy thinking per se but of a particular kind of nonsense and sloppy thinking: one that denies the existence of objective realities, or (when challenged) admits their existence but downplays their practical relevance. At its best, a journal like *Social Text* raises important issues that no scientist should ignore—questions, for example, about how corporate and government funding influences scientific work. Unfortunately, epistemic relativism does little to further the discussion of these matters.

In short, my concern about the spread of subjectivist thinking is both intellectual and political. Intellectually, the problem with such doctrines is that they are false (when not simply meaningless). There *is* a real world; its properties are *not* merely social constructions; facts and evidence *do* matter. What sane person would contend otherwise? And yet much contemporary academic theorizing consists precisely of attempts to blur these obvious truths.

Social Text's acceptance of my article exemplifies the intellectual arrogance of Theory—postmodernist *literary* theory, that is—carried to its logical extreme. No wonder they didn't bother to consult a physicist. If all is discourse and "text," then knowledge of the real world is superfluous; even physics becomes just another branch of cultural studies. If, moreover, all is rhetoric and language games, then internal logical consistency is superfluous, too: a patina of theoretical sophistication serves equally well. Incomprehensibility becomes a virtue; allusions, metaphors, and puns substitute for evidence and logic. My own article is, if anything, an extremely modest example of this well-established genre.

I'M ANGERED BECAUSE most (though not all) of this silliness is emanating from the self-proclaimed left. We're witnessing here a profound historical volte-face. For most of the past two centuries, the left has been identified with science and against obscurantism; we have believed that rational thought and the fearless analysis of objective reality (both natural and social) are incisive tools for combating the mystifications promoted by the powerful—not to mention being desirable human ends in their own right. The recent turn of many "progressive" or "leftist" academic humanists and social scientists toward one or another form of epistemic relativism betrays this worthy heritage and undermines the already fragile prospects for progressive social critique. Theorizing about "the social construction of reality" won't help us find an effective treatment for AIDS or devise strategies for preventing global warming. Nor can we combat false ideas in history, sociology, economics, and politics if we reject the notions of truth and falsity.

The results of my little experiment demonstrate, at the very least, that some fashionable sectors of the American academic left have been getting intellectually lazy. The editors of *Social Text* liked my article because they liked its conclusion: that "the content and methodology of postmodern science provide powerful intellectual support for the progressive political project." They apparently felt no need to analyze the quality of the evidence, the cogency of the arguments, or even the relevance of the arguments to the purported conclusion.

I'M NOT OBLIVIOUS to the ethical issues involved in my rather unorthodox experiment. Professional communities operate largely on trust; deception undercuts that trust. But it is important to understand exactly what I did. My article is a theoretical essay based entirely on publicly available sources, all of which I have meticulously footnoted. All works cited are real, and all quotations are rigorously accurate; none are invented. Now, it's true that the author doesn't believe his own argument. But why should that matter? The editors' duty as scholars is to judge the validity and interest of ideas, without regard for their provenance. (That is why many scholarly journals practice blind refereeing.) If the *Social Text* editors find my arguments convincing, then why should they be disconcerted simply because I don't? Or are they more deferent to the so-called cultural authority of technoscience than they would care to admit?

In the end, I resorted to parody for a simple pragmatic reason. The targets of my critique have by now become a self-perpetuating academic subculture that typically ignores (or disdains) reasoned criticism from the outside. In such a situation, a more direct demonstration of the subculture's intellectual standards was required. But how can one show that the emperor has no clothes? Satire is by far the best weapon; and the blow that can't be brushed off is the one that's self-inflicted. I offered the *Social Text* editors an opportunity to demonstrate their intellectual rigor. Did they meet the test? I don't think so.

I say this not in glee but in sadness. After all, I'm a leftist, too (under the Sandinista government I taught mathematics at the National University of Nicaragua). On nearly all practical political issues—including many concerning science and technology—I'm on the same side as the *Social Text* editors. But I'm a leftist (and a feminist) *because* of evidence and logic, not in spite of it. Why should the right wing be allowed to monopolize the intellectual high ground?

And why should self-indulgent nonsense—whatever its professed political orientation—be lauded as the height of scholarly achievement?

—May 1996

MYSTERY SCIENCE THEATER
A Forum on the Sokal Hoax

BRUCE ROBBINS AND ANDREW ROSS, *coeditors for* Social Text: What were some of the initial responses of the journal's editors when we first learned about Alan Sokal's prank on *Social Text*? One suspected that Sokal's parody was nothing of the sort and that his admission represented a change of heart or a folding of his intellectual resolve. Another editor was unconvinced that Sokal knew very much about what he was attempting to expose. A third was pleasantly astonished to learn that our journal is taken seriously enough to be considered a target of a hoax, especially a hoax by a physicist. Others were concerned that the hoax might spark off a new round of caricature and thereby perpetuate the climate in which science studies and cultural studies have been subject recently to so much derision from conservatives in science.

All of us were distressed at the deceptive means by which Sokal chose to make his point. This breach of ethics is a serious matter in any scholarly community and has damaging consequences when it occurs in science publishing. What is the likely result of Sokal's behavior for nonscientific journals? Less well known authors who submit unsolicited articles to journals like ours may now come under needless suspicion, and the openness of intellectual inquiry that *Social Text* has played its role in fostering will be curtailed.

However varied our responses, we all believe that Sokal took too much for granted in his account of his prank. Indeed, his claim—that our publication of his article proves that something is rotten in the state of cultural studies—is as wobbly as the article itself.

OBVIOUSLY, we now regret having published Sokal's article and apologize to our readers and to those in the science studies or cultural studies communities who might feel their work has been disparaged as a result of this affair. To give readers a clear sense of the circumstances underlying the publication of the article, we have taken the time to recount the relevant history of the editorial process. We regret that *Lingua Franca* did not provide us with such an opportunity when it decided to publish Sokal's statement.

From the first, we considered Sokal's unsolicited article to be a little hokey. It is not every day we receive a dense philosophical tract from a professional physicist. Not knowing the author or his work, we engaged in some speculation about his intentions and concluded that the article was the earnest attempt of a professional scientist to seek some kind of affirmation from postmodern philosophy for developments in his field. Sokal's adventures in PostmodernLand were not really our cup of tea. Like other journals of our vintage that try to keep abreast of cultural studies, *Social Text* has not published direct contributions to the debate about postmodern theory in a number of years, and his article would have been regarded as somewhat outdated if it had come from a humanist or a social scientist. As the work of a natural scientist, it was unusual and, we thought, plausibly symptomatic of how someone like Sokal might approach the field of postmodern epistemology—awkwardly but assertively trying to capture the "feel" of the professional language of this field while relying upon an armada of footnotes to ease his sense of vulnerability. In other words, we read it more as an act of good faith of the sort that might be worth encouraging than as a set of arguments with which we agreed. On those grounds, the editors considered it of interest to readers as a "document" in that time-honored tradition in which modern physicists have discovered harmonic resonances with their own reasoning in the fields of philosophy and metaphysics. Consequently, the article met one of the several criteria for publication that *Social Text* recognizes.

As a non-refereed journal of political opinion and cultural analysis produced by an editorial collective (and entirely self-published until its adoption four years ago by Duke University Press), *Social Text* has always seen its lineage in the "little magazine" tradition of the independent left as much as in the academic domain, and so we often balance diverse editorial criteria when discussing the worth of submissions, whether they be works of fiction, interviews with sex workers, or essays about anticolonialism. In other words, this is an editorial milieu with criteria and aims quite remote from those of a professional scientific journal. Whether Sokal's article would have been declared substandard by a physicist peer reviewer is debatable (it is not, after all, a scholarly contribution to the discipline of physics) but not finally relevant to us—at least not according to the criteria we employed.

Having established an interest in Sokal's article, we did ask him informally to revise the piece. We requested him (*a*) to excise a good deal of the philosophical speculation and (*b*) to excise most of his footnotes. Sokal seemed resistant to any revisions and indeed insisted on retaining almost all of his footnotes and bibliographic apparatus on the grounds that his peers, in science, expected extensive documentation of this sort. It was clear from this response that his article would appear as is or not at all. At this point, Sokal was designated as a "difficult, uncooperative author," a category well known to journal editors. We judged his article too much trouble to publish, not yet on the reject pile, perhaps of sufficient interest to readers if published in the company of related articles.

Sometime after this impasse was reached, the editors did indeed decide to assemble a special issue on the topic of science studies. We wanted to gauge how science critics were responding to the attacks by Paul Gross and Norman Levitt and by other conservatives in science. Contributions were solicited from across the field of knowledge—from humanists, social scientists, and natural scientists. (The final lineup included many of the more significant names in the field—Sandra Harding, Steve Fuller, Emily Martin, Hilary Rose, Langdon

Winner, Dorothy Nelkin, Richard Levins, George Levine, Sharon Traweek, Sarah Franklin, Ruth Hubbard, Joel Kovel, Stanley Aronowitz, and Les Levidow.) Most responded directly to the evolving controversy that some were calling the "Science Wars," while others wrote their own accounts of work in their respective fields. Here, we thought, was an appropriate and heterogeneous context in which Sokal's article might appear, providing a feasible solution to the editorial problem posed by his piece. He expressed some concern when asked if we could publish his work in this special issue (we assumed he wished to distance himself from the polemical company assembled for the issue) but reiterated his eagerness to see it in print. Our final decision to include him presumed that readers would see his article in the particular context of the *Science Wars* issue, as a contribution from someone unknown to the field whose views, however offbeat, might still be thought relevant to the debate. Since his article was not written for that special issue, and bears little resemblance, in tone or substance, to the commissioned articles, it was not slated to be included in the expanded book version of the issue (with additional articles by Katherine Hayles, Michael Lynch, Roger Hart, and Richard Lewontin), which will be published by Duke University Press in September.

In sum, Sokal's assumption that his parody caught the woozy editors of *Social Text* sleeping on the job is ill conceived. Its status as parody does not alter substantially our interest in the piece itself as a symptomatic document. Indeed, Sokal's conduct has quickly become an object of study for those who analyze the behavior of scientists. Our own role has also come under scrutiny, since, at the very least, the affair says something about our conception of how physicists read philosophy. As for the decision to publish his article, readers can judge for themselves whether we were right or wrong. But to construe this decision as proof of the bankruptcy of cultural studies is absurd.

WHAT ALAN SOKAL'S CONFESSION most altered was our perception of his own good faith as a self-declared leftist. However we feel about his deception, we do hope that the ensuing discussion has been, and will continue to be, productive and that interlocutors will resist the opportunity to exploit existing divisions and splits among committed people and seek instead to bridge and heal those differences. There is nothing we regret more than watching the left eat the left, surely one of the sorriest spectacles of the twentieth century.

Having talked with the (real) Sokal subsequently, we believe that most of the issues he intended to air are, at this point, rather well known to readers of *Social Text* and *Lingua Franca*. Indeed, they have been going the rounds in the academy since the first postmodern, social constructionist, or anti-foundational critiques of positivism appeared over thirty-five years ago. That many natural scientists have only recently felt the need to respond to these critiques says something about the restricted trade routes through which knowledge is still circulated in the academy, policed, as it is, at every departmental checkpoint by disciplinary passport controls. Nor are these critiques unfamiliar to folks who have long been involved in debates about the direction of the left, where positivism has had a long and healthy life. At this point in time, we have a vestigial stake in these critiques and debates but much less of an interest than Sokal supposes. Like Gross and Levitt, he appears to have absorbed these critiques only at the level of caricatures and has been reissuing these caricatures in the form of otherworldly fanatics who deny the existence of facts, objective realities, and gravitational forces. We are sure Sokal knows that no such persons exist, and we have wondered why on earth he would promote this fiction. He must be aware that early proponents of quantum reality encountered similar parodies of themselves in the opposition to their ideas. Physics is not the only field where this occurred. Comparable caricatures have figured in many different scholarly controversies, from early-twentieth-century debates about legal realism to more recent ones about genetic reductionism. It is time to put them to rest.

On the other hand, we recognize that professional scientists like Sokal do feel that their beliefs and their intellectual integrity are threatened by the diverse work done in the field of science studies. Doubtless, there have been distorted and reductive descriptions of scientists in many aspects of that work. Over the years, many scholars in the field have responded sympathetically to this grievance, and a good deal of common ground has been established. We share Sokal's concerns about obscurantism, for example. It is highly ironic that *Social Text* should now be associated with a kind of sectarian postmodernism that we have been at pains to discourage for many years. We would be all too happy if this episode cleared the air. Sokal has said that he agrees with many of the arguments put forth by other authors in the *Science Wars* issue of *Social Text*. Unfortunately, he declined to enter into a publishable dialogue with us for this issue of *Lingua Franca*. We are heartened, however, by the prospect of any level-headed discussion about the politics of science that does not rest exclusively on claims of expertise and that is shaped by the public interest.

Our main concern is that readers new to the debates engendered by science studies not be persuaded by the Sokal stunt that this is simply an academic turf war between scientists and humanists/social scientists, with each side trying to outsmart the other. Sadly, this outcome would simply reinforce the premise that only professional scientists have the credentialed right to speak their minds on scientific matters that affect all of us. What's important to us is not so much the gulf of comprehension between "the two cultures" as the gulf of power between experts and lay voices, and the currently shifting relationship between science and the corporate-military state. Nor are these concerns extrinsic to the practice of science itself. Prior to deciding whether science intrinsically tells the truth, we must ask again and again whether it is possible, or prudent, to isolate facts from values. This is a crucial question to ask because it bears upon the kind of progressive society we want to promote.

Why does science matter so much to us? Because its power, as a civil religion, as a social and political authority, affects our daily lives and the parlous condition of the natural world more than any other domain of knowledge. Does it follow that nonscientists should have some say in the decision-making processes that define and shape the work of the professional scientific community? Some scientists (including Sokal, presumably) would say yes, and in some countries non-expert citizens do indeed participate in these processes. All hell breaks loose, however, when the following question is asked: Should nonexperts have anything to say about scientific methodology and epistemology? After centuries of scientific racism, scientific sexism, and scientific domination of nature, one might have thought this was a pertinent question to ask.

ALAN SOKAL: I confess to amusement that one *Social Text* editor still doesn't believe my piece was a parody. Oh, well.

As for *Social Text*'s editorial process, readers can judge for themselves the plausibility of the editors' ex post facto explanations, which if true may be more damning than the incident itself. Some of their chronology is at variance with my own documentary record, but let me not beat a dead horse.

More interesting than the scandal provoked by the article's acceptance is, I think, the scandal that ought to be provoked by its content. My essay, aside from being (if I may quote Katha Pollitt's flattery) "a hilarious compilation of pomo gibberish," is also an annotated bibliography of the charlatanism and nonsense purveyed by dozens of prominent French and American intellectuals. This goes well beyond the narrow category of "postmodernism" and includes some of the most fashionable thinkers in "science studies," literary criticism, and cultural studies.

In short, there is a lot of sloppy thinking going around about "social construction," often abetted by a vocabulary that intentionally elides the distinction between facts and our knowledge of them. I'm no expert in epistemology, but some of this work is so illogical that it doesn't take an expert to deconstruct it. I've analyzed one representative example in an afterword submitted for publication in *Social Text*; I hope the editors will print it, perhaps along with replies. I'd suggest they also invite contributions from philosophers far sharper than myself, such as Susan Haack and Janet Radcliffe Richards.

Robbins and Ross say that I "declined to enter into a publishable dialogue" with them. Quite the contrary: we're having that dialogue right now. What I declined was an oral dialogue, which in my opinion usually yields a low ratio of content to words.

Robbins and Ross guess wrong when they say I feel "threatened" by science-studies scholars. My goal isn't to defend science from the barbarian hordes of lit crit (we'll survive just fine, thank you) but to defend the left from a trendy segment of itself. Like innumerable others from diverse backgrounds and disciplines, I call for the left to reclaim its Enlightenment roots. We're worried above all for the social sciences and the humanities, not the natural sciences.

In their last two paragraphs, Robbins and Ross bring up a plethora of real issues, but it would take quite a bit of space to disentangle the substance from the rhetoric. They conflate science as an intellectual system with the social and economic role of science and technology. They conflate epistemic and ethical issues.

These confusions lead Robbins and Ross into a serious error: setting up an opposition between science and progressive politics. They describe science as a "civil religion" that supports existing social and political structures. It is of course true that scientific research is skewed by the influence of those with power and money. But a scientific worldview, based on a commitment to logic and standards of evidence and to the incessant confrontation of theories with reality, is an essential component of any progressive politics.

Despite these differences, there is a potentially vast common ground between Robbins and Ross and myself. When scientific research is increasingly funded by private corporations that have a financial interest in particular outcomes of that research—is the drug effective or not?—scientific objectivity is undermined. (But to make this argument, one must first have a conception of objectivity: not as a state that human beings can ever attain, but as an ideal standard of comparison.) When universities are more interested in patent royalties than in the open sharing of scientific information, the public suffers. There are hundreds of important political and economic issues surrounding science and technology. Sociology of science, at its best, has done much to clarify these issues. But sloppy sociology, like sloppy science, is useless or even counterproductive.

EVELYN FOX KELLER, *professor of history and philosophy of science, Massachusetts Institute of Technology*: Alan Sokal's prank was a brilliant strategy for making an extremely important point, but what exactly is this point, and for whom is it important?

First, the point. Is it that the academy houses scholars who have the audacity to question the meaning of objectivity or to challenge the immunity of science from social forces? Or that some literary scholars have begun to write about scientific texts without first seeking the approval of scientists? Not only does Sokal seriously weaken his case with such suggestions, but he helps fuel the media's enthusiasm for the outlandish idea that a left antiscience conspiracy is perpetrating the claim that the world is not real. I wish he had let his ruse speak for itself, for its point is quite simple: the editors of *Social Text* have been shown to be unable to distinguish a hilarious jargon-ridden spoof from real argument. Or perhaps the editors were so eager to count a physicist as one of their own that they chose to publish an article they themselves regarded as "hokey."

Now, to whom should this matter? For many scientists, this episode will only bolster their fear that postmodernism (and science studies more generally) threatens the integrity and well-being of their own disciplines. But it is not science that is threatened by the hapless publication of gibberish; it is science studies itself. And the embarrassing defense offered by Ross and Robbins (not to mention the many counterattacks) just makes the problem worse. Scholars in science studies who have turned to postmodernism have done so out of a real need: truth and objectivity turn out to be vastly more problematic concepts than we used to think, and neither can be measured simply by the weight of scientific authority or even by demonstrations of efficacy. Yet surely the ability to distinguish argument from parody is a prerequisite to any attempt at understanding the complexities of truth claims, in science or elsewhere. How can we claim credibility for responsible scholarship—for the carefully reasoned and empirically founded research that makes up the bulk of science studies—if we do not recognize a problem here?

It saddens me that my scientific colleagues so readily confuse the analysis of social influence on science with radical subjectivism, mistaking challenges to the autonomy of science for the "dogma" that there exists no external world. And it alarms me to see the politicization of legitimate intellectual argument as a "left antiscience" movement versus a defense of traditional values mounted by the "right." But neither condones the failure of my colleagues in science studies to acknowledge so blatant a compromise to the integrity of their own discipline.

FRANCO MORETTI, *professor of comparative literature, Columbia University*: How did Alan Sokal fool the *Social Text* editorial collective? Simple: the members of that collective knew very little about physics (nothing wrong with that), and they didn't bother to ask an expert. They didn't do so, Ross and Robbins have told us, because "professional" standards are "not finally relevant to us—at least not according to the criteria we employed." This is a rather opaque justification, and no wonder. Basically, it means that *Social Text* doesn't care whether Sokal's work—or anybody else's—is solid or not. Nice to know, in general. But still, why did *Social Text* publish this particular article?

Because, the editors say, "[we] concluded that the article was the earnest attempt of a professional scientist to seek some kind of affirmation from postmodern philosophy for developments in his field." In plainer words: we publish Sokal not because he is interesting but because he says *we* are. This is a wonderful explanation, with a great hidden premise—that people in the humanities have nothing to learn from a scientist. He may be exhibited as a curious convert to theory, but we don't have to take him seriously. The *Social Text* board read and reread the article and didn't understand a thing—yet they didn't care, because at bottom they believe that physics has nothing to teach them. In the *Social Text* cosmology, science is a socially aggressive but intellectually weak enterprise that seeks "affirmation" from postmodern philosophy. This is why they didn't check Sokal's claims out: whether the physics made sense or not made no difference, because its value had to be in the philosophy anyway. So why bother?

This disciplinary narcissism, so typical of recent literary cultural studies, is a mystery to me. After all, the natural sciences have been quite successful with their object of study, and we probably have *a lot* to learn from their methods. But no: for Stanley Aronowitz (quoted in *The New York Times*), Sokal is "ill-read and half-educated." Well, then, how does it feel being duped by the half-educated?

Toward the end of their reply, Ross and Robbins state that "we must ask again and again whether it is possible, or prudent, to isolate facts from values." I would respond that yes, it is possible (though difficult), and certainly very prudent, because it's the only way to *learn* anything. If facts cannot be isolated from values, then values can never be tested, never contradicted, never changed. Research, experiment, evidence, and discussion all become useless. Only values, everywhere. A nightmare: Cardinal Bellarmino and Stanley Aronowitz, forever together.

Why Ross and Robbins like this scenario, and what makes it "progressive," is another mystery. "Science trades in knowledge," wrote Brecht at the end of *Galileo*, "which is the product of doubt. And this new art of doubt has enchanted the public. . . . They snatched the telescopes out of our hands and had them trained on their tormentors: prince, official, public moralist." Knowledge, doubt, enchantment, polemical unmasking: here is the science we need, not prudence. But, alas, much of the left has lost its passion for knowledge, and *Social Text* has proved it.

So far *Social Text* has not offered arguments but invoked all sorts of Victorian pieties ("deception," "breach of ethics," "irresponsible," "good faith," "confession") in the hopes of exorcising the hoax. Come on. You are a polemical journal, with an issue titled *Science Wars*. Drop the pose, accept the facts, and another, more interesting discussion may begin.

ELLEN SCHRECKER, *professor of history, Yeshiva University*: I find Alan Sokal's "experiment" and the furor it has caused more than a little disturbing. I agree with much of what he said: there is no justification for intellectual sloth, nor is opacity a virtue. Nonetheless, I am afraid that Sokal may not realize how potentially damaging his discursive booby trap may be.

Besides a real physical world, there is a real political one, a world in which conservative pundits and lawmakers are attacking not just the cultural studies departments but the entire academy. The battleground here is not a text but the bottom line. The right is fighting a broad-based campaign to demonize those sectors of the academic community that encourage critical thinking and offer an alternative perspective on the status quo. The Culture Wars have taken their casualties. Much of what we in the academy would consider mainstream scholarship is now under attack and continues to lose public support.

The onslaught against what academics do reinforces the efforts of the business-oriented Republicans and their allies to defund the public sector. So much the better if it turns out that much of the academy is not only economically irrelevant but also wrong. The defenders of the good old flag and canon, despite their alleged reverence for the liberal arts, rarely if ever confront the damage that bottom-line thinking and forced vocationalism are doing to their cherished institutions.

Alan Sokal is certainly no enemy of the traditional academy and is, in his way, trying to strengthen it. His demand for intellectual rigor is both refreshing and long overdue. There is no reason why conservatives should claim a monopoly on high standards and scholarly merit; leftists can be tough graders, too. Even so, I worry that Sokal's merry prank may well backfire and provide further ammunition for the forces that have damaged the academic community far more than a few trendy theorists.

—July 1996

THE REALITY GULF
Did the Gulf War Take Place?

SCOTT MCLEMEE

THE GULF WAR was a kind of video game—and not only for the millions of couch-potato noncombatants who watched it unfold on TV. High-tech weapons systems made combat an exercise in button punching (at least from the U.S. side). Generals at the Pentagon and in Baghdad monitored the war's progress via CNN's continuous feed of image and analysis. And a few weeks after it ended, the conflict went interactive when Time Warner released its Desert Storm CD-ROM.

Thus was the defining moment of the post–Cold War world downloaded into the data bank we call history. It was all very much like something from an essay by Jean Baudrillard, the French theorist of postmodernity whose writings on "the hyperreal" and "the procession of simulacra" present a metaphysics of cybernetic and video reality. And indeed, as the war began, Baudrillard directed his own attention to the mounting hostilities in the Gulf. Now a chapbook of his ruminations on the conflict, originally published by Editions Galilée in May 1991, is available as *The Gulf War Did Not Take Place*. (Baudrillard derived his title from Jean Giraudoux's 1935 play, *The Trojan War Will Not Take Place*.)

Baudrillard's first Gulf War essay, published in the Paris newspaper *Libération* on January 4, 1991, ventured in its title a bold prediction: "The Gulf War Will Not Take Place." Baudrillard argued that the vast apparatus of "deterrence" left over from the Cold War would contain the tensions between Iraq and the United States. "Western power in general," he announced, was "paralyzed by its own strength and incapable of assuming it in the form of relations of force." According to the theorist, the preparation for war, and especially the constant media coverage, ensured that war would never happen. "We are no longer in a logic of the passage from virtual to actual, but in a hyperrealist logic of the deterrence of the real by the virtual," Baudrillard explained. An English translation of the article appeared in the London *Guardian* just four days before January 15, when virtual missiles began hitting real targets.

So Baudrillard, with an air of determined nonchalance, did the only thing he could do. He wrote some more essays. And provoked some outrage. In his introduction to the book, Paul Patton—a lecturer in philosophy at the University of Sydney who put Baudrillard's prose into some approximation of English—defends the theorist from his most dismissive critic, the British writer Christopher Norris. In *Uncritical Theory: Postmodernism, Intellectuals, and the Gulf War*, Norris identified Baudrillard as the "purveyor of some of the silliest ideas yet to gain a hearing among disciples of French intellectual fashion." And with the beleaguered tone of a man who has finally been pushed too far, Norris asked, "How far wrong can a thinker go and still lay claim to serious attention?"

Pretty far, evidently. In the second essay—"The Gulf War: Is It Really Taking Place?"—Baudrillard neatly folded the spectacle on CNN into his theories. His translator, at least, is convinced. As Patton glosses it, "Real events lose their identity when they attain the velocity of real-time information, or to employ another metaphor, when they become encrusted with the information which represents them." *Id est*: If it's on television all the time, it quits being real. And in the final panel of his triptych, "The Gulf War Did Not Take Place," Baudrillard said the combatants were so grossly mismatched in firepower that the conflict was not really a war. Besides, he asked: "How is it that Saddam is still there as though nothing had happened?"

"That this is all sheer nonsense," wrote Norris shortly after Baudrillard's essays first appeared, "a postmodern update on well-worn sophistical themes, should be obvious to anyone not wholly given over to the vagaries of current intellectual fashion." Even more annoying to Norris than Baudrillard's cavalier indifference to events is his denial that, as Norris puts it, "there exists a truth 'behind' appearances, a level of rock-bottom factual appeal and ethical responsibility." Such irritation is particularly keen coming from Norris. His early books on Derrida and post-structuralist theory helped create an appetite for such French-fried notions as Baudrillard's among Anglophone readers. But Norris now positions himself as a partisan of the *hors texte.* "Reality" is, in a word, real. The truth is out there. According to an interview in the September 1995 issue of *Parallax* (subtitled *A Journal of Metadiscursive Theory and Cultural Practices*), he is working on a book about the philosophical implications of the history of aerodynamics. "I'm not quite sure," he says, "how all these jet-setting postmodernists can sit happily on airplanes and believe that aerodynamics is merely a product of this or that language-game or cultural code or whatever."

But in the United States, homeland of the simulacrum, Baudrillard's books do well. Colin Robinson, managing director of Verso Books, says that the English translation of Baudrillard's travelogue *America* has sold some twenty-two thousand copies since it first appeared in 1989. And most of the run of *The Gulf War Did Not Take Place* was promptly snapped up by distributors after Indiana University Press published it last October.

Only after the book was printed and shipped did anyone notice that the dust jacket claimed Baudrillard's essays were "written during the unfolding drama of 1992." So much for historical memory about the major international event of 1991. Since the world is on "a delusional course," as Baudrillard himself wrote in an earlier volume of essays, "we must adopt a delusional standpoint towards the world." Why not a delusional standpoint toward proofreading?

—May 1996

LAST WILL AND TESTAMENT OF AN EX–LITERARY CRITIC
A Theorist Rejects His Calling

FRANK LENTRICCHIA

I ONCE MANAGED to live for a long time, and with no apparent stress, a secret life with literature. Publicly, in the books I'd written and in the classroom, I worked as a historian and polemicist of literary theory who could speak with passion, and without noticeable impediment, about literature as a political instrument. I once wrote that the literary word was like a knife, a hammer, a gun. I became a known and some-what colorfully controversial figure, regularly excoriated in neoconservative laments about the academy.

The secret me was me-the-reader, in the act of reading: an experience in which the words of someone else filled me up and made it irrelevant to talk about my reading; an experience that I'd had for as long as I can remember being a reader. This secret life implicitly denied that any talk about what I had undergone could ever be authentic. My silent encounters with literature are ravishingly pleasurable, like erotic transport.

In private, I was tranquillity personified; in public, an actor in the endless strife and divisiveness of argument, the "Dirty Harry of literary theory," as one reviewer put it. My secret life eventually was to be shared with students in my undergraduate classroom, while my public life as literary intellectual continued to be played out in the graduate classroom. Two types of classroom; two selves unhappy with one another.

ONCE, AND ONLY ONCE, I posed the following question to undergraduate majors in a course I teach at Duke University on modern literature: "Anybody here like literature?" Looks of puzzlement and concern: *Is he stoned?* I like my undergraduates, with whom I share a bond of stubborn naïveté. We believe that literature is pleasurable and important, as literature and not as an illustration of something else. I've posed the same question in graduate seminars. The response never varies: knowing laughs, disturbing nods of recognition, a few stares of impatience and hostility. They assume I'm one of them. They say, "You don't believe that literature is important as literature." Then they point to the damaging evidence of some of my work in the field, usually to a book called *Criticism and Social Change.* I want to reply, "You need to understand the context." I say nothing. They believe that the book is clear, that no context can modify its essential meaning, and they're right. When *Criticism and Social Change* appeared in 1983, I was convinced that a literary critic, *as a literary critic*, could be an agent of social transformation, an activist who would show his students that, in its form and style, literature had a strategic role to play in the world's various arrangements of power; that literature wasn't to be relegated to the Arts and Leisure section of the Sunday paper as if it were a thing for weekend amusement only. I would show my students that what is called literature is nothing but the most devious of rhetorical discourses (writing with political designs upon us all), either in opposition to or in complicity with the power in place. In either case, novels, poems, and plays deserved to be included in the Sunday section called News of the Week in Review.

Over the last ten years, I've pretty much stopped reading literary criticism, because most of it isn't literary. But criticism it is of a sort— the sort that stems from the sense that one is morally superior to the writers that one is supposedly describing. This posture of superiority is assumed when those writers represent the major islands of Western literary tradition, the central cultural engine—so it goes—of racism, poverty, sexism, homophobia, and imperialism: a cesspool that literary critics would expose for mankind's benefit. Just what it would avail us to learn that Flaubert was a sexist is not clear. It is impossible, this much is clear, to exaggerate the heroic self-inflation of academic literary criticism.

To be certified as an academic literary critic, you need to believe, and be willing to assert, that Ezra Pound's *Cantos*, a work twice the length of *Paradise Lost* and which 99 percent of all serious students of literature find too difficult to read, actually forwards the cause of worldwide anti-Semitism. You need to tell your students that, despite what almost a century's worth of smart readers have concluded, Joseph Conrad's *Heart of Darkness* is a subtle celebration of the desolations of imperialism. My objection is not that literary study has been politicized but that it proceeds in happy indifference to, often in unconscionable innocence of, the protocols of literary competence. Only ten to fifteen years ago, the views I've cited on Pound and Conrad would have received barely passing grades had they been submitted as essays in an undergraduate course. Now such views circulate at the highest levels of my profession in the essays of distinguished literary critics.

I've never believed that writers had to be superior in anything except writing. The fundamental, if only implied, message of much literary criticism is self-righteous, and it takes this form: "T. S. Eliot is a homophobe and I am not. Therefore, I am a better person than Eliot. Imitate me, not Eliot." To which the proper response is: "But T. S. Eliot could really write, and you can't. Tell us truly, is there no filth in your soul?"

WHEN IT'S THE REAL THING, literature enlarges us; strips the film of familiarity from the world; creates bonds of sympathy with all kinds, even with evil characters, who we learn are all in the family. Each of these points has been made long ago in response to the question What is literature for? With no regrets, I tell you that I have nothing new to offer to the field of literary theory.

I confess to never having been able to get enough of the real thing. I worry incessantly about using up my stash and spending the last years of my life in gloom, having long ago mainlined all the great, veil-piercing books. Great *because* veil-piercing. Books propelling me out of the narrow life that I lead in my own little world, offering me revelations of strangers, who turn out not to be totally strange; a variety of real worlds, unveiled for me, for the first time.

If you should happen to enjoy the literary experience of liberation, it's not likely that you do so because you're able to take apart the formal resources of literature. All that you know is that you live where you live and that you are who you are. Then you submit to the text, you relinquish yourself, because you need to be transported. You know with complete certitude that when you are yourself, you are only, at best, half alive. Even if you can't say what it is, you know when you're in the thrall of real literature. You can't get your fix from reading the Op-Ed page or, for that matter, any other pages in discourses you think of as *not literary*. If asked to define "literary," you could not do it. If pressed, you'd say, "I'm not interested in the question." It's like asking me who God is. You might say, as I would, "The question 'What is literature?' is a question for those who secretly hate literature." If you put a gun to my head, I'll say, "All literature is travel literature, all true readers shut-ins."

The first time that I traveled it was 1956 and I was sixteen. I was in bed. Ever since, I like to do it in a bed, or reclining on a couch, or on the floor, with my knees drawn up—just like the first time, the book leaning against my thighs, nestled in my groin. The first booking was arranged by a high-school teacher named (honest) LaBella, who said to me out of the blue, "Live fast, die young, and have a good-looking corpse." He told me that he was quoting a line from a novel that I should read, *Knock on Any Door* by Willard Motley. I tried to take out the book from my hometown public library but was informed that I could have it only if I brought them a letter from my mother saying that it was okay, which my indulgent mother was happy to write.

After supper, I withdrew to my room, shut the door, and read deep into the night. Next morning, I didn't bother with breakfast. My mother looked in to ask if I was sick. I kept on going into the early afternoon, when I finished, still in my pajamas, unwashed and unshaven. Too bad I couldn't have hooked up a catheter.

I was living in the world of Nick Romano, a good Italian-American Catholic, an altar boy, who through a terrible unfairness is cast down into the mean streets of Chicago's West Side and eventually, at twenty-one, into the electric chair for a murder that he in fact committed and that I wanted him to get away with. "Live fast, die young, and have a good-looking corpse" was Nick's motto. He loved a girl named Rosemary, who loved him back passionately. They actually did it.

I was also a good Italian-American Catholic, crazy for a girl named Rosemary, but I never talked to her, never mind the other thing, which almost nobody in my teen world did. I lived in Utica, New York, a small ethnic town where parents were strict, where the streets were not mean. I had (and have) a dramatic life in books, not on the streets.

A couple of years ago, I learned that the late Willard Motley was gay and black and that he only rarely wrote about blacks. Occasionally I try to factor Motley's race and sexual orientation into what I experienced when I read his novel. I can't do it. Recently I learned that Motley said, in response to an obvious question, that he considered himself a member of the human race. In the current academy, there's no possibility of accepting that statement as anything but a pathetic dodge.

When I grew up and became a literary critic, I learned to keep silent about the reading experiences of liberation that I'd enjoyed since childhood. With many of my generation, I believed that my ability to say the words "politics" and "literature" in the same breath was the only socially responsible way to affirm the value of literary study.

Then, seven years ago, I lost my professional bearing and composure. The actual crisis occurred in a graduate class just as I was about to begin a lecture on Faulkner. Before I could get a word out, a student said, "The first thing we have to understand is that Faulkner is a racist." I responded with a stare, but he was not intimidated. I was. He wanted to subvert me with what I thought crude versions of ideas that had made my academic reputation and that had (as he told me before the semester began) drawn him to my class. And now I was refusing to be the critic he had every right to think I was. And I felt subverted. Later in the course, another student attacked Don DeLillo's *White Noise* for what he called its insensitivity to the Third World. I said, "But the novel doesn't concern the Third World. It's set in a small town in Middle America. It concerns the technological catastrophes of the First World." The student replied, "That's the problem. It's ethnocentric and elitist." I had been, before that class, working hard to be generous. After that class, I didn't want to be generous anymore and tried to communicate how unspeakably stupid I found these views but had trouble staying fully rational. There was an explosion or two of operatic dimension. I wasn't the tenor hero; I was the baritone villain.

So I gave up teaching graduate students. I escaped into the undergraduate classroom—in other words, slipped happily underground in order to talk to people who, like me, need to read great literature just as much as they need to eat.

I'M A TEACHER WHO believes that literature can't be taught, if by teaching we mean being in lucid possession of a discipline, a method, and rules for the engagement of the object of study. I believe that the finest examples of the object of study cannot be ruled and that, therefore, professional literary study is a contradiction in terms. Great writing is a literally *unruly*, one-of-a-kind thing, something new and original in the world of literature, which (like all cultural worlds) is dominated by the conventional and the rule-driven: the boringly second-rate. Where, then, is the teacher? In my classroom, I assume, but cannot prove, that there can be illuminating conversation about the peaks of unruly originality, from Homer and Dante to Joyce and

Proust. I assume that such conversation cannot be replaced by what goes on in the sociology or the economics classroom.

We do not, after all, tell economists that all economic data and systems are actually disguised examples of novels, poems, and plays. Yet this is precisely the form of absurdity that the professional study of literature has taken. The situation in the literary wing of the academy is that those who (when teenagers) spent the days and nights of their lives with their noses happily buried in imaginative literature now believe that they must look elsewhere, to academic disciplines, for the understanding and values of their happiness. And look elsewhere they do, with holy zeal. They embark upon a course and leave their happiness far behind.

I believe that what is now called literary criticism is a form of xeroxing. Tell me your theory and I'll tell you in advance what you'll say about any work of literature, especially those you haven't read. Texts are not read; they are pre-read. All of literature is x and nothing but x, and literary study is the naming (exposure) of x. For x, read imperialism, sexism, homophobia, and so on. All of literary history is said to be a display of x, because human history is nothing but the structure of x. By naming x, we supposedly name the social order (ordure) as it is and always has been. The point of naming it? Presumably, to produce a contagion of true understanding (the critic as social interventionist), from which would follow appropriate social change in wholesome directions, though it has to be noted that the literary academy has long been staffed by people with righteous understanding, who assiduously disseminate that understanding in the classroom, and still the world remains governed by sexism and so on. In the hearts of those who study literature lies the repressed but unshakable conviction that the study of literature serves no socially valued purpose. Too bad academic literary critics can't accept their amateur status—that is, their status as lovers.

If the authority of a contemporary literary critic lies in his *theory* of x, then wherein lies the authority of the theory itself? In disciplines in which he has little experience and less training. The typical literary critic who wields a theory is not himself a sociologist, historian, or economist as well as a student of literature. A scandal of professional impersonation? No, because the impersonators speak only into the mirror of other impersonators and rarely to those in a position to test their theories for fraudulence. An advanced literature department is the place where you can write a dissertation on Wittgenstein and never have to face an examiner from the philosophy department. An advanced literature department is the place where you may speak endlessly about gender and never have to face the scrutiny of a biologist, because gender is just a social construction and nature doesn't exist.

My reader has the right to pose some questions: You say that literature of original character can't be taught. So what is it that you do in your classroom? And you are obviously weary of the pounding chatter about sexism and so on. Are you saying that those subjects of academic literary criticism are not important just because they are fashionable? Is not literature significantly about such subjects, whether or not literary critics take them up? My answers: Literature is about homophobia and so on, but only because literature is about everything real and imaginable under the sun, including man as a political animal. Imperialism and so on are subjects for imagination, not agendas or ideas to be illustrated. Imaginative writers have but one agenda: to write beautifully, rivetingly, unforgettably.

What I see in the academy is an eager flight from literature by those who refuse to take the *literary* measure of the subject, whatever the subject may be. The literature student sees the objects that historians and sociologists see, but he ought to see them through the special lens of literature as objects in stylized and imaginative landscapes. The authentic literary type believes with Oscar Wilde that life is an imitation of art. Sociologists don't believe that; philosophers don't either. Why should they? They're sociologists and philosophers, who know that life is an imitation of sociology and philosophy.

I would take it as a sign of renewed health in literary studies if critics would recognize the value and authority of other disciplines in which they have (for the most part) but cocktail-party acquaintance, disciplines practiced by serious people, many of whom do not take literature seriously but perhaps more seriously than they take literary critics, whom they think of as charlatans deluxe. I would take it as a miraculous sign of full recovery if contemporary literary critics would recognize the impious comedic dimension of the most serious and weighty works of the literary tradition.

THE FIRST THING I DO in my classroom is shut the door and then make sure it's shut tight. (Unfortunately, on the windows of my classroom there are no shades.) Since I do not believe that, as a literary critic, I can have honest recourse to method, theory, and discipline—original writing being, by my definition, the antithesis of those things—I'm uneasy about what I do on university grounds, where those in charge have every right to expect professors to convey knowledge in systematic fashion, so that students might come away with an "education," rules of investigation that they might apply to texts that I haven't taught them. The academy doth make scientific impersonators of literary critics, who should, rather, be anarchists.

Behind closed doors, with only undergraduates in attendance, I become something of a rhapsode. As Plato says in the *Ion*, rhapsodes are enthusiasts. We're out of our minds. Like all rhapsodes, I like to recite from the text. I tell my students that in true recitation we're possessed, we are the medium for the writer's voice. I speak the text as the writer would speak it—this is my radical and unverifiable claim—and the phrases and sentences flow out of me as they flowed from him in the process of creating the text. The writer flows into me and out of me: my mouth his exit into our world.

My listener-students, in the moment of recitation, are infused, taken over by the writer's original voice embodied in me. They, too, become possessed. Rhapsode and audience assume a single strange consciousness not their own: "living," not "knowing," the text. We are simply, and collectively, mad.

Because I am an imperfect rhapsode, I bring to my students what I know about literary history, the author's life and times, literary forms, types, and styles: real knowledge, slowly and sometimes painfully gained over a lifetime, which takes me to the brink of the text itself.

My doctorate in literature helps, but it does not take me inside. I share this knowledge with my students, but it doesn't substitute for an honest act of reading. Then we face, let us say, James Joyce's *Ulysses* and quickly learn that, when we confront the page itself, calling *Ulysses* a novel, or a comic epic in prose, or an odd instance of satire, or a modernist experiment, doesn't do us much good, even if we have a sophisticated understanding of what these things mean. At the level of the page itself, all I have is my relatively informed sensibility and a number of years of reading as I fumble in the dark of originality. We try to describe what is on the page. That's all.

In my classes, we creep along (a whole semester, for example, on *Ulysses*). We tend to have difficulty getting through reading lists. I am a slow reader. We tend not to come to large conclusions. We don't know, at the end of the semester, what *Ulysses* means. We even have a hard time with the question What is *Ulysses* about? A harder time, I'm pleased to say, at the end of the semester than at the beginning. I'm not comfortable with questions about meaning or subject matter. I am a man flying from ideas, including his own.

Most of all, we get lost in the particulars of Joyce's writing. We like to wallow. We try to see "characters," "Dublin," "narrative," but what we only see is writing. Again and again we make the reader's equivalent of the discovery that Marcel Proust made when he finally knew that he was a writer. The young Proust was burdened with a sense that a mystery lay concealed behind certain objects of the world which he could not get out of his mind. His sense of concealed significance coincided with his despair of finding a literary vocation. Then one fine day the rind of things peeled away, and he saw that the mysterious significance was a phrase, perhaps a word, maybe a fragment of a sentence. And these were *his* words, first fruits of his wanting to write. Proust found his own writing as the secret concealed behind things. So the reader of Joyce, or of any writer of force, looking for the big things behind the text, will in the end find the only big thing, the writing in its specific shape and texture, and all that the writing incarnates, thanks to its specific shape and texture. The reader stays happily, then, at the surface of the text, where all the deep stuff resides,

trying to describe the surface—feeling about in the dark, then reporting back from the dark in words that would describe the encounter
with strange combinations of words.

My classes are an attempt to share a text in this way. The text so
shared is memorable, we remember it long, because we hover over the
surface untiringly; low-flying readers we are. We would memorize
Ulysses. Teacher and students textually bonded for about fifteen
weeks, becoming something cohesive and intimate, an enworded
community. Later, when we must part our ways (they graduate and
go away for good, only a few return), we will occasionally (in our privacy) see our lives through the world-bearing words of *Ulysses*, and
we'll recall each other and ourselves in that classroom, and we'll be
united again in a way, in Joyce's writing, as we travel again together in
a world made by Joyce. I think that's a good enough reason to teach
literature, in any classroom.

—September 1996

Dear Editors,
I'm delighted to read that Duke University professor Frank Lentricchia
has officially tendered his resignation from the party of hostility to litera-
ture. But while Lentricchia shuts the door of his classroom on the outside
world, teachers who care about literary values, few of whom enjoy situa-
tions as fortunate as his, continue to face hostile scrutiny from within the
academy and from without. Lentricchia's statement may offer them some
comfort, but little help in making their case to the skeptics that surround
them.

First, Lentricchia's presentation of his renewed appreciation for literary
values concedes far too much to the enemies of literature. While he does re-
fer to "the protocols of literary competence," his description of literary re-
sponse centers on rhapsodic enthusiasm; for him, the study of literature has
become a form of anti-intellectual escapism. Genuinely valuing literature
would involve seeing it not merely as a form of imaginary travel but also
as a form of understanding, which might appropriately inspire rigorous
and intellectually precise analysis as well as rhapsody. The ability to "de-

scribe the encounter with strange combinations of words" is grounded in sympathy, but it also demands skills and discipline, and a large part of helping our students become better readers is modeling those skills and that discipline for them.

Second, Lentricchia's withdrawal into the undergraduate classroom may be personally satisfying but does little to address the situation his critical writing helped to create. The persistence of the professional culture of hostility to literature means that undergraduates who share Lentricchia's love for good writing, however gifted they may be, must either betray that feeling or give up on the idea of attending graduate school and pursuing a career in the profession. It means as well that a generation of teachers shaped by the currently dominant attitudes are inculcating in their own students the facile moral smugness Lentricchia so deplores. Lentricchia helped soil the nest of literary study; the least he could do would be to help clean it up.

VERNON SHETLEY
Associate Professor of English
Wellesley College

Frank Lentricchia is hardly the first to express his distaste for what his chosen profession has become. Thomas Carlyle, for one, got there first. "Poetry, the workings of genius itself, which in all times, with one or another meaning, has been called Inspiration, and held to be mysterious and inscrutable, is no longer without its scientific exposition," Carlyle lamented in "Signs of the Times" (1829). "By arguing on the 'force of circumstances,' we have argued away all force from ourselves; and stand leashed together, uniform in dress and movement, like the rowers of some boundless galley."

But though his sympathies were clear, Carlyle knew, as surely Lentricchia must as well, not to throw out the baby with the bathwater. Great literature, alas, does not "teach itself," and neither does any other significant field of endeavor. Would that Carlyle would teach himself when I enter my undergraduate classroom tomorrow; he won't, and I will do what professors of literature have always done: explicate, historicize, ar-

gue, cajole, and question in order to get my students to think more clearly and deeply about the rhetoric of a man dead long before this century was born. Literary criticism, and even (horrors!) literary theory, have helped me do that, as they have helped Lentricchia. That he now finds these practices inappropriate for the undergraduate classroom says more about him, I think, than about the profession itself.

Lentricchia's diatribe against the methods he helped popularize caricatures the hard work of scholars who have never been satisfied with saying, for example, "Faulkner's a racist," but who nonetheless believe race is an inextricable element in Faulkner's genius. If Lentricchia did his job responsibly, he could make these subtleties clear to graduate students overeager to parrot back to him his pronouncements from the past. Instead, like Victor Frankenstein, he turns his back on the monster he's helped create, then curses its failures.

ELIZABETH ROSE GRUNER
Assistant Professor of English
University of Richmond

Like the talk-show guest who publicizes shameful secrets in an attempt to relativize his sin, Frank Lentricchia describes his addiction to critical theory as a malady affecting academe itself. And like the survivor he is, he prescribes cold turkey for the rest of us by arguing that "rhapsodic" reading is the only authentic way to teach literature.

The fallacy of Lentricchia's cure struck me immediately in the description of his two equally exaggerated classroom styles—the first from the heyday of his theory addiction, the second from his present abstemious mood. As a student, I had the opportunity to experience the same text, Rabelais's Pantagruel, *taught in the manner of both of Lentricchia's models but with opposite effects. My first exposure to Gargantua et al. was under the tutelage of a literary historian who reveled in Rabelais's strange and arcane references to texts high and low. Reading* Pantagruel *with this teacher was a boisterous passage on a sturdy flagship; we were tossed in the waves of occult knowledge and linguistic difficulty but held on for the sheer joy of the voyage. My second experience of Rabelais was with a pro-*

fessor who appeared so in awe of the text that he would venture little but to read passages aloud, as if aesthetic appreciation were alone sufficient. Granted, he read with feeling and gusto. But reading aloud leaves much to be desired, especially for a text as dense and obscure as Rabelais's. This second teacher left me bored and disappointed, and saddened for my fellow students, who would never enjoy Rabelais as I had done.

Lentricchia's advice to return to the text is not new; he merely echoes the hero of "intuitive" reading, Leo Spitzer. Like Spitzer, Lentricchia sees himself in the vanguard of a reaction against the excesses of the recent past. I have no problem with the critic's effort to heal himself. But I fear that the prejudices of his document, published with the apparent approval of an authoritative journal, may do more damage than good to the future of literary studies.

JULIA DOUTHWAITE
Associate Professor of French
University of Notre Dame

Praises to Frank Lentricchia for his confession and apologia. When Brother Lentricchia ceases to use the word "text" when he means "novel," we'll know his soul has truly come home.

JOAN MELLEN
Professor of English
Temple University

PAPER TIGERS

A Sociologist Follows Cultural Studies Into the Wilderness

MICHAEL SCHUDSON

IT CAN BE AN UNSETTLING EXPERIENCE for a sociologist to browse a university bookstore these days. It's easy enough to find the women's studies or gender studies section, African-American studies or cultural studies, but not so easy to locate sociology. This is especially unnerving when each of the other sections is full of books that look a lot like what sociology is supposed to be. Perhaps this is a victory, proof of what the journalist Richard Rovere wrote two generations ago: "Those of us who have been educated in the twentieth century habitually think in sociological terms, whether or not we have had any training in sociology." But somehow it does not feel like a victory. Something is missing. As the body of work called cultural studies has grown, the sociology of culture seems to have been elbowed aside.

Cultural studies refuses to be defined or to define itself. Still, some of its features can be discerned. It is something like the extension of literary studies to subjects outside a conventional canon—including science fiction, pornography, rock music, MTV, television generally, popular culture at large. It tends to embrace an anthropological understanding of culture as a whole way of life rather than as a set of privileged aesthetic objects. But if this new discipline sees culture as the universe of social practices, it also redefines social practices as an ensemble of texts, all susceptible to interpretation or deconstruction.

Cultural studies seems to promise a sociologically enriched analysis—
that is, one that locates cultural objects in relation to the social context in which people produce them and use them. But too often the
result is a sociologically impoverished view of politics and social action. Even more disturbing, cultural studies shows signs of becoming
an insulated and self-confirming field of study. Its most cherished
texts—including the one that this essay will examine, Donna Haraway's "Teddy Bear Patriarchy"—are rarely exposed to careful criticism from the outside.

If cultural studies tends to be shy about defining its boundaries, it
is often bold in proclaiming its politics. No conservatives need apply.
"Cultural studies," writes a leading proponent, Lawrence Grossberg,
"may have been (and I would hope still is) opposed to capitalism, its
structures of inequality and exploitation." Since cultural studies arose
as a rebellion within established university departments, and since it
has often found a home base in politically contested programs, like
women's studies, it is, not surprisingly, characterized by forms of address that testify to shared political principles. Because many scholars
who engage in cultural studies are self-proclaimed advocates for
women, gays and lesbians, or people of color in higher education, it is
easy to see why the fashioning of a distinctive intellectual vision becomes identified with political virtue. But even though political like-
mindedness is a familiar and valuable basis for human solidarity, it is
a dubious grounding for a whole field of study.

In contemporary sociology and many other social sciences, by contrast, it is taken for granted that conservatives, liberals, and Marxists
can and should coexist (though perhaps not too many conservatives
and not too many Marxists). In cultural studies, for all its fierce internal debates, there seems to be an unwritten loyalty oath to uphold the
trinity of class, race, and gender as the fundamental dimensions on
which difference is present in human experience. Moreover, on the
American scene, class regularly drops out of view. Actual work in cultural studies typically focuses on race, gender, and sexual preference.
Not only does class recede, but so do other major social bases of
discrimination, conflict, and differential power. A book like *Culture*

Wars, in which the sociologist James Davison Hunter argues that the fundamental divisions in American life today fall along religious lines, would not make sense or attract much interest in cultural studies.

Whatever the shortcomings of class, race, and gender as ways to discuss the basic dimensions of domination in contemporary societies, these terms certainly have a sociological ring. Equally sociological is the view that the privileged texts of literary or art-historical study should be forced to rub shoulders with rock lyrics, science fiction, talk radio, nursery rhymes, and appellate court opinions. Quintessentially sociological is the widespread notion that apparently "natural" categories are in fact socially constructed. Indeed, the whole cultural studies enterprise, as the British sociologist David Chaney suggests, might well be regarded as a subdivision of the sociology of knowledge, which has long taught that "traditions institutionalize ideologies and privilege."

WHY, THEN, do I believe cultural studies is more in need of sociology than the other way around? One significant problem is that the move from the sociology of culture to cultural studies often involves a slippage from a view that emphasizes the *social* construction of reality to a view that examines the *cultural* or *symbolic* construction of reality, as if this were a process that largely took place outside the social world.

The analytic distinction between the social and the cultural is not always easy to keep straight, but it seems to me fundamental. It goes like this: the "social" is people interacting, and the "cultural" refers to the perceptual frames, symbolic structures, and narrative conventions governing how they do so. For instance, "murder" is a cultural label that refers to one person's taking another person's life without legal warrant. "Murder is wrong" is a cultural injunction inscribed in religious and legal texts and available as a cognitive schema in people's heads. It is discourse, revisable and contestable. On the other hand, a given act of killing may or may not fit the legal and moral category "murder," but killing takes place regardless. It is social rather than cultural, behavior rather than consciousness. It makes a living person a dead one. While discourse affects the fate of the perpetrator (first- or second-degree murder? premeditated or not? mitigating or aggravating circumstances? justifiable homicide?), no words and no social constructions resuscitate the victim. Of course, we experience the world through culture. Different societies, and people differently situated in a single society, may see death, or aging, or kinship in very different ways. But no person and no society can escape addressing death, aging, and kinship.

Now, there are several cultural studies traditions, and my criticism is not applicable to all. One tradition grows out of the British effort to write about the relationship between culture and society in a way that keeps ever present the "lived experience" of human beings as they make use of a common stock of symbols and images, religious values, moral outlooks, and received attitudes toward the body, nature, work, and play. Richard Hoggart, for example, showed the complex ways in which working-class Britons drew meaning from pulp literature. And E. P. Thompson explained how the most politically active British workers of the early nineteenth century were able to condemn the capitalist order because of their long-standing belief in the "Englishman's birthright." While these writers, who did much of their best work in the 1950s and 1960s, took pride in their socialist political commitments, their intellectual orientation and methodological precepts were not essentially foreign to conventional sociology. Of course, followers of this tradition do not wish to distinguish between the social and the cultural; they insist strenuously that it is dangerous and misleading to draw such distinctions. According to Raymond Williams, the cultural, linguistic, and symbolic are "indissoluble elements of the material social process itself." The old distinction between "base" and "superstructure," they argue, has to be jettisoned. Although this seems to me a risky blurring of concepts, it works well enough in British cultural studies, which has as strong an identification with sociology as with literary studies and which keeps the study of culture anchored in "lived social experience" through a doggedly empiricist style of work.

But in the United States, where cultural studies has borrowed from

French more than British intellectual culture, a different tradition has grown. Here, a notion of lived experience figures only marginally; the primary concern has been to rethink the nature of the literary text itself. One of the goals of this multistranded line of work has been to demonstrate that each human "subject" is created by linguistic formations that exist prior to the individual's consciousness. No knowledge can be unattached to prevailing ideologies, and if a particular intellectual act is not directly subversive, it must by definition be involved in reinforcing the existing relations of power.

What follows from this is important: if knowledge (and culture) arises in a ready-made discursive setting, all knowledge is necessarily in the service of power—whether anyone intends it to be or not. After all, knowledge is inevitably knowledge "for." This is the common kernel of cultural studies and the sociology of knowledge. But if this insight becomes the end rather than the opening of inquiry, then trouble begins. "Knowledge for" is also "knowledge of," to adapt a distinction made by the anthropologist Clifford Geertz. This does not presume that "science" and other human representations must be accurate recording devices of a real world. But nor should we assume that knowledge is *only* ideology or only the projection of the "positionality" of the observer onto some object in the world. Neither the one extreme (that the object itself dictates how it will be known and represented) nor the other (that the object does not exist for human knowledge except as humans project themselves onto it) is defensible. Nor is either extreme position very interesting. The first denies human agency; the second denies the world. Both deny the problem— which is to comprehend the relation between human knowledge and the world that human beings seek to know.

IN ORDER TO BRING THESE GENERAL REMARKS down to earth, I would like to look closely at one much-admired paper in cultural studies, Donna Haraway's "Teddy Bear Patriarchy: Taxidermy in the Garden of Eden, New York City, 1908–1936." This paper was first published in *Social Text* in 1984 and was later incorporated into Haraway's influential 1989 book, *Primate Visions*. The essay was singled out in a review of *Primate Visions* by the historian of science Margaret Rossiter as a "stellar" chapter; it was hailed in a 1991 collection of essays on "the poetics and politics of museum display" as "the most compelling analysis tó date"; and it was reprinted in 1994 as an "exemplary" piece in a reader on social theory. If cultural studies has created its own canon, this essay has a strong claim to belong in it.

Haraway's essay presents New York City's American Museum of Natural History as an important participant in the politics of culture. She treats the powerful dioramas and artful taxidermy in the museum's African Hall as a readable text, one that purports to offer objective knowledge of the world of nature. In her view, however, the main purpose of African Hall is not to afford understanding of the natural world but to reproduce and naturalize a master narrative of race, class, and gender in a capitalist society.

The best way to grasp the hall's meaning, she implies, is to review its genesis—in this case, to tell the story of how its stuffed-animal specimens were collected on African safaris: "I want to show the reader how the experience of the diorama grew from the safari in specific times and places, how the camera and the gun together are the conduits for the spiritual commerce of man and nature, how biography is woven into and from a social and political tissue." Incorporated in *Primate Visions*, the essay becomes part of a sprawling, multifaceted ambitious attempt to describe Euro-American primate studies as a story Western science tells itself in ways that reproduce the social inequalities embedded in its own presuppositions. Considered on its own, the essay looks at the life of Carl Akeley, the taxidermist who designed African Hall, to show that the museum's exhibits display "a history of race, sex, and class in New York City." What is revealed in the hall is not Africa but America, "a tale of the commerce of power and knowledge in white and male supremacist monopoly capitalism."

At this point, a skeptical reader should be on guard—the leap from the specifics of reading a museum exhibit to these wooden and formulaic abstractions is risky, especially when the abstractions presume that "America" can be fully represented by a set of universal categories (white, male, capitalist) whose distinctly American inflection is nowhere broached. Still, the essay operates from what appears to be a sound sociological premise—that, as the late UC–San Diego sociologist César Graña wrote, "museums . . . have ideologies."

So, on guard or not, readers move on to a few engaging pages in which Haraway takes them into the museum through its great Central Park West facade, past the gift shop (stopping to read a photobiography of Teddy Roosevelt), and into African Hall. Haraway is a perceptive guide; some of her remarks on the dioramas are striking, especially her observation that in each diorama "at least one animal . . . catches the viewer's gaze and holds it in communion." This is an informative tour, though it is not clear what justifies Haraway's pronouncement that "the central moral truth" of the museum is "the effective truth of manhood," which is "conferred" on the visitor who "passes through the trial of the museum." Apparently deriving this claim from some of Teddy Roosevelt's words on the walls just inside the main building, Haraway concludes that any visitor to the museum—in the 1920s or today—becomes "necessarily a boy in moral state." (Or, as revised for the book, "necessarily a white boy in moral state.")

As Haraway understands it, the hall's grand theme is the use of "the hygiene of nature" to "cure the sick vision of civilized man." But she never explains how this cure is effected or what it has to do with the intentions of master taxidermist Carl Akeley. How a ritual that symbolically brings boys through "the trial of the museum" into manhood is equally a curative rite to repair decadent civilization is a neat trick never explained. Are the boys sick and decadent, too? Or does the curative trip to the museum inoculate innocents against a decadence that has not yet affected them?

Of course, the idea that "nature" can be a cure for the ills wrought by civilization is a long-standing theme in American thought, well marked in *Walden* and extending back at least to the agrarianism of Thomas Jefferson. But it does not necessarily entail the pessimism and sense of decline Haraway rightly sees in the views of some museum trustees. After all, it is possible to seek solace, even salvation, in nature without holding grand and dark views about the corruption of civilization. One of the most popular novelists of the second and third decades of the twentieth century was Gene Stratton Porter, whose novels were among the top-ten best-sellers in 1918, 1919, 1921, and 1925. Her belief in the redemptive quality of nature could not have been further removed from the cultural pessimism that Haraway attributes to the museum leaders. (" 'Good cheer! Good cheer!' exulted the Cardinal," is the opening of Stratton Porter's sunny account of bird life in *The Song of the Cardinal*.) Readers who felt lost or displaced in the onrushing, urbanizing society of the 1920s may have found solace in her pastoral ethic, but Stratton Porter herself seems to have shared none of the anxiety of the museum trustees.

So some people fretted about that "sick vision" of civilized society a good deal more than others. But Haraway does not specify where anxiety about civilization was located and how it was channeled. She suggests that Carl Akeley and the trustees believed civilization to be sick and the encounter with nature to be a possible cure. Yet the trustees may have worried more about socializing the not-yet civilized than about redeeming the civilized. After all, a large part of the museum's educational function was to reinforce the social control of New York's immigrants—not to provide therapy for its civilized elites. Museum president Henry Fairfield Osborn was frank about his hopes to reach the urban masses: "Nature teaches law and order and respect for property. If these people cannot go to the country, then the Museum must bring nature to the city." Haraway herself used this quotation as an epigraph for the version of "Teddy Bear Patriarchy" that appeared in *Primate Visions*. But it works against, or at the very least complicates, her argument.

Haraway's talk of "moral boys" and "sick civilization" may be just a bit of rhetorical excess as she warms to her theme. But these terms keep her from ever addressing the question of what message real-life visitors to the museum took from the exhibit. Haraway knows that different people experience a museum in different ways. But how, exactly, are readers to understand her insistence that African Hall encodes a single narrative about white, patriarchal capitalism and that it situates every visitor to the museum as a "boy in moral state"?

What I take to be going on here is a kind of experiment in interpretation. That it ultimately fails, as I will try to demonstrate, is no crime; that the essay is cited reverently rather than answered critically, however, should give us pause about the culture of cultural studies. This is not to deny the achievement of "Teddy Bear Patriarchy" as an original attempt to direct attention to museums as cultural constructions. My objection is not to the aim of the essay but to the superficiality of its sociology and its oddly ahistorical history. My objection, further, is to its celebrity. The wide use of the essay and the deference to its canonical standing seem to signal an interpretive community that shares with it several central assumptions. The first of these is that the important thing to know about the cultural world is that the discourses that govern it are the constructions of a system of monopoly capitalism and white patriarchy. The second is that it is an act of political virtue and intellectual courage to demonstrate the constructedness of these discourses or of the cultural artifacts to which they give rise. Finally, it is presumed in Haraway's essay (though not everywhere in her writings) that such demonstrations override any need to inquire about whether, how, or to what degree some aspect of what we can only term "reality" nonetheless constrains a given discourse.

I LEAVE ASIDE NOW the question of how real people read museums. Haraway's approach is literary rather than sociological. It tells us nothing about what meaning actual visitors take from African Hall. But it can still be examined on its own terms. Is the approach Haraway adopts to interpretation convincing in its own right?

Her essay relies on a series of synecdoches; in each instance, a single part of the museum stands for the larger whole. Each of these conversions has to be convincing for the analysis to succeed. That is, the reader must be won to the view that, first, the Theodore Roosevelt

Memorial entry and African Hall stand adequately for the AMNH. No other part of the museum ever speaks in this essay—no dinosaurs, no Margaret Mead Hall of Pacific Peoples, no Stephen Jay Gould columns in the museum's magazine, *Natural History.*

The second synecdochic link is that the meaning of African Hall lies in the original plans that were drawn up for it and in the collecting, by gun and photograph, of the materials that were to go into its dioramas. This link makes a powerful claim of authorship on behalf of the safari leader, taxidermist, and great white hunter Carl Akeley, whose life history takes up much of the essay. The fact that African Hall did not open until ten years after Akeley's death is mentioned, but no mention is made of how his original plans may have been altered by the passage of a decade; indeed, no mention is made of just how extensive or complete his conception of African Hall was at any point.

This second link may be justified—I have no evidence to the contrary. But museums are complex organizations that compete in a sometimes hostile environment for public notice, private donations, and academic approval. In Haraway's account, there is only a broad cultural discourse represented by the museum's trustees; the museum's president, Henry Fairfield Osborn; and the mastermind of African Hall, Carl Akeley. This discourse goes into the museum machinery at one end, and the African Hall exhibits come out the other. In between, a void: no social organization, no social conflict, no contention.

And no passage of time. The third synecdoche is that African Hall in 1921 (the year, Haraway reveals as if uncovering the deep secret core, of both a key collecting safari and the AMNH-hosted Second International Congress of Eugenics), or perhaps in 1926 (the year of Akeley's death), or at least in 1936 (the year of the hall's opening), represents the unaltered meaning of African Hall at the time of Haraway's essay in the 1980s. As white patriarchal monopoly capitalism is a transhistorical structure, so apparently are its expressions and representations. That the meaning of a cultural object can change over time does not stir Haraway's interest, at least in the main body of her essay.

But if there's anything that recent work in cultural history has established, it's precisely the variability of an object's meanings. We know, from Lawrence Levine, that Shakespeare was popular melodrama in America in 1850 and had become a high-culture classic by 1920. And we know, from John Higham, that even the meanings of cultural objects more fixed than a dramatic text—at least as fixed in time as a diorama—change radically in their meanings. In the 1880s, the Statue of Liberty was taken to be a symbol of how American republican government, established with the aid of France during the Revolution, served as a beacon to the world. By the 1920s and fully by 1940, it had come to have a meaning never dreamed of by any of the individuals or groups responsible for its development and installation in New York Harbor. It came to mean "Welcome to America!" It became an inspirational greeting to new immigrants, a meaning the immigrants themselves conferred on the statue. But Haraway generally proceeds as if the African Hall dioramas are preserved in historic amber, untouchable by the shifting interactions of text and context.

In her conclusion, Haraway does finally acknowledge that "basic ideologies and politics shifted." And, in the *Primate Visions* version of her essay, she adds that "even the racial doctrines so openly championed by the Museum were publicly criticized in the 1940s, though not until then." But this nod to history is too little and too late. And it does nothing to complicate her assertions about the museum's "central moral truth." Moreover, she is just plain wrong to claim that scientific racism was not publicly criticized until the 1940s. Haraway cites John Higham's *Send These to Me*, but she doesn't appear to have noticed one of its central points: "As early as the late 1920s, a decline of racism in intellectual circles set in. The eugenics movement waned; the Nordic cult lost its vogue. The change reflected the emancipation of American thought from biological determinism."

EACH OF HARAWAY'S SYNECDOCHIC LINKS stretches her materials to the breaking point. If we tried to walk a similar interpretive path with different materials, her sleight of hand might be more visible. For instance, let me propose that the essence of New York University is represented in its imposing Elmer Holmes Bobst Library, completed in 1973 as part of a major redesign and development of the Washington Square campus. Further, let me argue that the meaning of the library is biographically located in its architect, the modern master Philip Johnson. Johnson, into the late 1930s, was attracted to the Nazis. He was a vocal fascist sympathizer, and, like others who spoke the language of eugenics, he was anxious about "race suicide." If I am of a mind to see fascism as the dark truth of capitalism, I can proceed to argue with a logic parallel to Haraway's in "Teddy Bear Patriarchy" that the truth of NYU is fascism. I do not need to know what NYU students or faculty read or write any more than Haraway needs to know what visitors to the AMNH experience; I do not need to complicate the story with the plural or changing meanings of NYU to be assured that I have reached the central moral truth of the institution. If NYU is its library, the library its architect, and its architect a fascist, NYU is fascist.

If I made such an argument, would it be seriously entertained? Would people judge my work "stellar," "compelling," and "exemplary"? I do not think so. Why, then, has Haraway's essay escaped close scrutiny? Why has an argument stretched so thin seemed so attractive to so many? Her argument's logic is just the same: AMNH is its African Hall, African Hall is Akeley's and Osborn's visions, their visions were rankly racist and sexist, so the AMNH is racist and sexist, or an example of Teddy Bear Patriarchy.

Part of the appeal of Haraway's essay, no doubt, is its promise to take a close look at the racial thinking of the 1920s. About that Second International Congress of Eugenics that the AMNH hosted in 1921: Haraway is onto something here. AMNH leaders were indeed important figures in an effort mounted on behalf of scientific racism at the time. The trouble lies in her implication that this campaign was typical of racial discourse in the time span her essay surveys. The eugenics movement, after all, lost the battle for the hearts and minds of the American elite. In the 1930s and 1940s, scientific racism gave way to a greater recognition and acceptance of cultural differences. And no one played a more significant role in this development than a former

AMNH employee, Franz Boas, the most politically influential and very likely the most intellectually important American anthropologist ever.

SO WHY DOES HARAWAY HIGHLIGHT the 1921 conference as if it were especially indicative of the moral truth of AMNH? Why not the fact that the Eugenics Congress's next international conference, in 1932, also in New York, attracted fewer than one hundred people? Or the fact that later in AMNH history a hall would be dedicated to Boas's student Margaret Mead? Indeed, it is probably fair to say that the museum is today more closely identified with Mead than with Teddy Roosevelt or the relatively unknown Carl Akeley. Haraway reports correctly that eugenics was a significant movement in 1921, coloring the views of museum trustees and officials. But she fails to mention the conclusion of Higham and others that it was essentially dead by the time African Hall opened.

If description and historical accuracy were important here, the AMNH's connection to race, class, and gender would have been contextualized so readers could actually understand it. Haraway fails to do this. Implicit in today's coding of "class, gender, race" is that "race" refers to a distinction between white and nonwhite rather than, as was the case among Protestant elites in the 1920s, between Nordic and non-Nordic. Certainly racism toward African-Americans was part of the worldview of New York Protestant elites in the 1920s. Nineteenth-century Americans were taught in school about a hierarchy of races, with Caucasians invariably deemed the highest and Negroes the lowest. But the language of race shifted at the turn of the century, and the racial divide that elites worried most about was between people of northern European heritage and the immigrants from southern and eastern Europe, particularly the Jews.

Haraway observes that the notorious popularizer of scientific racism Madison Grant, an AMNH trustee, was worried about "the importation of nonwhite (which included Jewish and southern European) working classes." This aside is misleading. The immigrants Grant worried about did not simply include Jews and southern Europeans—

these were the *primary* groups that troubled and threatened him. In his influential racist tract *The Passing of the Great Race* (1916), a work that identifies its author as a trustee of the AMNH and includes a preface by Henry Fairfield Osborn, Grant makes this abundantly clear. He devotes the book to showing the differences among "the three main races of Europe"—the Nordic, the Alpine, and the Mediterranean—and the point of the book is to demonstrate the superiority of the Nordic to the others. Grant mentions but in no way dwells on "Negroids" and "Mongoloids." Of course, racism directed against African-Americans runs more deeply, more centrally, and more enduringly in American history than prejudice against Jews and southern and eastern Europeans. But this is not what was at stake in Grant's work.

The problem here is not only the imprecision about what "race" meant to the originators of African Hall. It is a failure to recognize how badly scientific racism was reeling by the 1930s, how genuine was the Boasian victory. Indeed, a new and powerful intelligentsia committed to a cosmopolitan vision of the world transcending race and ethnicity emerged and came to dominate intellectual life from 1930 into the 1960s, as the historian David Hollinger has argued. A powerful liberal consensus developed, cutting right across the lines that the Madison Grants of the world had wanted to keep strictly separate.

Of course, that liberal consensus was never complete. Anti-Semitic, anti-immigrant, and above all anti-black sentiment persisted and persists. But if the liberal consensus continues to be challenged, it remains very much alive. Many of this tradition's leading figures from the 1920s and 1930s, such as Walter Lippmann, Franz Boas, and John Dewey, are still read and argued about, whereas Madison Grant is at most a historical footnote. By what screwball logic, then, does Haraway land on Grant as the animating spirit of the white patriarchal capitalist vision that dominates American society?

WHY DOES IT MATTER if Haraway got the history wrong so long as her main point—that science is socially constructed in the service of power—remains correct?

If the past is dead and should be dead, as Haraway seems to believe, then it really doesn't matter a whit. But if, as William Faulkner put it, "the past is never dead. It's not even past," then it makes a very big difference that Haraway translated the 1920s "Nordic" into the 1980s "white" and blended in her postmodern Cuisinart the liberalism of Boas with the racism of Grant. If it is worth knowing what achievements in our past we can draw on for strength and inspiration, then the errors here are serious, and it is shocking that in the ten reviews of *Primate Visions* I have read, and the many mentions of the work I have come upon, not once has any of this been noted.

In the end, it is not Haraway's essay itself so much as the absence of serious published criticism that disturbs me. Cultural studies, especially in its postmodernist or post-structuralist vein, has features of a social movement and some of the edgy self-confidence of prior intellectual movements—psychoanalysis comes to mind. Psychoanalysis developed its own critical terminology, it offered an epistemology that ran counter to standard scientific practices, it promised emancipation through critique, and it took on a messianic cast. It also introduced new methods and frameworks for understanding human behavior that many people, even those who remain dubious about the project as a whole, have found valuable. Postmodern cultural studies may be following suit. I hope it does not follow psychoanalysis in constructing defense mechanisms. Psychoanalysis is famous for having perfected a method of discounting criticism by treating it as a symptom. "If you disagree, you are resisting." I see signs that cultural studies is succumbing to that sort of solipsism. It needs not only to generate criticism from within its own set of political assumptions (which it does, often and heatedly) but also to respond to criticism that calls those assumptions into question.

CULTURAL STUDIES CORRECTLY EMPHASIZES that no knowledge is innocent. But this dictum also applies to the fervent belief that "no knowledge is innocent." That claim serves ends just as the claim of scientists or journalists to objectivity does. Most obviously, it is a rationalization for expanding and making relevant the fading place of literary studies in our culture. It also protects political presuppositions from critical examination because it takes for granted that political and moral presuppositions are beyond rational debate. They are discourse in the service of power.

This shortchanges everybody. It cocoons the left from having to deal with the right—surely a bad idea at a time when the left's presence seems to be evaporating in the culture at large. Oddly enough, it also diminishes culture. If culture is only the discursive shaping and serving of power, there is no place for the radical assertion that forms of power are designed and valued to serve culture. Take, for example, Clifford Geertz's *Negara*, which argues that the elaborate court ceremonies of the Balinese state were not designed to reinforce the rulers' power but rather that the rulers' grasping for power was driven by their desire to perform and control the ceremonies. In a similar vein, Chandra Mukerji argues in *From Graven Images* that the Industrial Revolution served to justify a fashion for calicoes; it wasn't, Mukerji believes, that a fashion for calicoes served to enrich the emerging industrial bourgeoisie. If anything, culture is more important, not less important, than the theoretical presuppositions of cultural studies acknowledge. The tendency to reduce culture to the emanations of preconstituted power positions trivializes culture and ignores the complexity of politics. To improve on this with the familiar claim that culture is "contested terrain" is no solution. Yes, culture is contested terrain. And, yes—thanks in part to cultural studies—we can now say, "Of course it is." But when we say that, we have reached the beginning, not the end, of analysis.

—August 1997

ENJOY YOUR ŽIŽEK

An Excitable Slovenian Philosopher Examines the Obscene Practices of Everyday Life—Including His Own

ROBERT S. BOYNTON

AMID THE BUSTLE of Tony Blair's Britain, the tradition of the afternoon tea is one of the last remaining traces of the country's genteel past. There are few places that conjure up that past better than the oak-paneled King's Bar Lounge at the Hotel Russell, a fading Victorian pile that sits on the edge of Bloomsbury, only a few short blocks from the British Museum. On a drizzly summer afternoon, I sink into one of the lounge's overstuffed leather chairs, feeling as if I were being transported back to an earlier, more leisurely era—far from "cool Britannia" and debates over the future of the euro. The spell is abruptly broken, however, by the sudden, agitated entrance of the Slovenian philosopher Slavoj Žižek, who is in town to deliver a series of lectures at the British Film Institute.

"We must have the most fanatically precise English tea," Žižek insists, gesticulating dramatically in the style of a European dictator. "Everything must be exactly the way the English do it: clotted cream, cucumber sandwiches, scones. It must be the most radically English experience possible!"

Bearded, disheveled, and loud, Žižek looks like central casting's pick for the role of Eastern European Intellectual. Newspapers are lowered and conversations stop as a skittish waiter shows us to a small table in the far corner of the room. Barely pausing to sit down, Žižek launches into a monologue so learned and amusing that it could very well appear—verbatim—in one of the many books he has written about the obscene rules that sustain our supposedly civilized social practices. With lightning speed, he moves from the decline of British culture ("They took perfectly good tea, added milk, and made it look like filthy dishwater!") to Hollywood ("Brad Pitt's *Seven Years in Tibet*—a terrible movie!") to the Tibetan legal system ("a process of formalized bribery where opposing parties bid against each other in a ritualized auction—I absolutely love this!").

Žižek talks exactly as he writes, in a nonstop pastiche of Hegelian philosophy, Marxist dialectics, and Lacanian jargon leavened with references to film noir, dirty jokes, and pop culture ephemera. "Discussing Hegel and Lacan is like breathing for Slavoj. I've seen him talk about theory for four hours straight without flagging," says UC-Berkeley's Judith Butler. When not mediated by the printed page, however, the obsessive-compulsive quality that makes his hyperkinetic prose so exhilarating is somewhat overwhelming—even, evidently, for Žižek himself. Popping the occasional Xanax to settle his nerves, he tells me about his heart problems and frequent panic attacks. As his eyes dart around the room and his manic monologue becomes more frantic, I fear that I may be his last interviewer. Žižek is like a performance artist who is terrified of abandoning the stage; once he starts talking, he seems unable to stop. "You must be much crueler, more brutal with me!" he pleads, even as he speeds his pace to prevent me from cutting him off. "You should never enter a sadomasochistic relationship," he scolds, a sly smile peeking out from his bushy beard. "You wouldn't whip your partner hard enough!"

When the waiter returns, Žižek finally pauses, studies the menu, and orders a pot of mint tea and a plate of sugar cookies. Mint tea and cookies? What about our radical English experience? "Oh, I can't drink anything stronger than herbal tea in the afternoon," he says meekly. "Caffeine makes me too nervous."

FOR ŽIŽEK a conversation—whatever the topic—is an exercise in self-contradiction. When he thinks you are beginning to get a handle on his motives or desires, he pulls an about-face, insists he doesn't mean anything he has just said, that his own views are the exact opposite. His contrariness is famous, and it has generally served him well as a writer—helping to earn him a reputation as a dazzlingly acute thinker and prose stylist and to win him a cult following among American graduate students. In person, however, it seems that Žižek's contrariness is at least partly an uncontrollable compulsion. And yet his manipulations and subterfuges are so entertaining, and his intellect so stimulating, that it is far wiser to surrender without a fight than to try to trump him at his game.

Later that evening, I have an opportunity to watch Žižek's mesmerizing oratorical skills in action at the Museum of the Moving Image, where he gives a standing-room-only lecture on the erotic forces at play in science fiction. The audience is a diverse group, with hip, nose-ring-studded film theorists jostling for seats with graying, tweedy academics. Beforehand, I find Žižek pacing madly outside the auditorium, and he confides to me that this week's panic attacks have been so severe he nearly canceled tonight's engagement. A few minutes into his talk, however, he is fine; his emotional anxiety is quickly transformed into a blur of theoretical intensity.

By the time his two-week-long lecture series is completed, he has offered a succession of Lacanian interpretations—accompanied by visuals—of *Titanic*, *Deep Impact*, *The Abyss*, several works by Hitchcock and David Lynch, and even an episode of *Oprah* (with Slovene subtitles). At one point, he gleefully fast-forwards over a portion of Andrei Tarkovsky's *Solaris*, explaining that despite its theoretical value it is quite a dull film. "For me, life exists only insofar as I can theorize it," he confesses. "I can be bored to death by a movie, but if you give me a good theory, I will gladly erase the past in an Orwellian fashion and claim that I have always enjoyed it!" It is a bravura performance, replete with Žižek's trademark synthesis of philosophical verve and rhetorical playfulness—an intellectual style that recently led Terry Eagleton to describe him in the *London Review of Books* as "the most formidably brilliant exponent of psychoanalysis, indeed of cultural theory in general, to have emerged in Europe for some decades."

Of course, many readers are likely to feel disoriented by Žižek's fast-paced, densely associative writing, as well as by his reliance on the difficult notions of a notorious French psychoanalyst. Žižek's chief intellectual hero, Jacques Lacan, is a man whom recent critics have portrayed as an eccentric tyrant who may have perpetrated a grand intellectual hoax on his followers. But Žižek's appeal is due, in part, to his considerable ease with two subjects that most disciples of Lacan disregard: popular culture and politics. In much of his work, Žižek employs familiar concepts from the psychoanalytic and Lacanian lexicon—projection, inversion, the Real and the Symbolic—to explore the ideological contradictions of contemporary life. In books like *Enjoy Your Symptom!*, *Looking Awry*, *The Plague of Fantasies*, and *Everything You Always Wanted to Know About Lacan (But Were Afraid to Ask Hitchcock)*, he offers provocative, and always lively, readings of everything from Patricia Highsmith novels to the resurgence of nationalism in eastern Europe.

Politically savvy and deeply rational, Žižek's Lacan is a far cry from the abstruse guru of indeterminacy invoked by American literary theorists. In his writing, Žižek militates against the "distorted picture of Lacan as belonging to the field of 'post-structuralism.' " Rather, he argues that Lacan offers "perhaps the most radical contemporary version of the Enlightenment."

Žižek's Lacanian defense of the Enlightenment distinguishes him from many contemporary theorists. Indeed, the enormous popularity of Žižek's best-known book, *The Sublime Object of Ideology*, may owe something to the fact that it offers an alternative to two entrenched and antithetical bodies of contemporary thought: the French postmodernists' skepticism about the Enlightenment ideals of universality, truth, reason, and progress, and the German theorist Jürgen Habermas's attempt to vindicate those ideals with his theory of "communicative rationality." While Foucault and Derrida dissolve the human subject in a sea of discursive indeterminacy and historical contingency, Habermas's ultimately rests his defense of reason on a vision of the individual as an ethical actor in a functional community.

Žižek is sympathetic to many of Habermas's aims, but he offers a more complex psychoanalytic account of human thinking and desiring. Unlike Habermas, he assumes that communities are constitutively dysfunctional and that the human subject is always divided against itself by contradictory desires and identifications. And the rationalist project must proceed from the recognition of these fundamental truths. The thrill of reading Žižek (who, as a stylist, no one would ever confuse with the turgid Habermas) arises in part from the collision between the insanity he finds everywhere in our psychic and social lives and the rigorous clarity with which he anatomizes its workings. "He has almost single-handedly revived a dynamically dialectical Hegelian style of thinking," says Eric Santner, a professor of Germanic studies at the University of Chicago. "I think of him as a sort of 'logician of culture' who reveals the underlying structures of politics and ideology."

If Žižek's is not a household name in academe, this is not due to a lack of effort on his part. His ability to compose his books in English (parts of them are subsequently translated into Slovene) has so hastened his pace of publication that his various English-language publishers must occasionally scramble to keep him from flooding the market. No fewer than a dozen titles have appeared under his name since 1989, including several essay collections in the separate book series he edits for Verso and for Duke University Press. And 1999 will be a big year—even for Žižek Inc. Blackwell is publishing *The Žižek Reader*, and Verso is publishing *The Ticklish Subject*. Advertised as his magnum opus, *The Ticklish Subject* may be his most focused and most political book to date. Taking on contemporary intellectual bugaboos—from political correctness to multiculturalism—Žižek argues for a radical politics that will be unafraid to make sweeping claims in the name of a universal human subject. "A spectre is haunting Western academia," he writes, "the spectre of the Cartesian subject."

MANY OF ŽIŽEK'S DISTINGUISHING MARKS—his passion for psychoanalytic inversions, his fascination with Western popular culture, his resistance to the cynical logic of depoliticization—can be traced to the paradoxes of growing up under Yugloslav socialism. Born in Ljubljana, Slovenia, in 1949, Žižek was the son of devout Communists who grew increasingly disenchanted. He had a difficult relationship with his father, who wanted him to become an economist. Instead, Žižek divided his attention between reading philosophy and watching movies. Access to Western movies was easy because of a tradition requiring that movie companies deposit a copy of each film they distributed with the archives of regional universities. "The cinematheque theater was a miracle for us," remembers Žižek. "We were able to see unlimited Hollywood movies and European art films—one or two a day, five days a week."

Despite its relatively liberal cultural and political policies, Žižek argues, Tito's Yugoslavia produced a more repressive (though subtly so) brand of ideology than the other Eastern-bloc countries. While Czechoslovakian or Polish authorities made no secret of their authoritarian tactics, the more permissive Yugoslavian Communists sent out mixed signals about what was and was not permitted, thereby fostering an unusually effective, because at least partially self-regulating, system of censorship. By way of example Žižek tells the story of a Slovenian book publisher in the fairly tolerant late 1970s who wanted to collect some of the best-known Soviet dissident writing. "The party line fluctuated so much that the Central Committee of the League of Slovene Communists was terrified of committing itself one way or the other," Žižek explains. "So the members said, 'Wait a minute, you are yourself free to decide what to publish'—which was the really Kafkaesque situation. At least with Polish censorship, it was a strict bureaucracy, which would negotiate, reach a compromise, and give you a final decision. This would have been paradise for us! The nightmare of Yugoslavia was that you couldn't get a clear answer from anyone about anything."

The young Žižek was attracted to ideas that were relatively uncontaminated by ruling ideologies. After completing his undergraduate studies in 1971, he wrote a four-hundred-page master's thesis called "The Theoretical and Practical Relevance of French Structuralism," which canvassed the work of Lacan, Derrida, Kristeva, Lévi-Strauss, and Deleuze. Initially, Žižek was promised a university position. But when the evaluating committee judged his thesis insufficiently Marxist, the job went to another, less qualified candidate. "Slavoj was so charismatic and brilliant they were afraid to allow him to teach at the university lest he become the reigning sovereign at the department of philosophy and influence students," says the Lacanian social philosopher Mladen Dolar, who was also a graduate student at the time.

Žižek was devastated by this slight and spent the next several years virtually unemployed, supporting himself by translating philosophy from the German and living off his parents. In 1977, some of his former professors used their connections to win him a job at the Central Committee of the League of Slovene Communists, where, apart from assisting with occasional speeches (in which he would insert covertly subversive comments), Žižek was left alone to do his own philosophical work: the philosopher whose unreliable politics prevented him from teaching was now helping to write propaganda for the leaders of Slovenia's Communist Party. Žižek still revels in the irony. "I would write philosophy papers and then deliver them at international conferences in Italy and France—trips that were paid for by the Central Committee!"

If Yugoslavian socialism produced a thoroughly cynical citizenry, a country of people who understood that the last thing the regime desired was for them to believe too ardently in the official principles of Communism, this, argues Žižek, was ideology at its most effective. "The paradox of the regime was that if people were to take their ideology seriously it would effectively destroy the system," he says. In his account, cynicism and apathy are explanations not for the regime's failure but, perversely, for its success. "The conventional wisdom is that socialism was a failure because, instead of creating a 'New Man,' it produced a country of cynics who believed that the system is corrupt, politics is a horror, and only private happiness is possible," he argues. "But my point is this: perhaps depoliticization was the true aim of socialist education. This was surely the daily experience of my youth."

To counter this depoliticization, Žižek banded together with the Ljubljana Lacanians, a tight-knit group of Slovenian scholars that included Mladen Dolar, Alenka Zupančič, Miran Božovič, Zdravko Kobe, and Žižek's future wife, Renata Salecl. In their hands, French psychoanalysis acquired an often highly comic cast. The group took over a journal, *Problemi*, and founded a book publishing series, Analecta; inspired by Lacan's roots in the French surrealist movement (he was friends with André Breton and Salvador Dalí), they used these outlets to perpetrate several literary hoaxes. Articles in *Problemi* were frequently written under pseudonyms or left unsigned, in parodic imitation of Stalinist practice. Žižek once wrote a pseudonymous review attacking one of his own books on Lacan. On another occasion, *Problemi* published a fictional roundtable discussion of feminism in which Žižek played the boorish interlocutor, posing provocative questions to nonexistent participants. (Later, in *Enjoy Your Symptom!*, Žižek continued to engage in literary hoaxes with an essay on the films of Roberto Rossellini—none of which he had seen.) With the regime's aversion to Lacan on the rise, Žižek sensed a wonderful opportunity for mischief; writing in a widely read academic journal, *Anthropos*, under an assumed name, he published a deliberately clumsy attack on an imaginary book that allegedly detailed why Lacan's theories were wrong. The next day bookstores across Ljubljana received requests for the title.

Žižek spent 1981 in Paris, where he met some of the thinkers whose work he had been so avidly consuming. He would return often. In 1982, however, Lacan died and his mantle passed to his son-in-law, Jacques-Alain Miller—a man who would play an important role in Žižek's career. A former student of Althusser's, Miller had impressed Lacan with the coherence he brought to the master's sprawling theoretical system. While many Lacanians accuse Miller of simplifying Lacan (perish the thought!), others believe that Lacan's posthumous reputation would not have grown without Miller's ordering influence. A shrewd political operator, Miller was eager to expand the Lacanian empire farther than its progenitor had ever imagined. He taught two classes in Paris: one that was open to anyone, and an exclusive, thirty-student seminar at the Ecole de la Cause Freudienne in which he examined the works of Lacan page by page. After a brief interview, Žižek and Dolar were invited to attend this latter class. "Miller took

enormous interest in us because we came from Yugoslavia," Dolar remembers. "We had been publishing Lacan in *Problemi* and Analecta
for years, and he was grateful for that. He thinks very strategically and
didn't have anyone else established in Eastern Europe. To him, we
were the last stronghold of Western culture on the eastern front."

Žižek's Paris years, although intellectually stimulating, were not
very happy. Thanks to Miller, who got him a coveted teaching fellow-
ship, he was able to stay in Paris and write a second dissertation, a Lacanian reading of Hegel, Marx, and Saul Kripke, portions of which
would later become *The Sublime Object of Ideology.* But his first marriage, to a fellow Slovenian philosophy graduate student, had just
ended, and there were times he felt he was on the brink of committing suicide. His meager stipend barely kept him alive. He was a ripe
if reluctant candidate for psychoanalysis, and there were many days,
he says, when he skipped meals in order to pay for treatment.

In addition to being Žižek's teacher, adviser, and sponsor, Jacques-
Alain Miller became his analyst. While familiarity between analyst
and analysand is discouraged by Freudians, it was not unusual for Lacanians to socialize with their patients. Lacan's most controversial psychoanalytic innovation, however, was the variable, or "short," session
through which he tried to combat a patient's resistance by introducing an element of discontinuity into the therapeutic process. In contrast to Freud's fifty-minute "hour," Lacan's sessions ended the
moment he sensed the patient had uttered an important word or
phrase—a break that might occur in fifteen minutes or less. Miller
had fine-tuned the logic of therapy to the point that few sessions
lasted more than ten minutes. "To be in analysis with Miller was to
step into a divine, predestined universe," says Žižek. "He was a totally
arbitrary despot. He would say, come back tomorrow at exactly 4:55,
but this didn't mean anything! I would arrive at 4:55 and would find a
dozen people waiting."

One goal of the variable session is to keep a patient from preparing
material ahead of time. In this respect, Lacanian psychoanalysis met
its match in Žižek. "It was my strict rule, my sole ethical principle, to
lie consistently: to invent all symptoms, fabricate all dreams," he re-

ports of his treatment. "It was obsessional neurosis in its absolute purest form. Because you never knew how long it would last, I was always prepared for at least two sessions. I have this incredible fear of what I might discover if I really went into analysis. What if I lost my frenetic theoretical desire? What if I turned into a common person?" Eventually, Žižek claims, he had Miller completely taken in by his charade: "Once I knew what aroused his interest, I invented even more complicated scenarios and dreams. One involved the Bette Davis movie *All About Eve*. Miller's daughter is named Eve, so I told him that I had dreamed about going to a movie with Bette Davis in it. I planned every detail so that when I finished he announced grandly, 'This was your revenge against me!' "

As the head of the main Lacanian publishing house, Miller was in a position to turn Žižek's doctoral dissertation into a book. So, when not presenting his fabricated dreams and fantasies, Žižek would transform his sessions into de facto academic seminars to impress Miller with his keen intellect. Although Žižek successfully defended his dissertation in front of Miller, he learned after the defense that Miller did not intend to publish his thesis in book form. The following night he had his first panic attack, which had all the symptoms of a heart attack. Eventually he placed the manuscript with the publishing house of a rival Lacanian faction.

Before Žižek began shuttling between Paris and Ljubljana, his professional prospects had already taken a turn for the better. He was still unable to hold a university position, but in 1979 some friends intervened and got him a job as a researcher at the Institute for Sociology. Given the institute's social science orientation, Žižek was not allowed to do philosophy; instead, he announced that he would do research on the formation of Slovenian national identity. "I did the transcendental trick and said that although the long-term project is on Slovene nationalism, I must first sketch the conceptual structure of nationalism," he says. "Unfortunately, this 'clarification' has now gone on for two decades."

The job was a blessing in disguise. Once Žižek made his peace with the social scientists, he discovered that he was free to write, with none of the bureaucratic and pedagogical burdens of a Western academic. In essence, he is on permanent sabbatical. "Every three years I write a research proposal. Then I subdivide it into three one-sentence paragraphs, which I call my yearly projects. At the end of each year, I change the research proposal's future-tense verbs into the past tense and then call it my final report," he explains. Because the institute's budget depends on how much its members publish, Žižek—who publishes more work in international publications than everyone else combined—is left completely alone. "With total freedom, I am a total workaholic," he says.

Total freedom also allowed Žižek to play a role in Slovenian politics. Although not a full-fledged activist, he was intimately involved in the movement that helped hasten the end of Yugoslavian socialism. In the late 1980s and early 1990s, Žižek was a popular newspaper columnist for the weekly *Mladina* and helped found the Liberal Democratic Party, which opposes both Communism and right-wing nationalism and has stressed feminist and environmental issues. In 1990, he even ran for a seat on the four-member collective Slovenian presidency (he finished fifth). As Slovenia achieved a mostly peaceful independence, Žižek wrote frequently about the bloody conflicts nearby. And when the Liberal Democrats came to power in 1992, he found himself in the odd position of being an intellectual who wasn't marginalized. Žižek is quite proud of the "dirty deals" and compromises made by his party. "I despise abstract leftists who don't want to touch power because it is corrupting," he says. "No, power is there to be grabbed. I don't have any problem with that."

THE DAY AFTER ŽIŽEK'S LECTURE, he and his wife, Renata Salecl, meet me for lunch at a cozy Greek café just down the block from their London hotel. An attractive woman with a round face and short blond hair, Salecl is as calm and deliberate as Žižek is nervous and neurotic. Žižek, who claims he lacks the social graces to attend cocktail parties or schmooze with scholars and politicians, says that he relies on her to navigate the shoals of the outside world. She buys his clothes ("For me, shopping is like masturbating in public," he says), negotiates their teaching deals, and generally keeps him from having a nervous breakdown. Her first book, *Discipline as a Condition of Freedom* (which was recently staged as a ballet), was a Foucault-inspired analysis of Communist Yugoslavia. "Nobody believed in the rules, but they nevertheless kept following them obediently, and I wanted to know why," she explains. She has spent the morning at the offices of Verso, which will be publishing her book *[Per]versions of Love and Hate* this fall.

Together, she and Žižek have mastered the intricacies of American academic politics and established a congenial teaching ritual that keeps them in the United States for one semester every year. Recently they have held positions at Columbia, Princeton, Tulane, University of Minnesota, Cardozo Law School, and the New School for Social Research; this fall they are teaching at the University of Michigan. The duo has refined the process to a science. Each university must provide teaching positions, offices, and accommodations for both of them and agree that they will each teach one two-month course, consisting of one lecture per week on whatever subject they happen to be writing about. In addition to getting his U.S. pay, Žižek receives a full salary from his institute in Ljubljana. "When people ask me why I don't teach permanently in the United States, I tell them that it is because American universities have this very strange, eccentric idea that you must work for your salary," Žižek says. "I prefer to do the opposite and not work for my salary!"

Žižek has developed an elaborate set of psychological tricks to manipulate his American students and enable him to have as little contact with them as possible. At the first meeting of each course, he announces that all students will get an A and should write a final paper only if they want to. "I terrorize them by creating a situation where they have no excuse for giving me a paper unless they think it is really good. This scares them so much that out of forty students I will get only a few papers," he says. "And I get away with this because they attribute it to my 'European eccentricity.' "

Žižek says that he deals with student inquiries in a similar spirit. "I understand I have to take questions during my lectures, since this is America and everybody is allowed to talk about everything. But when it comes to office hours, I have perfected a whole set of strategies for how to block this," he says with a smirk. "The real trick, however, is to minimize their access to me and simultaneously appear to be even more democratic!" Initially Žižek scheduled office hours immediately before class so that students could not run on indefinitely. Then he came up with the idea of requiring them to submit a written question in advance, on the assumption that most would be too lazy to do it. (They were.) Žižek reserves what he calls "the nasty strategy" for large lecture classes in which the students often don't know one another. "I divide the time into six twenty-minute periods and then fill in the slots with invented names. That way the students think that all the hours are full and I can disappear," he explains.

UNDERGRADUATES ARE APT TO BE TOLERANT of their professors' idiosyncracies, but Žižek may have less luck hiding from critics when *The Ticklish Subject* is published this winter. Just as he once saw socialist Yugoslavia as a country that had been cynically depoliticized by its leaders, Žižek now believes that conservatives, liberals, and radicals have effectively stamped out genuine politics in the West. The modern era, he argues, is decidedly "post-political." Instead of politics, he writes, we have a largely conflict-free "collaboration of enlightened technocrats (economists, public opinion specialists . . .) and liberal multiculturalists" who negotiate a series of compromises that pose as—but fail to reflect—a "universal consensus."

Blair's New Labourites and Clinton's New Democrats are only the most recent depoliticized political parties to have made "the art of the possible" their modest mantra. Žižek also charges that sexual and ethnic identity politics "fits perfectly the depoliticized notion of society in which every particular group is 'accounted for,' has its specific status (of a victim) acknowledged through affirmative action or other measures destined to guarantee social justice." In satisfying grievances through programs targeted to specific groups, such as affirmative action, the tolerant liberal establishment prevents the emergence of a genuinely universal—and, in Žižek's definition, properly political—impulse.

For Žižek, all successful ideologies function the same way. If American-style consumer capitalism has replaced Yugoslavian Marxism as the antagonist, the battle is still the same: to create the conditions for what he calls "politics proper," a vaguely defined but deeply heroic and inherently universalist impulse in which a given social order and its power interests are destabilized and overthrown. "Authentic politics is the art of the impossible," he writes. "It changes the very parameters of what is considered 'possible' in the existing constellation."

This is a noble vision, but when Žižek turns to history, he finds only fleeting examples of genuine politics in action: in ancient Athens; in the proclamations of the Third Estate during the French Revolution; in the Polish Solidarity movement; and in the last, heady days of the East German Republic before the Wall came down and the crowds stopped chanting "Wir sind das Volk" ("We are *the* people!") and began chanting "Wir sind ein Volk" ("We are *a / one* people!"). The shift from definite to indefinite article, writes Žižek, marked "the closure of the momentary authentic political opening, the reappropriation of the democratic impetus by the thrust towards reunification of Germany, which meant rejoining Western Germany's liberal-capitalist police/political order."

In articulating his political credo, Žižek attempts to synthesize three unlikely—perhaps incompatible—sources: Lacan's notion of the subject as a "pure void" that is "radically out of joint" with the world, Marx's political economy, and Saint Paul's conviction that universal truth is the only force capable of recognizing the needs of the particular. Žižek is fond of calling himself a "Pauline materialist," and he admires Saint Paul's muscular vision. He believes that the post-political deadlock can be broken only by a gesture that undermines "capitalist globalization from the standpoint of universal truth in the same way that Pauline Christianity did to the Roman global empire." He adds:

"My dream is to combine an extremely dark, pessimistic belief that life is basically horrible and contingent with a revolutionary social attitude."

AS PHILOSOPHY, Žižek's argument is breathtaking, but as social prescription, "dream" may be an apt word. The only way to combat the dominance of global capitalism, he argues, is through a "direct socialization of the productive process"—an agenda that is unlikely to play well in Slovenia, which is now enjoying many of the fruits of Western consumer capitalism. When pressed to specify what controlling the productive process might look like, Žižek admits he doesn't know, although he feels certain that an alternative to capitalism will emerge and that the public debate must be opened up to include subjects like control over genetic engineering. Like many who call for a return to the primacy of economics, Žižek has only the most tenuous grasp of the subject.

What, then, are we to make of Žižek's eloquent plea for a return to politics? Is it just another self-undermining gesture? In part it is, but that may be the point. The blissful freedom of the utopian political moment is something, he believes, we all desire. But so too, he would acknowledge, do we desire ideologies and institutions. And these contradictory impulses—toward liberation and constraint—are not only political. A central tenet of Lacanian psychoanalysis is that the push and pull of anarchic desires and inhibiting defense mechanisms structures the psychic life of the individual. And why shouldn't this same dialectic characterize Žižek's own intellectual life, which has been devoted to proclaiming the universal relevance of Lacan's ideas?

"Do not forget that with me everything is the opposite of what it seems," he says. "Deep down I am very conservative; I just play at this subversive stuff. My most secret dream is to write an old-fashioned, multivolume theological tract on Lacanian theory in the style of Aquinas. I would examine each of Lacan's theories in a completely dogmatic way, considering the arguments for and against each statement and then offering a commentary. I would be happiest if I could be a monk in my cell, with nothing to do but write my *Summa Lacaniana.*"

But wouldn't that be lonely? Once again Žižek qualifies his qualification. "Okay, maybe not a solitary monk. I could be a monk with a woman."

—October 1998

PUTTING THE CAMP BACK INTO CAMPUS
Notes on a Fanzine
LARISSA MACFARQUHAR

AROUND THE TIME THE WORD "theory" started appearing in under-graduate circles without disciplinary modifiers and Andrew Ross started shopping at Comme des Garçons, it became inevitable that someone would take the glamorization of the humanities to its logical extreme. Someone would publish a fanzine. *Judy!*, a love letter to the Berkeley philosopher and gender theorist Judith Butler and to sec-ondary divas Gayatri Spivak ("hot"), Monique Wittig ("fabulous"), and Julia Kristeva ("the Garbo of theory stars"), may or may not be the first—fanzines generally fly too low to be picked up by media radar sweeps—but it's surely the most sex-positive. The zine is a seventeen-page photocopied newsletter written by a University of Iowa undergraduate who calls herself Miss Spentyouth. The cover of the premiere issue is a photo of diva-of-gay-males'-divas Judy Gar-land. "It's really hard to find pictures of Judith Butler, so here is an-other Judy," explains Spentyouth on page 1.

Judy! caters to a range of Butler-fan tastes, from the cute and campy to the pornographic (a naked-chick-with-dick ad for 970-JUDY, for example). "I dreamed that Kitty MacKinnon and Andrea Dworkin were in a mudwrestling match wearing small shiny bikinis and Judy was the ref," writes Spentyouth on page 3, in one of the many fantasy haiku to be found in the issue. "In my dream Judy looked red-hot despite the tacky Foot Locker outfit." The fanzine's centerpiece is a gay academic gossip column, Secrets of the Stars, which is best explained by quoting at length the item on last winter's MLA conference:

> The New York Hilton was SIZZLING this December as the famous theorists swarmed the lobby and the cash bars. The homo cash bar was a **star-fuckers** delight. **Eve Sedgwick** worked the crowd. **Kevin Kopelson** breezed in and out, looking very *Details* in a polka-dotted tie. The incomparably beautiful **Geeta Patel** oozed glamour in a full-length fur. **Judy** and **Diana Fuss** did a modest rock-star number in a corner. Were they reminiscing about Thanksgiving dinner at Judy's? Rumor has it that Judy and eleven of her closest girlfriends had **safe hot times** fisting the turkey with latex gloves. . . . These are the ladies who put the lay back in the MLA!

Miss Spentyouth talked with *Lingua Franca* by phone from her bed at about eleven in the morning, Iowa time, wearing nothing, so she claimed, but Chanel No. 5. "Is this shameless self-promotion?" she wondered aloud, drag-queenishly. "Should I be doing this? Or should I be more resistant? What do you think?" Spentyouth, who describes herself as "somewhere in between a junior and a senior—no one really knows," fell in love with Butler after hearing her lecture at Columbia in 1991. Since then she has been trying to get Butler to notice her and set her up in an apartment as a kept woman. She followed Butler out of the Hilton at the MLA conference last year but lost her in traffic. Out of the depression that disappointment engendered, *Judy!* was born. "The official line is that [the newsletter is] a critique of queer obsession with, and consumption of, celebrity," Spentyouth said. "The whole diva thing, extending to queer theory these days, with Eve Sedgwick and all these glamorous, incredibly famous women. It's really a critique of the whole theory circus—I don't know, don't say that. You have to make me seem incredibly clever."

It isn't only randy undergraduates who think Judy is hot right now. Butler was just wooed from the Johns Hopkins University Humanities Center by the floundering rhetoric department at Berkeley, which she has consented to sample with the understanding that she may return to Hopkins if she doesn't like it there. Butler's fame derives mostly from her two books: *Subjects of Desire*, which probes the problem of desire in French post-Hegelian philosophy, and *Gender Trouble*, a frontal attack on heterosexual hegemony. She's a philosopher with fingers in most of the tenure-friendly academic pies, including psychoanalysis, feminism, gay studies, and, for good measure, postcolonial theory. "Incredibly impressive, glamorous, charismatic," said Spentyouth, in search of an adjective. "She's an academic superstar."

The first issue of *Judy!* has been distributed haphazardly via a network of Spentyouth's friends in New York, Chicago, and California. At least one copy was touring the lesbian-gay circuit at Johns Hopkins—news to Spentyouth, who says she has no clue how many people have seen the magazine. Butler thinks the zine is a one-off, but Spentyouth already has plans for *Judy!* number 2, including an exposé of a conversation she had with Butler about *Judy!* number 1. "I'm having a little bit of that postpartum depression thing, and also I've been very busy with school," Spentyouth offered by way of explanation for the next issue's tardiness.

If Butler herself is secretly pleased by the adulation, she won't admit it. "I wish it hadn't happened," she said from her new California home during a telephone interview. "It draws attention away from my work and puts it on my person, and I would much rather have people pay attention to my work. I think it's unfortunate that this sort of culture emerges, because people just stop thinking carefully about things and take academia to be a kind of star culture or something." Asked why she thought she of all theorists had been chosen for divahood, Butler had an answer ready. "Because I'm not very personally revealing," she explained. "I believe that there are intellectually substantive issues that can be discussed without stating my most intimate or personal relationship to them."

"She's so mega," Spentyouth gushed in answer to the same question. "I mean, that's it—it's a celebrity thing, don't you think?" Spentyouth yawned. "I don't know. It's too early in the morning to talk about theory, but it's never too early to talk about theory stars."

—*September 1993*

Dear Editors,
I found your article "Putting the Camp Back Into Campus" to be an appalling and tasteless piece of journalism. Why would the writer of that piece, and Lingua Franca, *agree to protect the anonymity of Andrea Lawlor-Mariano, the undergraduate at the University of Iowa who edited the* Judy! *fanzine, if not to sanction and protect the circulation of the fanzine and its fully conjectured and debased speculations? By citing uncritically from the fanzine and protecting Andrea Lawlor-Mariano from publicity,* Lingua Franca *has effectively entered the homophobic reverie of the fanzine itself. If there is still some question over whether "Butler is secretly pleased by the adulation," let me clarify that I find this "adulation" to be slanderous and demeaning. If the fanzine signals the eclipse of serious intellectual engagement with theoretical works by a thoroughly hallucinated speculation on the theorist's sexual practice,* Lingua Franca *reengages that anti-intellectual aggression whereby scholars are reduced to occasions for salacious conjecture (pace Jim Miller on Foucault) rather than as writers of texts to be read and seriously debated. Whether this kind of trash emerges from within or outside gay communities, it remains an insult. I am poignantly reminded why it was I never subscribed to* Lingua Franca, *for it proves to have no more value than* Heterodoxy *or* The National Enquirer.

JUDITH BUTLER
Professor of Rhetoric
University of California at Berkeley

IS BAD WRITING NECESSARY?

George Orwell, Theodor Adorno, and the Politics of Language

JAMES MILLER

THESE ARE TRYING TIMES for the left in America, which may be one reason why a bitter debate has erupted among avowedly left-wing academics and intellectuals over a venerable topic—"Politics and the English Language," to borrow the title of George Orwell's famous 1946 essay. Must one write clearly, as Orwell argued, or are thinkers who are truly radical and subversive compelled to write radically and subversively—or even opaquely, as if through a glass darkly? That is the question.

On one side stand academic luminaries like the University of California at Berkeley rhetorician Judith Butler and the University of Pittsburgh English professor Jonathan Arac, who take their inspiration from critical theorists like Michel Foucault and Theodor Adorno. Arguing that their work has been misunderstood by journalists on the left, these radical professors distrust the demand for "linguistic transparency," charging that it cripples one's ability "to think the world more radically."

On the other side are ranged a variety of public intellectuals and journalists like the UCLA historian Russell Jacoby, the feminist writer Katha Pollitt, and the NYU physicist Alan Sokal. Intolerant of bewildering jargon, they cannot see how deliberately difficult prose can possibly help change the world. As their patron saint, they often nominate George Orwell, the very image of a man who spoke truth to power and spoke it plainly.

One thing the plain talkers on the left share is relatively greater access to a wider public. In part, this is because they know how to write with "linguistic transparency." But as Pollitt has ruefully pointed out, the proponents of plain talk have also doubtless benefited from the long-standing anti-intellectualism of the American mass media. Keen to simplify and wary of sustained argument, those who oversee the media are generally impatient with abstraction and complexity as well as the qualifications and nuances that might slow down the majority of readers. They want facts reported and explanations and arguments conveyed as painlessly as possible. As a result, writers on the left who can handle complex topics with terseness, clarity, and brio exercise an apparent influence on the wider culture out of all proportion to their standing, if any, in the academy.

This situation not only excites the envy of some left academics; it also fuels their suspicion that plain talk is politically perfidious—reinforcing rather than radically challenging the cultural status quo. Indeed, last year the academic organizers of a conference at the University of California at Santa Cruz made exactly this case, trying to pin the pejorative label "left conservatism" onto some of their most widely read critics.

If Orwell perfectly exemplifies the party of clarity, it might be said that the German philosopher Theodor Adorno has come to represent the party of opacity. Consider the most recent episode in this internecine Kulturkampf, which occurred this spring after the editors of *Philosophy and Literature* bestowed their annual Bad Writing Award on Judith Butler. Stung into action, Butler defended herself—in an Op-Ed piece of defiant lucidity—in the columns of *The New York Times*. And she cited Adorno to do so. But this was not the end of it. A few months later, when the literary critic Terry Eagleton complained in the *London Review of Books* about the labored style of Gayatri Spivak, the prominent postcolonial theorist, Butler weighed in to defend Spivak and denounce Eagleton. And once again Adorno served as her witness.

"Surely," Butler proclaimed in a letter to the editors, "neither the *LRB* nor Eagleton believes that theorists should confine themselves to writing introductory primers such as those that he has chosen to provide." Precisely because pathbreaking thinkers like Butler and Spivak are in pursuit of something bigger and better than a primer—Butler calls it "critical theory"—they refuse the "truisms which, now fully commodified as 'radical theory,' pass as critical thinking." If their prose is sometimes hard to read, that is because they, unlike Eagleton, are performing true critical thinking. "Adorno surely had it right," asserts Butler, "when he wrote—in *Minima Moralia*—about those who recirculate received opinion: 'only what they do not need first to understand, they consider understandable; only the word coined by commerce, and really alienated, touches them as familiar.' "

WHAT IS GOING ON HERE? And how have Orwell and Adorno, two long-dead figures, come to represent the poles of this debate? It was a half century ago that Orwell warned of the totalitarian use value of the evasive euphemism, the deliberately misleading oxymoron, and the proliferation of obfuscating abstraction in political prose, not least among academics on the left (a prime target of "Politics and the English Language" was Harold Laski, a leading light of the Labour Party). For a quarter century, Orwell's aesthetic convictions carried the day, at least on the anti-Stalinist left. In *The Sociological Imagination* (1959), the radical sociologist C. Wright Mills approvingly cited Orwell's example in contrasting the "confidence of the individual craftsman in his own ability to know reality" with the "bureaucratization of reason." Ten years later, Noam Chomsky used Orwell to throw darts at a different target, those segments of the academic left avowedly uninterested in practical politics: "George Orwell once remarked that political thought, especially on the left, is a sort of masturbation fantasy in which the world of fact hardly matters. That's true, unfortunately, and it's part of the reason that our society lacks a genuine, responsible, serious left-wing movement."

However plausible the position of Orwell and Mills and Chomsky, one cannot help but notice that Adorno's formidable *Minima Moralia*—the work cited in self-defense by Butler—was written at roughly the same time as Orwell's pioneering essay and commands a similar following among left-wing intellectuals.

Orwell and Adorno, both born in 1903, were early and outspoken foes of fascism and Stalinism. Both, deservedly, are icons of the independent left. And their worldviews overlapped in other ways as well. Each of them regarded the postwar world in the most dire terms: Adorno saw both western Europe and the Soviet Union as entirely "administered" societies where the prospects for genuine freedom were few; Orwell defined political speech as the "defense of the indefensible," adding that contemporary politics could be summed up by its "evasions, folly, hatred, schizophrenia." Both men also saw a close relation between the corruption of language and the corruption of politics. Orwell protested that "orthodoxy, of whatever color, seems to demand a lifeless, imitative style." Adorno wrote, "Where there is something that needs to be said, indifference to literary form always indicates dogmatization of content." Both were appalled by the replacement of evocative words with prefabricated, ready-made phrases. When Adorno asserted that "defiance of society includes defiance of its language," Orwell would have agreed.

And yet when it came to assessing the need for clear language in social criticism, they parted ways dramatically. In "Politics and the English Language," Orwell asserts that to write and think "clearly is a necessary first step toward political regeneration." In his 1956 essay "Punctuation Marks," Adorno asserts, just as boldly, that "lucidity, objectivity, and concise precision" are merely "ideologies" that have been "invented" by "editors and then writers" for "their own accommodation."

So whose views on language—Orwell's or Adorno's—seem most cogent in retrospect? And why did these two estimable authors come to such drastically different conclusions about the morality of style?

FIRST PUBLISHED in German in 1951, Adorno's *Minima Moralia* is one of the most intransigent pieces of cultural criticism in this century. The book was written in the 1940s, while Adorno was an unhappy exile in America. Divided into three parts—"1944," "1945," and "1946–1947"—the text consists of 153 numbered entries with deadpan titles ("They, the people," "Tough baby," and so on). Fragmentary and nonsequential, solemn and simultaneously offhand, each fragment circles briefly around a theme. Some of the book's most celebrated formulations are defiantly paradoxical: "In psychoanalysis, nothing is true except the exaggerations." Others issue in wild generalizations: "Normality is death." Still other passages combine a knowing allusiveness (for example, to Hegel's famous dictum that Napoleon was the world spirit on horseback) with a simple image ("Hitler's robot bombs," the pilotless V-1 and V-2 missiles that killed thousands of people in London) to insinuate, in a few elliptical words, a considered view about abstract philosophical matters: " 'I have seen the world spirit,' not on horseback, but on wings and without a head, and that refutes, at the same stroke, Hegel's philosophy of history." A topic that is provocatively formulated in one passage often reappears in another with a completely different, and sometimes inverted, emphasis. Adorno compared this way of writing to "spiders' webs." He hoped to snare readers in a tightly woven net of metaphors and ideas.

The distinctive features of Adorno's style owe a great deal to his rarefied upbringing. Born in Frankfurt am Main, Adorno inherited, and helped to renew, many of the most demanding currents in German high culture. Trained to become a classical pianist, he also studied sociology and philosophy before moving to Vienna in 1925 to study with the atonal composer Alban Berg. Discouraged from pursuing a career in music, he returned to Frankfurt and completed a dissertation on Kierkegaard.

Fluent in the specialized vocabularies refined by German philosophers from Kant and Hegel to Husserl and Heidegger, Adorno in these years also absorbed the key idea of reification from Marx and the Hungarian communist philosopher Georg Lukács. Capitalism, according to Marx, had produced a "topsy-turvy world" in which inanimate objects of every sort—from stocks and bonds to paintings and poems—were treated like fetishes with magical powers, while human beings were manipulated like inanimate objects, as if a laborer earning a salary were a mere tool with no independent mind or power. Adorno at the same time acquired a taste, which will seem rebarbative to most Anglophones, for dramatizing the wages of reification by attributing agency to impersonal nouns. (One example: "Topsy-turviness perpetuates itself: domination is propagated by the dominated.")

In 1938, old Frankfurt friends, led by Max Horkheimer, helped Adorno escape from Europe to join in research projects being organized in America by Horkheimer's transplanted Institute of Social Research (a.k.a. the Frankfurt School), based in New York City. At first Adorno earned a living working for the Princeton Radio Research Project, commuting daily from Manhattan to Newark, New Jersey, the site of the project's headquarters. "When I traveled there through the tunnel under the Hudson," he wrote years later, summing up his sense of displacement, "I felt a little as if I were in Kafka's Nature Theater of Oklahoma." Compared with a great many less fortunate émigré academics, Adorno had a good war. In 1941, after having moved to Southern California for health reasons, Horkheimer offered Adorno another job, this time conducting research into "the authoritarian personality." So, once again Adorno joined his German mentor, this time in the land of palm trees, balmy breezes, and movie stars.

He hated it.

Although Southern California in the 1940s was teeming with illustrious European exiles, including Arnold Schoenberg, Thomas Mann, Bertolt Brecht, and Igor Stravinsky, Adorno disappeared into his writing and research, repelled by the vainglory and vulgarity of the people he was expected to get along with amiably, in the American style. Outside the émigré community, Adorno's painstakingly acquired storehouse of knowledge—about modern opera, German philosophy, and the evils of the cash nexus and the commodity form—impressed no one.

"In America, I was liberated from a certain naive belief in culture," he confessed shortly before his death in 1969. In Europe, he had simply taken for granted "the fundamental importance of the mind—'Geist.' . . . The fact that this was not a foregone conclusion, I learned in America, where no reverential silence in the presence of everything intellectual prevailed."

Or, as he more tartly summed up the same sad experience in *Minima Moralia*, "Anyone who, in conversation, talks over the head of even one person, is tactless. For the sake of humanity talk is restricted to the most obvious, dullest, and tritest matters."

American anti-intellectualism has rarely had a more vicious critic. After completing a long collaborative essay with Horkheimer, *The Dialectic of Enlightenment*, Adorno set to work with a vengeance, organizing his thoughts about the wretchedness of his émigré experience. Composed in bits and pieces throughout his time in Southern California, *Minima Moralia* is, in part, the effort of a sensitive introvert, feeling lost and bereft of proper recognition, to conjure a cocoon of "reverential silence" around the words he has obsessively strung together, as if a perfectly taut sentence could be a talisman and helpmate, like the rosary beads of a pious Catholic.

He had no expectation whatsoever that the man in the street would have the faintest clue what he was up to. He didn't care. On the contrary: "For the intellectual, inviolable isolation is now the only way of showing some measure of solidarity"—and this isolation is to be ensured through the rarefied quality of one's prose.

Since Adorno obviously did not suppose that plumbers and soda jerks would be disturbing their dogmatic slumbers by laboring through his prose, what kind of reader was *Minima Moralia* meant to reach? Certainly someone who could pick up, and perhaps even find pleasure in, his many allusions (starting with the title, a play on *Magna moralia*, a digest of maxims and ethical arguments attributed in antiquity to Aristotle) and probably, too, a reader who shared something of his overwhelming disgust for modern-day popular culture.

But there are also hints that Adorno was appealing to a still-higher court of judgment. In a fragment on intellectual history, after survey-ing the damage done to Nietzsche's reputation by his posthumous popularity among neo-fascist bands of "Noble Human Beings and other riffraff," Adorno concludes that "even at that time the hope of leaving behind messages in bottles on the flood of barbarism bursting on Europe was an amiable illusion." The great solitary thinker, who had "wondered whether anyone was listening when he sang to himself in 'a secret barcarole,' " had suffered a fate worse than death: his work had become the plaything of ignoble fools. "Who, in the end, is to take it amiss if even the freest of free spirits no longer write for an imaginary posterity . . . but only for the dead God?"

Adorno's hidden premise seems to be this: any serious piece of writing, like any serious work of art, will be produced from the stand-point (in a mystical image borrowed from Walter Benjamin) of "the messianic light." Like Benjamin, Adorno wants "to contemplate all things as they would present themselves from the standpoint of re-demption"—an emancipated point of view, beyond the despair of liv-ing under the rules of capitalism. Insofar as such a work succeeds in single-mindedly addressing its proper audience, it may well be under-stood properly by no one—save the Messiah (who, of course, may never appear).

IT IS IN THIS FRANKLY ESCHATOLOGICAL CONTEXT, weirdly con-joined with what Jürgen Habermas once characterized as "self-affirmation gone wild," that Adorno most eloquently sums up his views on rhetoric in the fragment that Butler cites. It is titled "Moral-ity and style."

"It avails nothing ascetically to avoid all technical expressions, all allusions to spheres of culture that no longer exist," Adorno declares. "The logic of the day, which makes so much of its clarity, has naively adopted this perverted notion of everyday speech." (One can see here the roots of his postwar antipathy to the ordinary-language philoso-phy of Wittgenstein and J. L. Austin.) "Rigorous formulation" requires of a reader "conceptual effort," which Americans, with their dim-witted commitment to a superficial pragmatism (another one of Adorno's bêtes noires), will "violently resist." He adds: "Only what they do not need first to understand, they consider understandable; only the word coined by commerce, and really alienated, touches them as familiar. Few things contribute so much to the demoralization of intellectuals. Those who would escape it must recognize the advocates of communicability as traitors to what they communicate."

Since Adorno made no bones about his lack of interest in defining his terms or presenting a sequential argument ("In the emphatic essay thought divests itself of the traditional idea of truth"), it is worth pausing over three claims that can be distinguished in this remarkable fragment.

1) "It avails nothing ascetically to avoid all technical expressions." Serious writing sometimes requires jargon: the sorts of terms that circulate in any highly evolved science. It would be absurd to demand of a physicist like Einstein or Bohr that he write in prose intelligible to the layman. In Adorno's eyes, German philosophy has some claim to the title of science, and it certainly has evolved its own glossary of technical terms. Just because a bunch of American yahoos have never read Kant and Hegel is no reason to abandon an exacting vocabulary.

2) "It avails nothing ascetically to avoid . . . all allusions to spheres of culture that no longer exist." Seriously artful writing sometimes requires a license to range freely, drawing without inhibition on a rich store of cultural references, no matter how esoteric. It would be absurd to demand of a poet like Rilke or T. S. Eliot that he write lines that any old reader can appreciate. Adorno is a highly cultivated individual, a cosmopolitan, a musician of the mind. Just because a bunch of American yahoos have never read Goethe or listened to Alban Berg is no reason to give up referring to works by such artists, both classical and modern. Indeed, anyone aware of what modernism has wrought in the fine arts will feel further emboldened to reject, in a typically

modernist declaration of independence, "conventional surface coherence, the appearance of harmony, the order corroborated merely by replication."

3) "Only what they do not need first to understand, they consider understandable; only the word coined by commerce, and really alienated, touches them as familiar." Under capitalist relations of production, human beings exist in a state of alienation. Much of what they think they know must pass through a process of exchange, in which writers working for large corporations premasticate ideas, arguments, and the events of the day, and then deliver this information in measured portions to a starved and stunted public desperate for distraction and indifferent as to whether it is devouring thin gruel or a real meal. *Pari passu*, under current social conditions, as these are regulated by capitalism and the commodity form, truly unpopular writing willy-nilly becomes a locus of resistance to the powers that be: "He who offers for sale something unique that no-one wants to buy represents, even against his will, freedom from exchange."

Under these circumstances, the ideal of "universal communicability" is a sinister "liberal fiction," one that surreptitiously assumes the desirability of a "complete conformism." When even educated souls have internalized the "detritus" of a "barbarous culture—half-learning, slackness, heavy familiarity, coarseness"—the "desire to be understood by others" can only reinforce the "downward urge of the intellect." "Retention of strangeness is the only antidote to estrangement."

Q.E.D.: the most radical critic of alienation will be the most exquisitely aloof thinker, incomprehensible and unpopular by design, as if enraptured by his unswerving address to an ideal audience of one, a God who may not exist.

IT IS NOT TOO HARD to guess what Orwell would have made of *Minima Moralia* had he been able to read it. The scathing social criticism and the longing for a truly independent movement for social change

Orwell would, of course, have recognized and welcomed. But the style of Adorno's work would have offended all of Orwell's deepest literary instincts.

"Good prose is like a window pane," he once declared. True to this motto, he never stopped looking for the right frame for the right kinds of concrete images and turns of phrase, artfully enough rendered to conjure an illusion of perfect transparency.

That he was staggeringly successful in reaching the largest possible public, in a way that very few twentieth-century writers have been, is indicated by a few simple facts. Paul Berman has summed them up in one long sentence: "The writer who coined 'Hate Week,' 'Thought crime,' 'Thought Police,' 'vaporize,' 'Newspeak,' 'doublespeak,' 'Some are more equal than others,' and 'Big Brother is Watching You' has sold, between *Animal Farm* and *Nineteen Eighty-Four*, more than 40 million books in sixty languages which is, according to John Rodden, 'more than any pair of books by a serious or popular postwar author.' "

Orwell's views on politics and language were deeply shaped by his experience as the son of a British official in the Indian civil service. Christened Eric Arthur Blair, the boy was groomed to follow in his father's imperial footsteps. By the mid-1920s, while Adorno was in Vienna studying music with Berg, Blair was in Burma working for the police. In 1927, the year Adorno began his graduate studies in philosophy, Blair, renouncing his father's colonialism and resigning his police post, began to tramp around France and England, washing dishes in a Paris hotel, harvesting hops in Kent, and observing coal mining in the north of England. While keeping a diary of the injustices he witnessed, Blair discovered his vocation.

He would be a man of letters. He would "make political writing into an art." And he would make the world listen.

Diffident in private, Blair so feared failure in the literary marketplace that he invented a pseudonym for the book he wrote based on his diaries, *Down and Out in Paris and London*. Criticism would be directed at George Orwell, not Eric Blair. But since the book, when published in 1933, was a literary success, Eric Blair became George Orwell.

If the key experience behind Adorno's critique of mass society was his miserable exile in Southern California, Orwell's political epiphany could not have been more different. It happened in 1937 in Spain, where Orwell went to fight on the Republican side in the civil war against the fascists and to file reports for *The New Leader*. Enlisted in a Catalan militia organized by POUM (the Workers' Party of Marxist Unification), he was seriously wounded at the front and sent back to Barcelona to recover. There, Orwell was witness to a murderous power struggle between the Spanish Communists and the independent left, which in Catalonia consisted largely of anarchists and Trotskyists (who dominated POUM).

In the course of this struggle, the Communists falsely accused the Trotskyists of plotting with Franco. Determined to expose the lie, Orwell gathered documents and took notes for his great book on the civil war, *Homage to Catalonia* (1938). The experience left him with an admiration for the independent left and a hatred of the Communists. A decade later he claimed: "Every line of serious work that I have written since 1936 has been written, directly or indirectly, against totalitarianism and for democratic socialism, as I understand it."

Orwell's literary and political convictions only deepened with the passage of time. A political pariah by the time World War II broke out, Orwell tried to join the British army but was declared medically unfit (he seems to have suffered from tuberculosis, the likely cause of his premature death in 1950). Still anxious to lend his talents to the war effort, he took a position at the British Broadcasting Corporation in 1941, producing radio talks for the Indian section of the BBC Eastern Service, submitting himself to government censorship in order to make a contribution to the battle against fascism, writing news scripts, and broadcasting his sophisticated blend of political commentary and Allied propaganda. During the war, he also served as a literary editor and columnist for the *Tribune*, a weekly newspaper with an editorial board headed by Aneurin Bevan, the Labour Party leftist who would become a chief architect of Britain's National Health Service after the war.

As the war went on and Orwell developed a firsthand understanding of the difficulty in conveying facts and political ideals to the largest possible audience, his views hardened on the question of what Adorno had called "morality and style." For his wartime work, Orwell knew full well that critics would accuse him "of being an intellectual snob who wants to 'talk down to' the masses" or suspect him of "plotting to establish an English Gestapo." But he felt certain that he was on the right path, helping to establish the linguistic preconditions for a deeper democracy. "Some day we may have a genuine democratic government," he wrote in 1944, "a government which will want to tell people what is happening, and what must be done next, and what sacrifices are necessary, and why. It will need the mechanisms for doing so, of which the first are the right words, the right tone of voice."

In 1946, Orwell summed up his views in a short essay titled "Why I Write." In a passage of characteristically disarming bluntness, he listed four major reasons: "sheer egoism," the wish to be noticed; "aesthetic enthusiasm," the pure pleasure in arranging words in finely formed sentences; "historical impulse," the desire to bear witness to events and "to find out true facts and store them up for the use of posterity"; and "political purpose," the drive to "push the world in a certain direction."

To satisfy these ambitions, Orwell needed readers—the more, the better. "My initial concern is to get a hearing," he wrote. Neither his egoism nor his sense of political purpose could be gratified in any other way. What provoked his greatest works, from *Homage to Catalonia* in 1938 to *Animal Farm* in 1945 and *1984* in 1949, was his sense of moral outrage: at the mendaciousness of the Communists; at the barbarism of the Nazis; at the politically motivated obfuscation produced by the liars in every party. The bigger the audience he could reach, the more lies he could expose, the deeper his political impact would be.

AT THE CORE of Orwell's writing was his obsessive concern for factual truth, which, he could see, was an infinitely fragile thing, forever susceptible to the kinds of lies favored by those in power. Orwell's fixation may seem self-explanatory to anyone raised within the conventions of Anglo-American philosophy. But to a great many Continental philosophers, the empiricist assumption that there exists a pretheoretical world of facts just waiting to be described seems hopelessly naive. For the past two centuries, almost all of Germany's most eminent philosophers have subscribed to some version of the Kantian view that—in Hannah Arendt's formulation—"truth is neither given to nor disclosed to but produced by the human mind."

The philosophical issues at stake here are too complex to summarize briefly. Suffice it to say that Arendt herself was virtually unique, among German thinkers of her generation, in her refusal to give up the meaning of truth "in the sense in which men commonly understand it"—that is, as factual truth. Indeed, Arendt was, if anything, even more alarmed than Orwell about the fate of this form of truth: "The chances of factual truth surviving the onslaught of power are very slim indeed; it is always in danger of being maneuvered out of the world not only for a time but, potentially, forever."

Orwell, for his part, felt that his obligation to factual truth trumped even his unrelenting preoccupation with the style of his prose—or, for that matter, his loyalty to any particular political cause. In one of the longest chapters in *Homage to Catalonia*, he marshaled his evidence of Communist treachery with the painstaking thoroughness of a prosecutor at the bar of justice, knowing, as he later conceded, that he ran a risk of turning an otherwise lyrical piece of writing into a tedious exercise in topical journalism. "I could not have done otherwise," he explained: "I happened to know, what very few people in England had been allowed to know, that innocent men were being falsely accused. If I had not been angry about that I should never have written the book."

His erstwhile allies on the British left did not share Orwell's anger, arguing that the only hope for a Republican victory was a unified alliance under Communist control. And potential allies elsewhere did not always share Orwell's fierce commitment to the direct statement of factual truths. Indeed, members of the Frankfurt School were horrified by the "fetishization" of facts that they saw in the logical positivism of the Vienna circle, the value-free social science of the

American university, and the "tell it like it is" school of newspaper journalism. The problem was not only that a narrow emphasis on external facts sometimes obscured the mind's role in framing concepts (as Adorno protested, "something merely factual cannot be conceived without a concept, because to think it is always already to conceive it"); it was also that it obstructed the task of social criticism. In *Minima Moralia*, Adorno charged that the effort, so characteristic of Anglo-American investigative reporting, to give readers "the facts full in the face" succumbed to "the form and timbre of the command issued under Fascism by the dumb to the silent." For those who wished to achieve a measure of "comprehensibility to the most stupid" (as Adorno sarcastically put it), the critical theorist—in this respect indistinguishable from a Prussian autocrat—expressed nothing but contempt.

The contrast with Orwell could not be more stark. Whereas Adorno deployed a sophisticated philosophical framework, Orwell stressed brute facts. Whereas Adorno strove for modernist complexity, Orwell aimed at demotic simplicity. And even as Adorno was abjuring any effort to address a large audience of ordinary people, Orwell had bet his political and literary life on doing just that.

MANY INTELLECTUALS on the left today regard both Orwell and Adorno as hopelessly compromised figures, whatever their views on the politics of language and the morality of style.

Orwell's political sins were manifold: he disapproved of birth control, he was a Blimpish sort of British patriot, and (as one Web site put it in a warning against taking "Politics and the English Language" too seriously) he collaborated "with the B.B.C. against fascists in India in World War II, and wrote . . . in part to justify the work his journalism had done—for the Empire." Last year, controversy flared again over the fact that Orwell, shortly before his death, jotted down a list of people he regarded as politically compromised by their sympathy for Stalin and had it conveyed to the Information Research Department of the Foreign Office.

Adorno's case is almost equally vexed. There are some pretty strange lines in *Minima Moralia*—for example, "Totalitarianism and homosexuality belong together." In recent years, proponents of cultural studies have ridiculed Adorno's uninformed ranting about the evils of jazz and popular music. And then there is the matter of the great man's truly awe-inspiring capacity for contemplative passivity. This is someone (unlike his fellow critical theorist Herbert Marcuse) who steadfastly refused to be drawn into taking concrete positions on matters of pressing political importance. One of his oldest friends from Frankfurt, Leo Lowenthal (who ended up as a professor of sociology at the University of California at Berkeley), has said that Adorno had a simple motto: "Don't participate."

Orwell's political errors may well comfort academic critics of "left conservatism." But what about Adorno? For all his sins, can Adorno nonetheless be enlisted in the defense of the contemporary university?

Let us examine the arguments presented in Butler's letter to the *London Review of Books* by taking in turn the three claims that are implicit in Adorno's fragment "Morality and style."

1) On the matter of "technical expressions," a sympathetic reader must give Butler the benefit of the doubt. Like Adorno, today's critical theorists have steeped themselves in the vocabulary of German philosophy, from Kant and Hegel to Husserl and Heidegger, augmented by an infusion of terms from more recent French philosophers, especially Foucault. Jargon that is intolerable to a general reader is not only a source of power; it is also a convenient shorthand for conveying the results of inquiry in most academic disciplines, from physics to sociology, and not excepting feminist theory, literary criticism, and cultural studies.

At the same time, an unsympathetic reader is liable to feel put upon, if not bamboozled, by the constant barrage of technical terms found in the work of Butler and other contemporary theorists, such as Homi Bhabha and Gayatri Spivak. Quite often, one cannot help but suspect that this is a deliberate ploy, allowing the writer to accuse any critic of uncomprehending idiocy. Adorno himself once observed that "the thicket is no sacred grove. There is a duty to clarify all difficulties that result merely from esoteric complacency." Referring to Heidegger's prose, he complained that "he lays around himself the taboo that any understanding would simultaneously be falsification."

2) Adorno's staunch defense of the writer's right to deploy a dense network of cultural references that is liable to be appreciated by a relatively small number of people seems, on the whole, both reasonable and just. Anyone who has labored in the mass media knows that there is relentless pressure to dumb down every word of every sentence. Adorno's defiant display of erudition, by contrast, is a bracing rebuke to the ignorance and sharply diminished attention span of a great many ordinary readers and pundits, not to mention the blinkered narrowness of a great many university professors.

However, few writers, be they poets, scholars, or journalists, possess a mind as well furnished as that of Adorno. Certainly, few contemporary exponents of radical theory, Butler included, share his devotion to European high culture. His allusiveness is so pure, and so rooted in a specifically European sensibility, that it has been successfully emulated by only a handful of Americans—Susan Sontag, in her best essays of the 1960s and early 1970s, comes to mind, as does T. J. Clark, in his recent book, *Farewell to an Idea: Episodes From a History of Modernism.*

3) Adorno's last claim—that a style of writing comprehensible to only a few readers stands the best chance of evading the alienation of being turned into a mass-market commodity under conditions of capitalist production—is both the most radical and the hardest to know how to apply in practice. Apart from demonstrable inaccessibility, coupled with a lack of popularity, it is not clear how one is supposed to judge success, or failure, in this paradoxical venture. It is also not entirely clear from her references to Adorno whether Butler fully agrees with his position, at least in its most radical articulation in *Minima Moralia.* On the one hand, she agrees that resistance to capitalism requires the refusal of received opinions cheerfully expressed in

smugly measured periods. On the other hand, she holds out greater hope than Adorno does for the possibility of constructive social activism.

In her letter to the *London Review*, Butler, before quoting *Minima Moralia*, praises Spivak in terms Adorno would recognize—as a brave voice in the cultural wilderness. But in the same letter, she marvels at the sheer size of Spivak's readership and even claims that the "wide-ranging audience for Spivak's work proves that spoon-feeding is less appreciated than forms of activist thinking and writing."

While Butler may hope by endorsing Adorno's position to justify her style of writing, and that of countless other left academics, she cannot have it both ways. Either a key criterion of a truly radical theory is its austere indifference to being widely "appreciated," or it is not. If the criterion of a truly radical theory is its inaccessibility and consequent evasion of the cash nexus (Adorno's basic position in *Minima Moralia*), then a theory advertised as radical that nevertheless reaches a "wide-ranging audience" under conditions of commodity production must, ipso facto, not be truly radical.

Or consider another paradox of Adorno's position: if (in a typically exaggerated formulation) a literary "retention of strangeness is the only antidote to estrangement," then when the language becomes familiar, the antidote must lose its potency. (An overdose, even of critical theory, may prove fatal for the free spirit.)

Does this mean that Adorno's and Butler's most challenging ideas, precisely because of their relative popularity among a not-insignificant number of left-leaning intellectuals, have lost their antithetical use value and, by the infernal logic of exchange, been alienated and perhaps even dialectically transformed—turned into something hackneyed and predictable? If one accepts Adorno's position in *Minima Moralia*, there is no escaping the conclusion.

THREE YEARS AGO, Katha Pollitt summed up the problem with esoteric writing as a radical gesture in a world without real radical alternatives. When intellectuals on the left write in a way that excludes "all but the initiated few," she remarked, what almost inevitably results is "a pseudo-politics, in which everything is claimed in the name of revolution and democracy and equality and anti-authoritarianism, and nothing is risked, nothing, except maybe a bit of harmless cross-dressing, is even expected to happen outside the classroom."

Adorno himself was characteristically unapologetic about the apolitical consequences of his ultraradical critical theory: "Concrete and positive suggestions for change merely strengthen [the power of the status quo], either as ways of administering the unadministratable, or by calling down repression from the monstrous totality itself."

Orwell, by contrast, had little anxiety about making political suggestions, the more concretely put, the better. "If you simplify your [language]," he wrote in 1946, "you are freed from the worst follies of orthodoxy"—even the orthodoxies of a purer-than-pure critical theory. "You cannot speak any of the necessary dialects, and when you make a stupid remark its stupidity will be obvious, even to yourself."

Of course, it is dispiriting, particularly for anyone on the left, to be reminded that some things, including this debate, never change. But the next time one of our latter-day critical theorists attacks the desire for plain talk as a Trojan horse for "left conservatism," I suggest a thought experiment. Imagine poor old Adorno rolling over in his grave, still waiting for a messiah who may never come. And then picture Orwell, the "Maggot of the Month," as the Communists used to call him, doubled over in laughter and delighted to discover a brand-new oxymoron being deployed as a rhetorical weapon of perfectly Orwellian proportions.

—December 1999

PART II

The Tribulations of the
Academic Life

THE CANDIDATE
Inside One Affirmative Action Search

G. KINDROW

SEPTEMBER 23, 1989 The first faculty meeting of the term for the Department of English at Midwestern State. One of our assistant professors was denied tenure last year, and, given the financial constraints on the university, we were anxious to find out whether we would be able to replace him. The chair of the department told us the following: "The dean has authorized a search at the assistant-professor level for a 'minority' candidate."

Instantly the questions began. "Does the search include women or just ethnic minorities?" "What counts as a minority?" "What if we make a good-faith search and fail to come up with a suitable minority candidate? Can we then hire a nonminority candidate?" The answers: "No, women do not count." "I don't know exactly how 'minority' is being defined." "I don't know what would happen if we searched and failed to find a minority candidate." The department asked the chair to try and get some answers, from the dean, to the latter questions.

Most of my colleagues—largely liberal/left ideologically and disillusioned Democrats politically—were sympathetic to the need to have minorities and women on the faculty. The university, after all, had a substantial black and Hispanic undergraduate presence, and we believed that, in pedagogical terms, it was important for undergraduates to see that members of their community could be successful academics.

To this end, the department had been quite conscious of the need to hire women—who, as a consequence, were represented at all ranks, including full professor. Some years ago, we had a black assistant professor who left when he received a better offer from an eastern university. All this had been done without any specific pressure from the administration, other than the symbolic need to get approval from the Affirmative Action Office before any official offer went out. This approval was easily obtained by showing that we had advertised in places that would be the natural starting point for minority and women job seekers.

Many of us, myself included, felt at this point that it would be good if we could find a suitable minority candidate but that we were not prepared to make any concessions about quality. Others were prepared to lower standards, on the grounds either that the traditional standards were biased toward "masculine," "Eurocentric" criteria or that it was more important to provide a minority "role model" than to keep the same standards.

All of us agreed on one thing: that it was going to be very difficult to come up with a suitable candidate. Though we are a highly ranked department, we are not in the same class as Michigan and Harvard. And with the total pool of suitable minority Ph.D.'s dismayingly small and heavily recruited, especially by elite institutions, this was a severe liability.

Since time was running short (the annual conference for professors of English, which served as the main interviewing occasion for hiring, was in December, just three months away), we decided to put an ad in the principal English-literature-association newsletter for job hunters. In doing so, we made our first affirmative action compromise: although we had specific needs in certain areas, we decided not to limit the search by area. Quite simply, to do so would have reduced the minority-candidate pool to minuscule size, or even made it nonexistent. The advertisement could not exclude nonminority candidates from applying. It could only say that "Midwestern State is an Affirmative Action/Equal Opportunity employer. Minority candidates are especially encouraged to apply." Note: many academic job advertisements carry as a matter of course the "minorities urged to apply" tag, so there was no real way for a candidate to know what the real situation was.

In addition to putting an ad in our association newsletter, the chair placed an ad in a magazine I'll call *Black Opportunity*, which lists jobs specifically for minority candidates. In addition, we wrote letters to the major Ph.D.-granting departments asking them to recommend any minority candidates coming on the job market. Finally, a number of us who had minority friends in various departments called them and asked them to recommend minority faculty who already had jobs.

A search committee, of which I was a part, was set up to screen the forthcoming applications. In the current tight job market, we would receive about three hundred applications for this job.

OCTOBER 15 We now had answers to some of the questions our chairman had taken to the dean. Blacks, "Hispanic-surnamed" persons, and Native Americans counted as minorities; East Indians and Asians did not. Thus, the first absurdity emerged. Someone born in Argentina to a Jewish family named Mendoza would count. A "boat person" from Vietnam would not. The question of what would happen if we did not find a suitable minority candidate was left highly ambiguous by the dean. But the underlying message seemed to be, "Don't count on the position being available."

Applications began to arrive.

OCTOBER 17 In a conversation in the hall, the chair told me that he had gotten a bill from *Black Opportunity* for the advertisement we had placed. It was for three hundred dollars—approximately five times the cost of the advertisement in our association newsletter. This "academic mugging" seemed to me disgraceful, if also a nice lesson in affirmative action economics. To add insult to injury, when the chair asked the dean to pay for the cost of the ad (the departmental operating budget was ludicrously low and could not afford such a sum), the dean refused, with the helpful words "caveat emptor." So much for the "administrative commitment" to minority hiring.

NOVEMBER 2 I am screening the applications, which consist of a transcript of the candidate's grades, a curriculum vitae, three letters of reference, a cover letter, and a written sample of the candidate's research. A problem emerges: How do you tell who is a minority candidate? The applications, quite reasonably, have no place to indicate race. While names single out Hispanics—although a colleague and I spent most of an afternoon trying to figure out from clues in the vitae whether the clearly Romance-language surname of a candidate indicated he was Italian or Hispanic—they are no help for blacks. One looks for subtle, or not so subtle, clues. If the candidate has an undergraduate degree from a largely black school; if the candidate is working on a Ph.D. that involves minority issues; if the candidate belongs to a primarily minority professional organization; if the candidate was born in Ethiopia; if the thesis supervisor is wily enough to get in a reference (not so easy without being open to charges of patronizing or racist behavior).

I usually checked with one of my black professional acquaintances. The grapevine is sufficiently accurate that they are almost always able to make a positive identification. Only once did I actually have to call a department to ask bluntly if a candidate was black (he wasn't); it concerned an applicant from Princeton, and one of our assistant professors had heard that "a black" was applying from there.

At the same time that the applications were coming in, we began to call potential candidates who had been identified as minorities, asking them to apply.

NOVEMBER 10 At this stage, looking day after day at applications from hopeful Ph.D.'s, I began to develop moral qualms. Basically, I was screening them for indications of race, not scholarship. It was as simple as the two piles of applications on my desk: one for minority candidates, another for nonminorities.

My equivocal moral position soon took on a more personal cast. A candidate from a school where I had been a visiting professor called me to inquire about the job. While he was otherwise quite promising, I knew he did not stand much of a chance of even getting an interview. How much of the situation ought I to reveal? After some thought, I decided that if someone asked me whether the job was a "real one"—that is, competitive in the normal way—I would tell the truth: the position had been "designated" by the dean as a minority position; it was extremely unlikely that a nonminority person would be hired. On the other hand, if I was not asked point-blank, I would maintain silence about the limitations of the search. I would not volunteer information.

NOVEMBER 15 The search committee began to make a short list of candidates to invite for interviews at our annual association conference. Given the time and faculty available, we figured we could interview fourteen people, but it was clear that we didn't have fourteen potential minority interviewees. In fact, we had about twenty minority applicants in all, about half of whom were just not qualified. We decided on four people to be interviewed, all blacks, as it turned out, and none from this year's crop of Ph.D.'s. Rather, they were faculty members in tenure-track jobs. If we hired, we were going to be raiding other institutions. (The remaining ten interviews were scheduled with nonminority men and women.)

The list was brought to the department for general discussion. The discussion on the minorities was brief. There was general agreement that these candidates looked like reasonable bets—and, in any case, there were no other options. The candidates had Ph.D.'s from Princeton, Penn, CUNY, Rutgers. There was more animated discussion about the nonminority candidates, mainly because, in these cases, field was an issue.

DECEMBER 28–30 Nobody who hasn't sat in a stuffy hotel room for nine hours a day of job interviews can fully appreciate the horror of it all. I am not sure whether it is worse for the faculty or for the candidates. They, after all, get to talk about their work. We have to listen to nine mini lectures a day. After the first few interviews, the attention lags. Virtually everybody was worse in person than on paper, which was inevitable, given the implausibility of their letters of recommendation: every applicant was the "best in years." (This was true, in one professor's letters, for each of three candidates he was recommending.)

One candidate, however, the man from Rutgers, actually proved more lively, more acute, and wittier than his letters suggested. He displayed a wide range of learning and an analytic mind, impressing the entire committee. Of course, we now had to read his work in more detail, and he had to come give a paper to the department, but so far, so good. In addition, two other minority candidates were possibilities. Neither had done particularly well at the interview, but they both seemed to be good teachers and their letters were impressive. Among the nonminorities, two or three strong candidates stood out.

That same day, one of the nonminority candidates we had interviewed, an extremely promising young professor from a major graduate department, cornered me in the hall. He was currently in an unhappy academic position that left him little time for research, in spite of which he had just had a book published by Stanford University Press. He was desperate to get another position, and he knew we had nobody in his area of expertise in our department. "How did I do? Do you think I will get an invitation to campus?" Following my policy of not revealing more than I had been explicitly asked, I told him that while he had done well in the interview, the department would make the decision about whom to invite to campus, we had various needs and priorities, blah, blah, blah. But I knew that when he got the standard rejection letter, he would blame himself for not doing better in the interview, not getting that extra letter of recommendation. I don't know if he would have felt better if I had said, "You're not going to get an interview. You're white." But *I* would have.

JANUARY 5, 1990 The first faculty meeting after the holidays. The interviewing committee makes its report. We decide to invite three black candidates to campus; a fourth is held in reserve. The man from

Rutgers came, he saw, he conquered. His paper was interesting and thoughtful. He held up well under questioning, not overly defensive but holding his ground. The other two candidates more or less repeated their disappointing interviews. All three saw the dean, who did his best to persuade them of the virtues of the Midwest and of Midwestern State in particular.

JANUARY 10 Informal gossip in the hall serves as a commodities exchange for reputation. Wednesday: A is up three, B down one and a quarter. Thursday: A down a half, C up one and an eighth. The politically sophisticated are reading the candidates' work in preparation for the great debate to take place on January 12—the departmental meeting at which we will decide on a recommendation to make to the dean.

JANUARY 12 A startling development. The dean was so impressed with two of the people on the short list that he has given us permission to hire both of them if we so choose. A freebie.

We go around the room and get everyone's impressions. It becomes clear that the first offer is noncontroversial. Indeed it is unanimous: the man from Rutgers. He is in a field that we do not cover now. He is clearly highly qualified. He is not an American black (he's a West Indian), but that's the dean's worry. What about the second offer? Here things turn slightly nasty (in an academic way). It becomes clear that the people in his area do not think that he is good enough. They have read his work and do not think it original or well argued. But, the argument from the opposition goes, we can't be sure that he isn't good enough. Why not hire him and let the tenure process decide that issue? Meanwhile, we have an extra member of the faculty. How can it hurt?

But others, the majority, see another scenario as more convincing. In six years, this person will have a long publication list in respectable journals. He will have made the academic contacts to get good letters of recommendation. He will have made himself useful around campus. At that point, given that he is black, it will be impossible for the university to deny him tenure—no matter what the judgment of his peers. So if we think now that the person is unlikely to produce excellent work, we must not make the appointment in the first place. Ultimately that is the decision of the department. Ironically, in this case the candidate's race worked against him. Had he been white, many would have been willing to give him the benefit of the doubt, to give him the benefit of a trial period. But political realities made that impossible. It's also true that had he been white, he would not have made it to the interview stage.

To his credit, the dean does not question the decision of the department. The search is over. Now it is a matter of wooing.

JANUARY 17 I learn in the hall from the chair that the dean has made the candidate the following offer. (As with my disclosure-upon-request policy, the details of the offer are made known only to those who ask.) He will enter at a salary four thousand dollars greater than any other assistant professor, including those who had been in rank for five years longer, including an assistant professor who is nationally recognized as a "rising star." He is offered a research fund of ten thousand dollars a year for three years. Unlike other research funds awarded to professors in the department, this money could be used for summer salary. He will have a reduced teaching load for his first year.

JANUARY 27 The candidate, who was teaching at a state university in the Northwest, accepted. The score is Midwest 1, Northwest 0.

NOVEMBER 1 Now that it's all over, what is my view of how affirmative action works in the university context? It certainly does not conform to the picture painted by the opponents of "quotas." No unqualified individual was forced upon a department against its better judgment at the cost of passing up much-better-qualified nonminority candidates. Nor is it the case that the department had "internalized" the process so that, without being forced to, it voluntarily lowered its standards as a means to a good end. On the other hand, I do think that we were lucky: the outcome easily could have been worse. If we had been faced with the choice of the number-two candidate and a dean who said it was that person or the position goes back to the college, what would the department have done?

Had this been a color-blind competition, our winning candidate would almost certainly not have made it to the interviewing stage, where his talents were able to show. He was not from a major graduate department, his letters were not from major figures, and he was not teaching in a major department. These factors would have led to his being lost in the shuffle of nearly three hundred applications. His being black got him an interview.

In fact, since the candidate did not come from a major English department, and since his letters of recommendation were not from important people in his area, many of us worried that we had made a wrong decision even after he was hired. Sometime later, in conversation with a friend at Cambridge, one of the major figures in the area, the candidate's name came up in conversation, and I was relieved to hear his work praised.

As for our good fortune, one has to remember that what was fortunate for us was unfortunate for Northwest and not of any overall benefit to minorities on campus. The total number of blacks in faculty positions was the same after the search as before. I believe that, due to the demographic makeup of Midwest, the "role model" function is more important here than at Northwest. But to a large extent, the search for minority candidates is a game of national musical chairs. The result is that blacks at existing institutions get wooed away by impressive offers from institutions higher in the prestige hierarchy. It is a zero-sum game, with one institution losing minority presence for every one that gains.

Meanwhile, the procedure has real costs for those nonminority candidates who thought they were in an open competition and who lost out. And it inevitably breeds bitterness and envy on their part. My own view is that we should adopt a truth-in-advertising policy.

We now limit applicants by field, by rank, and de facto by quality of graduate school. If we believe it is desirable to hire a black or a woman (whether to rectify past injustices or to serve as a role model or to provide fresh perspectives in the discipline), why not just say so? I don't know about the legality of such an advertisement, but, morally speaking, it seems to me the right thing to do.

—April 1991

THE CANDIDATE'S STORY

On Being the Subject of an Affirmative Action Search

MICHAEL S. WARDELL

I AM CASUALLY LEAFING through my copy of the April 1991 issue of *Lingua Franca* when I come across an article by one "G. Kindrow" about an affirmative action search. As a professor who had himself been hired the previous year as the result of such a search, I naturally find the article of particular interest—an interest that increases as I discover several similarities between the case described and my own.

In fact, after several rereadings, the conclusion becomes undeniable: this article is about me! (A week or so later, Kindrow himself would give me a copy of the piece.) As I thumb back and forth, lingering over the juicy details, I begin to experience a certain unease. Despite the good things the article says about me, its overall message about affirmative action is far less positive.

Nowhere does Kindrow actually oppose affirmative action. On the level of explicit recommendations, his concluding paragraph says only that such procedures should perhaps be carried out with a "truth-in-advertising policy," which would formally announce the restriction of candidates. Yet in the tone of the article, the highlighting of certain kinds of costs and not others, the cues for engaging and disengaging our emotions, the message is one of dubiousness. Above all, there is very little in the piece about the circumstances and the past (and in some cases, ongoing) practices that made affirmative action necessary in the first place.

In fairness to Kindrow, he was not setting out to write a general, theoretical piece about the pros and cons of affirmative action. Yet whatever he may have intended, his article will be of far more service to those opposed to affirmative action than to those supporting it. At a time when the indications are that race and civil rights will be among the major issues of the 1992 presidential campaign, and perhaps of the 1990s in general, that slant is unfortunate and should not be ignored.

Here, then, is a counternarrative to redress the balance somewhat, from the minority candidate himself. I hope that my own story will help to show that the article reveals the failure of "Midwestern" University to reflect on the inherent biases of its procedures for evaluating minority candidates.

In a sense, my case is instructive precisely because of its atypicality. I had none of the handicaps with which the average black American must struggle. As the son of a university professor in the Caribbean, I grew up on a university campus in my native country and attended an elite high school. As a member of a privileged class, I suffered none of the psychic wounding and destruction of self-confidence that systematic racism often causes. After taking an undergraduate degree at home, I continued my studies at a university I'll call Big Canadian University and graduated with good grades and positive letters of recommendation.

I DID MY GRADUATE WORK in Canada (not at Rutgers), because the schools were relatively cheap there. My family is well-off by local standards, but their Third World dollars could not have come close to covering U.S. tuition. BCU has an international reputation, and the department I studied in (not English) is regarded as the best in the country, so this didn't, at first, seem to present a problem.

One of the most painfully illuminating points for me about Kindrow's article was that this was sheer delusion on my part, since, in the American scheme of things, BCU's program did not rank very high. This meant that, unbeknownst to me and largely for financial reasons, I was already disadvantaged in the U.S. job market. And I hadn't even had to face the kinds of hurdles most black Americans must surmount.

Kindrow admits that in screening applications the department routinely uses the quality of the graduate school as a de facto filter. But how many talented black students would have the resources to get into the schools on Kindrow's preferred list? Since getting into these schools requires surviving a whole pyramid of "screenings," mostly of a nonacademic kind, the uncritical application of this final filter is a de facto endorsement of a systematically biased status quo.

It has been observed of the free-enterprise system that the best way to get rich is to choose one's parents carefully. In an academic career, there is somewhat greater leeway for individual merit and effort to make a difference. But for those handicapped by race and class, the consequences of being limited to a less-than-stellar graduate program are likely to be far-reaching if not permanent.

Similar points can be made about the absence of big names on my CV (another revelation, this: so much for the standing of my Canadian referees!). If one has not been able to attend one of the top schools in the first place, how is one supposed to make contact with those rarefied circles?

My discipline is one in which the underrepresentation of blacks is so extreme by comparison with other branches of the academy that it has become the subject of ongoing discussion in the profession's newsletter. It is an underrepresentation sustained less by overt racism than by subtle networks of ethnicity, whole hidden structures of personal contacts. This is not a conspiracy theory but the truism that people in the same profession tend to socialize together and that to a significant extent in this country their socializing continues to be along racial lines. And this is bound to affect crucial decisions about whom to interview and hire, whom to solicit for letters of recommendation and other professional evaluations, whom to invite to conferences or to publish in journals. In their exclusivity, their reliance on who-knows-whom, these networks can also work against whites. But through race and class disadvantage, black academics will probably be handicapped to begin with in graduate school and in their profession and psychically burdened by their isolation. For them, the ethnic character of these networks represents a further heightening of these barriers that is not faced by white academics.

At one recent national meeting, I was regaled with horror stories by two black colleagues who graduated in the 1970s, when there were even fewer blacks in the profession than there are now. I heard the story of A, whose book, the result of years of labor, would have gotten only a one-paragraph note in one journal had another black American not gone out of his way to do a lengthier review of it. I was told of B, who, despite a publication list as long as your arm, seldom gets conference invitations or requests to do book reviews. Of C . . . D . . .

KINDROW ADMITS that without affirmative action I would never have made the interview list. Yet within the set of possibilities open to me, I had done what was necessary: gone to a good but affordable school, gotten strong letters of recommendation, and started publishing. But by Midwestern's standards, BCU wasn't good enough, my letters weren't from big enough names, and my publications were presumably insufficient or irrelevant. Had the search been conducted on ostensibly nonracial grounds, I would still be at "Northwest" (the first school that hired me) today. And if three years earlier the dean at Northwest had not put pressure on its department to conduct a minority search, and had there not been one individual in that department who insisted this recommendation be taken seriously, I would be out of the academy altogether. After graduating from BCU, I was unemployed in Canada for two years, and at the professional meeting where I got the offer from Northwest, I had decided that if nothing worked out there, it was time to cut my losses and try in midlife to change careers.

This needs some emphasis, since in a sense it is the whole point of my story: despite all the advantages with which I began, despite the abilities that Kindrow praises, it is only through affirmative action that I am a university professor today.

So my story is, in a sense, a success story: from unemployment in Canada, and the agonized thought that all those years in the dim, cobwebbed recesses of the BCU library had been wasted, to a tenure-track job in a top-twenty department in less than five years. The department at Midwestern has been very good to me, and I expect to be happy here.

But I have no illusions about how I came to be here. When I visit Canada or the Caribbean and friends or former fellow students ask me how I made it, I have a standard answer: "Ability, hard work, race, and luck—not 'not necessarily in that order' but necessarily not in that order."

All policies will have social costs, and I don't want to deny that occasional inequities may result from affirmative action. But the alternative is, it seems to me, to continue with a system that is not neutral but continues in diverse blatant and subtle ways to be stacked against racial minorities.

—August 1991

A MOST DANGEROUS METHOD
The Pedagogical Problem of Jane Gallop
MARGARET TALBOT

MOST ACADEMICS would just as soon forget the queasy intensity with which they both loved and hated their favorite professor in graduate school. To remember would mean recognizing how much their own graduate students hunger for their approval while longing to supplant them; how much students compete for their favor while winding around them ambiguous garlands of gossip. It would mean acknowledging that professors are often drawn to their protégés for reasons of their own—narcissistic, faintly unwholesome reasons not easily assimilable to a model of pure-hearted pedagogy.

If she is prudent, a professor won't speak too much in public about any feelings of identification or desire a student has stirred in her. Especially not now, when everyone is at such pains to avoid eroticizing the classroom. Better for an academic to err in the direction of a selfless, sexless schoolmarm than in that of a Miss Jean Brodie, triangulating her passions through the bodies of her girls. A prudent professor won't look too closely at the relationship whose potential for immoderation and transference German academics acknowledge by calling their thesis advisers *Doktor-Vater*s.

But Jane Gallop, the feminist theorist and literary critic, is not especially prudent.

FOR THE PAST YEAR, Gallop has been paying the price her kind of imprudence exacts these days. In November 1992, she was accused of sexual harassment. Her accusers were both women, both lesbians, and both graduate students; both were drawn to Gallop for the very reasons they later turned against her—the provocative role sexuality plays in her work and the flamboyant bad-girl persona she cultivates. Gallop, a celebrity in lit-crit circles, could be described as a sort of poststructuralist Mae West: in critiquing the notion of a disembodied mind, she loves to flaunt her own body, dressing up like a vamp in seamed stockings and spike heels when speaking at scholarly conferences, confessing in her essays to things like masturbating while reading Sade. Her prose and pedagogy are full of post-Freudian double entendres and titillating analogies—between sexual intercourse and writing, between seduction and pedagogy—clearly meant to shock. "My desire to be an academic, intellectual speaker is a desire to speak from the father's place," Gallop writes in *Thinking Through the Body*. "Yet the spiritual father's place (ideologically, the place of the academic, who was originally a cleric) demands separation of ideas from desire, a disembodied mind. I want to expose the father's desire so that I could take his place, but as a sexed subject."

For more than a year, while the two students organized demonstrations against Gallop on campus, gave interviews to the local newspapers, and told their peers and her colleagues that she was a sexual harasser ("Oh yeah, Jane Gallop," says a student who sees me photocopying articles about her. "Didn't she attack somebody or something?"), the University of Wisconsin at Milwaukee investigated Gallop's case. Her accusers dated their complaints from the afternoon Gallop stood up at a gay and lesbian studies conference and told the audience, in what she thought would be understood as a joke, that her sexual preference was graduate students. At that moment, they said, they realized that the playful sexual banter they'd willingly engaged in with Gallop was more, or maybe less, than they'd thought: Gallop wasn't trying to *teach* them anything; nor was she just being her weird and raunchy self; she was actually doing her ingenious best to talk them into bed. And because they'd rejected her advances, they argued,

she'd kept making one of them rewrite her papers and refused to provide the other with a letter of recommendation.

With one of the complainants, Gallop had indeed exchanged a
florid, public kiss. The most direct physical advance the other could
cite was the time Gallop rocked her rocking chair with one bare foot.
Both students, however, sought the same punishment for their professor. They wanted a letter of reprimand placed permanently in her file,
and they wanted her to "understand that making the complaint the
subject of intellectual inquiry constitutes retaliation." Gallop often
laces her essays with anecdotes about her students; her accusers
wanted to make sure Gallop never mentioned them in print, even if
she disguised their identities.

In August, I went to Milwaukee to interview Gallop, the two students, and their respective friends. I had spoken with Gallop on and
off throughout the spring and didn't know whether to see her saga as
a classic example of everything that's wrong with sexual-harassment
codes or just another case of someone smart exercising really bad
judgment. Gallop's relationship with the student she kissed, a thirty-
year-old Ph.D. candidate, sounded messy and complicated, lit up
with warning signals that both of them, sometimes willfully, misread.
But—the kiss aside—it didn't sound like harassment, or like anything
that could be resolved by a quasi-judicial process with a preordained
cast of student-victims and professor-perps.

It had always seemed to me that by pushing the academy to take
her as she is—dirty mind, long red nails, and all—Gallop helped
make it a less gray, and ultimately less sexist, place. But not all of her
feminist colleagues agree. Her accusers enjoyed a great deal of support
on the UWM campus and in Milwaukee newspapers. Even before the
charges were filed, she'd made herself unpopular by critiquing new
codes that frown on consensual sex between teachers and students.
UWM had adopted its version of these restrictions in 1988, but many
feminists on campus believed they had a long way to go before the
university took sexual harassment seriously. They had cause to think
that: in the past few years, the school had come under federal and
state scrutiny for its failure to record accurately and investigate fully

sexual-harassment charges brought by its students. Still, in this climate, campus feminists saw Gallop's objections as a betrayal.

So it was easy to imagine how, kiss or no kiss, Gallop's pro-sex feminism might leave her open to attack, how her outspoken classroom manner might be misread as sexual harassment in itself. Then, in late December, the university issued its findings: Gallop had *not* harassed either student. But in one of the cases, the affirmative action office said, she had violated the campus policy discouraging amorous consensual relations between professors and students. As a result, a letter of reprimand *will* go into her file. The decision, which Gallop is appealing, offers a curious and forbidding view of the limits of the professor-student relationship: "[The student] was a willing participant in the sexual banter; Professor Gallop did not condition [the student's] grades or participation in an academic program on [the student's] submission to sexual advances or sexual acts; [the student] was not and did not feel physically threatened, psychologically harmed or humiliated by any of Professor Gallop's conduct or words." And yet, the university ruled, Gallop, "the person in the more powerful position," did wrong by failing to report the relationship to a dean and failing to excuse herself from evaluating the student's academic performance or making decisions that had a financial impact on the student. "But for the sexual act," the university ruled, Gallop and her student "had an amorous relationship."

Since Gallop wasn't dating or sleeping with her student, the finding raises some disturbing questions. What exactly *is* an amorous relationship that excludes "the sexual act"? Does a close pedagogical relationship become "amorous" after one probably unwise but nonetheless anomalous step over the line? What do teachers do about students they come to care for and who like them a little too much in return? Refuse to teach them? What troubled me most about the case, however, was not the regime of chilly and spiritless professor-student exchanges it seemed to portend, though that was alarming enough. What bothered me was realizing that the trouble Gallop had gotten into was, in a way, inevitable. Gallop is not the first impassioned teacher to be tripped up by an increasingly elastic definition of sexual harassment and consent, and she probably won't be the last. But it seems telling that it was the very aspects of her teaching she considers the most feminist, the most subversive, as she would put it, of "phallic authority"—her emphasis on intimacy, on self-reflexivity, on rigorously working through the bonds of love that ensnare both teacher and student—that left her vulnerable to these charges. You can applaud Jane Gallop or you can find her excesses uncalled for, but there is no question that she believes in what she is doing and has thought about it long and hard. Close relationships between advisers and advisees may be rife with difficulties, but they are the best initiation into the academic life that anyone has yet devised. Gallop's story seemed to me the perfect opportunity to examine what it is we give up when we begin to police them.

"THERE ARE TIMES when I feel like what's at stake here is everything I value about teaching," Gallop says, "which doesn't involve having sex with students but does involve having such intense relations with students that when they go wrong they might, according to the new codes, be misconstrued as sexual harassment."

We are talking in the living room of the house Gallop shares with her boyfriend, a photographer and filmmaker named Dick Blau, and their seven-year-old son, Max. It's a comfortable two-story place on a shady street near the university—gingerbready and gemütlich on the outside, appointed with sleek 1950s furniture, like the boomerang-shaped aquamarine couch on which we're sitting, on the inside. After years of commuting between Milwaukee, where Blau chairs the film department at UWM, and Houston, where she taught at Rice, "she and Dick and Max are making a little home for themselves," as one of her students puts it.

It's cool and dark; we have the shades drawn to defeat the glare of the August afternoon. The doorbell rings and Gallop pads over in her bare feet to answer it. One of her graduate students, a slight, serious-looking fellow with lank strawberry-blond hair, wants to drop off the newest chapter of his thesis, which examines how feminism has changed the depiction of mother-son relations in literature and theory from Freud to Faulkner, David Leavitt to Adrienne Rich. He and Gallop arrange to meet for supper that evening to discuss it, but only after the two of them watch *Star Trek: The Next Generation* with Max. Later, they both tell me that they talked until midnight, first about the problems Gallop saw in the chapter, then about how he *felt* about the problems she saw in the chapter.

The kind of teaching Gallop does is by its nature—and hers—personal. She wants her students to learn to read texts as she does: symptomatically—alert, that is, to the clumsy metaphors, the little tics of syntax, even the mistranslations and typos that can betray an author's preoccupations or the unresolved contradictions of his or her argument. "She tries to teach a very particular method of close reading, which comes out of psychoanalysis and deconstruction," says Lynne Joyrich, a friend and colleague in the UWM English department. "It's very controlled. There's a lot of struggle. If she covers three sentences out of an article in one class session, that's a lot. It drives some students crazy."

In part, her teaching style reflects the theory behind it; in part, it's the natural expression of an intense personality. Gallop is in-your-face in a way some students find oppressive and others can't get enough of. "When she corrects your papers, it isn't as simple as saying, 'Here's a better way to put this'—she wants to know how it got there in the first place, and that means engaging with you at a personal level," says Chris Amirault, a doctoral candidate at UWM who did his undergraduate work at Brown, wears John Lennon-ish glasses and a flock of little earrings, and projects the bemused and tolerant cool of a counselor at an artsy summer camp. "Jane is deeply narcissistic, but her relationship to that narcissism is so developed, she's so committed to thinking about it, that she believes other people will be similarly committed. I completely respect that there are students who don't want to work that way, but I do."

We're eating breakfast at a diner the size of a small ranch, which Amirault has taken me to because it's regionally authentic, and between flapjacks he's been telling me about an unsuccessful paper he wrote several years ago for Gallop. "It was the most intense pedagogical experience I've ever had. We went through every sentence and what was behind it. Jane had covered the paper with 'I don't understand this'es, pointing out, for example, that I was using 'paradox' and 'contradiction' interchangeably. At first I felt very aggressed." And with the mixture of startling self-awareness and Gallopesque jargon I have noticed in several of her students, Amirault says: "Eventually I came to realize that it was written wholly within an unthinking transference. Its putative subject was how smart Freud was, but its real subject was how smart I was and how smart Jane was."

Amirault pulls out a more recent paper in which he has cast an unpitying eye on his Paulo Freirean fantasy of teaching as a political act and on his investment in a bright undergraduate named Shannon. Gallop has annotated it with standard editorial comments ("Nicely put" and "Sentence could be crisper" and even "This has yet to be sufficiently integrated/digested. Chew harder!") but also with remarks like "Your use of the adjective 'own' is truly interesting (symptomatic) in this paper. Of course, possession and boundaries are what's at stake" and "Would an explicit reference to the sexual version of this fantasy be helpful or is it just my ('own') wish for prurience?"

"It's teaching, not analysis, for her. She asks students to produce readings, and then she produces readings of those readings. It's not about explaining the psyches of the people in the room," Amirault says, taking a sip from one of his bottomless-cup-of-coffee refills. "But Jane makes you feel like your own position needs to be investigated. There has to be engagement, affect, discomfort sometimes. If those things aren't there, there's no learning. That comes in part from feminism—the idea that you have to reflect on who you are and where you are in society. And, of course, she has this deep commitment to a certain kind of post-structuralist psychoanalysis."

The student-teacher relationship holds such fascination for Gallop both because graduate school (at Cornell) was such a forcing ground of her own identity, the place where she'd dared her own *Doktor-Vater*s to accept her intellectual interest in sexuality, and because her relationship with her mentor, Jeffrey Mehlman, a theory-oriented professor of French, was particularly close: "That's where I really learned to do good work, that's where I learned my personal invest-ment in my professional identity—through my personal relationship to my teacher," she says. Gallop has borrowed from psychoanalysis much of the language in which she writes about graduate school and her own experience of it. She views crushes on professors as a form of transference—the endowing of new people in our lives with the emo-tional significance our parents once held for us. She has analyzed her own desire to be an intellectual as a yearning to usurp the place of the father and compel powerful men to recognize feminism's claims. And she has explored her relationship with Mehlman in terms of the push and shove of family love and sibling rivalry.

"Mehlman was my dissertation director," she writes in *Thinking Through the Body*, "the teacher who intro(se)duced me into the world of Lacan, French poststructuralist theory, and Freud." Gallop makes this remark in an afterword to one of her essays, in which she explains why she neglected to mention that the idea for it came from a former lover: "Argyros had been a student with me in graduate school; Mehlman was also his dissertation director. Argyros and I had lived together as best friends and lovers. Structurally, Argyros was my brother, Mehlman our father. I excluded Argyros to be textually alone with the father, out of my sense and fear that everything conspired to exclude me and to reinforce the academic father-son relation. This is not a commentary on the real men Mehlman and Argyros—both of whom took me quite seriously as a scholar, neither of whom seemed to want me to leave the room—but upon a structure which threat-ened to exclude me despite my having gotten myself into the room, despite any man's intentions toward me."

Nowadays Gallop—who at forty-one is no more than a decade older than some of her students—flirts and jokes with them not just for the fun of it, she says, but because it seems to her a good way to dispel a little of the parental authority they invest in her. When stu-dents develop crushes, as they frequently do, she thinks it best to talk about them openly, looking upon infatuation as an analyst looks upon transference: an instrument of understanding if acknowledged, a block to learning if not.

GALLOP HAD BEEN TEACHING for fourteen years—first at Miami University in Ohio, then at Rice—when she came to UWM in the fall of 1990. She'd been hired after a contentious search for a senior feminist theorist, a search whose smoke signals the English department's sizable detachment of feminist graduate students had observed closely. "She's a big name in feminist theory," says one student. "She filled a big teaching vacuum in the department, and I think a lot of people were hoping for a nurturer."

That's not exactly what they got. Even students who love Gallop say she's a tough grader and a harsh critic, that she has been known to push them through four or five drafts of a paper. "A lot of grad students are into various kinds of warmed-over liberal pedagogy," says Amirault. "And Jane is authoritarian in the sense that she believes she has something to teach you and you have something to learn. She's opinionated and abrasive. Of course, there are male professors who are exactly the same way, but it's not a problem for them." Jeff Walker, the grad student whose dissertation is on mothers and sons, makes a similar point: "Grades are meaningful to Jane in a way that they aren't to many professors. She's given Bs and Cs to graduate students. And there's a tension, I think, between her rigorous pedagogy and high demands and her casualness in other respects, her willingness, for example, to socialize with graduate students. In psychoanalytic terms, she's playing two parental roles: one embodies the law of the father and the other the presumed supportiveness and informality of the mother."

Elisabeth Ladenson, a former protégée of Gallop's who is now an assistant professor of French at the University of Virginia and who calls Gallop's teaching "unconventional, self-referential, sort of dangerous," tells a story about sitting in on a feminist lit-crit seminar that Gallop taught for graduate students at Rice. "One day a woman gave a presentation, and she had basically ignored everything Jane had asked her to do in the assignment: she talked about five or six essays instead of one, she argued with them instead of doing a close reading, and after the allotted fifteen minutes were up, she showed no sign of stopping. Jane asked her quite directly to think about the fact that she hadn't fulfilled the assignment—very firmly and very neutrally, sort of like an analyst. And the woman started crying. Frankly, it would have thoroughly disarmed a male professor. But Jane didn't let it go. She began talking about how the precise way this woman had flouted the rules was symptomatic of something larger in feminism, a kind of resistance to theory. She turned this excruciating situation into an edifying pedagogical moment." Did the tearful student get much out of it? "I don't think so," says Ladenson. "Except maybe some feminist jargon. On the last day of class, she complained about having been victimized."

Though Gallop seems the soul of friendliness, I can see how she might be formidable. She has a deep voice, and she talks loud and fast, hell-bent on making her points. "Students are blinded to her nice-guy side," says Ladenson, "because she's very smart, she doesn't suffer fools gladly, and when she's in the classroom, well, she thinks about what she's thinking about. She's not worrying whether you have a comfy chair." Her appearance challenges, too, in part because she pulls off the curious sartorial trick of looking both clothes-conscious and utterly indifferent to fashion. Her outfits and accessories—the skirt made of men's ties, the glove-tight Joan Crawford suit she sometimes dons for conferences—seem to announce themselves with quotation marks as "parody" or "eccentricity" or "fetish." For both of our interviews, she is casually dressed in shorts and a brightly colored vintage shirt and wears no makeup. But a single rat-tail braid hangs from her tousled shoulder-length hair, and she flashes a *Married to the Mob* manicure—long crimson nails, except for one gold pinkie nail. Jeff Walker says he was "terrified of her on the first day of class, because, first, she was wearing this bright-red power suit with all these wild accessories. And second of all, she started out by telling us we'd have to work harder to satisfy her expectations than we ever had before."

The work she wanted the students to do in that class—the first she taught at UWM, and a repeat of the feminist theory class Ladenson describes—focused on her book in progress, *Around 1981*, and its main theme: the acceptance of feminist criticism as a legitimate branch of literary studies. They were to analyze its institutionalization in the academy at a time—the early 1980s—when, as Gallop writes, "feminism as a social movement was encountering major setbacks in a climate of new conservatism." But Gallop tends to underestimate the extent to which some of her own feminist students perceive her as an exponent of institutional power, resent her for it, and wish to make *that* the subject of the class. In each of the three feminist theory seminars she has taught since 1985, she says, "some subset of the seminar decided to band together to try and challenge me because they thought I was authoritarian." And in the sexual-harrassment complaints, her accusers also seem disgruntled with her status, stressing Gallop's "fame" as a theorist (as one of their supporters explains to me, though the students didn't have to take courses with Gallop in order to complete their degrees in their chosen fields, they felt "pressure" to do so "because she is famous"), her position as the only woman at UWM to have achieved the rank of distinguished professor, and the "extremely unequal power differential," as one of the complainants puts it, that separates professors and graduate students.

"One of the misunderstandings I had with that class," Gallop says, "is that they somehow saw my giving them my writing as a way of redoubling my authority, whereas I saw it as a way of making myself more vulnerable, because, after all, these were drafts."

In hindsight, Gallop wonders whether offering up her unfinished work was the only "gesture of informality" that her students misinterpreted in light of that "power differential." Early in the semester, she started going out after class with a group of female students who wanted to continue the discussion, maybe get a little more airtime than they had managed to snag in the overenrolled seminar. They'd drink beer and joke around; the conversation would often turn to sex.

Gallop joined in; she welcomed the opportunity to remind her new students that, though she sometimes sounded pontifical in class, she was a real person, not "some kind of totally professional being."

"Certainly part of who I've always been socially since I was an adult, or even a semi-adult," Gallop says, "is someone who makes sexual jokes with just about anybody, aside from strangers on a bus. I am someone who is sometimes flirtatious and who likes acting somewhat outrageous. So with grad students in a social situation, I find myself reacting as I would to anybody in a social situation. And with a sense that that is what they want. I mean, grad students are always trying to get professors to go out drinking with them, to come to their parties; they seem to want to break down some of that distance."

In the past, that flirting was apparently understood more in the spirit that Gallop intended it than as, say, a proposition. The university's finding in the sexual-harassment case states: "None of Professor Gallop's students [an unspecified number were interviewed for the investigation], either former students or UWM students, had any personal knowledge of any sexual relationship, consensual or otherwise, that Professor Gallop had had with any student. None of her former Ph.D. candidates felt any sexual overtones in her dealings with them. Each described her as either 'provocative' or 'performative.' " This accords with my own picture of Gallop, which is not of a coy or predatory flirt but of a rather straight shooter.

"Jane flirts with everybody," a friend of hers says. "She flirts with inanimate objects. That's just Jane. Always has been as far as I know." But these days when Gallop throws back a few beers and pals around with her grad students, it has a different meaning than it had when she was younger, untenured, less published, about as unfirmly ensconced in the academy as feminism itself. It was naive, perhaps, not to realize that sooner. "I now have students like [one of her accusers] who come to work with me because they've read my books on the reading lists for their M.A.'s, students for whom I am an authority because I'm an author," Gallop says with a Rodney Dangerfield grimace of disbelief. "I still look at my writing as something I hope is good enough, something I'm anxious about the unfinished drafts of. But for my graduate students, I am the author of *The Daughter's Seduction*, the author of *Reading Lacan*. They perceive me as something that is still barely imaginable to me—as what I call Jane-Gallop-in-quotation-marks."

After talking with several of her students, I begin to realize that Gallop makes some of them angry because she reminds them that distinguished female professors aren't necessarily any nicer, more indulgent, more intuitively ethical than their male counterparts. Just like the guys, they sometimes hand out bad grades, refuse to write letters of recommendation, pack reading lists with their own books, turn importuning freshmen away at their office doors. Only it's worse, because students, especially women, want more time and expect more comfort from female professors. There are still so few in the higher ranks of academe—women make up more than half of all college students but only 11.6 percent of full professors nationwide—that each one must carry an unwieldy burden of expectation. They must embody with George Sand–like brio what it means to be women and intellectuals, while nurturing every tender ego that comes into their orbit. If they should happen also to be feminist scholars, they raise the further hope, fed by much of the writing on feminist pedagogy, that their classrooms will be havens of sisterly equality where the gladiatorial rivalries of the "patriarchal" seminar are given no quarter.

The feminist students now working toward doctorates are the first to study under feminist teachers with tenure and clout, and this has produced some curious reactions. "One of the things I have experienced is that our students tend to imagine we have more power than we do," says Nancy K. Miller, a feminist literary critic at the City University of New York. "Our generation had no women ahead of us. We were rebelling against father figures, and that was simpler in some ways. Now I'm the same age as some of my students' mothers, and I stir some of those feelings of identification and repudiation you might expect."

But rebelling against Gallop is peculiarly tricky, because she's such a figure of rebellion herself. The authorial voice Gallop adopts in *Thinking Through the Body* is boldly exhibitionist and coolly self-critical. ("In the original paper I talk about the 'American feminist' and her investment in the clitoris. If I am distancing myself from that, it is both mas- turbatory guilt and more general embarrassment with the celebration of the self. . . . The attack on the American celebration of the self has become stock discourse contrasting American and French feminism. Yet who am I when I say that? . . . Encoding the guilty as American acts out an identification with the 'French woman' and an aggressive distancing from the 'American feminist.' ") She's only too happy to disrupt her sophisticated discussion of the distinction between "phal- lus" and "penis" in Lacanian thought with a Borscht Belt dirty joke. ("Anna Freud was reaching maturity and began to show an interest in her father's work, so Freud gave her some of his writings to read. About a month later he asked her if she had any questions about what she had been reading. 'Just one,' she replied. 'What is a phallus?' Being a man of science, Freud unbuttoned his pants and showed her. 'Oh,' Anna exclaimed, thus enlightened. 'It's like a penis, only smaller!' ") And she's eager, in her readings of the big boys like Roland Barthes, "to outdo the fathers at their own game," as Ann Snitow put it in a re- view of *Thinking Through the Body*, "to seduce them, too, until they are forced to subvert their own rules, or to admit the failure of their systems to contain everything and particularly to contain the unread- able, unresolvable body." Students seem to like the way Gallop swag- gers across the page, but a lot of them, I suspect, would rather be her than be taught by her.

Gallop knows she is caught in a bind: "I'm realizing that one of the reasons I can't undercut my authority with students by being shock- ingly informal is that my authority is based on an authorial persona or a theoretical persona that is itself shockingly informal—that's part of its authority. It seems like a terrible contradiction." Gallop pauses to take a long sip of mineral water. "The sexual innuendo that func- tioned ten years ago to mark me as one of the girls with my students now marks me as one of the guys."

ÐANA BECKELMAN WAS NOT one of the students who bristled at Gal- lop's authority. At least not at first.

When Beckelman, a second-year Ph.D. candidate in the rhetoric and composition program within UWM's English department, signed up in the fall of 1990 for Gallop's graduate seminar on feminist theory, she was already, as she puts it, "smitten." In an autobiographical paper she later wrote for another professor, Beckelman recalls how she'd fantasized all summer about "sprawling" under the oak trees in her backyard with Gallop, discussing writing with her, playing Phaedrus to Gallop's Socrates.

At thirty, Beckelman was in search of a mentor to foster her own flamboyant style. A lesbian with the muscular build of the Texas state shot-put champion she had once been, a talented writer torn between fiction and literary criticism, she wasn't sure where, or even if, she belonged in the academy. "But I figured, here's Jane Gallop, this person who's not your typical academician, someone who could be a role model for how to be yourself and still be a successful academic. We're both sort of bad, boisterous, outrageous. We enjoyed that about each other," Beckelman tells me on the telephone from a friend's house in California.

Even better, Gallop was, in a manner of speaking, famous. Not Madonna famous; not even k.d. lang famous. But a name with real pull in high-theory and feminist circles. "I'm a Capricorn. I'm very ambitious, very driven," says Beckelman. "And I'd gone to Milwaukee to get on the fast track by hooking up with someone well known. I was dazzled by Jane—it was the first time I'd ever worked with a scholar who had a national reputation." At another point in the conversation, she says, "If Jane had approached me for a fling during the first few weeks of school, I think it would have happened."

Two weeks after enrolling in her course, Beckelman asked Gallop to be her adviser, and Gallop accepted. The women became friendly outside of class. Beckelman concedes that she participated in, and even initiated, much of the beer-drinking banter (she remembers holding forth one night about her "very 1970s, Marge Piercy–esque we're-all-nonmonogamous theory of open relationships"), though the sexual-harassment complaint she filed two years later suggests that Gallop's contributions to that same banter amounted to an abuse of power. "Look, I'm five feet nine, 170 pounds, and very dykey," Beck-elman says. "People look at me and say: 'How could this happen to *you*? How could you let Jane do this to you?' But grad school is a pretty weird, paranoia-inducing place. I was trying to work with someone who was well known, and I liked her. She's gregarious; she has a certain amount of charm. When she flirted, I flirted back. It re-minded me of the wordplay in her books, and I thought, 'Hey, this must be the latest hip and trendy theoretical thing.' But then I began to be confused by what she intended with some of her remarks."

By way of example, Beckelman says Gallop told her that she had "beautiful deltoids" and that she liked Texas women. After Beckel-man's open-relationships speech, she says Gallop remarked, "From all that practice, you must be quite a good lover." Gallop remembers similar themes, different inflections: she says she kidded Beckelman about how she showed off her deltoids when she talked; told her she enjoyed hearing a Texas accent because she missed Texas; and said, "in a spirit that was sarcastic, not admiring," that it sounded like Beckelman was trying to impress the group with her "experience."

At first, their work together seemed full of promise. Beckelman was eager to try out her own version of Gallop's confessional style and pleased when Gallop gave her an A/A− on her first class presentation, which blended analytic work with a memoir of her grandmother. But Gallop's reaction to her second presentation came as a blow. "It had a lot of inside Freudian jokes," Beckelman recalls, "so I thought she'd think it was funny. But I was questioning her position as a woman who says she's attracted to women of another class, even though she lives with a man and has a son."

Beckelman is citing a parenthetical remark in one of Gallop's es-says that jumped out at her the first time she read it. By the time Beckelman told me about it, she had come to regard this comment as the key to Gallop's "eroticization" of graduate students. Gallop deliv-ers the aside in "The Other Woman," an essay about an essay in which the French feminist Annie Leclerc explores her sensual fascina-tion with the maid depicted behind her mistress in Vermeer's *The Let-ter*. Gallop is interested in what Leclerc's reverie might disclose about the fantasy of a classless sisterhood, oceanic and all-embracing, so attractive to so many feminists. In typical Gallop fashion, she chides Leclerc for romanticizing the working class while congratulating her for owning up to a desire that others share but deny: "Of course, there is a long phallic tradition of desire for those with less power and privilege (women, for example) and I cannot but wonder about the relationship of Leclerc's desire to that tradition. Just as I cannot but be reminded of the romantic and essentially conservative tradition of the happy and beautiful folk, the earthy, free working class. . . . Despite these problems I have with Leclerc's desire for the maid (an erotic attraction to women of another class which I share, I should add), I think it valuable as a powerful account of just that sort of desire, a desire that is frequently hidden under the 'mantle of redressers of wrongs.' "

In early October—before the second presentation—Beckelman told Gallop she needed to talk with her, and they went out to dinner. She wanted to clarify, Beckelman now explains, what the "woman wanted from me." She quoted Gallop's glib remark in the essay on Leclerc and said it bothered her. Was Gallop just striking a theoretical pose, or did she really have lust in her heart for other women? Gallop told her it was none of her business. Beckelman persisted: "Are you coming on to me or just flirting?" "Just flirting," Gallop replied, adding that she thought of flirting, theoretically, as a way of seducing students to learn and that she was most definitely pursuing a pedagogical, not a sexual, relationship with her. Gallop recalls that Beckelman seemed relieved. And they agreed for a time to drop their ribaldry.

But in that second class presentation later that month, Beckelman again brought up Gallop's "erotic attraction to women of another class"; as Gallop understood it, Beckelman was accusing her of pretending to a fashionable lesbianism. (For the record, Gallop says she has slept with both men and women and in the early 1970s identified herself "publicly and politically" as a lesbian. She has been involved with her current boyfriend, however, for the past thirteen years.)

Gallop gave this talk a lower grade than the first—an A double minus—because, she says, the ideas were muddled and it lacked the kind of narrative passages in which Beckelman shone. But Beckelman took the grade hard; to her it was evidence that Gallop "loathed" her work, that she "just went ballistic when I challenged her position." Beckelman felt reassured when Gallop gave her an A /A+ on her final paper, which alternated between a scholarly analysis of *Thinking Through the Body* and a series of sexually explicit love letters to an unnamed woman. The grade was unusually high for Gallop—so unusual that she called Beckelman at home in Texas over Christmas vacation to tell her about it—but for Beckelman it was just a sign that she and her mentor were "back on track."

Hearing Beckelman talk about her excitement when Gallop liked a paper and her dark suspicions when Gallop didn't, I remember the sensation of yearning for an adviser's approval, feeling embarrassed about the childlike quality of that yearning and yet knowing that, professionally speaking, the approval is necessary. At one time or another, most graduate students have entertained the suspicion that their adviser controls their destiny, and it's true in just enough ways to make paranoia seem justified. "The professor combines the transferential authority of the parent with the actual power of a director of graduate studies," writes the historian Peter Loewenberg in a smart essay on the sticky emotional climate of graduate school. "The faculty-student relationship, particularly on the graduate level, is not that of equals. It is one of domination and submission. Whereas reality factors in other professional relationships such as attorney-client or doctor-patient are limited to a contractual transaction whereby the latter agrees to pay and obey while the former ministers with the promise of relief, in academia the reality gives the professor authority over the student's finances, employment, academic record, references—to say nothing of the emotional rewards—heightened self-esteem, enhanced prestige, and the fantasy of eventual inheritance of power. . . . For any student who has been an independent adult on his own, a return to graduate school most certainly represents an emotional regression."

On at least one occasion that they both confirm, Beckelman seems to have been trying to impress Gallop with her sexual savoir faire. One fall afternoon, Beckelman showed up at Gallop's office with a package she had received from her lover in Texas: Beckelman described it as a "Freudian fantasy kit"; Gallop describes it as a bundle of "sexual props." Gallop was, she wrote in her official response to Beckelman's complaint, "horrified" and asked Beckelman "to put it away, told her that her fantasies [were] and should remain a private thing between her and her lover, and that [she did] not want to see or hear about this package."

In the spring semester, Beckelman opted to take an independent study with Gallop in which she would read Freud, Barthes, and Lacan, as well as her adviser's two books on Lacan. It was the low point of their pedagogical relationship. When they held their first meeting, to discuss Freud's *Beyond the Pleasure Principle*, Gallop felt, as she wrote in her reply, that Beckelman's "readings were very uninformed and extremely inaccurate. Dana had never studied Freud and, I believe, had never even read him before but had, as does the culture in general, a lot of presuppositions about him. When I would try to point out the ways that her readings were implausible, wrong, or didn't make sense, or when I tried to ask her leading questions to get her to see these problems, she simply argued with me, defending her 'position.' " Gallop suggested they try something different. Beckelman would come in with questions about what she didn't understand in the text; Gallop would clear them up. But this approach, too, soon dissolved into argument. When I ask Beckelman about it, she agrees that their meetings were often combative but offers a different interpretation: "It was frustrating. I'd want to talk about my ideas, and she'd just want to talk about hers. I felt like she was threatened by me, but I thought, 'This is weird: this woman is very secure; she's got her books. How could a grad student be threatening to her ego?' But the more I said things that went against her ideas, the more she'd say, 'That's not valid.' "

Gallop considered it a breakthrough when she and Beckelman began openly discussing the tensions between them. At one point, Beckelman accused her of wanting to relegate her to student status forever so that she could continue to exert control over her. She worried, she said on another occasion, that Gallop would never be satisfied with anything she did, and then confided that in this sense her adviser reminded her of her father, a high-school football coach who wanted Dana to excel at sports but couldn't show any pleasure when she did. ("I told her about my father," says Beckelman. "But I also told her I'd been through therapy and didn't have those issues anymore.") Later, Gallop says, Beckelman told her that when she was a student in the master's program at UT-Arlington, her female adviser had seemed put off by both her lesbianism and her outrageous style. (Beckelman denies having said this.)

Gallop, reluctant to be miscast as either withholding father or prissy professor, reverted to the light, slightly off-color teasing that she believed was "comforting" to Dana because "it was where I treated Dana as a peer and showed her I was not a judgmental authority."

When I try to puzzle out how Beckelman must have felt, one of Gallop's colleagues' remarks sticks in my mind: "I never thought what Jane did was sexual harassment. But I wondered about her judgment. Dana idolized her, and I think she should have realized that with this student she was on shaky emotional ground." Gallop figured she could handle whatever ambivalent feelings a bright, audacious student like Beckelman might have about her. "I think I had a kind of hubris in which I felt I could teach any student," she says. "I could get over their resistance or whatever. I hesitate to say this in print, because I don't tell the students this, but I actually agree to work with any student who asks to work with me, because a lot of students get very intimidated by me at first."

IN FEBRUARY 1991, Beckelman interviewed Gallop for a publication called *Composition Studies: Freshman English News*, and both women think of it as a reliable document of what was best about their exchanges. It makes a lively read, yet there are stretches of the interview where both Gallop and Beckelman seem not so much to be swapping ideas as thinking aloud in each other's presence. When one or the other hears the word "sex," they seem to have found their point of connection, but it's illusory. Gallop compares writing to sex, for example, while Beckelman seizes on the sexual analogy to steer the discussion to their relationship:

JG: I had a realization sometime last fall about my specific relation to writing. It's not the actual writing that is difficult, but there's something I'm terrified of that makes it very hard. I feel like I don't want to write, I don't want to sit down to write, I don't want to start, I want to get up right away, yet when I say it's very hard I'm exaggerating because I sit down and do it every day and once I start it's extremely pleasurable. So I had this realization that I felt the exact same way about sex.

DB: Something told me that we'd get to sex sooner or later.

JG: Of course, but I want to explain because I had one of those moments like light bulbs going on in the sense that I avoid doing both, or think I want to avoid doing them. I mean, I've been living with someone for years, and every night we get into bed together, but that doesn't necessarily mean we're going to have sex, and my first response is to think I want to watch TV or I want to go to sleep. But a lot of times, particularly if a couple of days have gone by, I make myself start having sex, and as soon as I cross over some kind of threshold in which I commit myself to having sex I find that it's extremely pleasurable. But there's something in me that doesn't want to do it so that I have to make myself do it, and I have the exact same relation to writing, which is that once I start writing I very seldom have trouble, I very seldom get stuck, I very seldom write much that I have to throw away, so that I actually write well and get a lot of pleasure from it. So they're both sources of great gratification and yet also things that I'm terrified of and resistant to.

DB: But it's more than just a fear of failure—

JG: Yes, I think that there's some fear that I will be confronted with some terrible inadequacy about myself, but it's also about how one constructs one's self-image—

DB: In the sense that you don't want to be someone who writes about sex and doesn't have it—

JG: Right. Jane never has sex, she just theorizes it.

DB: Well, speaking of sex and writing, where does your view of teaching as a form of seduction fit in?

GALLOP THINKS SHE MADE MISTAKES with Dana Beckelman, but not the one that everybody else seems to think she made, which was to kiss her at a crowded bar in the presence of other graduate students. Indeed, it's hard to find anyone other than Gallop herself who will defend the "twenty-second soul kiss," as one witness described it. Especially since it occurred the evening after Gallop jokingly referred to herself as someone whose "sexual preference is graduate students."

Gallop's remark was intended to be provocative, she says, but she made it in the service of an intellectual critique. Taking the floor at a gay and lesbian conference after one speaker had waxed enthusiastic about butch and femme roles, Gallop remembers saying something like, "As one of the few people here who is not a graduate student, as someone who might say her sexual preference is graduate students, I want to ask why you are celebrating all sorts of differences, thinking it progress that they are no longer denied, while one kind of difference is bad, remains something that should be reduced as much as possible— the difference between teacher and graduate student."

That evening, Beckelman, Gallop, and a handful of grad students who had been at the conference went out drinking at a local lesbian bar. For a long time, Beckelman and Gallop talked about their troubled relationship, with Gallop sitting on a bar stool swigging beer and Beckelman standing between her legs. Gallop kept making the point that no amount of repartee could alter the fundamental fact of their relationship: she was the teacher, Beckelman the student. Beckelman hadn't been able to accept that, she said, and had wanted to "fuck the teacher out of her." Beckelman says Gallop touched her breasts and stroked her shoulders as they talked; Gallop says she may have touched her arms for emphasis, but not her breasts. After half an hour or so, Beckelman broke up the tête-à-tête by urging the group to dance—a moment she describes in a paper she wrote for another professor as "egging" Gallop onto the dance floor, then smirking with her friends about what a lousy dancer she was.

Before Beckelman left the bar, she and Gallop embraced, as they sometimes did when parting. According to Beckelman, Gallop then "mashed her lips against mine" and "shoved her tongue in my mouth." According to Gallop, Beckelman was the one who turned a peck into a French kiss. But both women say that from there on in, the smooch was mutual. Gallop says they were engaging in a "performance," not acting on desire. Beckelman, in her complaint, describes her apparently enthusiastic participation this way: "So I kissed her until she responded, more as a vindictive act than a reciprocally sexual one. I was angry and hurt, and saw kissing her as a form of revenge, a way to manipulate her desire, knowing I would never go any further." In our interview, Beckelman sticks with this oddly pulp-fiction-ish scenario. "My attitude," she recalls, "was, sure, I'll kiss you. I will give you the kiss to end all kisses, and then I'll never touch or flirt with you again."

According to the university's finding, "the individuals who witnessed the kiss varied in their perceptions of what they saw," proving, one supposes, that a kiss is neither still nor just a kiss: "Some thought it was a performance. One saw it as 'humorous' that a student who had been flirting with Professor Gallop had finally kissed her. Another surmised that outside its context, others would 'miss the point.' One student stated that Professor Gallop 'definitely forced [Ms. Beckelman] between her legs while they were at the bar.' "

By Gallop's logic, it was the very fact that she kissed Beckelman so brazenly that exonerated her from sexual harassment: if she were trying to hide either a coercive or a consensual relationship with Beckelman, she wouldn't have stood there twisting tongues with her before a semicircle of gaping students. And, in fact, several of her friends and colleagues talk to me about Gallop's "masquerade" or "performance" as a "bad girl"; much of what Gallop would do in public, they say, is precisely what she *wouldn't* do in private. Her critics on the UWM campus, though, could interpret the kiss only as a tip-of-the-iceberg anecdote: if this is what Jane Gallop does in the open, just imagine what she does behind closed doors.

Gallop's own account of the barroom clinch does more to advance her pedagogical theories than to clarify her motives. "I wanted the other graduate students at the bar to think about the erotics of the relation between teacher and student," she says. "You know, a lot of the reaction, both gossipy and official, to my case is that what I have done in general, and what I must have done that night, was to make students uncomfortable. And the way things are going with sexual-harassment policy, people are beginning to interpret 'hostile environment' as anything that makes students uncomfortable. Well, I have a problem, because I feel that part of my *job* as a teacher is to make students feel uncomfortable, to ask them questions they don't necessarily want to face."

Gallop may have been deluding herself when she assumed that she and Beckelman shared the same playfully transgressive agenda or that Beckelman could ever resist the opportunity to use the kiss against her. She probably should have paid heed to the barely contained rage in Beckelman's conference presentation the next day, when she amended the paper she was giving to include the lines "I don't have a problem fucking Jane Gallop as long as she practices safe sex. After all, she is merely an 'other woman.' I do have a problem fucking my dissertation adviser." Beckelman says she meant this as a "public rejection of any intent to have sex with Jane." Gallop says she didn't think of it much one way or another, since the paper dealt with her work and was full of bold puns; besides, she says, she already took it for granted that she and Beckelman would never sleep together. In fact, Gallop told her afterward how much she liked the paper, though she challenged Beckelman's interpretation of the nurse on the cover of *Thinking Through the Body* as "a lesbian figure." (The cover photograph shows a nurse assisting at a birth.)

If Beckelman felt any lingering anger over the kiss, she didn't show it. She and Gallop continued to work together during the spring and summer; they went out at least once for Mexican food and once for beer and, Gallop says, hugged "in the manner of old friends" when they said good night. Though Beckelman told Gallop that her girl-friend, who had been at the bar the night of the kiss, had been made jealous by it, Beckelman never said she was disturbed by it herself. The trouble came, as it always had with Gallop and Beckelman, when Gallop began passing judgment on her work.

Beckelman was writing her preliminary proposal—the three- to five-page essay in which she was to define the field she'd be examined in and which Gallop thought of as a key intellectual exercise, the first step in transforming a grad student into "a mature, autonomous, and original scholar." Gallop found Beckelman's initial attempts to formulate her field (she wanted to work on some aspect of feminist academic writing) confused, and the teacher marched her student through four or five drafts (Beckelman says five; Gallop remembers four). "I was very frustrated," Beckelman says. "I called it the rigor patrol. The second version I thought was very good, the third draft I thought was better, but the fourth and fifth got worse. I realized that the first three were all trying to articulate my ideas, but the fourth and fifth were trying to articulate hers." (In her complaint she writes, "I feel at this point there is a direct relationship between Jane's rejection of my proposals and my rejection of her advances, but I cannot, of course, prove this.")

The following December, Beckelman wrote to Gallop to tell her she had decided to withdraw from the rhetoric and composition program and switch to the creative-writing concentration. Gallop was disturbed by the wistful and intimate tone of the letter—Beckelman, she says, wrote that she had been sweeping her new apartment in the nude, it was four o'clock in the morning and she was thinking of Gallop, feeling sad about her plan to switch to a program in which Gallop could no longer advise her. (Beckelman's recollection of the letter varies slightly from Gallop's: she says that when she mentioned sweeping in the nude, she was alluding to a photograph of Gallop taken by Blau that hangs on Gallop's office wall.) Gallop showed the letter to a colleague, who remarked that it sounded like a letter from a lover mulling over a breakup and urged her to talk to Beckelman about the basis for her decision.

Here is where Gallop's and Beckelman's accounts diverge most markedly: Gallop says this conversation occurred over coffee a few weeks after she got the letter; Beckelman says it happened earlier, in September, when Gallop would have still been her adviser. Whenever it took place, the conversation began amicably. Beckelman said she had always wanted to pursue fiction writing but had worried about making a living at it. Gallop said she respected her decision to develop her talents as a prose stylist because it was her narrative writing that, as her teacher, Gallop had always thought the strongest. (In her complaint, Beckelman says she was forced to switch to creative writing by Gallop's amorous attentions—a problematic claim, since Gallop doesn't teach in the rhetoric and composition program or serve on its advisory committee and Beckelman had gone out of her way to work with her in the first place.)

But later in that same conversation, Beckelman returned to an old theme: Had Gallop *ever* slept with women? Had she ever *really* been attracted to a student—to her, say? "Attempting to be fully honest in my answer," Gallop writes with astonishingly reckless—yet typical—candor in her official response, "I said that I had in general not felt any attraction to her" but that she remembered noticing on one occasion how nice her breasts looked in a silk tank top and had once "wondered to myself and in conversation with Dick if Dana's sexual experience with women meant she knew something that could free me from a pattern of increasing sexual rigidity." Why would she say all this to a student, even a former student, who brought more baggage than a Ryder van could hold to this particular conversation? The titillation of resurrecting a fleeting desire, perhaps. Or Gallop's compulsion to confessional honesty. Or her reluctance to be thought of as some goody-two-shoes hetero chick. Her explanation is that she was "trying to say that although I do not have sexual relations with students, I do sometimes experience real desire. I said this because I was also responding to her earlier suggestion that I was playing with a kind of fashionable lesbianism, pretending to feel attraction to women when it was in fact a pose."

For almost a year, Beckelman pondered filing a complaint but didn't. She eventually earned her Ph.D. in creative writing (and now holds a teaching post at a university in Tokyo). She still talked about Gallop but usually only to express the congealed scorn and pity of the up-and-coming for the old-and-out-of-it: "It's a boredom thing," she tells me. "She's done everything she set out to do. I mean, I'd feel like I was just hitting my stride, like Madonna. But maybe she feels, 'Hey, I've done the book thing, I've done the child thing.' "

What finally convinced her to file charges, she says, was hearing that another grad student, a friend who was also a lesbian, felt she, too, had been badly treated by Gallop. Beckelman told the friend that together they could stop Gallop. As Beckelman explains in her complaint, while she couldn't "link Jane's sexual behavior toward me with her negative responses to my proposals," the other student's story "showed that Jane uses academics vindictively against sexual rejection." Besides, Beckelman had worried that if she was the only student lodging a complaint, she would be "constructed as having implicated myself by having kissed [Gallop] in the bar."

The truth was that Beckelman not only had implicated herself but also seemed at times to revel in her implication. When she brought the case up in a column she wrote in March 1993 for the *Lesbian and Gay Studies Newsletter*, Beckelman sounded less like an aggrieved victim than a P.C. Hedda Hopper, hard as nails and almost gleefully dishy: "Gossip has it, my dears, that at the MLA the rumors were flying (or being whispered discreetly) that I and someone else had filed sexual harassment complaints against Jane Gallop, so I don't think it's entirely out of line to confirm those rumors here. Yes, the investigation is in progress, and yes, as a result, that's all I can divulge (at least publicly). I can say, however, that the entire ordeal has been cause for my thoughts to be preoccupied."

WHATEVER ONE ULTIMATELY CONCLUDES about Beckelman's complaint, it's not hard to see why it warranted investigation. But why did the university treat the second student's complaint with equal seriousness? The charge was bolstered, of course, by its coupling with Beckelman's, but it's also useful to remember that in the fall of 1992, UWM had a strong incentive to treat sexual-harassment complaints with elaborate deference—it had a P.R. nightmare on its hands that had everything to do with its record on such cases.

The second student (she has since transferred from UWM, declines to be interviewed, and prefers not to be named) focused her complaint on Gallop's refusal to write her letters of recommendation to Brown and Johns Hopkins, though Gallop had previously written a letter on her behalf to the University of California at Santa Cruz. She admitted that she had willingly "engaged in a mode of sexual/ intellectual pedagogical exchange with Gallop," but, she claims, Gallop then made sexual advances and when they were thwarted retaliated by treating her in "an inconsistent and conflicted" manner—that is, writing a letter of recommendation to one school but not to two others. In au courant, if somewhat confused, diction, the student goes on to explain that "it is at the level of the institutionally enforced power differential (which Professor Gallop knowingly exploited) that I wish to locate the harassment."

The notorious rocking-chair incident occurred one night in June 1991 when the student dropped off a paper at Gallop's house. It was raining, she was riding her motorcycle, and she asked to stay for a while. They sat in the living room talking and had a few drinks. When the student said she was hungry and couldn't drive home until she ate something, Gallop poked around in the fridge and pulled out some leftover tabbouleh. On her way to the kitchen, she walked past a downstairs bedroom and seemed to pause, which the student found insinuating. At another point, Gallop reached over with her foot and rocked the rocking chair, which the student also found insinuating. Much is made in the complaint of Gallop's foot being bare. The student also mentions that a few months earlier, at a party after the gay and lesbian graduate student conference (the same conference during which Gallop was supposedly pursuing Beckelman), she felt Gallop was hovering in or around the groups of people with whom the student was talking. (Since the student's complaint alleges quid pro quo harassment—that is, that Gallop refused to write the letters of recommendation because her sexual advances had been spurned—it seems worth noting that Gallop wrote the one letter and declined to write the others within the same three weeks in December, more than six months after the alleged come-ons occurred.)

Gallop says she could support the student's application to UC–Santa Cruz because the student had told her she wanted to pursue gay studies and Santa Cruz was strong in that field, but she could not endorse her for a more general graduate program in English at schools not known for gay studies. The student had taken only one class with her—an undergraduate lecture course she had actually audited—and she had been faltering at UWM, picking up incompletes and growing ever more frustrated with the scarcity of gay studies offerings there. In her official response, Gallop also says she cannot see how declining to write a letter of recommendation constitutes a form of retaliation against a student.

When UWM's Office of Affirmative Action/Equal Opportunity finally released a finding on the case in December, it agreed with her, and in strong language: "While [the student] claims she felt these acts were 'sexual in nature,' she does not describe a single incident that could be defined objectively as such. Such feelings, unaccompanied by words or actions on Professor Gallop's part, are not contemplated within the definition of 'sexual harassment' by either the Equal Employment Opportunity Commission's regulations or courts. . . . Professor Gallop's reasons for refusing to write letters of support for her are entirely reasonable and plausible."

The second student's complaint may have been patently, even comically, flimsy, but it's important to remember how inflamed the atmosphere was when the charges were filed. A state legislative audit performed in the spring of 1991 had faulted UWM for not taking complaints of discrimination and harassment as seriously as the law demanded. The affirmative action office, it said, did not keep adequate records of student complaints, dragged its feet when it looked into them, and sometimes lost files altogether. Meanwhile, a routine U.S. Department of Labor investigation had revealed that the university had not filed the affirmative action report required by federal law for five years. So the Department of Labor decided to look a little deeper: in the fall of 1992, it issued a stinging report that identified "patterns and or practices of discrimination" in UWM's hiring and promotion of women. It threatened to freeze federal grants for the entire UW system—some $350 million worth—if UWM didn't take steps to rectify the problem. (The university has since reached an agreement with the federal government in which it promises to revamp its affirmative action procedures and offer jobs and back pay to a number of female faculty members who left or were not promoted.)

None of this was happening quietly. For months, Milwaukee newspapers and politicians had been taking UWM to task. State senator Barbara Notestein had declared that "something was rotten at UWM" and called for the resignation of Chancellor John Schroeder unless he took steps to correct sex discrimination on his campus. Somebody organized a Victims of UWM Support Group, which advertised its mission in the student paper: to aid "healing by acknowledging what the UWM families will not—the covert nepotism, patronage, unethical practices and discrimination by UWM Families based on gender (male and female victims), race, economic class and ethnic or religious affiliations" and by pursuing remedies such as discrimination suits for those "crippling abuses."

Moreover, the individual cases of discrimination and harassment that had come to light were embarrassing in the extreme. The best known—it even showed up as a segment on NBC's *Street Stories*—was the Ceil Pillsbury case. Pillsbury was an accounting professor in the UWM business school who filed a sex-discrimination suit against the university for denying her tenure in 1989 while granting it to three similarly qualified men. Last year she settled with UWM, winning tenure plus back pay and legal expenses. In the meantime, Pillsbury proved to be a stunningly marketable injured party. A Republican and born-again Christian who had never been, as they say, a troublemaker, she was fresh-faced, preppy-looking, and married to a wealthy businessman who did not begrudge her the mounting costs of battling the university. Worse still, she told tales of a sexism so crude and retrograde you wondered whether her colleagues had been cryogenically preserved since the Barney Rubble era. After deep-sixing Pillsbury's tenure bid, for example, the business school's tenured professors, all twenty of them men, issued a memo defending their decision. In it, they saw fit to mention that Pillsbury had once attended an office Christmas party clad in "a sweater that had a small boot suspended from each breast." Their argument seemed to be that because Pillsbury wore sexy sweaters, she could not be a feminist, and because she was not a feminist, she could not accuse them of sex discrimination. The offending sweater, which Pillsbury brandished on *Street Stories* and in the pages of *The Chronicle of Higher Education*, turned out to be a bulky wool number featuring a fireplace bedecked with Christmas stockings, one of those special holiday purchases you see advertised in Spiegel-style catalogs. Even if Pillsbury's wearing of sexy sweaters were remotely related to the tenure decision, this was not a sexy sweater.

And if the business school excelled at what's-*she*-doing-in-our-clubhouse sexism, the art department distinguished itself with tacky sex scandals. Students complained that it had become a place so preoccupied with frantic coupling, it was not only hard to get work done but sometimes downright unsafe. In the fall of 1992, for example, the university initiated dismissal proceedings against one Gary Schlappal, an associate professor of ceramics upon whom, one imagines, the pottery-wheel scene in the movie *Ghost* had a big impact. Students claimed Schlappal (who did not contest the charges of professional misconduct and later resigned) said things like "Let's go back to your place and party" (to a female undergraduate) and "I had her in a motel room for a month with nothing but a bare bulb swinging over us, and she still doesn't get it" (to one undergrad about another). In addition, Schlappal allegedly had sex with a student in his office one night while other students were working nearby in the ceramics studio. They might not have noticed, except that the woman closeted with Schlappal had left her kiln unattended, causing it to become, as the university report on Schlappal puts it, "red hot": "This created an embarrassing and awkward situation for students J and K as they felt helpless to do anything as Gary Schlappal was in his darkened office with Student I at least until past 12:30 a.m."

Chancellor Schroeder thought one way to diffuse the embarrassing and awkward situation in which cases like this had landed the university would be to ask the sociologist Eleanor Miller, one of his critics on campus, to head the affirmative action office and see what she could do to clean it up. Miller had held the post for less than a year when the Gallop complaint came in. Though both feminists, Gallop and she were not allies—Miller had objected strenuously and publicly to a conference Gallop had proposed on teacher-student sex—and Miller says now, "There was no complaint I wanted to deal with less." Though she worked on the case initially, she recused herself a few months into the investigation, because "there were reasons I felt I wouldn't be seen as an unbiased judge in the case." (The finding was written by Barbara J. Meacham, a lawyer from outside the university who succeeded Miller.)

There were others on campus who wanted to see the case against Gallop pushed as far as it could go. They saw it as a chance to prove the integrity of sexual-harassment codes by applying them as stringently to a prominent feminist as they would to some unrepentant Lothario. "Jane Gallop is as bad as—no worse than—the men who do this kind of thing," says Christine Ruh, a former student and self-declared "Victim of UWM" who has devoted much of the past eight years trying to get the university to redress her grievance—a complaint against a professor with whom she had a consensual relationship and who later, she says, treated her badly in class. "[Gallop's] research is about the empowerment of a group of people who have been discriminated against for millions of years. But this case completely negates all that stuff she has said. It's a betrayal of her work."

Gallop's two accusers took advantage of sentiments like these when they began to organize against her on the UWM campus. Last spring, although the investigation was still in progress and was supposed to be confidential, they called a meeting of their fellow grad students to air their complaints against Gallop and to urge a boycott of a conference

she was organizing under the auspices of UWM's Center for Twentieth Century Studies. During the conference itself, they formed an ad
hoc group called Students Against Sexual Harassment and set up a
table immediately outside the hall, at which they sold cookies,
muffins, and Day-Glo bumper stickers that read "Distinguished Professors Do It Pedagogically." Students also passed out flyers exhorting
conference participants, "Do not allow yourselves to be co-opted into
Jane's deluded world."

When Gallop first proposed the conference, she had imagined that
it would focus on sexuality and learning and would serve as an occasion for speaking openly about and maybe even critiquing the new
generation of sexual-harassment and consensual-sex policies. But so
many feminists on campus protested the idea that Gallop expanded
the conference to embrace any sort of personal engagement in teaching—everything from the trials of black female professors whose students are mostly white to the graduate student's ambiguous position
as both student and teacher.

The conference, "Pedagogy: The Question of the Personal," attracted speakers from all over the country, from the anthropologist
Sharon Traweek, who studies the socialization of male and female scientists in graduate school and who is now at UCLA, to Joseph Litvak,
a gay studies scholar at Bowdoin. Some of them talked about transference or erotics or sexual identity and some didn't; most of them apparently felt unsullied by their participation in it. Yet some students
and professors at UWM continued to insist that the conference was at
worst mere window dressing for Gallop's antic libido; at best, an incitement to too-frank discussions of sexuality in the classroom, which
would discomfit or compromise women.

SASH's leafleting incensed many of the professors who spoke at
the conference. One of them, Litvak, says it created "an atmosphere
of intimidation, of ideological policing" and led him to formulate an
angry critique of the entire case. "I can't speak to [its] particularities,"
he says. "But I think that a lot of the aggression against Jane that
seemed to be about sex was really about professional resentment. The
leaflets played heavily on Jane's status as a distinguished professor, as

though that were in itself culpable. Her salary was mentioned also. It seemed like a lot of displaced status envy getting played out, like what was really behind it was the unhappiness of grad students, their feelings of powerlessness, of abjectness. That's something that people don't talk about very much in the academy, but it's as much a force as some of the other things we're starting to talk about, like sexuality. I guess you could call it the class issue, and it's the last taboo."

In the rhetoric of the protesters and the account of the conference in Milwaukee's alternative newspaper, the *Shepherd Express*, the difference between, say, criticizing sexual-harassment policy and sexually harassing, writing about sex and forcing it on your students, seemed to have been handily erased. The *Express* trotted out the titles of conference papers—"I Walk the Line: The Body of the Graduate Student TA in the University"; "Discipline, Spectacle, and Melancholia in and Around the Gay Studies Classroom"; and "On Waking Up One Morning and Discovering We Are Them: Power and Privilege on the Margins"—imaginatively detecting sexual messages in papers with little or no sexual content. The article was reprinted in UWM's conservative student newspaper and in *Heterodoxy*, the right-wing academic scandal sheet.

The irony of all this was that even in its original, more provocative incarnation, Gallop's conference was at least arguably a feminist enterprise. "What I wanted to do when I proposed this conference two years ago was to take this issue and open it up to the debate about sex in feminist theory," she says. "I thought, 'Great: now we can really talk about the ideas about sex, education, and women that are behind these policies.' And I was truly shocked to have a phalanx of feminists tell me we couldn't discuss this issue publicly; that to publicly show that there were feminists who were asking questions about sexual-harassment policy would weaken the policy, would hurt women students, would hurt the victims."

What Gallop had hoped to do at the conference, she elaborates, "is make these policies better, more feminist, and more likely to work. It is my belief that the reason universities have very tough policies on sexual harassment—and very bad records on enforcing them—is that the definition of sexual harassment is being expanded to include many things people don't really think are bad. If you include consensual sex in sexual-harassment policy, then you make it easier for a lot of my colleagues around the country, men in their fifties who are married to someone who was their student twenty or thirty years ago, which is not only respectable but maybe a little dull, just to wink and laugh off the whole idea of sexual harassment. When sexual harassment sounds just like sex, then what you get is a situation where everybody officially says it's bad but everybody does it, which is what you have in a society that thinks sex is bad. Societies that have very strong strictures against sex are not made up of people who don't have sex; they're made up of a kind of vast discrepancy between official discourse and practice—which is what I think we're getting with sexual-harassment policy."

BEFORE I LEAVE MILWAUKEE, I talk with a group of three women: Christine Ruh; Margo Anderson, the brisk, forthright chair of the UWM history department; and Leslie Fedorchuk, a soft-spoken former art professor at UWM. As we sit around the worn picnic table in Anderson's backyard, they explain why they support the university's policy against consensual amorous relationships between teachers and students, despite the difficulty of enforcing it. "It's hard," Anderson admits, "to imagine my colleagues voluntarily fessing up to a relationship with someone under their supervision." Fedorchuk chimes in, inadvertently echoing Gallop: "There are a lot of faculty in the art department—men and women—who are married to former students. So this policy becomes really interesting to enforce if you have the bulkhead of the department who has not only done this but doesn't see much wrong with it or thinks this is just the way it's always been done."

One way to encourage professors to pay attention to the policy is to discourage them from seeing students outside the classroom at all. Ruh tells a story about an art-professor friend named Jill who drew the line in what she thought was an admirable way: "Jill had this new student in one of her classes who was handicapped and new in town and didn't have a lot of friends. She was trying to befriend Jill—you know, 'Can we just go out for a pizza and a beer after class?' And Jill sat her down and said, 'Excuse me, but no. The important thing here is that we maintain the professional relationship. Anything outside of that betrays the professional relationship, not only with you but with all other students, because I'm not going out for beer with any of them.' "

Since Anderson nods emphatically, I ask her if she ever worries that something worthwhile might be lost under a rule of conduct so geared to protecting both teacher and student from any unguarded moments. "I think," she says, "that the issue is whether you're favoring one student over another. And you have to ask yourself whether you're getting more out of this than the other person. Why am I doing this? Why would I want to go have beer with my students? Is it because it's part of their education, which is what I'm here for? Or is it because I'm lonely and want to have beer with somebody? And if so, are my students the appropriate people?

"We're working through a whole new series of relationships here. When you look at the broad spectrum, women haven't done very well under the old way of doing things in academe. I mean, I'm the only female full professor in the history department. I look around at the meetings and it's just me and all these guys. So I don't think the old way of socializing or fraternizing your way to the top works very well. I think women lose out."

It's easy to sympathize with Anderson, with her conviction that women would do better if only some of the clubby informality of academic decision making could be dispelled, the unwritten rules made more explicit for the benefit of newcomers to the game, like women and minorities. And it's certainly easy to understand her frustration with the scarcity of women in the professoriat, where the funnel effect—the more prestigious the school and the higher the rank, the fewer women you see—still prevails.

But the aspect of her solution that calls for purging teacher-student relationships of as much of the personal as possible in an effort to level the playing field for women strikes me as wrongheaded, a kind of dystopia of sterile professionalism. It makes me think about the intemperate professor who urged me to be an academic and makes me wonder whether someone has since clipped her wings to fit the times. She was the sort of person who allowed her passion for ideas and history to spill over the edges of class time into long drunken dinners with students, and because she did, she convinced us that what she called "the life of the mind" was a fuller thing than we had ever believed. Even as undergrads, we knew there was something silly and pompous about a phrase like that applied to us, but we loved her for it anyway, for the way she made a job—professor—sound like a wildly inspired vocation. And because she wore little black-leather skirts and played up her resemblance to Jeanne Moreau and had a lover and a baby whom she sometimes told us about, she made it seem possible to lead the life of the mind with no apologies for leading it in a woman's body.

Like Gallop, my teacher was a feminist who set herself against the movement's more censorious faction; she must be appalled to see how utterly it has succeeded in imposing its ascetic vision of sexual politics on university life. Remembering her, I remember something Gallop said to me. We were talking about the startling fact that while in the realm of feminist theory the dispute between MacKinnonite and self-declared bad-girl feminism remains lively and unresolved, in the realm of campus policy the MacKinnonite side has clearly won: it has convinced the world outside the academy that it represents a feminist consensus. "I haven't taught a feminist theory seminar in maybe five years in which I had one student who thought she was in the MacKinnonite camp," Gallop says. "So what I find amazing is that those classrooms in which the pro-sex side of feminism dominates and feeds into things like queer theory are ensconced within an institution in which the other side has already defined the rules. It's not so much that one side won the debate as that the other side went to another discursive space, went to the space of law and policy, and got the upper hand. Whereas the people on my side were still busy teaching classes, writing articles, and arguing with each other."

There is no question that with Beckelman, Gallop made big mistakes. She underestimated the impact that her roster of publications and her grand title had on her students. She gave in to an exhibitionist streak and perhaps to a fleeting attraction when she kissed Beckelman. Again and again she ignored signs that Beckelman's feelings about her were volatile and ambivalent and only made more so by their friendship.

Yet there is also little doubt that Gallop is one of those exhilarating teachers who make a difference in their students' lives and that her kind of teaching is at risk. When university policy makers try to eliminate the possibility of injured feelings or misunderstandings or erotic currents between teachers and students, they run the risk of sanitizing all the life out of pedagogy. Nobody likes to talk about it much these days, but professors who spend a great deal of time and energy on particular students generally do so not out of selfless devotion (academics are not a notably selfless lot) but out of fondness or identification or the sense that these students will reflect well on them in the wider world—what Freudians might call a libidinal engagement. And these feelings are stirred not only by what happens between teachers and students in class but also by what happens in unexpected moments outside it. As Gallop writes in her appeal, "Have we decided that students and teachers should not go out to eat together, should not become friends, that it is inappropriate if a student comes to care what a teacher thinks of her? It would be unconscionable to make such a radical change in the nature of education without engaging in extended community discussion."

There is something lost when we get too punctilious about defining teaching as a business relationship. And what's lost isn't trivial: it's the glimpses of the professor as a whole person that many students thrive on; the sense that learning isn't confined to the fifty-minute lecture; the passions of teachers like Jane Gallop.

—January 1994

THANKS FOR NOTHING
How to Lose Friends and Sabotage Your Thesis
EMILY NUSSBAUM

ON A BRIGHT MORNING LAST JUNE, Chris Brown stepped into the cool of the UC–Santa Barbara library clutching his master's thesis: seventy-three pages on the growth of abalone shells. His thesis committee had signed off on his work, and it was now bound for the silent grave of the archives. Brown would not continue into the doctoral program. It was the last day of his graduate career—or so it seemed.

There was only one problem: Brown had appended an unusual two-page statement to his thesis, a dramatic *j'accuse!* both profane and hilarious and aggressively specific in its grievances. "I would like to offer special Disacknowledgments to the following degenerates," Brown railed, "for being an ever-present hindrance during my graduate career." The dean and the staff of the Graduate Division, he wrote, were "fascists . . . the largest argument against higher education there has ever been." All dealings with the administration, he complained, "have ended in sheer frustration. I'd rather take a hot stick in the eye than deal with your bureaucratic nonsense."

The Davidson Library was a morass of "incomprehensible fines, unwillingness to help and general poor attitude"; Professor Fred Wudl was cited for "arrogance and proclivity at being an ass"; former California governor Pete Wilson was lambasted as "a supreme government jerk who has personally overseen the demise of the university." The

University of California regents panel was cursed for "continued suppression of graduate students, your most loyal employees. . . . May your continually biased and corrupt practices be fraught with continued controversies brought upon by the students who you offer a fatuous disservice."

As a final flourish, Brown denounced science itself "for being a hollow specter of what you should be": "Your vapid conceits have rendered those in your pursuit lifeless, unfeeling zombies. If I can forever escape you, the better I will be."

Famous last words. Not only has Brown failed to escape the gravitational tug of UCSB's material-science department; he remains in the orbit of the very administration he despises. Soon after Brown deposited his thesis, a library assistant spotted the two pages of disacknowledgments and sent them to the dean, who called Brown's thesis committee to check that everything was aboveboard. It wasn't. The committee members were incensed that Brown had added his angry words to the thesis after they had signed off on it; only if he removed the pages would they approve the work so he could receive his degree. Brown refused—eventually allying with the Foundation for Individual Rights in Education and mounting an elaborate Web site, www.disacknowledged.org.

Legal threats have blossomed on both sides. The high-profile civil-liberties lawyer Harvey Silverglate, a director of FIRE and the co-author of *The Shadow University: The Betrayal of Liberty on America's Campuses*, argued in a letter to the university that it had a constitutional duty to grant Brown his degree: "These are sacred obligations that transcend your dislike of Mr. Brown's political opinions and criticisms." Thor Halvorssen, executive director of FIRE, terms Brown's situation "a slam-dunk First Amendment case."

Is Brown tilting at windmills, fighting the good fight—or engaging in some bizarre amalgam of both? "There are two different issues here," argues Brown. "There's what I wrote, my complaints. And then there's the whole concept of academic freedom." His initial impulse, he concedes, was a desire for catharsis—"I'm certain it was written with a great deal of frustration," he notes with an odd detachment.

But in Brown's eyes, the administration's response converted his prank into a crusade for freedom of expression. "They were like, 'Let's silence him! Let's discipline him!' " he says. " 'Write a letter of apology and remove these pages, or you don't get the degree!' That has *nothing* to do with my science."

"I've told Chris many times that I really want him to get his degree," responds Charles Li, the dean of UCSB's Graduate Division. "But this is not a free-speech issue." Brown, he argues, can print anything he likes in the newspaper or on his Web site, but he cannot force the university to "collaborate" with him. A master's thesis, Li maintains, is a form of publication—and publishing Brown's accusations could potentially expose the university to claims of libel. Moreover, he argues, a thesis committee has the absolute right to approve a student's work from cover to cover, up to and including the acknowledgments page.

Nonsense, says Brown. However dramatic their rhetoric, the disacknowledgments are merely his opinions. What's more, he points out, students regularly put personal notes into such documents—without administrative repercussions. He cites one thesis in the UCSB archives in which the author singled out "the inept facilities management monkey who raised the cooling water pressure" and "the dumb ass who left his cooling water *on* for a laser that was *off* for 2 years and subsequently flooded my lab, desk, and my most important files"; the author went on to suggest that their "lifeless, bloated, limb-less bodies" should wash to shore and "be picked clean by seabirds and maggots."

Brown believes the administration is refusing to grant his degree in a fit of pique. But why bother pressing the matter? Why not just remove the pages and move on? "There's a serious issue here!" Brown insists. "I can't just walk away." A former Austin, Texas, scenester (he worked with *Slacker* director Richard Linklater and befriended *Beavis and Butt-head* creator Mike Judge), Brown claims he went back to school to "bring my knowledge to the next level." Instead, he says, he found himself learning more from co-workers than from professors. The administration blocked him from dropping a biology class after the deadline, despite his professor's assurances that he could do so. And in classic graduate student fashion, he began to bubble over with rancorous disillusionment—working sixteen-hour days, never leaving the lab, hashing away at a seemingly endless project. The disacknowledgments may have started as a nasty joke, but in the wake of their exposure Brown appears to have attempted an act of alchemy: transforming bile into chicken soup for the constitutional soul.

He's not finding allies where he might have expected them, however. UCSB Academic Freedom Committee member Constance Penley—a film scholar who teaches a popular course in pornography—says that in her view Brown's case "trivializes" the cause of academic freedom. "I think it's very unfair to try to deceive people into endorsing your speech," she notes, adding that Brown "lost all credibility" by trying to sneak the disacknowledgments into the library behind his committee's back.

Are there any professors who take a more favorable view of Brown's maneuver? Well, there's at least one—Fred Wudl, the very man vilified in the disacknowledgments as an "ass." Brown never studied with Wudl, but his ex-girlfriend and several friends did. According to Brown, the professor regularly reduced students to tears. When reached by *Lingua Franca*, Wudl claimed to be unfamiliar with the controversy. But on hearing Brown's characterization, he was nonplussed. "I've survived other evaluations of my character," he noted dryly, adding that "occasionally graduate students do cry." As for Brown's academic status? "I'd give him the damn master's, get him out of there!" he exclaimed. "It's his document, it's his creation, he can use it for anything. So what?" Wudl wouldn't be surprised, he added, if other students had quoted from the Kama Sutra. "The acknowledgments section," he pointed out, "is a very personal thing."

—May 2000

THE STAND
Expert Witnesses and Ancient Mysteries in a Colorado Courtroom

DANIEL MENDELSOHN

EVEN AFTER IT WAS ALL OVER—when, nearly three years after it had started, the United States Supreme Court finally handed down a decision—no one who'd been part of it from the very beginning, who knew about the perjury accusations and the legal threats, about the real meaning of the Greek word *tolmêma*, about Plato's *Laws*, paragraph 17, and the question of anal penetration—nobody could say for sure whether any of it had, in the end, made a difference. The lawyers and the journalists can't agree; nor can the protagonists themselves, the three scholars who served so controversially as expert witnesses. At Oxford, John Finnis, professor of law and legal philosophy, prefers not to discuss the matter; at Princeton, associate professor of politics Robert George has become disillusioned about the role of public intellectuals because of it; while at the University of Chicago, Martha Nussbaum, the charismatic and controversial classicist who is now a professor of law and ethics, continues to be voluble and impassioned about her own role in the public arena, despite what her two critics have said about her.

"It" is what happened after Finnis and George made what one shocked lawyer called an "extraordinarily serious accusation": that Nussbaum had, essentially, perjured herself while serving, along with Finnis and George, as an expert witness in *Romer* v. *Evans*, the 1993 case more commonly known as the Colorado Amendment 2 case, or sometimes just as the Colorado gay-rights case. (The case ultimately went to the Supreme Court, where Colorado's anti-gay Amendment 2 was ruled unconstitutional this past May.) Nussbaum, an authority on Aristotle and ancient moral philosophy, was testifying on behalf of the plaintiffs—that is, the "pro-gay" side trying to overturn Amendment 2; Finnis and George, both eminent conservative legal philosophers, gave evidence meant to justify the state of Colorado's attempt to ban legal protections for homosexuals. Strictly speaking, "perjury" itself was not among the tens of thousands of words that would be printed about the controversy; but it may as well have been. Nussbaum's testimony, George later wrote, "amounted to a series of misrepresentations, distortions, and deceptions" involving material that lay within her area of expertise.

Even without Finnis's and George's accusations, *Romer* v. *Evans* would have been an unusual trial. Because some of the legal strategies pursued by both sides depended on testimony offered by classical scholars, natural-law theorists, and specialists in ancient philosophy, the case became a lightning rod for discussion about the relevance of the humanities to "real" life—and, by implication, about the motives and methods of public intellectuals. Not all of this discussion was especially respectful of the life of the mind. There were those—among them writers at *The New Republic* and *The New Yorker*—who found something comic in the sight of academic superstars earnestly debating Plato's views on anal intercourse in a Denver courtroom a good twenty-three hundred years after Plato himself presumably rejoined the realm of pure Ideas.

But the nature of Finnis's and George's allegations against Nussbaum did raise a serious question, one closer perhaps to the concerns of tragedy than those of comedy: Must scholars sacrifice their intellectual standards when they enter the public arena? Finnis's 1994 article about the case in *Academic Questions*, a journal published by the anti-P.C. National Association of Scholars, is titled " 'Shameless Acts' in Colorado: Abuse of Scholarship in Constitutional Cases." It begins with a description of how, according to him, flawed expert-witness testimony affected the outcome of *Roe* v. *Wade*; it ends, after a lengthy discussion of Nussbaum's role in *Romer* v. *Evans*, with an almost evangelical denunciation of "the evil implications of scholarly willingness to lie or to speak with reckless disregard for the norms governing the inquiry and discourse of truthful scholars." If that jeremiad continues to resonate, it's because it presents the Colorado case as yet another engagement in the Culture Wars, yet another cautionary tale of the contemporary academy run amok. In an article in *The Times Literary Supplement*, the Wellesley classicist Mary Lefkowitz cited Nussbaum's testimony as a telling instance of how "culturally correct arguments" are used to promote "higher ethical values at the expense of some historical and linguistic precision." But others, including Nussbaum's supporters, are not so sure. For these cultural warriors, what happened in Denver is less a matter of a latter-day *trahison des clercs* than an example of the moral ambiguities that attend an effort to fight even a good fight on unfamiliar terrain.

THE ANCIENT POETS who sang of the Trojan War took pains to identify the *arkhê kakôn*, "the origin of all the evils," that befell the Greeks and Trojans. In the case of Finnis versus Nussbaum, the *arkhê kakôn* was considerably less lovely to look at than Helen of Troy. It took the form of a referendum, passed in 1992 by 53 percent of the voters in Colorado, that created an amendment to the state constitution making it illegal for any state agency to designate homosexual, lesbian, or bisexual "orientation, conduct, practices, or relationships" as the basis for protected legal status. Almost immediately after the measure passed, a group of plaintiffs that included everyone from Martina Navratilova to the cities of Boulder and Aspen (whose gay-rights ordinances would have been nullified by Amendment 2) sought an injunction against it. The injunction was promptly granted by district court judge H. Jeffrey Bayless and was later upheld by the Colorado Supreme Court, which sent the case back to Bayless for a full trial—the trial in which Nussbaum and Finnis and George were to play their controversial roles.

You might wonder how three authorities on the remote past found their way into a 1990s courtroom. Yet the legal rationale for having these very different thinkers participate in the Colorado case, though complex, was not as baseless as some would claim. In a pretrial brief, the Colorado plaintiffs (the "pro-gay" side) claimed that because "the 'moral judgment' expressed by Amendment 2 is nothing more than irrational hostility toward lesbians, gay men, and bisexuals, Amendment 2 does not serve any legitimate purpose." It was to counter this claim, to demonstrate that there could be a legitimate, rational basis for the state's unfavorable singling out of homosexuals, that John Finnis was called as an expert witness by the state. A highly regarded moral philosopher who is also a devout Catholic, Finnis is the author of definitive works on natural-law theory and moral absolutes, as well as the leading practitioner's book on the constitutional laws of the British Commonwealth nations. This intellectual and political résumé made him ideal for the role in which Tim Tymkovich, the Colorado solicitor general who argued the state's case in 1993, had cast him. "It was a very controversial case, so I wanted people with significant academic credentials," Tymkovich says.

Finnis would argue that the state's position was a wholly secular one that traced its roots to long before the rise of Christianity and that, if anything, owed much to the founders of the Western tradition of rational thought. In a lengthy affidavit submitted on behalf of the state, Finnis asserted that "all three of the greatest Greek philosophers, Socrates, Plato, and Aristotle, regarded homosexual *conduct* as intrinsically shameful, immoral and indeed depraved or depraving. That is to say, all three rejected the linchpin of modern 'gay' ideology and lifestyle."

It was these claims about the Greeks that Martha Nussbaum was brought in to rebut. She, too, was an obvious choice. Over the past decade, Nussbaum has become a controversial figure in the world of classics and classical philosophy, famous, as the classicist David Sedley has written, for "straddl[ing] boundaries conventionally drawn between philosophy and literature, and between scholarship and the social sciences." Nussbaum, who sees herself as a Socratic "gadfly," passionately believes in what the classical philosopher Phillip Mitsis calls "full-frontal philosophy"—in robustly using intellectual inquiry to improve the quality of life. She hasn't hesitated to practice what she preaches. She's spoken about Plato on the Discovery Channel; is an adviser to the World Institute for Development Economics Research (a UN-run project); and has contributed to, authored, and edited a spate of books on everything from the need for gay rights to the dangers of patriotism to the importance of novels to public life. Denver was hardly her first performance on a public stage.

In her preliminary Witness Summary statement, Nussbaum challenged Finnis's central thesis about the Greeks and homosexuality. Contra Finnis, she declared that "prior to the Christian tradition there is no evidence that natural-law theories regarded same-sex erotic attachments as immoral, 'unnatural,' or improper." Hence any natural-law theory that "condemns gay or lesbian sexual conduct and relationships as a violation of natural law or the natural human good . . . is inherently theological."

The closing bit about "inherently theological" positions was more than a rhetorical flourish. If the plaintiffs could use Nussbaum's rebuttal arguments to show that the underpinnings of Amendment 2 were in fact inherently theological, they might conceivably succeed in advancing one of the more far-fetched of their legal objections to it: that it was unconstitutional on the grounds that it constituted "establishment of religion."

The establishment-clause objection "wasn't that serious," Peter Cicchino admits, "but we had to argue all the different levels." Cicchino, thirty-six, is the director of the Lesbian and Gay Youth Project at New York City's Urban Justice Center and was a member of the American Civil Liberties Union team that helped argue the plaintiffs' case. A fluent and impassioned speaker who was trained as a Jesuit and who has taught classical Greek, Cicchino takes pains to emphasize the sequence of events. He reminds me that it wasn't the pro-gay plaintiffs who dragged in all this sentimental stuff about Platonic love and the golden days of Greek homosexuality. From the very beginning, in fact, the plaintiffs tried to have the state's arguments from moral philosophy dismissed as irrelevant. It was only after they failed that Nussbaum was brought in—as a *rebuttal* witness.

"You can do a journalistic first," Cicchino tells me. "Everyone from *The New Yorker* to *The New Republic* has made fun of this," he sputters—"this" being the use of scholars of ancient philosophy to further a court case late in the twentieth century. "It's been painted as a story of a country-yokel judge who was totally overwhelmed by high-powered litigators and Ivy League academics. But you can explain two things: one, why it was perfectly understandable that the plaintiffs called in Martha Nussbaum and engaged in this debate. And two, why there is very sound legal reason for doing so."

Interestingly, Cicchino's opposite number on the conservative side concurs. "This is not just an academic issue," Tymkovich says, echoing the conclusion of Finnis's *Academic Questions* article. "Our courts make *decisions* based on this material."

IT IS A SPECIAL IRONY of the Nussbaum controversy that so much of it boils down to a very academic issue indeed: the meaning of the term that Plato, in an influential text on morals, uses to characterize homosexual acts. Although it began as a fairly minor, almost incidental part of Nussbaum's argument, the *tolmêma* debate exploded into one of the trial's most controversial episodes. The debate revealed not only the wildly divergent readings of the ancient philosophers offered by the two sides in the case but also their competing worldviews.

It would have been hard to predict any of this when Nussbaum took the stand on the afternoon of Friday, October 15, 1993. She began by confirming that she was there "to express opinions in response to John Finnis and other witnesses [for] the state." (Finnis's testimony took the form of an affidavit that had been entered into testimony a week before; he himself never appeared as a witness in Denver.) Coaxed along during the direct-examination portion of her testimony by the plaintiffs' attorney Greg Eurich, a pro bono litigator from the prestigious Denver firm of Holland & Hart, Nussbaum testified that although Finnis represented his argument as being based "in reason and based in particular on what he calls the Platonic-Aristotelian tradition of moral philosophy," it was no such thing. Why? Because Finnis's understanding of Plato and Aristotle, she argued, was based on erroneous, outdated, and moralizing English translations of the original Greek texts of those philosophers' works.

On the face of it, few people were better qualified to judge such matters than Nussbaum: as the plaintiffs reminded the court, she has been retained by the trustees of the Harvard Loeb Classical Library, the most widely used of the bilingual editions of the Greek and Latin classics, to examine all the translations of Greek philosophy in that series and to recommend revision or even retranslation where necessary. (Finnis says he reads Latin well but needs a dictionary for Greek.) What Nussbaum said on the stand that day suggests why her testimony was potentially so devastating—not only to Finnis's argument but to his intellectual amour propre as well.

"Now," Eurich asked, "you've just summarized John Finnis's view and justification for Amendment 2 on moral grounds?"

> NUSSBAUM: Yes, I have.
>
> EURICH: Now, let's break that down a little bit. He talks, I gather, in part or bases his conclusion in part on the Greek classical tradition, is that correct?
>
> NUSSBAUM: Yes, that's right.
>
> EURICH: Would you comment on the extent to which his reading of that classical tradition is an accurate reading in that respect?
>
> NUSSBAUM: Yeah, I have to say that Finnis is no classicist. He's a distinguished philosopher and religious authority, but he has no training in classics, and he has access to the ancient texts only through translations. He's made a pretty cursory examination of even those, but I have to say that the texts he selects, the translations he uses of those texts are some of the worst that I did identify in the assessment that I made for the Loeb Classical Library.

Because of this kind of translation problem, she said, Finnis's conclusions about homosexuality in the Greek tradition were "simply false." What was more, she suggested, Finnis's positions ultimately had more to do with affairs of church than state: "Finnis's particular views . . .

deriv[e] from the Thomist tradition of Catholic moral philosophy. . . . Finnis conceals those specifically religious purposes and misrepresents his argument as a secular, rational argument."

Nussbaum then provided a single—and, as it turned out, ill-fated—example of how Finnis was "tripped up" by poor translation: a passage in a late (and notoriously difficult) Platonic dialogue called the *Laws*. In this passage, which had been cited by Finnis in his original affidavit, Plato talks about people who mate with members of their own sex and concludes (in the 1926 Loeb translation cited by Finnis) that "those guilty of such enormities were impelled by their slavery to pleasure." The word that R. G. Bury, the Loeb translator, renders here as "enormities" is *tolmêma*, a Greek word that has a variety of connotations ranging from an "act of bold daring" to an "act of outrageous effrontery," depending on the context. Arguing that Bury's word choice here was the result of "a great deal of shame and embarrassment about homosexuality in the British and American cultures," Nussbaum asserted that the phrase in question ought properly to be translated in a "morally neutral" fashion. She herself suggested that "those who first venture to do this" was a more appropriate rendering of the *tolmêma* passage than "those guilty of such enormities."

Although it must have seemed pretty recherché at the time, all this fuss about a single word did have larger implications. Nussbaum's own take on *tolmêma* allowed her to argue that "in Greek culture of the fifth and fourth centuries BC . . . homosexual acts between consenting males . . . are attested as received with great approval"; Finnis, of course, believes otherwise.

By challenging Finnis on *tolmêma*, Nussbaum had fired the first salvo in the Translation Wars; from the Translation Wars it was just a short way to the Dictionary Thing. Both, of course, led inexorably to paragraph 17.

"WHAT GOT NUSSBAUM INTO TROUBLE," says Robert George, "is this preposterous claim that moral objections to homosexual conduct in the West originate with Christianity." George, who studied with

Finnis at Oxford, is so boyish-looking that he seems somewhat out of place in a crammed office in Princeton University's Corwin Hall; you're somehow not surprised to learn that he goes by "Robbie." Three years after his Colorado testimony, he still discusses the case with considerable fervor. Some of this enthusiasm, you can't help thinking, is a former star pupil's delight at finding himself playing alongside his onetime teacher; but there's something else, too, in his manner—a righteous indignation that reminds you of the peroration of Finnis's *Academic Questions* article. (Finnis himself declined to be interviewed for this article. "I've said what I want to say about both the precise question at stake in the controversy with respect to Professor Nussbaum's statements, and also in relation to general questions about the abuse of scholarship," he says from his office in Oxford. "I've said it in print." George wasn't surprised: "He's a very meticulous and careful scholar. He wouldn't talk off the top of his head about scholarship. He's a real library guy.")

It was George, at any rate, who first questioned Nussbaum's testimony. As a defense witness, George testified after Nussbaum did—just a few days later, in fact, on October 20, 1993. Under direct examination by Tim Tymkovich, George baldly stated that Nussbaum's testimony was "almost all totally misleading or false." Although he was referring here to a number of claims made by Nussbaum—for example, George alleges that she, in responding to Finnis, had misrepresented Finnis as claiming that sex must be procreative in order to be moral—he zeroed in on her argument about *tolmêma*, which he describes as being "entirely unsuccessful" and, in his view, "inexplicable." George, who admits to having no Greek at all, continued: "I went ahead and gathered all the major translations that I could get my hands on, and I found that Finnis's view was supported unanimously."

It was as a result of Nussbaum's effort to counter this contention of George's that the Dictionary Thing began.

Since Nussbaum had already testified, she replied to George's allegations in a sworn affidavit dated October 21. Her own interpretation of *tolmêma*, she wrote, was borne out by "the authoritative dictionary relied on by all scholars in this area." She then proceeded to give the dictionary entry, which indeed lists no pejorative connotation of the word. But what "authoritative dictionary" did she have in mind? The answer to that question would soon land her in trouble.

Nussbaum's affidavit is organized as a series of numbered paragraphs. In paragraph 10, the name of the lexicon in question appears this way:

Liddell, Scott   *Lexicon of the Ancient Greek Language.*

The possible significance of the blank space—a blob of Liquid Paper on the original document—leaped out at Finnis and George. The authoritative dictionary that is relied on by all Greek scholars is, in fact, customarily listed as "Liddell, Scott & Jones, *A Greek-English Lexicon.*" Without the "& Jones," "Liddell, Scott" necessarily refers to an 1897 edition of this basic lexicographical reference tool—a long-superseded edition that in fact lists no pejorative meaning for the word *tolmêma.* The Jones edition, on the other hand, published in 1940, includes extensive revisions made under the direction of the scholar Henry Stuart Jones. Among the revisions, as both Finnis and George are quick to point out, is the inclusion of "shameless act" as a possible translation of *tolmêma.*

Had Nussbaum resorted to a bibliographic sleight of hand? Since Finnis first published his observations about Nussbaum's use of the superseded dictionary, the lengths to which Nussbaum has gone to justify herself have been considerable—and, in the eyes of some, embarrassing. "I like Martha, and I admire her a lot," one classicist, an expert in Hellenistic philosophy, told me. "But with this dictionary thing, she's really pooping all over herself." For instance, Nussbaum claimed in a letter to George that the edition she used was the one *without* the supplementation by Jones—a claim rendered somewhat dubious, as George tartly observed in a 1995 *Academic Questions* article, by the fact that the edition she regularly cites in her own published work is the later, 1940 Jones edition. Nussbaum went on to suggest, in the same letter, that the Jones revisions were at any rate immaterial with respect to the lexicon's treatment of the classical philosophers, since, she claimed, the 1897 edition was "more reliable on authors of the classical period," while the material added by Jones pertained to "late and Christian-era authors." Unfortunately for Nussbaum, her claims seem to be forcefully answered by the words of Henry Stuart Jones himself. "[T]he references to Plato and Aristotle," Jones writes of the treatment of those authors in the older, superseded edition, "needed careful revision and some amplification."

When I bring up these objections in a conversation with Nussbaum, she seems exasperated by the whole issue. (Although the matter is now three years old, George's attack on her in *Academic Questions* came out only last winter.) Nussbaum in conversation comes across as forceful, articulate, and not at all unsympathetic; you get the impression that she can't quite understand how a disagreement over the interpretation of ancient Greek texts could have metamorphosed, like something out of Ovid, into a lawyer-headed hydra. "A lexicon is a useful collection of passages, but the interpretations that are made in it have about the same status as any scholar's interpretation," she tells me, somewhat impatiently. "Of course the lexicon that I consulted, the older edition, gave *only* the meaning that I preferred. But in any case, never would I use a lexicon as a crucial determinant of meaning."

According to Nussbaum, what matters is providing the right translation, not using the right dictionary. But it's still not clear how this point jibes with her own implication that her claims about *tolmêma* should be accepted on the grounds that they are supported by an entry in "the most authoritative" lexicon used by classicists. Those sympathetic to Nussbaum—and there are many, starting with the legal team who argued successfully for the plaintiffs in *Romer* v. *Evans*—may wish that she had dispensed with the whole Dictionary Thing. Instead, she made a dramatic claim in paragraph 17 of her affidavit. In it she asserts in connection with *Laws* I 636 C, "[T]he word that I have translated 'venture' . . . cannot reasonably be claimed to convey a nuance of guilt"—that is, a pejorative nuance.

"Cannot reasonably be claimed" is what finally got to Finnis.

"[T]he issue is not whether the translation offered by Professor Nussbaum for [*tolmêma*] is correct," he wrote in his *Academic Questions* article. "The issue raised here . . . is exclusively whether the translation . . . by Bury in the Loeb edition *falsifies* or *substantially misrepresents* the sentence, the passage, or the thought of Plato"—in other words, whether someone could reasonably claim that *tolmêma* conveyed moral condemnation. It seems clear that someone could. Which is why Finnis ended up asserting that "the gist of paragraph 17, like that of paragraph 10"—the paragraph with the Liquid Paper—"is false, and thoroughly deceptive."

And, therefore, perjurious.

THERE WERE OTHER STATEMENTS that Nussbaum made during her testimony which George later claimed were false. Among them was Nussbaum's representation of the views of the eminent classicist Sir Kenneth Dover, author of an enormously influential study of classical Greek popular attitudes about sexuality titled *Greek Homosexuality*. Under cross-examination by the state, Nussbaum was asked whether Dover had concluded that Socrates, Plato, and Aristotle had "condemned homosexual conduct." Her answer was that Dover had not. George responded vigorously, even dramatically, to Nussbaum's testimony when he took the stand. Flourishing Dover's book, he read aloud the passage in which Dover describes the character of Socrates, as it was depicted by both Plato and his contemporary Xenophon. "There is no doubt that both of them condemn homosexual copulation," Dover had written. Closing the book, George charged that Nussbaum had "misrepresented the view of Dover on Socrates and the view of Socrates himself."

(After the trial, remarkably enough, Nussbaum persuaded Dover both to modify some of his views about the meaning of *tolmêma*, which he'd originally translated as "crimes" in *Greek Homosexuality*, and to further refine some of his views about Socrates and homosexual acts. In an appendix to a 1994 article about the case, written by Nussbaum for the *Virginia Law Review*, Dover goes on record as saying that although Socrates condemned homosexual copulation, it was not because he thought it was "wicked, shameful, and depraving.")

Nussbaum was incensed by the charges George made against her during his testimony. And after consulting with her attorneys, she requested in a letter that George officially retract his accusations before the record for the case was closed. George's charge that she had misrepresented Dover's views was, she wrote, "(*a*) false, (*b*) produced with reckless disregard for the truth . . . [and] (*c*) damaging to my reputation as a scholar." George—who, like Finnis, is an attorney—did not fail to understand the import of these three allegations. "Those are the actionable elements of libel," he notes. "It was an outrageous implied threat."

"I suppose that he interpreted that language to be a threat of a libel suit," Nussbaum says when reminded of her letter to George. "He can interpret it as he likes, since I don't have any actual intent of bringing an action for libel. I am a great believer in respectful dialogue." But given the seriousness of George's accusations against her, it's George's retort, rather than Nussbaum's, that keeps ringing in your head. "If Nussbaum really believed she was in the right," George says heatedly, "why *hasn't* she sued us?"

ONE REASON SHE HASN'T, if you ask Nussbaum, is that she's not a litigious person. When you see her, a striking woman of considerable personal charm and great presence, you're not surprised to learn that her first love was acting. (Peter Cicchino recalls how Nussbaum's good looks and stylish clothes "floored" the court when she entered. "They were fixated on her," he says, recalling the dismayed reaction of the state's attorneys, who presumably were expecting someone with a gray bun.) But this flair for the theatrical apparently doesn't include courtroom drama. "Until I went to Colorado, I'd never been in a courtroom, and I prefer not to be in a courtroom," Nussbaum tells me. "It was in consultation with the lawyers that I used that language [in her letter to George]. They thought that it was a good thing, because they were hoping that once [George] realized he was in error, he would—before the deadline—change some of his statements for the record."

Nine days after she sent that letter, Nussbaum wrote a second letter to George. It couldn't have been more different from the first. "Now that we are through with the trial and may resume our lives as scholars," it began, and it certainly sounded like Nussbaum was relieved to be back home. The Nussbaum that emerged in the second letter was quite different from the feisty and defensive Nussbaum of the affidavits and the courtroom, the Nussbaum of paragraphs 10 and 17. Here she was eager to persuade rather than dispute: the letter contained a lengthy explication of the Liddell-Scott affair and of her views about *tolmêma*. "All my cards are on the table," she wrote. "[L]et's go over the passages." In the spirit of "spirited scholarly debate" that she so highly praises, Nussbaum went on to invite George to speak before a working group in law and philosophy that she was to conduct the following spring at Chicago.

But George remained unimpressed—and, perhaps, unconvinced. "Yes, she invited me out to meet her fancy friends," he says. "But my feeling was that it *wasn't* just an honest disagreement over scholarly issues." After showing Nussbaum's second letter to a trusted friend, he became convinced by the friend's interpretation: that the second letter was "a blatant attempt to suborn" him—to charm him into softening his views. He declined her invitation.

George's refusal to accept Nussbaum's overture, his decision to linger over the question of her "honesty" rather than to engage her in open debate, isn't all that easy to reconcile with his and Finnis's commitment to "the discourse of truthful scholarship." Even if you tend to agree with George's and Finnis's interpretation of Nussbaum's statements during the trial, the stuff about blatantly suborning him may be a bit much. Your sense of Nussbaum, both in person and from what you can make of the Colorado affair, is precisely the opposite—that she's *not* all that calculating. This is, in fact, something she's rather proud of. "If they knew anything about me," she says of Finnis and George, "they'd know that even when I got divorced, I didn't have a lawyer of my own. I really don't think litigation is a very appropriate project." Nussbaum's actions in Colorado and afterward have, if anything, an oddly ad hoc feeling about them, as if she can't quite believe that Finnis and George are as intent on pursuing her as they are.

Something Nussbaum tells me suggests why—and helps to explain not just what happened in Colorado but *why* it happened as it did. Talking with her, you get the impression that she went to Colorado thinking she'd be participating in some kind of seminar, with all the expansiveness and room for exegesis you get in scholarly debate. The narrowness of the discursive space she found herself in seems to have surprised and frustrated her. "I'd never been an expert witness before, and I'd never been a part of a trial before, actually, and I felt it's not an ideal situation in which to engage in philosophical and scholarly arguments," she says. "You know, to me, it was mysterious how one could be examined by lawyers who were not themselves trained in these issues. So that's one problem."

That problem was all the more unfortunate because an extended, far-ranging inquiry of the sort Nussbaum was interested in could have illuminated the vast complexities of the very issue that the state wanted to represent as being relatively straightforward—that is, Plato's attitude about human sexuality. By keeping the argument narrowly focused on *copulation* (which Plato seems to have been less than thrilled with in general), the state successfully deflected discussion of what any reader of the *Symposium* and the *Phaedrus* knows: that the philosopher saw homoerotic *affect*, if not acts, as fertile ground from which philosophical inquiry can spring. At one point in her oral testimony, Nussbaum tried to open up a discussion on this point; but it was too late. The terms of the debate had been limited, fatally, to "what Plato thought" about sex acts.

As indeed they had to be. From a legal point of view, the question of homosexual desire isn't especially relevant. After all, there's no way to prohibit homosexual affect; you can only outlaw—and punish—acts. Perhaps the greatest irony of the Colorado case is that anything *unequivocally* positive that Nussbaum could have said about Plato's attitude toward homosexuality is essentially beyond the scope of the law; whereas the Platonic and Greek attitudes about homosexuality that could have an effect on the living law—that is, attitudes about sex *acts*—are negative pretty much down the line.

As attorneys, Cicchino and George seemed immediately to grasp this. "It probably wouldn't have gotten them all that they needed," George said, referring to a hypothetical, *Symposium*-based approach. Listening to him, you realize that the entire legal controversy was played out on Finnis's and George's terms: acts rather than affects, strict definitions rather than open-ended discussions. An unconscious frustration over this predicament colors Nussbaum's testimony, perhaps; at any rate, it's surely why the plaintiffs tried to have the moral philosophy stuff thrown out from the outset.

This sort of frustration is hardly unique to the Colorado Amendment 2 case. Indeed, it may occur whenever humanists, who are typically more comfortable speaking of interpretations than of proof, show up in the courtroom as expert witnesses. In 1979, the Equal Employment Opportunity Commission filed a sex-discrimination suit against the Sears, Roebuck company in which two feminist historians were asked to testify. (Sears's witness was there to argue that there were "fundamental differences" between men and women that could explain disparities in Sears's hiring record; the EEOC's, to prove that disparities between male and female hiring were a consequence of employer preferences rather than employee choices. The judge sided with Sears.) In an essay titled "The Sears Case" that appeared in her book *Gender and the Politics of History*, the historian Joan Wallach Scott tartly characterized what happened when humanists took the stand. "In a kind of parody of positivism," she wrote, "they were forced to swear to the truth or falsehood of these generalizations that had been developed for purposes other than legal contestations and they were forced to treat their interpretive premises as matters of fact." This appraisal suggests that there's a generic problem with certain kinds of expert-witness testimony; at any rate, it helps explain—even if it does not justify—Nussbaum's actions. And Scott's conclusion—that "only in a courtroom" could differing interpretations of highly complex material be taken "as proof of bad faith"—certainly goes a long way toward accounting for Finnis's and George's reactions.

Joan Scott's comments about expert-witness testimony echo another conversation I'd had in connection with the Colorado case—one that vividly restated Scott's point. In defending Nussbaum's behavior, Peter Cicchino talked about different "discourses" of the law and of scholarship. When it comes to expert witnesses, he suggested, it may be the discourse of persuasion rather than the discourse of absolute truth that ultimately matters. "Experts who are recruited to assist legal arguments argue with a different form of rhetoric," he remarked. "And this," he went on, referring to Nussbaum's testimony, "is a different species of rhetoric. It's not lying, and it's not throwing out the ordinary canons of scholarly investigation. You may not agree that it flies on the level of scholarship, but given what we accept as reasonable or respectable or at least as admissible into the discourse of the debate as scholarly positions, her testimony certainly crosses that threshold. It is not, as the law says, *prima facie* an absurdity. It certainly passes the laugh test."

Cicchino's attempt to defend Nussbaum ends up backfiring, of course, if what you're interested in is what Finnis and George say they are interested in—the "discourse of truthful scholars." Among many scholars who prize philological meticulousness, what Nussbaum did in Colorado hasn't passed the laugh test: "pooping all over yourself," after all, is the stuff of low comedy, not high tragic earnestness. That Nussbaum's eagerness to act with high moral seriousness should have led her to that most Aristophanic of all fates is an irony that only a Greek tragedian, perhaps, could appreciate; but the fact that Cicchino, an attorney, thought Nussbaum had passed the test confirms Scott's conclusion: that the gap that separates law and scholarship may well be as unbridgeable as the gap that distinguishes tragedy from comedy.

All this suggests that the question of whether Nussbaum misled the court may be the wrong question to ask. A more important question may be why—or even whether—any of this matters outside the court-room. It does matter, but in ways that could never have been apparent when Nussbaum and George flew to Denver in October 1993. The case is significant. It is significant precisely because it suggests that ex-pert testimony by humanities scholars is bound to be fraught with problems not because the humanities are silly or irrelevant to the is-sues at hand—the case demonstrated quite the opposite—but because of the unbridgeable gap to which Nussbaum, Cicchino, and Scott re-ferred in their different ways. It may be that the requirements of legal discourse, which, if anything, seeks to eliminate ambiguity wherever possible, may ultimately be incompatible with the practice of human-istic inquiry, which revels in the ambiguities of human experience.

WHAT EVERYONE WILL MAKE of all this is another matter. For now, at least, George professes himself disillusioned with the role of public intellectuals; Nussbaum certainly does not. Tim Tymkovich doesn't think that the scholarly testimony had any impact on the judge; Peter Cicchino is confident that testimony by humanists like Finnis and Nussbaum will bear importantly on future cases involving issues of public morality. The Supreme Court, at any event, seems not to have been overly influenced by classical scholarship when it struck down Amendment 2 in May. The list goes on.

The cacophony of divergent views about the ultimate significance of the case reminds you, perhaps, of Cicchino's jarring reference to laughter, to the piquant comedy that characterizes unbridgeable gaps. As it happens, all these things have a special Platonic resonance. The *Symposium*—a dialogue that happens to be about the differences be-tween spiritual and physical love, between affect and acts—also ends with the sound of contentious voices. Near the conclusion of the eponymous drinking party at which the debate about love takes place, only three protagonists are still awake and arguing: the newly crowned tragedian Agathon, the comedian Aristophanes, and Socrates. The narrator forgets most of what the gadfly-philosopher was telling the other two as they, too, finally nod off; but on one point he's clear. "The upshot of it," he says, "was that Socrates was trying to compel them to agree that a single man could write both comedy *and* tragedy, and hence that in respect to his craft the tragic poet and the comic poet were one and the same." You don't doubt that it was an interesting argument. It's just too bad everybody missed it.

—September 1996

LETTERHEADS
Who Are the Real Public Intellectuals?
CHRISTOPHER SHEA

THE OP-ED PAGE of *The New York Times* is a familiar venue for the public intellectual. There, academic mandarins descend from their rarefied chambers to offer eight-hundred-word distillations of their views. It's less well recognized, however, that the *Times* has another arena for intellectuals with an appetite for the public eye—a forum that requires an even greater talent for pithiness. It's just a few inches, a turn of the head, to the left: the letters page.

Although Alan Wolfe and Kathleen Hall Jamieson may be better known to the Op-Ed editors, Felicia Ackerman, a professor of philosophy at Brown University, *owns* the *Times* letters page. Since 1991, the *Times* has published seventy-four of her epistles, including six so far this year. And were it not for the *Times*'s notorious stringency, readers would see far more of Ackerman: she estimates that for every letter that runs, she's written three or four others. That comes to at least a couple of hundred letters to the editor of America's newspaper of record—to say nothing of the missives she's published in the *Utne Reader*, *The American Prospect*, *The New Republic*, and *Lingua Franca*, among other places.

Critics of twentieth-century analytic philosophy portray the field as hermetic and self-regarding. But who better than an analytic philosopher to expose the contradictions and weaknesses embedded in the daily news? A typical Ackerman letter appeared in the April 29, 2001,

New York Times Magazine in response to an article called "How to Be Popular." The piece included an anecdote about a junior-high society queen who deigned to give comfort to a victim of bullies. Ackerman wrote: "Tory's act of taking the victim's hand and walking him 'to the nurse and then the guidance counselor' illustrates our tendency to see all problems as psychological ones. It is insulting to take the victim of bullies to a guidance counselor, as if he were the one who needed to change."

On March 18, Ackerman criticized a piece in the Travel section. The reporter had waxed nostalgic for Samoa, where she'd lived as a child, and rued the changes she had seen there on a recent visit. If the author "longed for 'simple childhood pleasures like McDonald's' " when she herself lived there, Ackerman demanded, "why does she begrudge Samoan children the pleasure they will get when McDonald's comes to Samoa? And why does she consider it a 'downside,' instead of a sign of wonderful progress, that 'the islanders seem to take a certain comfort level for granted'?"

Certain subjects almost always get Ackerman's blood boiling: corporate invasions of privacy, activists who want sitcom characters to be "role models" ("Eek! Eek!" she exclaims when a reporter uses that phrase while interviewing her), and—absolutely above all—anyone who thinks high-tech health care for the elderly is dehumanizing. A few years ago, when the *Times* writer Vicki Goldberg sang the praises of hospices, Ackerman retorted: "Being, as Ms. Goldberg put it, 'locked in the cold, metallic embrace' of a life-sustaining machine, like a ventilator, is just as compatible with being 'wrapped in the love of family' as is writing articles with the aid of a cold, metallic word processor."

Although an against-the-grain, anti-P.C. strain gives some of her letters a neoconservative flavor, Ackerman is a solid lefty. She simply prefers, she says, to comment on subjects that she thinks no one else will write letters about. As crunchy *Utne Reader* subscribers have discovered, however, there's one area where she doesn't hew to the left-wing party line: "I like the kind of liberalism that is about people, not California condors or whooping cranes," she observes.

As it happens, Ackerman's interest in extra-academic prose is long-standing. She also writes fiction. In fact, her 1988 short story "The Forecasting Game," published in *Commentary*, won her an O. Henry Prize. As for her strictly academic work, Ackerman is trained as a philosopher of language—formerly writing papers pointing out flaws in the ordinary-language wing of that subfield. She now writes about medical ethics, particularly end-of-life issues, and also about the fifteenth-century English writer Sir Thomas Malory, who is something of an obsession for her. (She has been known to end conversations and personal letters with a phrase from Malory's *Le Morte d'Arthur*: "Have ye no drede.")

As prolific as she is, Ackerman is not likely to challenge the epistolary record of Louis J. Herman, a retired United Nations translator who published 123 letters in the *Times* from the time he left his job in 1987 until his death in 1996. (He submitted 859.) In recent years, *Times* policy has limited readers to one item on the main letters page every two months.

Ackerman does, however, have one rival to the throne of top academic letter writer: Norman F. Cantor, the retired New York University historian of the Middle Ages. Cantor's output is less impressive by some measures—fewer letters in the *Times*, a more variable voice—but he is Ackerman's equal in range of subjects and far surpasses her in vitriol. When Lawrence Stone, the distinguished English historian, died in 1999, Cantor published a letter in *The Times Literary Supplement* calling Stone's book *The Crisis of the Aristocracy, 1558–1641* "second-rate R. H. Tawney Marxism" and charging that the historian's work generally was "verbose, disorganized, and often erroneous." When C. Vann Woodward died last year, Cantor did a similar, if slightly less withering, number on him in the *TLS*.

"I don't have any compulsion about this," protests Cantor, whose book *In the Wake of the Plague: The Black Death and the World It Made* hit best-seller lists this year. "I don't turn them out three times a week."

Explaining his motivations, he says: "There are a million copies of my medieval books in print, but I regard myself as a cultural critic as well as a historian. I'm particularly concerned with the training of historians, and who trains them, and how that impacts on the general culture."

Those who rallied to Stone's defense implied or said outright that Cantor was a crank. It's the inevitable charge leveled at a frequent letter writer. Ackerman says it's an unfair one: "Why is it more likely that a person who writes letters to the editor will be called a crank than someone who writes Op-Eds, or short stories, or essays—all of which I've also written?"

—September 2001

IN THE FRANKLIN FACTORY
Slow-Motion Scholarship in an Age of Academic Obsolescence
JACK HITT

ON THE SECOND FLOOR of Yale's Sterling Memorial Library, the visitor exits the elevator into a vacant hall and takes a short silent walk to a door stenciled ROOM 230. Overhead is a placard set in a plain wood frame that reads simply, THE BENJAMIN FRANKLIN COLLECTION. The lowercase *c* and *t* of the last word are connected in a tiny curl of old script—the first clue that what happens behind this door dates back to some earlier time. The six scholars inside are engaged in one of the longest ongoing projects in modern academe. They are editing and annotating, in chronological order, a thirty-thousand-document cache known as the Franklin Papers—a collection of everything we currently know that the Founding Father ever wrote or received. Now at work on volumes 34 and 35 of a projected forty-six-volume set, the editors and their predecessors—some long ago recommitted to dust—have been steadily at work since Yale set the project in motion in 1954.

When I first spoke with one of the editors, Ellen Cohn, I asked how long she had been working there. "Oh," she said, "it was around the time Franklin left for Paris." Cohn has a soft, cautious voice—one, I imagine, born of the painstaking work of moving through a great man's life almost in real time. I found myself cupping the telephone as if I were protecting a candle flame from the wind. "Yes, I see," I said, my usually garrulous roar retreating to a sympathetic whisper. "But, um, could you translate that into the Julian calendar?"

I could hear Cohn scratching something out on the other end of the line. Perhaps it's been a while since she thought this way. "Seventeen years," she said finally, "I've been here seventeen years. Nineteen seventy-nine."

Nested in the less frequented warrens of the academy, a number of such projects plod on at their largely uneventful labor: setting out for posterity the works of some of our culture's most prolific correspondents. Yale has the Franklin Papers. Scholars at Princeton have been assembling Thomas Jefferson's opus since 1944. There are James Madison and John Adams projects ongoing. The Alexander Hamilton Papers began in 1959 and closed up in 1979. When I called Dorothy Twohig—now working on the Washington Papers at the University of Virginia, late of the Hamilton project—to find out why the Gentleman of the Grange was given such short shrift, I thought I was onto something, maybe an academic bias or a historical insight. "No, no, it was just that Hamilton produced a lot less paper," she said. "The project was made easier to finish," she added, pausing with impeccable comic timing, "by Aaron Burr."

According to the Association for Documentary Editing, there are more than seventy such projects currently under way. Although the historical efforts might be the best known of a little-known field, there are also literary-papers projects out there—constituting the other camp of "the hits and the lits," as they're known. A few philosophers have received the full documentary treatment, most notably John Dewey at Southern Illinois University and William James at the University of Virginia. So far the only scientist whose lifetime work is being annotated is Albert Einstein at Boston University. In a time when the vanguard of academe has taken to aping our flighty pop culture, with lit professors strutting around the MLA in sharkskin suits and plundering the tabloids for book topics, these projects continue to attract the kind of scholar unafraid to devote half, sometimes all, of a career to a single long undertaking.

The world that develops in places like Room 230 has its own distinctive culture, typically with its own founding legend, language, and habits; and, for those willing to linger, the folders of yellowing documents will eventually spill their stories of ancient dramas and hidden ambitions and old scores. Since many if not most of these editors lack doctorates (four of the six at the Franklin Papers), the culture of achievement is not measured by the usual perks of tenure or the prestige of an endowed chair but rather by an Old World–style guild system of long, hard work. Knowledge is a rarefied privilege gained only after proper devotion to the documents. In Room 230, as I would come to learn, an ignored clerk seated in the corner can rise—apprentice, journeyman, master—to become a scholar of international standing. It only takes a lifetime.

MANY OF THESE PROJECTS date their origins to the early and middle decades of this century, when capturing the papers of a great person was "considered a feather in the cap of the university," said the Franklin editor Barbara Oberg. As incredible as it may seem today, when the competition for the James Boswell Papers ended in 1949, the news of Yale's victory was reported on the front page of *The New York Times*. A widely published photograph showed the papers being trundled into the Yale library under armed guard. For the Founding Fathers projects, most of which started up right after World War II, "it was part of the Cold War," Oberg said. "That sense that Americans should understand where they came from, and know their own history, and that a good way to do that is to collect and publish, in verified form, texts of the Founders."

As if the shifting fashions of academic hipness weren't enough of a threat to such flat-footed pursuits, the end of the Cold War can be felt even here, in perhaps its farthest-flung precinct. This year, the National Historical Publications and Records Commission, a federal agency that owes its grant-making privileges largely to the founding-era projects, demoted those endeavors to second-priority status. In November, the commission passed a new funding plan that elevates several other grant categories to top priority, including the block grants that are given to state agencies to fund local projects. In the past, these bequests have ranged from funds for Seminole history in

Florida to a $450 grant to pay an intern in South Carolina to process a collection at the Beth Shalom Synagogue. Another $5,000 went to establish an archives at a small seminary.

One might presume that the NHPRC was just falling in with the Washington zeitgeist of preferring state efficiency over federal ineptitude or, more cynically, that the NHPRC is pulling the oldest bureaucratic ploy in town: scattering its money over as many congressional districts as possible to survive the knife at appropriations time. The NHPRC's executive director, Gerald George, says that the new plan was a matter of "leveraging" the funds and getting a "multiplier" effect for money. But whatever the explanation, the result is plain: next year, the letters of George Washington and Thomas Jefferson must get in the back of the line, hat in hand, behind the memos of ex-governors and the collected receipts of beloved town clerks. According to Oberg, it's particularly painful to be troubled by funding doubts now. "We are so close to ending," she said. "We are shooting to finish by 2006, the three hundredth anniversary of Franklin's birth."

Oberg said this without a trace of irony in her voice because, in the unique time frame of these endeavors, she doesn't experience any. Dorothy Twohig was just as earnest when she told me how exciting it was to be able to have the end of the Washington Papers in sight. "We're projecting 2015 to 2017 as our completion date," she said. It is this sense of time that gives these places their particular character and attitude. Oberg told me that she was hired to serve as the fourth editor of the project, "in the middle of Franklin's mission to France" (which by then I could practically translate myself to be 1986). She had been the editor of the Albert Gallatin Papers at Baruch College in New York City when she was asked to devote, essentially, the rest of her career to Franklin. "I came in as editor when I was forty-three," she said, "with the expectation that I would be strong and young enough to finish it, which I think I am."

It takes a person of rare temperament for this kind of work, Twohig explained. "I interviewed a scholar recently who had written a paper on an obscure address," she said. "The work required a lot of labor among army materials and historical records. I knew right away he would be perfect. It's really historical detection. You either love it or hate it. But you have to be careful with hiring. I have seen perfectly good scholars go quietly berserk."

A good deal of the patience required is for sifting through a lifetime worth of paper and deciding precisely what gets included and what does not. When I jokingly mentioned including a laundry list, I was caught up short. "Well, yes, we included an absolutely fascinating tailor's bill in the last volume," Oberg said. "It revealed that, contrary to his simple, Puritan image, Franklin bought a very luxurious, elaborate suit to wear when he presented his credentials at the court of Versailles. Bills are quite revealing. But we wouldn't include every receipt from a grocer." She paused. "We'd summarize those in a headnote on accounts."

Those who sign on no longer view the volumes that slowly emerge as mere books but rather see in them the kind of enduring work that Aquinas imagined for *Summa theologiae* or Ptolemy for his *Almagest*. And they are probably right. The Franklin Papers publishes about one thousand copies of each volume, priced at eighty dollars a book. Most of them are sold to libraries. A few are sold to collectors or manuscript dealers. The bulk of scholars in the future studying the Founding Fathers or their era will invariably turn to these editions. The original documents are often too frail to withstand the constant contact typically required by contemporary scholarship.

Of course, it could be a good half millennium before a massive theoretical shift drives scholars to revisit all six thousand pages of James Boswell's manuscripts or the complete diaries and correspondence of George Washington.

"My personal feeling is that these papers constitute a general contribution to knowledge," says the Boswell Papers' managing editor, Gordon Turnbull, taking an expansive view of his labors. "As long as literary and historical study continues, these volumes will have a value and a place, and that is not true of most of the books that many, many, many worthy people have written for the purpose of getting tenure. I don't want to diminish one at the expense of the other, but the critical, theoretical book is not really a book in the sense that these editions are books. Most academic books are self-consciously polemical, openly acknowledging that they are contributing to a continuing debate. They may well be eclipsed by a computer bulletin board or a home page.

"The 1950s, 1960s, and 1970s saw a spectacular rise to professorial glamour and a premium placed on the theoretical, interpretive book. This was associated not only with deconstruction but with the more sociological movements that made their way into criticism for very good reasons—feminism, political leftism, et cetera. They were long overdue. But the critical waves have broken and crashed. They have been engaged in a very spectacular tussle and collision with each other. And I have enjoyed the whole thing. But in the meantime, these scholarly editions march on."

Turnbull's tough standards for durability can be applied just as rigorously to the scholarly editions themselves. Consider the edition of George Washington's papers that was completed several decades ago.

"The John C. Fitzpatrick edition in the late 1930s and 1940s produced thirty-seven volumes and a two-volume index," Twohig said. "But it was one side of the correspondence and without annotation. It's a decent job." She paused, not wanting to damn with faint praise, but on reflection could only add, "Quite decent."

None of the scholars I talked with conceived of their work as narrow or dull. The great person under consideration was seen as a broad matrix for a much bigger view of history. Because of Boswell's extensive correspondence with the overseer of his Scottish estate, Auchinleck, Turnbull said, he "is really a window on Scottish agrarian culture at the eve of the Industrial Revolution." Likewise, said Ellen Cohn, because Franklin helped instigate the American bid for independence, revolutionized journalism, overwhelmed science, and rather notoriously dallied with the society of Paris during his mission there, he is really "a window on the eighteenth century."

Plus, reading someone else's old mail, when you know the outcome, does provide a voyeuristic sense of drama. "We had Benedict Arnold's treachery in volume 33," Oberg said, "but Franklin does not learn about it until volume 34, so you have this dreaded sense of how it's going to feel when he opens this letter."

BECAUSE FEW OF THE SCHOLARS working on these projects were employed when the university first obtained the precious cargo, the facts surrounding that moment take on the elements of a founding myth. The central characteristic of the plot always seems to be a delicious fluke that set fate in motion. For instance, the Franklin Papers were said to owe their origin to a chance remark made by a Yale graduate and engineer named William Smith Mason. He had casually dismissed Franklin for not being a serious theoretical scientist. When Mason was told that Franklin's jolly persona was actually a mask that hid the greatest mind of his century, he decided to find out the truth firsthand. His obsession resulted in thirteen thousand letters, busts, paintings, and written works that generally fall under the rubric "Franklin and his times." The collection came to Yale in 1936, and when the money began to appear after the war, the Franklin Papers were off.

The legend of the Boswell Papers, on the other hand, is so complex and comical it has been made into a book, *Pride and Negligence: The History of the Boswell Papers.*

The short version is that Boswell died with an extensive paper record packed away at Auchinleck. But the papers were ignored and then forgotten because of the misreading of a single letter in one word. Scholars kept reading a phrase as "burned at Auchinleck" until it was discovered centuries later that the phrase was actually "*buried* at Auchinleck," meaning stored there. By this time, Boswell's descendants, the Lords Talbot of Malahide, were in dire financial straits and happy to sell to a rich collector. Enter a flamboyant American, Lieutenant Colonel Ralph Isham, who bought the papers in the early 1920s, and then went bankrupt trying to purchase additional discoveries for his collection.

After a tangle of lawsuits was settled, the papers came into play among the universities on this side of the ocean. Though the great Boswell scholar at the time was a Yale professor named Chauncey Brewster Tinker, Harvard desperately wanted the papers for reasons that have since been revealed to be somewhat less than noble. In a letter dated March 30, 1929, the Harvard librarian George Winship wrote the papers' owner to explain why America's first university was so eager to take possession: "One special reason would make it particularly delightful if we could get these papers for Harvard. This is the fact that for many reasons Yale wants them very much indeed," Winship wrote. "The man on the Yale faculty whom we envy Yale more than anyone else is Chauncey Tinker; could we make Tinker come up to the Harvard library for the material which he can interpret better than anyone else now living, it would give some of us a very pleasant feeling."

Such tiny treasures, constant and forever, provide a unique satisfaction. Still, I wanted to know how devoting one's life not only to one subject but to one person affects the papers' employees. Did they come to think of their man any differently after living with him for ten, twenty, thirty years? What was it really like to get up every morning, without exception, and all day long regard the minutiae of Ben Franklin's life? In order to understand the culture of one of these enterprises a little better, I arranged to meet with some of the scholars at the Franklin Papers and to attend one of their weekly staff meetings.

EVERY TUESDAY at 11 a.m., the six Franklin editors gather around a small table at the end of the long shotgun space of Room 230. The length of one wall is lined with desks and bookcases, which look out of Gothic windows onto the quad below. The other walls are filled with caged bookshelves holding the crumbling texts of Frankliniana, the eighteenth-century works that Franklin's own library might well have comprised. In the center of the room is a simple shelf sprouting thousands of elephantine folders, each holding an individual document under consideration. On a nearby wall, twenty-nine pages of yellow lined paper, listing the names and dates of the 840 documents that will potentially become volume 34, are stapled to a board. Crammed throughout the room are busts, portraits, medallions, and other objects of the era.

Here and there, Franklin kitsch sits on the scholars' desks, while the high walls are filled with gold-framed engravings of Franklin, the ladies of Paris, the evangelist George Whitefield, and other Franklin contemporaries. The first matters under consideration one chilly morning were whether Franklin played the violin and whether he had read the Talmud. Both questions had arrived from regular folks in the mail, as questions often do. Since no one knew, the task of finding out the answers was shelved until some later occasion when someone would be given the research assignment. I'm certain the inquirers will get an answer sometime before the dawn of the new millennium.

There was great excitement that morning because Ellen Cohn had come upon a new version of what Franklin called a "bagatelle"—one of the light essays he wrote while living in Paris. This particular bagatelle, traditionally titled "The Handsome and the Deformed Leg," is a classic Franklin performance. It is a parable of sorts, drawing a distinction between two types of people—those who strive to see "the Conveniencies of Things, the pleasant Parts of Conversation, the well-dress'd & well-tasted Dishes," and those who "speak only of the contraries." Franklin writes of a man who could instantly distinguish between the two types of people because he had one leg "by some Accident crooked and deform'd." If a visitor stared long at the bad leg, the man knew to have nothing to do with him. So, concludes our pithiest philosopher, "I therefore advise these critical, querulous, discontented unhappy People, that if they wish to be loved & respected by others and happy in themselves, they should *leave off looking at the ugly Leg.*"

The thrill that morning stemmed from Cohn's discovery of a new version that has Franklin translating his own French title from "La Belle et la Mauvaise Jambe" to "The Ugly and the Handsome Leg" rather than "The Handsome and the Deformed Leg." Seated as if for a Moravian dance, her hands folded in her lap, a modest babushka restraining her hair, Cohn stated softly that she thinks the papers should run with it.

"Fabulous," Oberg pronounced, "we will publish a different title and a version no one else has." There is a murmur of merriment at this stroke of good fortune.

At one point in the meeting, a fairly recent newcomer to the enterprise, Karen Duval, was asked to report on her work. Speaking in a deep velvety voice of scholarly authority, she mentioned a particularly flirtatious series of bagatelles addressed by Franklin to a Madame Brillon. When Oberg asked her to explain to me who this lady was, she balked, and then blurted out a phrase so antique I suspected it must be Franklinian.

She said, "I daren't."

Knowing history's bawdy rendition of Franklin's life in Paris, I at first suspected her modesty had something to do with maintaining a protective decorum around the group's eponymous hero. I picked up on a number of quick glances and looks of hesitation that finally culminated in a bowing of the head toward the most senior member of the team, Claude-Anne Lopez, known affectionately as Claude.

"Her husband acted as go-between," Lopez pronounced in her Belgian accent, her blue eyes flashing wickedly around the table. "It was all very French."

What I had observed, I would discover, had nothing to do with Franklin. Duval's demurral was not a display of discomfort but a ritual of deference: Lopez has been employed in Room 230 almost from the beginning, more than forty years of intimacy with the central rack of giant folders. Over the years, she has published three highly regarded studies of Franklin (one devoted three chapters to Brillon). But when Dwight Eisenhower was struggling with his first term in office, Lopez took her first job here as nothing more than a Yale faculty member's wife desperate for some engaging work. Being a polyglot, she was hired to transcribe the collection's French documents from eighteenth-century calligraphy into typed pages that would eventually be read and annotated by real scholars for publication. For this job of copying clerk, she was paid sixty-five cents an hour.

OVER A LONG LUNCH of lemon chicken soup and carrot cake at the Yorkside restaurant in New Haven, I asked the project's master scholar to fill in the forty-year blank.

Lopez was a classics student who fled her native Belgium with her mother to escape Hitler. She came to America and eventually married an Italian man with a Spanish surname who went on to teach history at Yale. An admitted "Ph.D. dropout," she was hired by the project's first editor, Leonard Labaree, solely because of her fluency in French. For most of her career, she labored alone because her work concentrated on Franklin's mission to Paris, from 1776 to 1785, while the team was plowing through the documentary record of Franklin's life in chronological order, beginning in the 1720s. To add insult to isolation, Labaree refused to acknowledge his lowly clerk on the title page or even in the office.

"When there was a meeting," Lopez said, "I would be the only person not asked to join. I would be sitting right there, yet I was the only one not asked. It was very frustrating." This lasted a decade.

But by the mid-1960s, she had transcribed and become intimate with most of the documents central to an era that is arguably the most important, if not the most notorious, in Franklin's career. One night at a dinner party, an academic overhead her spinning an anecdote about Franklin. The next day he called Lopez, because the speaker scheduled to address a congregation of French professors had canceled. The faculty wife was asked to fill in.

"It turned out I am a good speaker," she said, "because I always stop after forty-five minutes." After a few years of giving talks, she gathered her ideas into a 1966 book about Franklin's Paris years called *Mon Cher Papa*. The book was praised widely in *The New York Review of Books* and elsewhere for its smart analysis of Franklin's relationships in Paris. By examining Franklin through the prism of his female friends, and by doing so in 1966 no less, Lopez had presciently produced a pioneering work of history—a kind of feminist approach that predated gender studies by decades. She published another book on Franklin and his family several years later, but still the boss of Room 230 could not find space on the papers' masthead for the woman who was now the most celebrated scholar on his team. Only his death would change the situation. In 1972, the new editor, William Willcox, was embarrassed by the omission and altered the title page at once. Still, the team was years behind Lopez's work.

"As of volume 15, my name appeared in the books, but Franklin doesn't get to Paris until eight more editions," she said. "It wasn't until volume 23 that, at last, I felt like part of the team." That was in 1983, twenty-seven years after she was first hired.

After Willcox's death, Lopez was made "acting editor" for volume 27, the only tome that bears her name at the top of the page. There had been talk of Lopez's taking over permanently.

"By then, I was in my sixties," Lopez recalled, "and I really wasn't very lucky. That was also the time my husband became very ill." She explained that another editor took a leave of absence. "It was a very difficult time. I soon found out my husband had cancer. There were numerous trips I had to make."

She momentarily quit sipping her soup and looked away. "Let's see, I took over in 1983, or was it '84? It's all such a blur now. I did publish my volume as editor, volume 27. It's a number I will never forget." She clinched her spoon; her voice remained steady, without emotion.

"The board kept me waiting all my life, and then they said I was too old," she said, allowing a moment of silence before returning to her soup. "But I don't want to sound bitter. I consider myself lucky to have had a career, considering I had no degree."

TODAY THE MASTHEAD of the Franklin Papers lists Claude-Anne Lopez as a consulting editor. But perhaps what is most interesting when one examines that page is that the staff, which four decades ago was dominated by men, is now, with one exception, all women. In many ways, Franklin has benefited from the personnel change. I, for one, grew up believing that Franklin was a rogue and a wencher, especially in his Paris days.

"I don't know if he had affairs with those women," Lopez said of Franklin's alleged dalliances. "Look, he was in his seventies. He had gout. It was only for the ladies that he wrote in French. These were the bagatelles. And the ladies would go over his grammar and correct it. See, I think it was just another way that Franklin plunged into French culture. To him it was all part of his political mission. He was comfortable around women, and they adored him as a father figure. They called him 'Papa.' That's where I got my title."

How fitting that men read these famously flirtatious letters and assumed (hoped?) that such sentiments were followed by Franklin's boffing all the lovelies of Paris. How astonishing to have the same letters read by a woman with a gimlet eye on Franklin the man and conclude that the flirtations were more likely consummated with a game of chess or a cup of tea. Now that we all have sobered up in this postfeminist age, who would like to wager which of these hermeneutical analyses is more likely accurate?

What is also revealed by spending some time with Lopez and her colleagues is just how differently they think of Franklin from the rest of us. Like Lopez discussing those letters, the editors I interviewed talked about Franklin in the way one might gossip about somebody alive and nearby. At one point, Lopez said that she "could never have fallen in love with Franklin because he was not emotional, except in his politics." Oberg mentioned how upset she was at an unnecessarily sharp letter Franklin had written to his distressed daughter that seemed to reveal a man incapable of empathizing with someone else's suffering.

They acknowledge Franklin's brilliance, but they cite specific moments and actions, without engaging in the typical sentimental inflation that often plagues discussions of great figures from history. Ellen Cohn said she admired Franklin for putting his appreciation of good science before his emotions, even during the Revolution. While at war with King George, she said, Franklin personally issued to all American ship captains and privateers a passport guaranteeing safe passage to

Captain Cook. Because Cook was on a mission of science, Franklin ordered that the explorer be allowed to return to England unmolested. (Franklin could not have known that Captain Cook by this time had been murdered.)

I never heard anything approaching Parson Weems–style adoration or the hagiographic impulses that often exude from biographers, eager to convince everyone that the guy *they* are studying is the most important person in the world. I asked several of the editors if they dreamed about Ben Franklin. And all of them said that he hadn't invaded their night life. He was not an icon; rather, he was a real presence for them during the day. They thought of him as someone they sort of knew.

"I talk to him every morning," Oberg confessed at one point, "when I come into my office. There's the wonderful 1782 Joseph Wright portrait of Franklin on the wall, and he's looking down at me. I try to explain to him what we're doing, what folders we'll be looking at that day. He probably thinks it's all a bit too much. Then he does this tiny tight smile, probably because he had such bad teeth, and then he tells me, 'Continue on, continue on.' "

AT THE MEETING, I was invited to question the group. So I asked the scholars what document would likely end the collection. Franklin's will? Each person at the table looked at me as if I had stabbed one of them in the head. "I forget that Franklin dies in the end," Oberg said quietly. Then everyone began tossing out ideas, particular letters they thought might be the very last.

Finally someone announced, hopefully at first, that there would be more work to do because they would have to issue an edition of errata. But the very admission that a half century of the most punctilious and exacting care going over every semicolon and ampersand would, nevertheless and always, require a list of errata plunged the group's mood into even more despair. I felt utterly, albeit politely, despised. Then Claude put her hands on the table, and the staff turned their lonely eyes to her.

"We shall call it an addendum," she said.

"Addendum." Each one of them said the word several times, as if trying on a new hat. "Addendum." "Addendum." Another murmur of merriment swept the room as chairs scraped back from the table and the scholars returned to their desks.

—February 1997

THE MAN WHO KNEW TOO MUCH

A Professor's Probing Teaching Methods Land His Career
in Jeopardy (and His School in Court)

RUTH SHALIT

THREE YEARS AGO on Christmas Day, Adam Weisberger, a young professor at Maine's Colby College, settled into an overstuffed armchair and began to make his way through a batch of student papers for Sociology 215. The course, a review of the classical works of social theory, was Weisberger's pride and joy. Students were encouraged to engage in "critical self-reflection"—to use the abstract theories of Hegel, Marx, Durkheim, and Weber to reflect on problems in their own families. As Weisberger saw it, the approach had been a great success. In a sixth-semester review of his performance at Colby, colleagues had singled out the class as especially powerful and illuminating: "Students found he did an excellent job of making the material relevant to their lives." But this time, as he worked his way through the student assignments, Weisberger became aware that the course was far from universally admired.

Instead of writing about their family troubles, three female students had penned angry indictments of Weisberger's teaching methods. Adam had pressed them too hard, they wrote, forcing them to disclose more than they wished. "How does it do me any good to recognize how external social forces are operating in my family's dilemma with my brother?" wondered one student. "This class is not the appropriate place for psychoanalysis." Wrote another: "Not every-

one is ready or able to get deep into some of their family stuff. . . .
How do you grade something like that? No one can assess the value of
my pain."

In theory, the student backlash was an unobjectionable, even desirable, development. At the professor's urging, no aspect of SO 215 was
exempt from scrutiny, least of all Weisberger himself. At the same
time, Weisberger was troubled by these papers; he detected a tone of
belligerence and personal hostility. "I really didn't mind students' getting angry with me or challenging me," he says. "But there was something qualitatively different about this. Just instinctively I thought:
'There might be an issue here,'" he says. "I had a vague premonition
that this did not bode well for me."

At the time, however, even Weisberger couldn't have predicted just
how ugly things would get—for him, for Colby, and for the growing
cadre of female students who would come to define his pedagogical
tactics as a violation of privacy and an abuse of power requiring action
at the highest levels of the administration. In the months following
the first stirrings of discontent, the charges would spread like a cancer,
as three, then seven, and finally seventeen female students came forward to register their objections to Weisberger's teaching style. The
gravity of the charges varied. Some branded his approach merely intrusive. Others went further, arguing that, because Weisberger's assignments made them feel upset and uncomfortable, his classroom
represented the kind of "hostile environment" that can constitute sexual harassment under the law. And one student, Jamie Geier, went
further still, alleging that Weisberger had used her private travails not
only as a source of prurient fascination but as an instrument of romantic pursuit. According to Geier, Weisberger not only pressured
her to write papers on the nonparental sexual abuse she had suffered
as a child but exploited her vulnerability by calling her up and asking
her out on dates. Such transgressions, Geier and her mother later
stressed to a Colby dean, were far from isolated incidents; they were
"just an extreme form of what [Weisberger] has been doing . . . to
other women [students] in the sociology department."

The charges of impropriety, all of which Weisberger has apoplectically denied, would have large and cascading effects, culminating in the denial of his 1996 bid for tenure and the end of his career as a sociology professor. The case would become a legal soap opera and an academic cautionary tale, a parable of gender politics, faculty intrigue, and a campus response lacking in the rudiments of due process. It would expose the perilous byways of a fashionable new teaching style that relies on a considerable degree of personal disclosure from students. And it would cast a harsh spotlight on the methods of a brash thirty-seven-year-old professor who is now suing Colby to get his job back.

FROM THE TIME WEISBERGER ARRIVED on campus in the fall of 1989, students say, he established himself as a vivid presence. His office was a haven for those stressed out about schoolwork, mad at their roommates, or just looking to shoot the breeze. When distressed coeds showed up with weepy tales of personal tribulation, he'd close the door, hand them a tissue, and try to lift their spirits. Weisberger befriended individual students, cheerfully inviting them to go running with him, baby-sit his two young daughters, or join him for lunch at a local coffeehouse.

Even as he broke down barriers outside the classroom, Weisberger pursued a strategy inside the classroom that was bolder still. For SO 215, there were no assigned paper topics. In the course's syllabus, Weisberger described his approach:

> What I am aiming for in the assignments is for you to reflect on the class readings and discussion by means of analyzing an important part of your lives—namely, your family. I am willing to entertain other ideas as written work, but you must make a persuasive case. You may be as personal or impersonal as you wish. . . . The outward form of the papers is less important than your using the ideas to investigate the relationships in your family.

Weisberger insists his approach was warranted precisely because the texts on his syllabus were so torturous. "Hegel's language is so highly compressed and abstract," he says. "But these books are there to serve human purposes. They help us to understand inequality in everyday social relationships. . . . And when you know how to tease out some of the implications, you see just how relevant they are." After the students submitted their assignments, Weisberger would meet with them to discuss their work and to suggest possible topics for subsequent papers. Though many of the students chose to write about sad or traumatic aspects of their personal life—depression, childhood sexual abuse, or rape—Weisberger, in these conferences, did not offer them the kind of sympathetic understanding one would naturally extend to victims of such misfortunes. Unlike many devotees of experiential teaching, he had no desire to "reinforce the validity" of their personal narratives. "I didn't want any of this boo-hoo, I'm-a-victim stuff," he says. "That's bullshit. I've heard it a million times."

And so, when students presented to him what he considered a shopworn account of their personal travails, he bombarded them with countervailing interpretations. "Why should I, as a teacher, simply accept formulaic kinds of self-insight, whether it comes from male or female, left or right?" he asks. The encounters occasionally took on a needling, discomforting quality. "There would sometimes be anger from students," he says, "because I didn't give them the obligatory empathic response. But again, why should I?"

Weisberger cites one student's paper about her father; it focused on "how he would sabotage himself in his desire to achieve status and success," he says. Although the student had intended her paper to be a candid examination of the impact of social class on her family life, Weisberger found her analysis somewhat oversimplified. "She wanted to criticize her father to the exclusion of her mother," he recalls. Weisberger urged the student to think of her family as a system rather than as isolated individuals acting autonomously. "I asked her, 'What role does your mother play in this miniature drama?'" he recalls. When he suggested writing a paper on the topic, she agreed but without enthusiasm. "Here was a student," he concluded, "who was ideologically inclined to find fault with maleness."

How could he be so sure that the young woman was interpreting her own experience in a false or inauthentic fashion? In his zeal to discourage students from fitting their lives into a preordained script, hadn't he imposed an equally formulaic script of his own? He shakes his head impatiently. "I wanted students to see that that which we believe to be most personal is where the categorical lives most deeply. I was striving against pat formulas. Maybe I didn't do it successfully. But I tried."

WHATEVER THE PITFALLS of this teaching method, it was initially well received by students and faculty at Colby. In 1992, the authors of his sixth-semester review reported that Weisberger was "doing an exceptional job teaching" and that "he would be a very strong candidate for tenure if he continues to perform in the manner he has to date."

But by 1994, when Weisberger's troubles started, several important things had changed. Weisberger had gotten divorced and moved on campus. "As a faculty resident," he says, "I felt my responsibility was to bridge the gap between the classroom experience and outside-the-class experience. And so I made a policy of eating with students from my dorm or students who were in my classes." Colby's handbook for faculty residents encourages this sort of interaction: the guidelines mandate "substantial contact with students who reside in your hall or Commons," "dining with the students in your Commons," and "providing opportunities for faculty-student contact within your residence hall."

Yet it's not hard to see how Weisberger's ubiquity in the residence halls, taken in combination with his bold, probing teaching method, contributed to a mounting sense of unease in a predominantly female department. All of a sudden the same instructor to whom students were confiding their darkest family secrets was also hanging out in their dorms, throwing birthday parties for them, sitting across from them at dinner. And he wasn't wearing a wedding ring.

INDEED, it was in this climate of moist overfamiliarity that the charges against Weisberger would take root and flourish. One evening

shortly after Thanksgiving in 1994, a student named Pam Herd but-
tonholed her classmate Adrienne Clay in the dining hall. "I introduced myself," she says, "and I said, 'I was just wondering what you
thought about SO 215, and about Adam in particular.' At the time, I
really felt like no one else in the course seemed to have a problem. I
thought: 'Is it just me?' " As Herd outlined her concerns—Weisberger
was pushing too hard and violating boundaries—Clay's mouth
dropped open. "She said that she couldn't believe it, that another student had approached her about that very thing just the day before."

Adrienne Clay was deeply affected by her conversations with Herd
and with another classmate, Amy Brown (a pseudonym for a student
who asked that her name not be revealed). Clay began thinking, she
says, about Hegel's master-slave dialectic—a topic of discussion in the
class. She asked herself "about what happens when one slave starts
talking to other slaves about what they've experienced collectively. All
of a sudden they stand back and see their situation whole. They see
that this is a shared role that they're in. And they say, 'Wait a minute.
This sucks.' " Within a few weeks, Clay, Herd, and Brown had each
independently decided to compose term papers that sharply challenged Weisberger's conduct as a teacher.

How did the students come to choose such a course of action?
Adrienne Clay says she liked Weisberger initially. "He was trying to
relate sociology to a personal level," she says. "I thought it was a great
idea. I would have lunch with him. Take walks with him. He really
likes that." Clay's problems began after she wrote a paper about her
father, a gynecologist, interpreting his strong protectiveness of her "as
resulting, in part, from some of the terrible things he saw happening
to some of his young female patients." Weisberger, intrigued, suggested she read a book called *Bonds of Love*, about Oedipal relationships between fathers and daughters. Clay was horrified. "I realized
that his picture of what I meant when I said that my father thinks of
me while seeing patients was literally one of a doctor examining a
woman in stirrups."

In hindsight, says Clay, she is "disgusted" by the papers she wrote
in Weisberger's course. "They were awful and wrong," she says. "I was

exploiting my family members for a grade. I didn't realize that until about two-thirds of the way through the course. All of a sudden it was like, 'Oh, yuck. What am I doing?' "

Weisberger loved to act the analyst, recalls Pam Herd. She says she expected her first conference with him to focus on the way she had tried to bring sociological theory into her paper. "This was a theory course," she says. "I thought he was going to say, 'Well, gee, Durkheim wouldn't necessarily have put it quite that way.' " Herd says that, far from representing the apotheosis of "high theory," as Weisberger now claims, the conferences devolved into painful discussions about problems in her family. "He was asking me all sorts of questions about my mother," she says. "I was responding . . . but with some discomfort. I'm a relatively open person, but this wasn't the right place."

Herd, who is now planning to attend graduate school in sociology, is a devoted reader of the playwright Ntozake Shange. "I've read a fair number of interviews with her," she says. "Anything that's inside you, she refers to as 'stuff.' The only way I can describe what happened with Adam is that I have this . . . stuff. And I'm careful with it." She sighs.

"Adam," she says, "wanted my stuff."

Unlike Herd and Clay, Amy Brown disliked the course, and Weisberger, from the very start. "Right away," she says, "there was an initial gut feeling that made me uncomfortable." After talking to friends, Brown came to the conclusion that Weisberger was probing into topics that were better left unplumbed. "A lot of women in the class were writing about powerful personal issues," she says. "I knew that some of the women were writing about things like child molestation and rape. . . . He wasn't equipped to deal with that." Worse, she had the sense that he was motivated less by intellectual curiosity than by a kind of voyeuristic titillation. "He wanted students to floodgate all this vulnerable stuff into his lap, so that he could feel good," she says. "It seemed important to him to develop dependent relationships with women. . . . I think it was a kind of power trip for him."

Weisberger denies the suggestion that he forced students to write about sordid or sensational subjects. "They're saying that I crammed these assignments down their throats over their protests? These students uttered not one word of protest the entire semester!" The students, for their part, respond that they couldn't protest, that the impact of the professor-student relationship was too powerful. "Adam thought that because he criticized social hierarchy, and how unfair it was, somehow it didn't apply to him," says Amy Brown. "And that's where he made his major goof. Authority relationships don't dissolve after six weeks of class."

AFTER HE READ THE FINAL PAPERS for SO 215, Weisberger called up the aggrieved students and asked to meet with them individually. "I thought we could resolve our differences," he says. But when the meetings seemed tense and unhelpful, he decided to bring the matter to the attention of Terry Arendell, the newly appointed chair of Colby's sociology department. Arendell would not comment for this story, but according to Weisberger she initially seemed cordial and sympathetic, offering to meet with the students in hopes of "defusing the situation." Weisberger consented. "I asked her to please report back to me about the meeting," he recalls. "I also asked her to notify me of any other meetings she might have" with students from his classes. A week later, Arendell told Weisberger that she had spoken with students in the class. "In her opinion, the problem had something to do with gender issues," he recalls.

Arendell then offered to look over Weisberger's teaching evaluations. When she called him at home that night to tell him she'd read them and they were "wonderful," Weisberger breathed a sigh of relief. "I thought the issue had been put to rest," he says. Just to make sure, he took the step of appending to his official personnel file a memo in which he acknowledged the student complaints and vowed to rethink his approach to the course. "I recognize the potential for this approach to go awry," he wrote. "In the future, I will adopt a more traditional approach and focus on the texts of Marx, Weber, Durkheim, and others."

In fact, Weisberger's relief was entirely unjustified. Unbeknownst to him, Arendell was continuing to meet with SO 215 students, receiving feedback about his teaching method. She had also begun escorting students to see Robert McArthur, dean of the faculty. At these meetings, students complained that Weisberger's approach to SO 215 was unethical and intrusive.

Listening to the complaints, the dean seemed "concerned," recalls Pam Herd. "He didn't like what he was hearing." But rather than asking the students to file an official complaint against Weisberger, McArthur adopted a wait-and-see attitude. "He told us that in about a year letters would be solicited for Adam's tenure review," says Herd. "And that if we were having a problem with someone, well, then this would really be the perfect opportunity to express our concern."

When a student who was sympathetic to Weisberger informed him that Arendell was taking students to meet with Dean McArthur, he was flabbergasted. Far from "defusing the situation," he says, his department chair seemed to be reinforcing the backlash against him. The junior professor called his own summit meeting with McArthur in which he denied any wrongdoing and railed against Arendell: "I said, please tell me you're not going to let her do this. Please give me some guarantee that you're not going to let her run amok and screw up my life." Weisberger recalls that the dean's response was noncommittal. As Weisberger remembers it, the dean said, "I have no position [on the complaints]. I'm merely a neutral conduit for information."

BEFORE LONG, the scandal began to sprout branches. In December 1995, almost eight months after Weisberger's frustrated approach to McArthur, the dean summoned the sociologist back to his office. There, Weisberger learned that a student named Jamie Geier had shown up in the dean's office the previous week, accompanied by her parents, to accuse Weisberger of sexual harassment. Geier's charges, McArthur stressed, were serious. She maintained that in the fall of 1994, when she had been a student in SO 215, Weisberger had pressured her to write papers about the (non-parental) sexual abuse she had suffered as a child. That he had repeatedly telephoned her, saying things like "You look lovely today. . . . I really like that skirt" and asking her to have "breakfast, lunch, dinner." That he had said, "I have feelings for you I don't know how to deal with." And that when she had finally confronted him, a year later, he had burst into tears, admitted that he had behaved improperly, and pleaded with her not to tell.

Weisberger adamantly denied to McArthur that he had made any suggestive remarks to Geier, that he had complimented her on her appearance or pursued her romantically. He also denied Geier's allegation "that I had forced these assignments down her throat, over her opposition, against her resistance." Geier, Weisberger insisted, had chosen her own topics. Furthermore, he said, it was Geier who had attempted to violate student-teacher boundaries. As Weisberger later put it in his appeal to his tenure committee:

> On or around November of 1994, we were walking across campus when she told me she had a dream about me. She said that in the dream I was her doctor and I was delivering her baby. "You were going in but it didn't hurt," she said. I was embarrassed and alarmed by her remark, and said, "I think this might be a little dangerous." To which she said, "Don't think so much."

As a member of the faculty, Weisberger was familiar with Colby's harassment policy, which stipulated that "each reported incident" of harassment would be "investigated carefully, promptly, and thoroughly." Weisberger asked that McArthur conduct a formal investigation into Geier's charges. Such an investigation, Weisberger insisted, would prove his innocence. To Weisberger's astonishment, McArthur declined. Geier, he explained, had asked that her charge be considered "informal" rather than "formal": according to her mother, she did not want her name to appear in a "public forum." As an informal charge, Geier's complaint fell outside the purview of Colby's policy. (Geier would not be interviewed for this story.)

But even if Geier did not wish to issue a formal complaint against Weisberger, she did want to see him punished. On February 5, 1996,

she sent McArthur a letter informing the dean that "it is my preference that Mr. Weisberger's employment at Colby be terminated immediately." She urged this course of action for several reasons.

First, she wanted to "send a message to students, staff and
faculty . . . that sexually or other harassing behavior will not be tolerated." Such an action, Geier wrote, was necessary to protect the
"other students who have documented their complaints against Mr.
Weisberger's harassing and inappropriate behavior"—a reference to
those students who had criticized Weisberger's teaching method in
meetings with Arendell. Geier added that if the college elected not to
fire Weisberger, she believed that at a minimum:

> (1) Mr. Weisberger should move off campus immediately; (2) Mr.
> Weisberger should be required to teach all of his classes on campus
> in regular classrooms; (3) Mr. Weisberger's contact with students
> should occur only during regular class and office hours; (4) Mr.
> Weisberger's presence in the sociology department should be limited
> to his three weekly scheduled classes and his posted office hours; and
> (5) a monitor . . . should sit in on each and every one of Mr. Weis-
> berger's classes.

When McArthur forwarded a copy of Geier's letter to Weisberger, demanding his immediate response, Weisberger became incensed.

In a series of angry replies, he told McArthur he considered Geier's
requests beyond the pale. "My job is within the sociology department," he wrote. "The ability to conduct scholarship in my office is at
the core of my job. . . . I am not a threat to anyone, and I refuse to assume the role of a subdued aggressor." Weisberger also made further
requests for a formal investigation. "I cannot overemphasize the deep
concern I have for the irreparable damage that these false allegations
are doing to my career and reputation," he wrote. "Why does the college not intervene to protect me from Ms. Geier's demands?"

Weisberger's consternation was understandable. In her tape-
recorded interview with Dean McArthur, Geier had claimed that
while a student in SO 215 she had felt "sick, tense, ill, scared, embar-

rassed" in Weisberger's presence. This claim came as a surprise to Weisberger, who remembered her liking the course. Indeed, by the time of his letter to McArthur, Weisberger had fished out of his file cabinet a copy of Geier's course evaluation. In the evaluation Geier had written:

> I wish I knew that the evaluations were going to be handed out today because I would have prepared something to say. Adam has made social theory interesting and has taught me to apply my major to what happens in everyday life. He is open-minded, well-prepared for class, gives thought-provoking lectures, and respects his students' opinions. I also appreciate the time he gives to his students in and out of class. This class is stimulating and his questions force me to analyze my views and interpretations of the readings. He is a wonderful professor and I hope every sociology major/minor has the good fortune to have him as a professor.

Though Weisberger forwarded a copy of the evaluation to McArthur, the dean did not acknowledge its receipt. Instead, he sent Geier an apologetic e-mail, a copy of which he forwarded to Weisberger. "Dear Jamie," he wrote. "Despite our attempt to find a mutually agreeable resolution, I am sorry to report that I have now been advised by Professor Weisberger that he is unwilling to move from his campus apartment until the end of this semester."

AS WORD OF GEIER'S HARASSMENT CHARGE spread across campus, the student revolt against Weisberger heated up. In February 1996, Weisberger learned from Dean McArthur that no fewer than seven students had now come to his office to complain about SO 215. And there was another, equally disturbing development: in the minds of some students and administrators, Geier's complaint and those of Herd, Brown, and Clay had merged into a single, powerful indictment. Weisberger "made female students uncomfortable," says Laura Schmishkiss, a friend of Adrienne Clay's who had taken the class in

1992. "Not physically uncomfortable, necessarily, but intellectually and emotionally uncomfortable. I would certainly call it an abuse of power, which is at root what sexual harassment is."

Several of Weisberger's detractors object to any conflation of their charges with Geier's. Although Adrienne Clay contends that there was an "undercurrent of sexual tension" behind the complaints, she says, "We weren't claiming sexual harassment at all." Amy Brown also says she "never used the term 'sexual harassment.' I thought what we were talking about was a more general abuse of power." Even so, Brown says she can understand why some of Weisberger's detractors apparently felt differently: "It would have been a lot simpler if we had had a special term for what happened in Adam's class. We all watched the Thomas-Hill hearings. It's like, if you can't use the phrase 'sexual harassment,' then your experience doesn't have validity."

In March 1996, at an open forum with the administration, a senior sociology major named Beth Wallace stood up and spoke for about five minutes about Jamie Geier's sexual-harassment charges against Weisberger, all but naming him directly. Wallace wondered aloud about the right of victims of sexual harassment to discuss their experience. "As far as freedom of speech," Wallace asked administrators, "How much can the victim talk about her experience without being hit with a slander suit?" "That's a very good question," President William Cotter replied. "Our policies don't really say." Though Colby's policies mandate that allegations of sexual harassment be kept confidential, rumors were spreading around campus, says Heather Sprague, a 1996 Colby graduate. She recalls being approached by a male classmate with a particularly distorted view of the facts. "He asked if I knew that Adam was being charged with thirty-nine counts of sexual harassment."

As the talk about him proliferated, Weisberger, once a popular figure, found himself a pariah. "Students would literally lower their heads and walk in the other direction when they saw me coming," he says. The day after the semester ended, he moved far off campus. As his ordeal unfolded, Weisberger says, "I kept defining for myself what form vindication would take." First, he says, it was having his name cleared by some sort of investigative tribunal. Then, when Colby refused to investigate, it was receiving tenure. "I felt that if I could get tenure, I would be vindicated symbolically," he says.

IN FACT, Colby administrators had already taken steps that would reduce the likelihood of such a favorable outcome. In August 1996, Weisberger's tenure file was presented for the first time to Cheryl Gilkes, a tenured sociology professor who had agreed to serve as chair of the tenure committee after Arendell had recused herself. Though Gilkes had already been informed by Arendell of the harassment charge against Weisberger, she was nonetheless surprised to find a detailed synopsis of the charge included in her colleague's tenure dossier. The package included Geier's letters to Dean McArthur, a cassette recording of what Geier referred to as her "testimony" to the dean, and a personal plea to members of Weisberger's tenure committee in which Geier outlined her harassment complaint and asked that the committee deny Weisberger tenure. Following Colby policy, it also included more than a hundred solicited letters from Weisberger's former students; several of these referred to Jamie Geier's charges.

Gilkes decided to remove Geier's material, and all references to it, from Weisberger's tenure dossier. She then informed the dean she had done so. "Put it back in," he said. Gilkes would not be interviewed for this story, but according to two sources at Colby she received a surprise visit later that day from an agitated Arendell. The Geier material, Arendell said, had to be put back in. Why? Gilkes asked. Because, Arendell replied, students had been told they would have the option of communicating their unhappiness with Weisberger to the tenure committee. Unsure of how to proceed, Gilkes consulted two friends who worked as provosts at other universities. Both confirmed her instinct that these proceedings were "highly irregular" and that Geier's uninvestigated harassment charge, and all letters associated with it, should be pulled out of Weisberger's tenure dossier and dealt with separately and confidentially. Gilkes, confused and upset, visited McArthur in his office. Who, she asked, told students they would have the option of airing their complaints by writing letters to Weisberger's tenure committee? I did, the dean replied. Realizing she had no choice in the matter, Gilkes called up Weisberger to relay the bad news.

Of the 116 letters received by Weisberger's tenure committee, a good three-fourths or so are unequivocally positive: "A gifted and brilliant professor with a passion for teaching"; "The finest teacher I ever had"; "Adam's insights became the foundation of my belief system, making me the person I am today." A few are neutral. Then there are the nearly 20 negative letters. Almost all came from female students who were likely to have been aware of the harassment charges against Weisberger; many addressed the myriad complaints against him directly: "Students are not taking his course to be objects of play or a means of voyeurism for his personal use"; "If he is granted tenure I am certain as I can be the behavior I have described will continue"; "A close friend of mine was sexually harassed by Professor Weisberger"; "I just want to state that what I have seen and heard about Mr. Weisberger is a clear example of sexual harassment."

As the tenure committee prepared to meet, McArthur sent summaries of the student letters to Weisberger, adding that the young professor was being offered an "unprecedented opportunity to have these summaries prior to your department tenure committee's deliberations." Attempting to rebut the students' charges, Weisberger did the best he could. "I categorically deny the allegation that I pressured students to reveal details about their personal lives, as well as the insinuations of voyeurism and lurid fascination," he wrote to members of the committee. "At no time during my years at Colby have I ever abused my position as a professor."

But it wasn't enough. In December 1996, Weisberger received a call from Dean McArthur informing him that his bid for tenure had been denied due to concerns about his teaching. Weisberger, believing that the school had violated basic norms of procedural fairness and academic freedom, appealed the decision. His efforts were unsuccessful. "There is no evidence that the college's Promotion and Tenure Committee based their decision to deny Adam Weisberger tenure on the style of his teaching, rather than on his effectiveness as a teacher," concluded Colby's appeals committee.

Weisberger was furious. The explosive nature of the allegations, he believed, had cast a shadow over the objective evaluation of his scholarship, dooming his tenure bid from the start. Even worse, the tenure process, he felt, had become a sexual-harassment investigation in disguise, "which means that, when they denied me tenure, ipso facto they found me liable for sexual harassment."

Weisberger's concerns about the damage to his reputation mounted as friends at other schools gently disabused him of his hopes to remain in the profession. The market was tight, they said, and word of the harassment charges had already spread through the informal job networks of academic sociology. After hearing this prognosis, Weisberger decided to give up his teaching career. In the fall of 1997, he enrolled as a first-year law student at Boston University, resigning himself to "three years of peanut butter and jelly and a mountain of debt."

BUT OVER THE COMING MONTHS, Weisberger's encounters with the law will be more than academic. On April 25, 1997, he filed a civil-rights complaint with the Maine Human Rights Commission, accusing Colby College of gender discrimination and—in an ironic twist—sexual harassment. The civil-rights charge is twofold. First, Weisberger alleges that the complaints about his teaching style would not have been allowed to grow and fester were it not for his male gender. "When female professors solicit personal experiences from students, they're not intrusive or invasive," Weisberger says. "They're caring and nurturing! When I, a young divorced male, do it, I'm this lecherous, slimy professor who's trying to pry open their legs." Second, Weisberger contends that in refusing to investigate and dispose of the students' charges, thus allowing a campaign of defamatory rumors to sprout and flourish unchecked, Colby created an "abusive working environment"—an environment that was "so pervasive and hostile" that it "altered the conditions of my employment," amounting to, yes, sexual harassment.

At the moment, it seems almost certain that Weisberger will be far from the only victim in this bitter and costly legal drama. Weisberger has supplemented his discrimination claim with a civil suit against Colby, seeking damages and equitable relief for "defamation, intentional infliction of emotional distress . . . invasion of privacy, reckless or negligent failure to investigate, and breach of contract." Already Weisberger's legal team is preparing discovery requests for students' course evaluations, academic transcripts, even psychological records. As the case goes forward—and if it proceeds to trial—the students will surely be in for a grueling ordeal. Their accounts of family dysfunction, breakdown, and betrayal—the seamy details of which they say they were loath to share with Weisberger—will move from the classroom to the courtroom, a cold-eyed realm of discovery, subpoena, and unfriendly cross-examination. A more hostile environment could scarcely be imagined.

Administrators at Colby College refused repeated requests to comment for this article. "In response to the general question, Did we violate our own policies and treat Adam Weisberger unfairly: To that general question, I would reply, absolutely not," was all Dean McArthur was willing to say. But the essence of Colby's position on the discrimination suit can be gleaned from the Weisberger team's written response to the school's response, a copy of which was provided by Jonathan Shapiro, Weisberger's lawyer. In its statement, Colby repeats the claim that Weisberger was denied tenure due to his inferior teaching abilities. But an examination of the committee members' summary statements—which Weisberger has acquired from Colby—suggests otherwise. Of the nine faculty members on Weisberger's tenure committee, six voted to reject tenure. The statements of all six focus on the complaints about Weisberger's methods—not on his effectiveness as a teacher. One professor noted that while "the vast majority of students evaluate Adam's teaching quite positively, in fact, they rave about him," he or she was unable to vote for tenure because "a smaller minority has suffered very adverse consequences as a result of his teaching methodology." Another chides Weisberger for "abusing the imbalance of power between students and teachers," adding: "It is remarkable that far more radical steps weren't taken . . . to expunge the problems [of] too much personal contact with students and a pedagogy that seems, despite Weisberger's denials, to have made the critique of the *political* very *personal* and painful to a significant number of female students."

Colby's reaction to Weisberger's claim that the school violated its own procedures is one of blanket denial. To Weisberger's charge that McArthur and Arendell solicited and encouraged female students to write negative letters to be included in his tenure dossier, the school's reply is that the charge is "unfounded." As for Weisberger's charge that Colby violated its own policy by failing to investigate Geier's charges "carefully, promptly, and thoroughly," the college simply reiterates that Geier's complaint was only "informal." There is no attempt to answer Weisberger's protest that the word "informal" appears nowhere in Colby's sexual-harassment policies.

It's curious, then, that Weisberger has chosen to battle Colby over "gender discrimination" rather than focus his legal ire on the apparent lack of due process and fair play the school showed when it allowed Jamie Geier's uninvestigated sexual-harassment charge to play a role in the tenure committee's decision making. On this last score, however, Colby's behavior may well be legally defensible under Equal Employment Opportunity Commission guidelines, which stipulate numerous legal protections for sexual-harassment complainants but none for accused harassers. If anything, the law's presumption against suspected harassers is taken only too literally by Colby, which appears to put a greater premium on pleasing students than on ensuring justice for a lumpenproletariat faculty. ("At bottom, it's the cash nexus driving all of this," says one Colby professor. "The model of the suburban mall has encroached on higher education.") In this context, Laura Schmishkiss's expansion of sexual harassment to include any situation in which a student is made to feel "intellectually and emotionally uncomfortable" may represent a whole new vision of liberal education. Says Weisberger, " 'Uncomfortable' is a word I came to despise at Colby. It's the tyranny of absolute subjectivity, a way to censure another person without having to give any content. And it absolutely seeps into the classroom. You can't even have intellectual debate because someone's feelings might get hurt."

To be sure, none of this is to exonerate Weisberger—to see him, as he appears to see himself, as a blameless victim of this shrill campus melodrama. After all, he should have known that in today's charged climate, entangling himself with the personal secrets of female students was a volatile—and potentially foolhardy—thing to do as a teacher. Even so, Colby's actions seem excessively punitive. Colby officials could have undertaken an investigation into Geier's sexual-harassment charge, as required by the faculty handbook. They could have attempted to mediate informally the more tentative complaints about teaching methods. Such measures, of course, presume a modicum of good faith toward an embattled faculty member, something that seems to have been missing in this case.

COLBY'S CRUDE RESPONSE to Weisberger's alleged transgressions seems particularly unfortunate, considering that the sort of complaints he generated are far from uncommon on college campuses. In "When the Personal Becomes Problematic," a recent article in the journal *Teaching Sociology*, the Purdue University sociologist Elizabeth Grauerholz and her student Stacey Capenhaver explore the ethics of using teaching methods that "rely on students' own life experiences and often involve a high degree of self-disclosure." Such methods, Grauerholz and Capenhaver write, not only are crucial to the formation of what C. Wright Mills calls "the sociological imagination" but can have therapeutic benefits as well, reinforcing "the validity of personal experience" and enabling some students to "deal with personal victimization which they had denied."

But there's a hitch. "If we encourage students to think about the connections between their personal lives and the world around them—a major goal of sociological teaching—we are putting some students at risk," write the authors. "We may be doing untold damage to our students by requiring or encouraging them to reveal difficult, perhaps traumatic, details of their lives in class assignments or classroom projects." In the article, Grauerholz offers up her own experience as an object lesson. During a seminar she taught titled "Gender Violence," she required Capenhaver and other students to write an autobiographical journal in which they explored the impact of violence on their lives. The goal "was to empower . . . students, as they gained knowledge of themselves and the social forces affecting their lives." But things didn't quite work out as planned.

Grauerholz "didn't learn that any students had problems with the assignment until after she collected the autobiographies," at which point "three students felt comfortable enough to write notes to me." One student wrote, "I felt somewhat exploited and exposed by this paper." Another ventured that "assigning a grade to a person's feelings and life experiences is difficult at best." Grauerholz was surprised by the response. "I suppose I thought, naively, that if anyone had a problem with any assignment, they would be able to talk about it with me and that we would work out a mutually agreeable solution." She realizes now, she writes, that such an assumption was "unrealistic in a relationship in which the power difference is as great as that between professor and student."

In a final comment, Capenhaver adds a note of special caution for male instructors, urging them to consider how other variables, "such as gender," might "affect the power relation between student and professor." When a female student is required by a male instructor to write anything about her personal life, Capenhaver writes, she "is surrendering even more control to someone who already has emotional and social power over her. . . . Instructors could use knowledge about a student's past to identify the most vulnerable female students, or possibly could use such information to blackmail or sexually harass a student."

In the aftermath of the Weisberger case, Grauerholz and Capenhaver's cautionary tale has particular resonance for Colby faculty. "When students start talking about their personal lives, they're talking about issues that you're not prepared or trained to handle," says one male professor. "You should stay the hell away from it. You'd have to be a fool after what happened to Adam." This professor, a teacher of foreign language, says he recently asked students in his intro class to compose a letter in the foreign language. One student chose to write a letter to her mother. "In terms of technique and sentence structure, the letter was well written," says the professor. "In my conference with her, my only criticism was: 'This doesn't read like a letter from a daughter to her mother. This is like a letter you would write to your accountant.'" The student began to weep. "That *is* my relationship to my mother," she told him.

It was then, says the professor, that he realized, "I'm out of my depth. I don't know what I'm doing here. And that's when I said, forget it. I'm not prepared to play with this." From that point on, he says, when students suggest that they write something involving their personal life, "I say no."

Other professors, particularly women, are still willing to experiment—if they forgo the kind of abrasive approach that was Weisberger's stock-in-trade. Phyllis Mannocchi, a fifty-two-year-old English professor, teaches a popular course called "Passionate Expression" focusing primarily on sexuality. "I've developed a kind of writing assignment that is both personal and analytic," Mannocchi says. "I call them 'Reflections.' Students do things like describe what is erotic. . . . I don't think you can do that in the context of a formal essay." Mannocchi's teaching presumes an impressive level of student trust. A few years ago, one of her students chose to perform a scene from Tony Kushner's play *Angels in America*. "It was a nude scene," she says—though underwear was worn. "Now, I mean, I didn't broadcast that all over campus. But that happened. I told students they didn't have to come to class if they didn't want to. But why am I allowed to do that?" Mannocchi laughs nervously. "I don't know," she says.

Told of Weisberger's inclination to "challenge" or criticize student papers, Mannocchi recoils in horror. "I always use the voice of my shrink," she says. "She never would have said, Well, what about your mother? It's all about nudging along responses rather than directing them." Indeed, far from seeking to unsettle or discomfit students, Mannocchi soothes them. "Because I came through the women's movement, and really through a lot of consciousness-raising, I'm very careful about the comments I make," she says. "I help students to see their own experience. I don't judge the way they've expressed it. My comments are always as an equal."

Of course, Mannocchi is not quite her students' equal; after she comments on students' papers, she presumably goes on to grade them. But there, too, Mannocchi is not out to rock the boat. "I judge students holistically, on all their work in the semester," she says. "Somehow we come to an agreement about grades. Students write or talk to me about what they feel they deserve." Mannocchi leans forward in her chair and smiles. "Usually," she says, "I'm very generous."

Adam Weisberger, of course, thought he was being generous as well. Within the precincts of his classroom, students were urged to view Hegel's master-slave dialectic not only as an object of scholarly examination but as a central trope of their interactions. "One of the things you can do with the master-slave relationship," Weisberger says, "is to see how it might be played out in the context of student and professor. Hegel writes that the slave has repressed knowledge about the nature of inequality, by virtue of having to act in service to the master. . . . There are some things a student knows which the teacher is himself unconscious of." For this reason, Weisberger admits, "the students who rose up against me were acting out some of the very things I wanted them to understand."

But while applauding their cheekiness, Weisberger stops well short of endorsing the students' uprising. "I used to say in the course that there were two destructive tendencies a student could bring into it: blind obedience and blind rebellion," Weisberger says. "Sometimes the reaction against the way you were conditioned to respond to authority can be just as blind as the original conditioning." The first-year law student sighs. "Especially," he adds, "when you have people reinforcing you."

In the end, Weisberger's chief regret is not that his students learned the material all too well but that they didn't learn it well enough: "They were using Hegel . . . to fight something oppressive. But that's not who I am! It was a great delusion, a massive displacement." What the students failed to understand, Weisberger says, is that there were two categories of masters at Colby. "Untenured professors are the lower masters," he says. "The upper masters are tenured faculty and administration."

Weisberger grows agitated. "Don't you see?" he asks. "The upper masters instrumentalized the discontent of the student slaves to impose social control on a recalcitrant member of the lower category of master. That's what happened here. The students thought they were freeing themselves. They weren't freeing themselves. They were running into the arms of their masters! You think the administrators of Colby College are more likely to want to see you liberate yourself?"

In any case, no one associated with the Weisberger affair is likely to find liberation any time soon. "Colby wanted to get rid of a problem in the least costly way," Weisberger explains. "They miscalculated. Now it's going to cost them. It's going to cost them a lot of money. It's going to cost them faculty morale. It's going to tarnish their reputation."

For the first time all day, Adam Weisberger smiles.

—February 1998

PART III

The Political Professor

THE KILLING OF PROFESSOR CULIANU
Chronicle of a Death Foretold
TED ANTON

ON THE LAST MORNING OF HIS LIFE, a charismatic University of Chicago Divinity School professor named Ioan Culianu taught a class on gnosticism, the study of secret mystic sects. One of his graduate students, Alexander Arguelles, was presenting a paper to the faculty for the first time that day. "I was nervous. He said, 'It's nothing to fear, just a rite of passage,' " Arguelles recounts. "He patted me on the back and smiled." Arguelles stops. "I'll never forget that smile."

Two hours later Culianu was dead of a single .25-caliber bullet wound to the back of the head. His execution-style murder in a campus bathroom stunned the school, terrified students, and stumped the Chicago police and the FBI. Now, after sixteen months, the crime looks more and more like what Culianu's friends suspected it was all along: the first political assassination of a professor on American soil.

AT FIRST THE POLICE THOUGHT the killing might be the act of a disgruntled student or colleague, perhaps even a practitioner of the occult arts Culianu studied. But investigators turned up no evidence to corroborate these theories. What they did discover is that for almost two years Culianu, a Romanian émigré, had been attacking the new Romanian government in journals, broadcasts, and interviews around the world. He had received death threats, as have other Romanians-in-exile since his murder.

At forty-one, Professor Culianu was adored by students and admired by scholars from Umberto Eco to Harold Bloom. Fluent in eight languages, the author of seventeen books, and the holder of three Ph.D.'s, Culianu was "brilliant, famous in Europe," says Dr. Moshe Idel, a Hebrew University professor and expert on Jewish mysticism. Tall, with a dimpled smile and deep eyes that looked somewhere beyond you, Ioan Culianu proposed that multiple universes coexist, that the mind creates reality, and that magic can outperform modern science. In the weeks before his murder on May 21, 1991, he was finishing three books, planning his wedding, preparing for a long-anticipated return to Romania, and hosting a conference in Chicago with the retrospectively haunting title "Other Realms: Death, Ecstasy, and Otherworldly Journeys in Recent Scholarship."

But it is the prophetic quality of the victim's own political statements and Borgesian fiction that add the eeriest dimension to this chilling story. A specialist in the occult, Culianu liked to tell his students' futures and often came up with predictions that were unnervingly on target. At one Hyde Park party, he uncovered a graduate student's concealed panic over her career. He told another that she was "humiliating herself in a love triangle," and his accuracy, she says, "knocked the wind out of me." In the fantasy and detective stories he published in avant-garde literary magazines like *Exquisite Corpse*, Culianu wrote of political events that materialized months or years later, of secret sects, and of murders remarkably like his own. This crime is an academic whodunit, touching on the tortured intricacies of Romanian history, on myth and mysticism, and on the buried connections between a scholar's political and intellectual passions. As fiction, it makes uncanny tragedy. The tragedy is it's not fiction.

AS A TEACHER, Ioan Culianu was open, funny, and unforgettable, but as a friend he was secretive and insular. He was born January 5, 1950, into a prominent family in the Romanian town of Iasi near the

Soviet border. Iasi had majestic boulevards, stone cathedrals, crooked cobbled alleys, and, for Culianu, ghostly memories of his boyar family's former glories. Culianu's great-grandfather and grandfather had presided over its university, Romania's oldest. During Romania's era of fascism and Axis alliance, his grandfather was famous for defending Jews by wielding a marble-handled cane against their tormentors.

The boy grew up under the Communists, who came to power just after World War II. The Party seized his family's mansion, confining them to four rooms infused by the "bitter smell of decomposing upholstery," Culianu later wrote. Forbidden to play with other children, he amused himself with solitary games in the estate's walled garden. On his office desk after the murder police found three walnuts from the tree in that garden.

"We lived in fear of Securitate, the secret police," recalls Culianu's sister, Therese Petrescu, now married to one of Romania's leading dissidents. His father, an opposition lawyer and mathematician, could not publish or find a job; he died, a broken man, at fifty-one.

At the University of Bucharest, Ioan Culianu and his friends reveled in mind games, teasing their professors by inventing elaborate bibliographic citations to scholars with outlandish names. When he placed first in national literature and language exams, Securitate tried to recruit him, as it did most top graduates. A so-called Captain Ureche (Captain Ear) took him "walking through many alleyways," urging him to inform on colleagues, Culianu wrote in a 1989 statement to the U.S. Immigration and Naturalization Service. When Culianu refused, he, like his father, found he could not get a decent job or publisher.

Unlike his father, though, Ioan Culianu escaped. On July 4, 1972, he defected while in Italy on scholarship. Romanian writers abroad have been beaten or killed, in incidents that usually suggest Securitate involvement, and Culianu's subsequent achievements all came as he moved in fear of reprisal through Italy, France, and Holland. Exile, however, gave him excellent contacts around the world, especially with another Romanian expatriate, the late Mircea Eliade, the University of Chicago's acclaimed religious scholar. Eliade encouraged the younger scholar's exploration of mysticism and astral religion and helped bring Culianu to Chicago as a visiting professor in 1986. At the time of his death, Culianu held a professorship in the history of Christianity and the history of religions; the University of Chicago had promised him tenure when his immigration proceedings were concluded.

In Hyde Park, Culianu expanded his research beyond the study of religion, working to recast our concepts of magic, sex, death, and the self. His interests ranged widely—from the study of multiple universes to the mind's phantasms, from literary theory to the spiritual techniques of ecstasy. "He had," says Michael Fishbane, a divinity school colleague, "the linguistic capacity, the originality, the boldness, and the energy to produce an enormous life's work." His three posthumously published books suggest the scope of his ambition. One covers the history of gnostic sects, another explores afterlife journeys, and the third is a comprehensive dictionary of world religions.

Because he linked the occult, physics, magic, Eros, and history, his scholarship was mislabeled New Age. It was far more. Culianu sought the underlying structure of fanaticism and faith to find "the patterned predictability of thought itself," writes Lawrence Sullivan, director of Harvard's Center for the Study of World Religions. "He made two key contributions," says Carol Zaleski, a Smith College professor of religion. "One was in the sheer mass of his erudition. But his main interest was in understanding how the mind invents imaginary worlds and makes them so real they in effect become real."

Yet more than his scholarship, his personality is what students still talk about. "He met us and greeted us by name," says a former graduate student, Michael Allocca. "I looked forward all summer to seeing him," says Greg Spinner, another of Culianu's students. "I'll just never know anyone like him again." Spinner and Allocca persuaded him to give them a course in his specialty, divination. The final exam was to predict the future.

On the university quad in 1986, Culianu met Hillary Wiesner, a Harvard graduate student with whom he would co-write most of his later works. She became his fiancée and the object of his mystical chivalry. "He invented a kind of religion focused on me," says Wiesner. "My friends couldn't believe him." When Culianu and Wiesner saw the movie *Cyrano de Bergerac*, though, she understood, at least a little. "He cried at that movie," she says. "In his mind he *was* Cyrano, alone, on a secret ideal quest against impossible odds to avenge his father and the past."

A WILLING EXPATRIATE, Ioan Culianu followed Romanian politics from a distance for seventeen years. But after the Romanian revolution in December 1989, he became a firebrand. In his last fifteen months, Culianu wrote more than thirty articles attacking Romania's new leaders in *Lumea Libera* (Free World), a New York–based émigré newspaper, and in *Corriere della Sera*, the Italian national daily. He made scathing Radio Free Europe and BBC broadcasts; the BBC even told him to tone them down. He wrote prescient short stories about a country called Jormania, his fictional version of Romania.

History helps explain his "latent explosion," Norman Manea's term for the belated political engagement of the Romanian intellectual in exile. Squeezed by the old Russian, Ottoman, and Austro-Hungarian empires, Romania is a poor, mountainous, oft-conquered country haunted by identity crises and susceptible to corrupt and sadistic leadership, both foreign and native. (The most famous Romanian, Dracula, is a fictional character based on the aptly named fifteenth-century prince Vlad the Impaler.) Democratic traditions have never really taken root; xenophobia and anti-Semitism have often flourished and, as Manea points out, kept many young intellectuals aloof from national politics.

In the late 1930s, a fascist party called the Iron Guard grew in power. Nurturing its own version of blood-and-soil mythology, the Iron Guard, in the words of the historian Vlad Georgescu, "brought a death cult to Romanian politics" and took even the Nazis aback with the barbarity of its pogroms. Aware that much of this history had been suppressed in the postwar era, Culianu had called for an investigator like Elie Wiesel to uncover the full truth of the Romanian holocaust.

In 1944, Romania's young king Michael infuriated the Iron Guard by turning his back on Germany and bringing the country into the antifascist coalition—or, as the ultranationalists saw it, capitulating to the Russians. When the Communists took over in 1947, many Iron Guardists escaped—to the United States. As it happens, Chicago harbors one of the largest concentrations of these exiles. "You have an old but active fascist community here," says a source who asked not to be named. "They still recruit," adds another.

The revolution against Nicolae Ceausescu seemed at first a joyful reversal of Romania's dark history. But a number of recent books that examine the events of December 1989, including those by the National Public Radio commentator Andrei Codrescu, the journalist Edward Behr, and the Radio Free Europe correspondent Nestor Ratesh, have confirmed what Culianu and others said early on about Eastern Europe's last and bloodiest revolt. They argue that what began as a genuine popular uprising in the city of Timisoara was soon co-opted by factions within Securitate, the army, and the party that had long been planning to topple the Ceausescu regime. Accounts differ as to how quickly and definitively the revolt was hijacked. Some commentators argue that much of the revolution we saw on TV was staged and even claim that the KGB had a hand in it; others say the uprising was genuinely popular and spontaneous but soon provided a pretext for the coup plotters to make their move. All agree that many officials in the postrevolutionary government are veterans of the Ceausescu regime and share much of its contempt for democracy. As Ratesh puts it, the struggles of December resulted in "the striking paradox of a basically anti-Communist revolution producing a regime dominated by former Communists." Romania's government faces a stagnant economy and frequent protests, but the opposition is fractured, and the current regime may well be returned to power in national elections this September. An anti-Semitic right—to which some of Ceausescu's former associates have gravitated and which appears to be funded by a faction of Securitate—is on the rise.

Unlike other governments in Eastern Europe, the Romanian government today retains most of its secret-police force (though it does have a new, more benign-sounding name: the Romanian Information Service). Even abroad, the former Securitate, or at least remnants of it, apparently continues to engage in dirty tricks. An official in the FBI's Intelligence Division testified before Congress last November, for example, that while Czechoslovakia, Poland, and Hungary have significantly scaled back their intelligence operations in the United States, "we cannot say the same thing for Romania. . . . We're still very concerned about their intentions."

Ioan Culianu was among the first and loudest to label Romania's revolution a coup. His fiction had been even more perceptive: six months before anyone thought Ceausescu could fall, Culianu published a short story in Italy, "The Intervention in Jormania," that described a rebellion similar to Romania's. A second story, "Free Jormania," told of a coup in the midst of a genuine revolution, in which secret-police factions battle and coup leaders film exhumed corpses to inflate the number of combat deaths and confuse the public. An ABC *Nightline* investigation later revealed that the leaders of the Romanian revolution had resorted to just such a grisly strategy—videotaping rows of corpses dug up from paupers' graves and claiming they were the bodies of demonstrators killed by Ceausescu forces. In Romania, as in Culianu's fiction, political reality had become a mind game.

A month before Culianu died, a wide-ranging interview with him appeared in the Romanian dissident magazine *22*. "He gave the most devastating indictment of the new union of far left and far right in Romania," says Vladimir Tismaneanu, a University of Maryland political science professor and author of *Reinventing Politics: Eastern Europe From Stalin to Havel*. At first reluctant to talk, Culianu went on to call Securitate a force "of epochal stupidity and yet unseen profundity." Asked about Romania's free elections and press, he replied that the main benefactors were newly free fascists. The professor antagonized not only far left and far right but even the interviewer, calling the revolution a "tragic waste" dictated by the KGB. "It was his death sentence," says Ion Pacepa, a former chief of the Romanian Foreign Intelligence Service who defected in 1978 and is now hiding in America.

It is not surprising that Ioan Culianu worried about retaliation and thought he saw evidence of it. A month before the revolution, his Hyde Park apartment was ransacked. The Chicago police report shows that a TV, a computer, floppy disks, and bottles of wine were stolen. Culianu, who was petitioning to get his sister and brother-in-law out of Romania, felt that Securitate was warning him, says his friend Stelian Plesoiu.

Others disagreed. "It was nothing political, just a bad neighborhood," says Greg Spinner, who helped his professor move out and into a high-security high-rise on Lake Shore Drive.

Culianu never mentioned to university friends or the police the death threats he had begun getting. "He was a stiff-upper-lip type," says Spinner, to whom Culianu did once confide he was getting into "dangerous territory" in his political writing.

One person to whom he did mention the threats was his friend Dorin Tudoran, a dissident publisher and poet. "They came in letters or over the phone. He didn't know the source," Tudoran says. "They said they would kill him if he kept writing about Romania. First he was amused. Then he became frightened."

Yet he got himself even more involved in exile politics. In April 1991, a month before he was killed, Ioan Culianu hosted the elderly king Michael at the University of Chicago, later concluding that the exiled monarch was the best hope for stability in their country. Three days before his murder, he decided to cancel his trip to Romania, during which he had planned to visit his ailing mother and attend a conference of the American-Romanian Academy, a scholarly group known for its anti-Communist activity. He told his sister he was receiving threats from the powerful far-right group called Vatra Romaneasca (Romanian Hearth), "for all practical purposes an organ of the Romanian Information Service," according to a retired Securitate captain.

He then changed the locks on his office door.

THE THIRD-FLOOR BATHROOM where Ioan Culianu was slain is a serene place. Etched into one toilet-roll holder is a swastika, probably unrelated to the crime. Culianu died during the lunch hour on a sunny May afternoon as hundreds of people filed through Swift Hall for the annual divinity school book sale. His killer apparently perched on a toilet seat in the stall next to Culianu's and pointed the gun down at his head. The single shot sliced through his brain and exploded out a nostril. No one saw the killer flee. The gun was never found. Culianu's keys and wallet were still in his pocket, and his black-opal watch was still fastened to his wrist. The killing was so precise that when a student entered the bathroom minutes later, there was almost no blood yet, just a bluish arm dangling below the partition.

"These people knew what they were doing," observes Cook County chief medical examiner Robert J. Stein. "To kill with one shot from a gun as small as a .25—that's not easy." The former intelligence chief Ion Pacepa goes further: "It's a typical KGB-style type of execution, one shot to the back of the head."

Culianu's killing uncoiled a string of strange events, rumors, and instances of disinformation. A day after the murder, a gift of his books that Culianu had sent to King Michael's home in Geneva, Switzerland, arrived in its Jiffy Pak envelope—opened and empty. The day before the murder, someone phoned the family and many of the business associates of Andrei Codrescu to tell them that Codrescu, a Romanian exile and a friend of Culianu's, had killed himself. Codrescu says he eventually learned that the calls had been made by "an individual in California." But he says that he is afraid to reveal the caller's identity, commenting only that "the spread of disinformation is a typical Securitate strategy."

In the following days, the widow of Mircea Eliade, a woman Culianu doted on, began receiving menacing calls at her Hyde Park home. Eliade had named Culianu his literary executor, but in recent years the elder scholar, who died in 1986, had come under attack as an apologist for the Iron Guard, and Culianu himself had criticized his mentor. Mrs. Eliade changed her number and has declined to talk.

A few weeks later, the American-Romanian Academy meeting in Bucharest fizzled when a number of scholars from the West who'd been scheduled to attend bowed out. "It was crucial for free opposition in our country," says Mircea Sabau, a physicist at the University of Chicago's teaching hospital and a friend of Culianu's. "But after the killing, few people showed up."

According to Culianu's sister, Romania's official newspaper, *Libertatea* (Freedom), then published what it claimed was a Chicago police report asserting that no foreign intelligence service was involved in the crime. But the Chicago police say they issued no such report. In a June 7, 1991, press conference, Romania's president, Ion Iliescu, also commented on the crime, stating a "high American official" told him it was not a political murder. A State Department expert on Eastern European affairs, however, disclaims any knowledge of such a comment by an American official.

Other Romanian writers in the United States and abroad began getting death threats. The far-rightist newspaper *Romania Mare* (Greater Romania), published by former Ceausescu supporters, attacked the political science professor Vladimir Tismaneanu: "Watch out, rat, the rat patrol is after you." In Washington, the dissident Dorin Tudoran began receiving threats naming Culianu. "I got calls that said, 'We'll send you after your friend Culianu. We have a bullet with your name on it.'" The FBI eventually caught the Romanians making the calls, but neither Tudoran nor the bureau will say who they were.

In Athens, a Romanian writer and close friend of Professor Culianu's was threatened twice during the week his article on the murder appeared. In New York, a journalist received threats similar to the others. In Chicago, a Romanian radio announcer who has sponsored the king's visits got menacing phone calls and a letter naming Culianu.

Some of the threats may be spurious, traceable to a lone exile nursing old resentments. But there is something odd, and perhaps significant, about the way most of these messages are worded: they borrow the archaic language of the Iron Guard's mystic nationalism. In Athens, the letters even featured obsolete accent marks. Most observers say this is an old Securitate cover tactic. In his book *Red Horizons*, Pacepa details international smear campaigns in which Securitate used nationalist rhetoric to intimidate dissidents, sometimes inventing new right-wing groups.

A February 1992 article in *Romania Mare* adopted similar language to applaud Culianu's murder. Filled with vulgar references to the murder site, the article said Culianu was appropriately killed on a "lethal toilet prepared for him as if by destiny."

A MURDER SITE IS A TEXT, and on a quiet May afternoon the divinity school professor Anthony Yu analyzes the bathroom site of his friend's murder, close to his book-lined office. "It's ritually significant," he says. "It conveys symbolic and physical humiliation, stain, impurity, a most profane site to end a life. In fact, I've wondered if this was a cult killing."

The police haven't ruled out the possibility that it was a cult killing—or the act of a disgruntled colleague, student, or lover. But if there is such a motive, it is well hidden. "He just didn't have any enemies," says Nathaniel Deutsch, Culianu's graduate assistant, and others concur.

On occasion, though, Culianu's avid research into the occult had gotten him into trouble. At a lecture he gave in France on Renaissance magic, three self-described witches objected to his meddling in their realm. He, his co-lecturer, and several in the audience became seriously ill. Lectures on that topic were "an enterprise," he noted wryly in his book *Eros and Magic in the Renaissance*, "from which I shall refrain in the future."

Many Romanians themselves are skeptical about a political motive in this murder. Why would even an unbridled faction of Securitate bother with a professor in Chicago who was not a player? The question is a cultural knot; its answer may lie less in the rational than in the mythical, indeed cultist, fanaticism Culianu studied and critiqued.

First, discard the idea that a professor's writings could not inspire enough anger to get him killed. Many compare Culianu's death to the 1940 murder of Nicholae Iorga, a famous Romanian historian who had antagonized the Iron Guard and is thought to have been killed by them, outside of Bucharest. "I know the people who murdered Iorga," says Dr. Alexander Ronnett, an elderly dentist and general practitioner who is a self-proclaimed Chicago spokesman for the Iron Guard. "The only thing they did wrong was to be too kind," he says. "They should have skinned him alive in public."

To Romania's new far rightists, Culianu was a traitor to his kind— a writer whose attacks were more direct and personal than those of people like Tismaneanu, Codrescu, or Manea, who are all Jewish and therefore excluded, in the neofascist view of things, from the circle of Romanian patriots. He was the intellectual heir to Eliade, one of Romania's most famous scholars abroad. But while the old Iron Guard had proudly called Eliade "one of our own," the new Romanian rightists loathed Culianu. The article in *Romania Mare*, signed by Leonard Gavriliu, the Romanian translator of Freud, offered its own harrowing commentary on the murder site: referring to the "seething, fermented vision of Culianu's fecal brain," it called him "a piece of excrement over whom not enough water was flushed." It said that Culianu, "a refugee in the gangster megalopolis of Chicago," had no right to criticize Romanian anti-Semitism or to demand a reckoning with the country's recent past.

Securitate, too, reserves special vengeance for anyone who puts their criticisms of Romania in writing. In 1991, Dimitru Mazilu, a former high official of the ruling National Salvation Front who had just completed a manuscript critical of the new regime, was beaten and slashed in his Geneva apartment. The two hooded men who attacked him with razors spoke Romanian—and they left with Mazilu's manuscript. Other writers and publishers have been beaten or killed in France, Germany, and Canada. According to Pacepa, the Ceausescu-era Securitate used radiation to surreptitiously poison dissident writers it had detained.

Still, even those who are convinced that Culianu's was a political murder are puzzled about why he in particular might have been targeted. One explanation may be the breadth and passion of his attack on Romania's new government. Appearing in April 1991, a month before he died, Culianu's interview with 22 was one of the first broadsides on the ruling National Salvation Front and the December revolution to be published in Romania itself. In it, he "combined the emotionalism of a poet with the depth of a political scientist," says Tismaneanu. He castigated not only Securitate but the Iron Guard, cultist nationalism, the Orthodox Church, and Romanian culture. He called for an investigation of Romania's genocide of hundreds of thousands of Jews. Any one of these could provoke reprisal in a country that has never confronted its recent past. "His criticism was complex, nonlinear, subtle. You must put it together," says Sabau. "Then it's devastating."

The 22 interview would have "hit them [members of the current Romanian government] hard," say Pacepa. "They'd say, 'This guy's trouble. He's only going to get worse. Let's get rid of him.' It may not even have been a government decision."

The fact that Culianu was not known outside the academic world may also have made him more vulnerable. "They go after those less well known to confuse the police and scare the rest of us," says Sabau.

When it comes to Balkan intrigue, the Chicago police proceed pretty much as usual. "The FBI handles the international dimension," says Chicago police commander Fred Miller, who will say only that he's recently gotten a new lead in the Culianu case.

The enigmatic killing grips those who knew Ioan Culianu. "Losing him was like the burning of the Library at Alexandria. There's so much he knew, it'll take years to sift what he could tell you in a second," says Greg Spinner. "I can't stop thinking about him," says Nathaniel Deutsch. Beyond the senseless loss, the correlation between his research and his murder is the most unsettling element of this crime. Ioan Culianu believed in multiple universes—perhaps because he lived in multiple worlds himself. He taught his students to suspend disbelief to become good detectives of the occult; he believed Eastern Europeans had to do the same in order to uncover the occult political twists of a deeply divided region. He believed in the power of the past and the power to rewrite it, as he saw such power used in his country. "His scholarly interests were almost a mirror image of the organization that was plotting to kill him," says Tismaneanu.

Culianu's last short story, "The Language of Creation," appeared in Codrescu's magazine *Exquisite Corpse* the month Culianu died. It tells of a historian "forty years old, living in a high rise security building on the Lake." He teaches at a "grey and renowned Midwestern University." And one day he comes to possess a strange music box that contains in code the language spoken by God: the language of creation. The three former owners of the box have met with murder in centuries past.

The current owner considers using the box against a "distasteful political regime" but fears he will suffer the same fate as those who came before him. As much as he tries to break its secret code, he never can. After much indecision, he finally leaves the music box at a yard sale and escapes to freedom from what had become the intellectual prison posed by its secret.

One wonders why, after twenty years of exile, with all those accomplishments behind him and so many ahead of him, Ioan Culianu didn't leave his own past at a yard sale. Did he sense the full extent of the danger he was in? At times it almost seems he did. If one looks deep enough into the story of his murder, one may see a professor unconsciously grappling in his fiction and scholarship with the very real forces that combined to kill him.

—September 1992

THE CRITIQUE OF PURE POP
A Philosopher Takes On the Pet Shop Boys
HILLARY FREY

IT GOES WITHOUT SAYING that philosophers rarely get into brawls
with Top 40 musicians and parents. But Roger Scruton, Britain's outspoken conservative philosopher and critic of things cool, is anything
but typical.

Late last March, Scruton found himself the object of considerable
attention when the Pet Shop Boys, a venerable British techno-pop
band, filed an eighty-thousand-dollar libel suit against him and his
publisher. The specific offense? It's in the pages of Scruton's most recent book, *An Intelligent Person's Guide to Modern Culture*, in which
the fifty-five-year-old philosopher evinces contempt for most things
modern. In a chapter called "Yoofanasia," Scruton puts forth the following: "Sometimes, as with the Spice Girls or the Pet Shop Boys, serious doubts arise as to whether the performers made more than a
minimal contribution to the recording, which owes its trade mark to
subsequent sound engineering."

The offending statement is less a critique of the bands in question
than an extension of Scruton's ongoing efforts to explain what's
wrong with modern music. In his book *The Aesthetics of Music*, Scruton defines good musical taste as "the sum of those preferences that
would emerge in a well-ordered soul." And what would such a soul
shop for at Tower Records? Mozart and Vivaldi, apparently. "Classical harmony provides us with an archetype of human sympathy,"

Scruton muses. "The ability to notice a bass line, to feel the rightness of the notes and of the harmonies that erupt from them, is the ability to respond to a wider world, to value the other voice, and to situate both self and other in a moralized universe."

By this measure, most of us are in deep trouble. To Scruton, today's pop music, which bonds its listener to the performer rather than the song, is almost entirely devoid of musical merit. A tune by Nirvana's Kurt Cobain offers only a "ghostly resemblance to melody," and its harmonies swim in a "soup of amplified overtones." R.E.M.'s "Losing My Religion" is dismally "shapeless": "No triad is ever inverted, and nothing moves between the chords, so that all is absorbed in rhythm." And electronic dance music is even worse. The Pet Shop Boys' mechanized thumps and illusory heartbeats are an assault on his classically trained ear: "Beat is not rhythm," he explains, "but the last sad skeleton of rhythm, stripped bare of human life."

Who, then, is to blame for shifting the public ear from Performance Today to K-Rock? In *An Intelligent Person's Guide to Modern Culture*, he points his accusatory finger at "a new human type" emerging in modern cities—a.k.a. the youth of the 1990s: "Youth culture is a global force. It has its own language, its own customs, its own territory and its own self-contained economy." It also has its own music, whose sound, according to Scruton, is defined by bands like R.E.M., Prodigy, and Oasis (whom he once denounced in a lecture as "mindless oafs").

These bands aren't taking Scruton to court, but they do have their defenders, even among the intelligentsia. John Sutherland, a well-known Victorianist and University of London professor, argues that "there is certainly more to [R.E.M.] than meets the jaded ear of Roger Scruton." In a February issue of the *London Review of Books* he went on to point out, "The notion that this group [R.E.M.], at this moment, represents the 'voice of youth' is peculiar enough. . . . Michael Stipe [R.E.M.'s lead singer] is knocking on 40!" Indeed, skin-and-bones Stipe is looking much worse for wear than his "aesthetician critic," whose author photo consumes the entire back cover of *An Intelligent Person's Guide to Modern Culture*. (Sutherland also unravels

"The Sad Professor," a dirgelike track on R.E.M.'s album *UP* that tells the story of a boring, drunk, and miserable literature professor. "Michael Stipe is serenading me and Roger Scruton," he surmises.)

Apparently, Scruton not only dislikes the "new human type" created by youth culture; he also wants to keep this type out of his home. In an April feature story in the London *Guardian*, Scruton described how he will bring his five-month-old son, Samuel, through his formative years, steering him as far away as possible from toxins like pop music, baseball hats, and baggy pants. "My wife Sophie and I have decided to offer Sam a genuinely deprived childhood," Scruton explains. "Sam is being educated not so as to enjoy himself, but so that other people will enjoy him." For the duration of what Scruton calls Sam's "ordeal," the boy will not watch television or play with toys or drink Coca-Cola. He will, however, read Greek by age six, play the piano and viola, and attend church regularly.

The education of Samuel Scruton is not exactly a Dickensian horror, but it's not a walk in the park, either. Even Scruton acknowledges that Sam may "just become a cruel experiment in parenting." Think of John Stuart Mill, who, raised by a philosopher father with a Scruton-like strong arm, suffered a terrible breakdown at twenty. Rejecting his father's teachings, Mill found inspiration in Wordsworth, the Oasis of his day. *Guardian* readers predict that a troubled adulthood lies ahead for young Sam Scruton, too. Suggested one letter writer, "The *Guardian* should invite Mr. Scruton to provide us with a regular column on bringing up young Samuel, the proceeds to be invested to pay for therapy required in later life."

For the moment, the new father has more immediate concerns—like his pending lawsuit. The Pet Shop Boys could still drop the charges, since the financial stakes are not terribly high. Nor is it too late for Scruton to make nice and apologize: weirdly enough, after news of the suit first broke, he told one reporter, "Actually, I quite like the Pet Shop Boys—certainly the early stuff."

—July 1999

WHO OWNS THE SIXTIES?

The Opening of a Scholarly Generation Gap

RICK PERLSTEIN

ON AUGUST 13, 1994, some quarter-million pilgrims journeyed to up-state New York to experience Woodstock II. They were searching for the spirit of the sixties. What they found was a messy debate over whether that staggeringly commercialized event was a proper tribute to the decade or its proper burial.

For many sixties faithful, the commemoration was plainly a sacrilege, and it fell to Maurice Isserman, a historian at Hamilton College, to explain why the original Woodstock was superior. "Partially by design, partially by accident," he wrote in *The Philadelphia Inquirer*, the 1969 Woodstock "evoked and jumbled together many of the most cherished myths enshrined in the national self-image: self-reliance, agrarian simplicity, and providential mission"—this, "despite the entrepreneurial ambitions of its promoters, its slick promotion, and the miracles of sound technology and stagecraft which made it possible."

Another historian, however, begged to differ. "Most of the big figures at Woodstock in 1969 were hucksters," insisted Thomas Sugrue of the University of Pennsylvania, quoted in a *Washington Post* story the same day. "They were trying to make a buck and trying to make a name." And what of those who cherish memories of Woodstock as the apotheosis of the good, the true, and the libidinal? "It was just a rock concert," said the professor, "and it was memorable for two reasons: because there were gate-crashers, and because the weather was bad."

Isserman, now forty-nine, had been a reveler at Max Yasgur's farm and a member of Students for a Democratic Society. Sugrue, who is thirty-three, says his most powerful sixties memory is of watching National Guard tanks roll down the riot-torn streets of his Detroit neighborhood; he was five years old at the time. Isserman and Sugrue are both historians of the sixties, and they are contending over the interpretation of a decade that remains among the most powerful historical reference points in American politics. That grand theme of the 1960s—the generation gap—has come to sixties scholarship, and it has come to stay.

FEW HISTORIANS are more aware of this gap, or have done more to widen it, than David Farber, who, at thirty-nine, is the elder statesman of the post-sixties sixties interpreters. His first book, *Chicago '68* (1988), presented that year's tempestuous Democratic National Convention from three different sympathetically presented perspectives: the protesters who came to Chicago to disrupt the convention, the cops who beat them, and the Daley administration officials who presided over the whole mess. "I don't know if my book was the very first of its kind," says Farber in the faculty cafeteria at Barnard College, where he is assistant professor of history. "But it was certainly among the first studies to treat the sixties as an era, an era that is *over*."

When Farber's book was published, a review in *The Village Voice* by baby-boomer novelist Carol Anshaw brooked no such revisionism. Next to sidebars of dewy sixties reminiscences by *Voice* staffers ("I was plotting the overthrow of my high school," began one), Anshaw argued that "perhaps [Farber] wasn't the person to write this book." His study didn't convince, she harrumphed, because he "had no experience of a decade that was primarily experiential."

At the Barnard cafeteria, Farber recalls snatches of this seven-year-old review verbatim: "She said that the book was 'dangerous' for 'giving the establishment its due.' " He pauses, and continues: "I think the sixties generation of activists saw themselves as acting *in* history. 'The Whole World Is Watching'—they were literally chanting it in the streets. And that's the irony that's heated up this debate so much. Because in the end, well, maybe they weren't the historical agents of change quite as much as they hoped."

For Farber, this irony has powerful consequences for his generation of scholars. The task of writing about the sixties, Farber argued in a 1994 polemic in *The Chronicle of Higher Education*, "has been complicated . . . by generational politics within the academy, as older scholars who participated in the Sixties defend interpretations that stem from their own experiences." His conclusion: "People in the academy are kidding themselves if they believe that a young scholar is not bucking the already long odds of finding and keeping a decent job if he or she challenges certain myths of the Sixties."

Not surprisingly, many of the tenured radicals beg to differ. Todd Gitlin, professor of journalism at NYU and a former president of SDS, admires Farber's scholarly work. But he finds Farber's assault on his elders in the *Chronicle* to be "reeking of resentment" and rooted in a mythologization of its own: "It's conventional for young people today," says Gitlin, "to say that the sixties people, whoever they were, had all the fun, and none of the AIDS, and were cushioned by endless prosperity."

Whatever the merit of Farber's charges, there's little doubt that younger scholars are challenging "myths of the sixties" from any number of—often contradictory—angles. Some argue that the New Left had a far broader base than previously supposed. Others suggest that its base, and its impact, were extremely narrow. Still others believe that the real story of the sixties was the rise of a grassroots, antiestablishment movement called . . . the New Right.

DUSTUPS OVER "THE SIXTIES" are as old as the 1960s themselves. In 1960, the radical sociologist C. Wright Mills boasted in his "Letter to the New Left" that, after decades of left-wing doldrums, radicalized students were finally turning the political tide against an entrenched liberalism. A book published the same year by M. Stanton Evans concurred, sort of. In *Revolt on Campus*, Evans argued that students' frustrations "with the conformity of liberalism" promised that the 1960s would be the decade of student conservatism.

By the early 1970s, though, a consensus about the decade had begun to form in the scholarly literature: a salutary upsurge of democratic promise at the beginning of the 1960s was subverted by the dark seeds contained within it. That unsparing thesis was codified most influentially by the Rice historian Allen J. Matusow in his magisterial 1983 work, *The Unraveling of America: A History of Liberalism in the 1960s*. Matusow laid the decline of America's grand liberal tradition at the feet of student radicalism's excesses; and he exerted a quiet influence on the writing of movement veterans such as Todd Gitlin, James Miller, and Maurice Isserman. In 1987, this trio's works appeared in rapid succession: Gitlin marched through the signal events of the decade in his encyclopedic *The Sixties: Years of Hope, Days of Rage*; Miller proffered a rich collective biography of SDS's early leadership in *"Democracy Is in the Streets": From Port Huron to the Siege of Chicago*; and Isserman chronicled the political roots of the New Left in *If I Had a Hammer: The Death of the Old Left and the Birth of the New Left*. All three books related the story of the sixties in terms of the inspiring rise and tragic fall of the student protest movement. They were sympathetic to student radicalism but sober-minded about its consequences. And with their rich detail and acute analyses, they set a standard for the writing of sixties history that has yet to be equaled.

The insider accounts of the sixties kept on coming; more than a score appeared in 1987–1988 alone. And, for the most part, they followed the Gitlin-Miller-Isserman narrative arc, which has become known among historians as the "declension hypothesis." It goes something like this: As the 1950s grayly droned on, springs of contrarian sentiment began bubbling into the best minds of a generation raised in unprecedented prosperity but well versed in the existential subversions of the Beats and *Mad* magazine. At the beginning of the 1960s, students went south to fight for civil rights with the Student Nonviolent Coordinating Committee and came back to elite universities with the audacious goal of changing the world. They created new kinds of political organizations, foremost among them SDS, which were driven by a vague ideal called participatory democracy. The new politics was to be scrupulously nonhierarchical and pragmatic, promising a humane alternative to both sectarian radicalism and technocratic liberalism.

Meanwhile, in a haze of marijuana smoke, the counterculture tested the limits of personal freedom. At first the hippies maintained an arm's-length relationship with the politicos. But as the Vietnam War escalated, the line between activist and Aquarian began to blur— to the detriment of each. Writers sympathetic to the counterculture believe it self-destructed under the pressures of politicization; New Leftists see their movement folding under a crush of countercultural hedonism. Both agree that the movement ended five years before the Vietnam War did, in a blaze of numskull adventurism and Maoist masquerade. ("The future of our movement," went one particularly unfortunate slogan, "is the future of crime in the streets.") When it was all over, the sixties left behind as its bittersweet legacy an America both more free and more divided than ever before.

THAT'S A STORY, say the Young Turks, that's by turns misguided, distorted, irrelevant, or just plain wrong. Take the case of SDS. In the accounting of Gitlin, Isserman, and Miller, the radicals who built Students for a Democratic Society were, like their historians, secular, well-off denizens of elite universities like Harvard and Michigan, often Jewish, and typically refugees from either suburban ticky-tacky torpor or Old Communist Left families. Doug Rossinow, a Johns Hopkins Ph.D. who's finishing up a study of the SDS chapter in Austin, Texas, uncovers a different story. Rossinow is twenty-nine, and his attraction to his subject has little to do with any residual memories: "I never heard about SDS until I was in college. I got interested in this topic because I came across some reference to it in books, and there didn't seem to be a lot of scholarship."

When Rossinow set out to study the New Left, he chose to use a methodology born of the sixties: he would write political history from the bottom up, from the experience of the rank and file rather than the leadership. Ironically, from Kirkpatrick Sale's *SDS* (1973) to Wini Breines's *Community and Organization in the New Left, 1962–1968* (1982) to James Miller's 1987 *"Democracy Is in the Streets*," historians had typically written the history of student radicalism as the story of its leaders. But, notes Rossinow, "When you look at SDS from the grass roots, you find surprising things." For example: in Texas at least, the most important inspiration for SDS's put-your-body-on-the-line brand of radicalism was not C. Wright Mills or Eldridge Cleaver but the action-oriented Christianity imbibed at the local YMCA. With this point in mind, Rossinow presents the antiwar movement as one in a long line of Protestant reform movements stretching back to the American Revolution.

Rossinow's revisionist efforts are complemented by those of Ken Heineman, author of *Campus Wars: The Peace Movement at American State Universities in the Vietnam Era* (1995). Heineman, who comes from a blue-collar family and calls himself a "reluctant Republican," finds working-class folk conspicuously absent from the existing historiography (excepting the figure of Joe Sixpack, the movement's archetypal proletarian spoiler). Yet kids from blue-collar backgrounds formed a large portion of the antiwar activists at the nonelite schools he studied: SUNY-Buffalo, Michigan State, Penn State.

And Kent State. Heineman challenges the conventional wisdom on the Ohio National Guard's 1970 massacre there. Conventionally, it was Kent State that brought the sixties to the blue-collar belt. The university, remarks Todd Gitlin in *The Sixties*, "was a heartland school, far from elite, the very type of campus where Richard Nixon's 'silent majority' was supposed to be training." If such naked repression could be visited on such sleepy backwaters (four dead in *Ohio* of all places), then few partisans of the movement, and certainly none in its vanguard, could be safe from state terror.

The only problem with this interpretation, Heineman points out, is that Kent State *was* the movement's vanguard. Kent Staters protested for the right to organize on campus a full year before the Free Speech Movement at Berkeley supposedly gave birth to white student activism. The Ohio school's first antiwar group was founded a year ahead of Berkeley's. And Kent State students were even among the founders of SDS's ultravanguardist terrorist spin-off, the Weathermen.

Kent State also raises another pointed question: Did sixties radicalism really implode at the end of the decade? Or might it, in fact, have expanded its reach in the 1970s? According to the declension hypothesis, Kent State and other end-of-the-decade disasters sounded the death knell for a broad-based popular movement to change American society (after the shootings, wrote James Miller, "the New Left collapsed, plummeting into cultural oblivion as if it had been some kind of political Hula-Hoop"). In a 1994 article in *American Quarterly*, Rossinow challenges this downbeat assessment: "It is difficult to see how one can view the post-1968 Left as a complete disaster unless one is unsympathetic or unaware of the women's liberation movement, which first emerged in 1967–1968." America *changed* in the 1960s, Rossinow insists. Most palpably, it changed in its gender arrangements—a shift in which the New Left and the counterculture played an important but limited role.

This argument about the broader, less visible influence of sixties radicalism was made most pointedly by Sarah Evans in her 1979 book, *Personal Politics: The Roots of Women's Liberation in the Civil Rights Movement & the New Left*. Alice Echols, the author of *Daring to Be Bad: Radical Feminism in America, 1967–1975* (1989), concurs: "For Gitlin and Miller et al., the tragedy of the late Sixties was the fracturing of the Movement. And the New Left pretty much *does* go up in flames. Even so, I think the only way that women could have their own movements, and black people and gay people"—whose struggles likewise produced real changes in the structure of American society—"was, unfortunately, *outside* the larger movement."

ECHOLS'S GUARDED OPTIMISM about the sixties legacy is shared by many former activists. But what veteran would applaud the message of another camp of scholars, led by U. Penn's Thomas Sugrue, who argue that the Promethean adventures of the New Left and the counterculture aren't all that relevant to understanding the sixties in the first place? "There's more to the sixties than social movements," says Sugrue, "a lot more. Let's think about the Black Panthers as an example, or SDS. They had very small memberships. They were made a big deal of in the media in the 1960s. But if you think about the long-term consequences of those groups in building political organizations, their power isn't as great as it appears. To talk about black power, let's look at the election of blacks to local offices after the Voting Rights Act passed. It's not as glamorous a story as Huey Newton walking up the steps of the California state capitol with a rifle. But in many ways it's a far more important story for its enduring effect on American politics.

"Sixties historiography is still so limited," he adds, "and sixties veterans still have the corner on the market." Sugrue is talking not just about the likes of Todd Gitlin and Maurice Isserman but also about a group of influential writers that includes Allen Matusow, the Clinton pollster Stanley Greenberg (*Middle Class Dreams: The Politics and Power of the New American Majority*), and Thomas and Mary Edsall (*Chain Reaction: The Impact of Race, Rights, and Taxes on American Politics*). Call them the liberals-mugged-by-radicalism school: they see a Democratic Party that scared away its mass base when it veered from its early-1960s blend of Keynesian economics, labor-management cooperation, and racial integration toward a McGovernik capitulation to radicalism. Says Sugrue: "My argument"—supported by his research on housing riots in Detroit since the 1940s—"is that white working-class and middle-class members of the Democratic coalition were *always* very tenuously allied to the liberal tradition."

One of the most powerful insights of new sixties scholarship, then, may be that Reagan Democrats were a long time in the making. It was the nomination of Barry Goldwater in 1964, after all, that first turned the Republican Party toward a right-wing populism cemented by "anti-sixties" themes of law and order, patriotism, and "family values." This is the story told by Mary Brennan, a thirty-five-year-old historian at Southwest Texas State University, in her book *Turning*

Right in the Sixties: The Conservative Capture of the GOP (1995), one of many new projects that takes chronicling the rise of the new conservatism as a central task of sixties history. Attention to social movements on the left, says Brennan, misses a scorching irony of the decade: the real masters of grassroots organizing were on the right. "Right-wingers succeeded by exploiting hitherto untapped sources of discontent," she notes. "Moreover, building a political movement from the bottom up allowed conservatives to . . . avoid the [Republican Party's] liberal-controlled national organization."

Brennan could, of course, have written pretty much the same thing about SDS and the Democrats. That irony has not been lost on sociologists of political movements. UC–San Diego's Rebecca Klatch, author of *Women of the New Right* (1987), is just now finishing up a comparative study of activists in SDS and in Young Americans for Freedom, the conservative group formed in 1960 on William F. Buckley Jr.'s Sharon, Connecticut, estate. Klatch finds striking parallels, including the groups' common sense of generational mission and their shared revulsion (voiced in almost identical language) for the liberal managerial state. She has even uncovered a long-forgotten solidarity movement between the libertarian right and left, which had its own organ, the journal *Left and Right*.

Maybe M. Stanton Evans's quixotic prediction that the sixties would be the decade of student conservatism wasn't so quixotic after all. Cadres of Young Americans for Freedom activists, Pat Buchanan among them, formed the shock troops for the right-wing capture of the GOP (and later the nation). Nine years after the publication of his book on the rise of SDS, James Miller regrets having missed this story. "In terms of the political history of this country, the New Left just isn't an important story," he says. Focus on it, says Miller, and you "evade the extraordinary success of the forces that first supported Goldwater, then Reagan as governor of California, and then Wallace. I can't help but see that absence in the historiography as integral to the mythologization of the sixties."

THE MYTHOLOGIZATION OF THE SIXTIES: that, according to David Farber, is exactly what is still wrong with sixties scholarship today. Is his charge fair? Certainly many of the sixties insiders have written books that are fragrant with self-criticism. But are other New Leftists manning the barricades again, this time to fight a rearguard battle against revisionism?

Richard Ellis, a political scientist at Oregon's Willamette University, thinks so. He's completed several chapters of a study called *The Illiberalism of Egalitarianism*. It's a carefully argued work that provides a theoretical buttress for James Miller's and Todd Gitlin's insights into the fall of SDS. Like Miller and Gitlin, Ellis believes that the group devolved into dogmatic factionalism because its commitment to internal democracy and moral purity frustrated its attempts to work democratic reform in the larger society. When he submitted a version of this argument to *The Journal of American History* in 1994, he says, "the three readers I could identify were former members of SDS. It's as if you were writing on the Reagan administration and the journal sent your paper to Jeane Kirkpatrick, Ed Meese, and Casper Weinberger!" (One vet's reader's report: "I don't think the author is asking the right questions and I disagree with her/his answers. I do not think her/his thesis is borne out by what I know. . . . I think it is a fundamental misreading of the New Left." The reviewer left it at that, without going on to explain what the right questions might be.)

It's hard enough to write the history of people who are still around to argue back; it's harder still if they're the ones who are evaluating your work professionally. Alice Echols tells a chastening story. Shortly after the publication of *Daring to Be Bad*, she learned that a Bay Area feminist study group was reading her book. At one meeting, says Echols, "a prominent women's historian said I'd written an inaccurate history." According to this critic, Echols had overplayed the women's movement's fractiousness. Other veteran activists in the study group disagreed—their memories pretty much squared with Echols's account from the archives—and eventually the dissenter came around and admitted that Echols's history was accurate. "But she said that even if the book were true, I shouldn't have written it."

Peter Braunstein, a graduate student at NYU who's writing a history of the counterculture as his dissertation, calls this phenomenon "possessive memory" and has delivered a theoretical paper on the subject at several sixties conferences. Participating in a sweeping social movement, he reasons, creates a sense of self-regeneration so powerful that it can become a constitutive part of the activist's later identity. Possessive memory, he writes, "leaves the person and his memories in a lover's embrace: the person is in possession of his memories, and no one else can touch them; at the same time, his memories are in possession of him."

Pity the poor young historian who tries to pry them loose. "You interview people who defined themselves by their orientation to the drug culture," Braunstein observes, "and you take out a copy of *The East Village Other* and say, 'Here you say that LSD is the solution to all the world's problems. What was going through your head back then?' They'll say that drugs were merely fourteenth on the list of motivating factors for the counterculture." Braunstein marvels at this kind of revisionism. Then again, perhaps it's not surprising that historians of psychedelia encounter a memory lapse or two along the way.

Whatever difficulties are posed by studying the counterculture, the subject looms larger in current scholarship than it once did. And much of the new work is dedicated to demystification. Never mind the glamour of Hendrix or Joplin. From the perspective of the Woodstock II generation, the sixties counterculture doesn't look that radical at all. Tom Frank, editor of the cultural criticism journal *The Baffler* and a University of Chicago Ph.D., makes the now-familiar point that the sixties rebel mystique was better suited to retailing than to revolution. In a forthcoming book on sixties advertising, he writes: "When business leaders cast their gaze onto the youth culture bubbling around them, they saw both a reflection of their own struggle against the stifling bureaucratic methods of the past and an affirmation of a new dynamic consumerism that must replace the old."

David Farber, for his part, seconds Frank's argument. He likes to explain sixties libertinism by quoting Ernest Dichter, a prominent corporate consultant in the 1950s. "One of the basic problems of prosperity," Dichter wrote, "is to demonstrate that the hedonistic approach to life is a moral and not an immoral one." This was the story corporate America was telling on the eve of the 1960s, says Farber, and it shouldn't be surprising that impressionable young Americans took businessmen at their word, with consequences Wall Street could neither have anticipated nor have countenanced.

ONE MIGHT ASK, THEN: Is a 1960s bell-bottom merely a 1950s tail fin rendered in cloth? It's a question that's bound to rankle sixties veterans, of both the reconstructed and the unreconstructed variety. After all, was there ever a society more self-conscious about its own historical identity, its role as an *agent* of history, than America in the 1960s? In January 1960, Arthur Schlesinger Jr. wrote in *Esquire* that "from the vantage point of the Sixties, the Fifties . . . will seem simply a listless interlude, quickly forgotten, in which the American people collected itself for greater exertions and higher splendors in the future." At the decade's close, a Berkeley DJ used to sign off his newscast in the same spirit: "If you don't like the news, make some of your own."

At their boldest, the sixties revisionists say farewell to this brand of sixties exceptionalism. They argue that, *pace* Schlesinger and that Berkeley DJ, the sixties may not have been all that special in the first place; that "the sixties" can't survive distanced scholarly treatment of the sixties. SDS, for all its searing drama, was not something new in the world—just another religiously inflected reform movement like the teetotalers. Liberalism began its decline not in the 1960s but in the 1940s. The counterculture was not a blot on the American creed but its apotheosis.

And, some add, only those who weren't part of the action have the perspective to see it all so clearly. "I teach a course on the sixties now," says Thomas Sugrue. "But in fifty years there won't be courses on the history of America in the sixties. When I look at the land of *Leave It to Beaver* and then look at the sixties, I see a bunch of commonalities. The sixties memoir writers and historians see radical discontinuities. And that's because we're of different generations."

Different generations, perhaps; but ask Todd Gitlin, and he'll tell you that the more things change, the more they stay the same. Those who would normalize the sixties may declare themselves impervious to the decade's blandishments. But this, says Gitlin, "sounds to me like an example of a parricidal impulse."

"It's reminiscent," he hastens to add, in the most piquant possible rebuttal to the sixties revisionists' pretensions, "of one of the least attractive features of sixties thinking."

—May 1996

GENOVESE'S MARCH
The Radical Reconstructions of a Southern Historian
JAMES SUROWIECKI

EUGENE GENOVESE didn't want to be an intellectual. In fact, he didn't even want to go to college. At the age of seventeen, the future historian and academic controversialist was a member of the Communist Party in Brooklyn and training to be a trade-union organizer. He wasn't looking to be anything else. "I really wanted to be an organizer. And believe it or not, I was very good at it," he says. "In fact, I was such a whizbang as an organizer that they made an exception for me and let me join the Party before I was eighteen."

All Genovese wanted was to organize, but his father insisted on college, and the Party agreed. "My Party comrades said a college education would be a useful tool," he recalls. "So I went, but I knew I was going out there to be a Party organizer, a union organizer. I was a working-class kid, and I was rather anti-intellectual. As far as I was concerned, intellectuals were people who talked a lot, and when they went in to do a job they screwed up."

Whatever the Party might have wanted, Genovese did go on to become an intellectual, albeit a persistently unconventional one whose work has made him among the most esteemed figures in his profession, and among the most unpopular. His first book, *The Political Economy of Slavery* (1965), startled liberal historians of the American "consensus" by insisting that the antebellum South had little in common, culturally or economically, with the market-driven North. And

his second, *The World the Slaveholders Made* (1969), offered a provocatively sympathetic account of George Fitzhugh, the Old South's leading pro-slavery apologist, while investigating the relationship between
the South's economic system and its dominant cultural values. With
these works, Genovese almost single-handedly made Marxist history
respectable, to the point that C. Vann Woodward would write in
1971, "The arrival of Eugene Genovese on the American academic
scene marks a significant change." But it was the publication of *Roll,
Jordan, Roll,* in 1974, that brought Genovese the greatest renown.

With sweeping drama and detail, Genovese showed how the plantation system was shaped by the slaves as well as the slaveholders and
depicted a highly complex slave society, which depended on both accommodation and resistance to the master class. In doing so, Genovese laid to rest the notion that slaves had been so brutalized by their
experience that they were unable to develop a culture of their own.

Roll, Jordan, Roll remains among the most widely read works of
American history. But Genovese himself is no longer the central
figure among historians that he once was. His long journey from an
uncompromising Marxism to an equally uncompromising brand of
cultural conservatism has brought him to the periphery of his mostly
left-of-center profession. His recent scholarly writings are unfamiliar
to many historians, and even his earlier work seems in danger of being
eclipsed by his bitter polemics against political correctness and multiculturalism in the pages of *The New Republic*, *The National Review*,
and elsewhere. Genovese, who is now retired from his position at the
University Center in Atlanta, remains a serious historian, and the upcoming publication of *The Mind of the Master Class*, the history of the
slaveholders he and his wife have been working on since the early
1980s, should remind everyone of that. But at the moment, "historian" seems not to be the first word that comes to mind when his
name is mentioned.

"I think that there's a whole generation of scholars who were not
there in the late 1960s and the 1970s who don't even want to look at
Roll, Jordan, Roll because of Genovese's later political positions," says
Robin Kelley of NYU. "I think the book is brilliant, but when I tell

people that *Roll, Jordan, Roll* was for black history what E. P. Thompson's *The Making of the English Working Class* was for working-class history, they look at me like I'm crazy."

And what are the recent political positions that have made Genovese's work so hard to see? One might begin with his most controversial essay of recent years, "The Question," which appeared in *Dissent*'s Summer 1994 issue. The article was a public recantation of Genovese's long-held Marxism and a broad indictment of the left for its willingness to tolerate the crimes of Stalin and Mao and for its refusal "to subject our basic premises to stern review." It was also, and perhaps more significantly, an attack on multiculturalism, feminism, and political correctness, all of which Genovese depicted as dominating "deranged and degraded college campuses."

From there, one might look at Genovese's passionate defense of Dinesh D'Souza's *Illiberal Education*, in which he lamented "the atrocities that ravage our campuses," labeled political correctness "a new McCarthyism, in some ways more effective and vicious than the old," and, most striking, called for the "unleashing [of] counterterrorism against cowardly administrators and their complicit faculty." Then there are his many essays seeking to rehabilitate the importance of Christianity for any serious politics, claiming greatness for any number of Old South intellectuals, defending the doctrine of states' rights, and attacking what he has called the "reigning moral degeneracy and irresponsible individualism that are paraded as 'alternate lifestyles.' " On top of this place the seemingly endless series of stories circulating in the academy about Genovese's alleged temper, his vindictiveness, and his ideological absolutism, and Genovese's marginalization from the academy comes to seem more inevitable than surprising.

Still, the common view of Genovese as an embittered reactionary is hardly a complete or accurate one. His recent essay collection *The Southern Front* contains an elegant and thoughtful defense of the Communist historian Herbert Aptheker and a respectful call for some form of black nationalism. And perhaps most important, Genovese's abandonment of socialism has not made him a partisan of the free market: "I . . . am no more enamored of capitalism than I ever was," he wrote in 1994, in calling for "one or another form of social corporatism." Genovese's story is not, then, the story of how a committed socialist evolved into a *Wall Street Journal*–style pundit. It's the story of how a contentious and restless intellectual moved from the milieu of the Communist Party to the milieu of southern conservatism while remaining very much the same man.

EVEN TODAY, Genovese uses the word "bourgeois" as an epithet. Born in 1930, he grew up in the working-class neighborhood of Bensonhurst in Brooklyn. His father, Dominick, and his mother, Lena, were both the children of immigrants from Sicily. Eugene and his brother, Bob, were the only Italian kids on their block who didn't speak Italian, though. Their father refused to teach them.

Dominick Genovese worshipped FDR, and though he was not a radical, he was, in Eugene's words, "proud of being a working man, and he hated the bosses." His son shared those feelings. "Look, I grew up in a house that was very class-conscious," he says. "And as an eight-year-old kid, I hated the bosses with a passion that only an eight-year-old kid can feel, and it took many years to overcome it." That Genovese and I are sitting in the comfortable living room of his elegantly furnished Atlanta home as he tells me this seems at once incongruous and appropriate. After all, membership in the working class has never been something American parents have sought to pass on to their children.

Given Genovese's background, the Communist Party had little trouble convincing him to join. He left the Church, started going to nightly meetings of the Communist front organization American Youth for Democracy, and spent the summers running floating picket lines in Manhattan's fur district for Party unions. "We had to send in flying squads to keep the places closed," he says. "I was just a kid, but I was told, 'Nothing goes in and nothing goes out. We don't want to hear any excuses, and if you wind up in jail, we know nothing about it.' " The clarity of that approach must have appealed to Genovese.

No complaining was allowed. Everyone was expected to do the tasks they had accepted responsibility for. No one held your hand. Party organizing was the same way.

So, too, was college. Genovese entered Brooklyn College in 1948, and he still speaks of his time there with reverence. "Brooklyn College was mainly working- and lower-middle-class kids, and, boy, it was good," he says. "Most of the students were hard-driving, and it was full of professors who were slave drivers. They were magnificent. They were there to shake you up. They were there to create the most hostile environment possible, and anyone who whined about it would have been thrown out."

Initially Genovese spent as much time politicking as he did studying. In 1948, as the Cold War began to alter the fabric of American life, he was an open member of the Communist Party, serving on the College Council as the Party's official spokesman. In 1950, though, his political career fell apart precipitously when he was expelled from the Party. Genovese had violated Party discipline, and in retaliation charges of "anti-Semitism" and "white chauvinism" were hurled against him. Julius Jacobson, a classmate of Genovese's who remembers him as "the leading intellectual Stalinist on campus," says that "the whole thing was the usual Stalinist frame-up." He adds: "God knows what was behind it."

Genovese, for his part, remains understanding of the Party's decision. "I zigged when I should have zagged," he says. "The Party was taking an ultraleft line, and I knew it was suicidal. But look, I was a very neurotic kid, and I behaved in a very undisciplined, even childish way. I wouldn't have respected them if they hadn't booted me." At age twenty, Genovese saw that his career as an organizer was over. His friends and comrades stopped talking to him. "It was traumatic," he says. "I was a dedicated young Communist, and this was like being excommunicated from the Catholic Church."

The excommunication, though, freed him to become an academic. By his senior year, the former anti-intellectual had decided to become a historian. The distinguished economic historian Hans Rosenberg, who despised Marxism but nonetheless respected Genovese's commitment to it, convinced Genovese that the Southern slaveholders represented a perfect case study of "how a ruling class really rules" and that the South therefore was the ideal place to figure out if a Marxist analysis could really explain what it was meant to explain.

In the early 1950s, Genovese served briefly in the U.S. Army, where he passed much of the time teaching himself Italian by reading Gramsci. When the army purged itself of political undesirables following the Army-McCarthy hearings, Genovese was hastily given a general discharge (which was later upgraded to an honorable one). In 1955, he entered Columbia on the GI Bill, where he worked with the historian Frank Tannenbaum, whose book *Slave and Citizen* was already an acknowledged classic. Astonishingly, Genovese turned in a manuscript of more than six hundred pages for his dissertation on the Southern master class and saw it rejected, and then went back and wrote a substantially different one. "The story was that there were two faculty members on the committee who said they would not sign any Marxist dissertations," Genovese says. "But David Donald and Richard Morris also said that I was trying to run before I could walk. Modesty was not one of my strong points." Eventually the reactionaries were removed from the committee, and the second version of his dissertation was accepted. Because of his onetime Party membership, Genovese never expected to get an academic job. But in 1958, Brooklyn Polytechnic Institute offered him a position. And five years later, he moved on to Rutgers. When he arrived there, Genovese went out of his way to make sure that the school understood the nature of his politics. Years later his department chair assured him, "I'm not interested in your religion."

THE MID- AND LATE 1960S were as turbulent for Genovese as they were for the nation. He would publish two major books, feud publicly with the New Left, support the antiwar movement, get married and divorced several times, and do all this while undergoing psychoanalysis. There were also the death threats.

In 1965, before the U.S. Marines had landed at Da Nang, Genovese spoke at a Rutgers teach-in on Vietnam and said: "I do not fear or reject the impending Vietcong victory in Vietnam. I welcome it." For the John Birch Society and assorted other right-wing groups, this was tantamount to treason; and soon enough the threats poured in. Before long, Genovese had also become a major issue in the 1965 New Jersey gubernatorial campaign. The Democratic incumbent, Richard Hughes, took the position that Genovese's statements fell under the rubric of academic freedom. His Republican opponent called for Genovese's immediate removal and brought in Richard Nixon to lead the charge. Nixon traveled around the state attacking Genovese. Hughes won. Genovese stayed.

DESPITE THE CONSIDERABLE UPHEAVAL about him, Genovese's scholarly work steadily accumulated. *The Political Economy of Slavery*, published in 1965, challenged prevailing views of the Civil War as either the product of irrepressible moral conflict or a pointless shedding of blood that could have been prevented by more adept statesmanship. Instead, Genovese insisted that the South was bound to collide with the North, since slave owning "imparted to Southern life a special social, economic, political, ideological, and psychological content."

Using hordes of comparative data, Genovese showed that slaveholders were more concerned with the maintenance of slavery than with increased efficiency and productivity. Compared with farmers in the North, for example, they produced little milk and raised rather lean hogs. And they often ignored simple innovations in soil fertilization and crop rotation that would have increased their profits. Most of all, Genovese argued the slaveholders were not "merely ordinary capitalists who happened to have money in slaves": they had a distinctive set of values, and they believed in them deeply. While some critics took Genovese to task for underplaying the importance of race—a criticism that would be echoed throughout his career—the historian David Potter called the book "one of the landmarks of Southern historiography . . . one of those books that rearrange basic concepts," and *The Nation* praised it for "showing Marxism to be a useful tool for historical analysis."

Remarkably, Genovese's Marxism did not prevent him from admiring the Southern planters, who captivated him with their evident seriousness of purpose and their rejection of the cash nexus as the arbiter of life. "Theirs was an aristocratic, antibourgeois spirit with values and mores emphasizing family and status, a strong code of honor, and aspirations to luxury, ease, and accomplishment," he wrote. "The planter typically recoiled at the notion that profit should be the goal of life." To some of his critics, Genovese's admiration for the slaveholders implied that he would have supported them politically. His response at the time is instructive:

> In irreconcilable contradictions, as Comrade Stalin, who remains dear to some of us for the genuine accomplishments that accompanied his crimes, clearly understood, it is precisely the most admirable, manly, principled, and, by their own lights, moral opponents who have to be killed; the others can be frightened or bought.

Elsewhere he added: "If a radical regional revolution and the genuine liberation of black people were to be effected, the slaveholders as a class would have had to be exterminated." Understanding how a ruling class ruled, in other words, and recognizing the degree to which the worldview of that class was internally consistent and subjectively moral were not the same as sanctioning what Genovese called "an objectively immoral system." It was possible to respect the slaveholders and still believe that they needed to be done away with.

WITH THE EXCEPTIONS of Herbert Aptheker and perhaps William Appleman Williams, Genovese was the first serious American historian to consider himself a Marxist. But from the beginning of his intellectual career, Genovese was resolutely opposed to the dogma of economic determinism. In the preface to *The World the Slaveholders Made*, he insisted on "the necessity to recognize that ideas, once called into being and rooted in important social groups, have a life of their own." In other words, culture was not reducible to class. More important, this implied that a struggle over ideas and over culture was essential to any attempt to transform society.

Genovese's emphasis on culture was especially evident in his acceptance of a black nationalist interpretation of black identity. "American blacks constitute not so much a class as a nation," Genovese told a Boston-area gathering of Students for a Democratic Society in 1968. On another occasion, he praised black jazzmen for "demonstrating that black jazz and white jazz are not, and could not be, quite the same." And he argued that black people had to "play the main role in the formation of [their] own intelligentsia and national culture" (though he also insisted that the idea that only blacks could teach black history was an "ideologically fascist position").

In light of Genovese's contemporary attacks on what he terms "the Left's program for the Balkanization of the American nation," his endorsement of a black nationalist politics may seem surprising, but, in fact, his position has been remarkably consistent over time. Genovese has always believed that the situation of black Americans is unique, both culturally and politically; what is true of them is not true of any other racial or ethnic group. As he put it in a recent piece in *The New Republic*, "[A] case can justly be made for a measure of black autonomy that cannot be made with the same justice for any other group in America."

In making that case, of course, Genovese departed considerably from the tenets of traditional Marxism. To assume that black assembly-line workers and black members of the upper middle class share a common culture is to assume that race can be more important than class in structuring one's experience of the world. And to endorse the goals of black nationalism is to assume that one's racial identity should continue to be more important, both culturally and politically, than one's class position.

Genovese himself would have rejected the idea that black nationalism was necessarily opposed to a class-based politics. But if nothing else, his early embrace of black nationalism shows that for him tradition and custom always bear down with a heavy weight upon the living. A people's beliefs are shaped as much by the past—by the traditions of family, community, and church—as by the present. And as a result, social change cannot occur without great resistance. Like his love of order and clarity, Genovese's belief in the endurance of culture is a key to understanding the person he has become.

EVEN WHILE HE WAS BURROWING HIMSELF into the archives for *Roll, Jordan, Roll*, Genovese was also deeply enmeshed in the antiwar movement and in his struggles with the New Left. Though he respected the movement's recognition that culture mattered, for the most part he was scornful of sixties-era radicalism. "What I always hated about the New Left was its lack of political seriousness," he says. To Genovese, the New Left was more interested in personal liberation than in the disciplined effort required to achieve revolutionary, and sustainable, social change. The movement's faith in participatory democracy challenged everything he believed about the importance of, and need for, authority and hierarchy. Its view of history and of the future he thought naive.

Then, of course, there was Staughton Lynd.

Lynd was an assistant professor of American history at Yale, an early activist in the civil-rights and antiwar movements, and the author of numerous essays on American radicalism. Lynd's politics were in the best tradition of homegrown American egalitarianism, inflected by a Quaker faith. "When I first met him, I thought the world of him, and I believed, as a lot of people did, that he was going to be the future," Genovese says. "But if you decide someone's going to be the messiah and he disappoints you, it's not his fault. In time, I hated everything he stood for as I came to know it. He was really one of the most appallingly self-righteous people I have ever met in my life."

Genovese and Lynd clashed over tactics, over theory, over morality, and over scholarship, most notably when Genovese published an absolutely scathing piece on Lynd in *The New York Review of Books*, in September 1968. Genovese called Lynd's book *The Intellectual Ori-*

gins of American Radicalism "a travesty of history" and wrote that Lynd's politics led him "to do violence to almost every historical question he touches." Why the anger? Lynd's attempt to discover the ancestors for what he called "the existential radicalism of today," and his open admission that his real concerns were "ahistorical," were tailor-made to incite Genovese's wrath. So was Lynd's claim that slavery was wrong in all times and places; in Genovese's view, this sort of thinking ignored the necessary role that slavery played in the historical development of capitalism. In a later exchange in the *NYRB*'s letters pages, Genovese expressed "a deep abhorrence" for Lynd's politics and, stunningly, said that Lynd's attempt to apply an "absolute morality" to political questions ended up serving as "an incitement to totalitarian violence." Given Lynd's explicit commitment to pacifism, this was a remarkable contention.

The substantive differences between Lynd's and Genovese's politics were certainly real. At the same time, the problem seems to have been as much stylistic—cultural, if you will—as anything else. Genovese suggests as much. "Lynd was a bourgeois academic, a WASP," he says. "Maybe it's just the difference between a WASP and a Sicilian." What that seems to have meant in practice is that Lynd's more reticent and circumlocutory style struck Genovese as condescending and insulting. Genovese's in-your-face approach must have hit Lynd similarly hard. Today Lynd says of the *New York Review of Books* piece, "It really stuck under my skin. This struck me as the kind of thing Marx wrote when he really wanted to wipe someone off the map."

In December 1969, Genovese and Lynd clashed again, this time at the American Historical Association's annual convention. In what Genovese labels "a cheap factional ploy," Lynd had been put forward as a candidate for president of the association on a platform that would have committed the AHA to coming out against the war in Vietnam. Genovese was unremittingly opposed to the war, and had been since it began. But he led the successful effort to reject both the platform and Lynd on the grounds that professional organizations should not have ideological criteria for membership. In what might be seen as a moment rich with foreshadowing, Genovese, at that time the most important radical historian in America, gave a rousing speech to a divided hall. The heated cries of support that filled the room came from people with whom Genovese had nothing in common politically. But he remained convinced that the need to keep the profession free from ideological criteria for membership outweighed other concerns. As he says now, "I go to conventions to meet people I disagree with."

IN 1968 AND 1969, Lynd and the AHA were hardly the only important matters Genovese had to think about. He was dating Elizabeth Fox, a graduate student at Harvard whom he later married. And he was also in the midst of a two-year appointment at Sir George Williams University in Montreal, where he was once again threatened with death. This time, however, the threats apparently came from the left, not the right.

In the winter of 1969, the campus left at Sir George Williams rose up and called for the removal of a professor who had been accused of racism. Along the way, students burned the school's computer center and created general campus havoc. A group of professors on the left, including Genovese, refused to support what he would later call "reactionary nihilism masquerading as revolutionary action." As a result, they were labeled traitors to the cause. "It's an interesting experience to walk around campus and see signs with your picture on them labeled, ENEMY OF THE PEOPLE: WANTED DEAD OR ALIVE," says Genovese. "But not for a night, not one night, did I lose sleep because of it."

Eventually it was revealed that the leader of the student activists belonged to the campus conservative party and was not, as he had claimed to be, a Maoist. Genovese and his colleagues emerged unscathed. They were also confirmed in their attitudes toward student radicalism. "I didn't think anything was going to happen," he says. "People who are advertising that they are going to kill you aren't dangerous. It's the people sitting alone in their rooms brooding that you worry about."

The summer after the Sir George Williams crisis, Genovese and Elizabeth Fox were married, and that fall they moved to the University of Rochester, where Genovese had been appointed chairman of the history department. He would remain there for more than a decade. It was in his first years at Rochester that Genovese completed *Roll, Jordan, Roll*, which was published in 1974.

SYNTHESIZING HARD FACTS about life in the slave quarters, in the fields, and in the churches with a provocative interpretation of the planters' means of control, *Roll, Jordan, Roll* was social history on a grand scale. Perhaps the book's most important feat was its refutation of an argument the historian Stanley Elkins had advanced in his 1959 book, *Slavery*. According to Elkins, the slaves had been crushed by slavery just as concentration camp inmates had been crushed by their ordeal; thus the demeaning figure of Sambo was not a racist stereotype but an accurate depiction of what slavery had done to black Americans. After *Roll, Jordan Roll*, Elkins's position was impossible to take seriously.

More positively, Genovese showed how slaves transformed the custom of receiving pay for work on Sundays into something approaching a right and how those slaves who received surnames did so only at their own insistence. Surprisingly often, he argued, slaves refused to be whipped and got away with it. The underlying point, for Genovese, was that slave society was fundamentally a "paternalist" one, in which slaves and slaveholders accepted that they had specific rights and specific duties toward each other.

While Genovese recognized the importance of coercion, he insisted that, by itself, coercion could not explain why black slaves defended a white woman from a drunken Union soldier on the streets of Charleston, South Carolina, or why a young master wrote an eight-page letter describing his sorrow at the death of his servant. In *Roll, Jordan, Roll*, Genovese tried to take slaves and slaveholders at their word when they described their experiences. His argument was not that the slaves had reconciled themselves to their oppression but that they had recognized the need to construct a real life within it. For Genovese, nothing was more important in this regard than slave religion. The church served as a source of cultural unity and consolation for the slaves, even if it was devoid of any revolutionary spirit. Genovese's emphasis on slave religion led C. Vann Woodward to describe the book as "preeminently the religious history of a people."

Upon its publication, *Roll, Jordan, Roll* was widely praised by the historical establishment; it was acclaimed by Woodward in *The New York Review of Books*, David Brion Davis in *The New York Times*, and David Donald in *Commentary*. Yet Genovese's reliance on the idea of paternalism—which he derived from Gramsci's notion of hegemony—to explain the successful functioning of a slave society struck some of his critics as tendentious. Was the slaves' consent, however tentative, necessary to keep the system afloat? Were coercion and the impossibility of successful revolt not enough to keep the slaves in line? These were hard questions to answer. And Genovese made things more difficult for himself by saving an extended discussion of slave rebellions for a later book, a decision that made him appear to be short-changing the importance of slave resistance and of slaveholder violence.

NYU's Robin Kelley, though, thinks the attacks on the book are misplaced. "I think a lot of people misread the book," he says. "Force is a central theme throughout. I don't think Genovese is arguing that it was cultural hegemony as opposed to force, but that force backs up the kind of cultural and social consent that's required not only for a plantation to run but for it to become a family. The book shows how much African people's resistance really shaped the system of consent and really defined the whole plantation culture."

Resistance, in the form of day-to-day struggles, is there in *Roll, Jordan, Roll,* but Genovese was always more skeptical of the political value of everyday forms of resistance than his New Left colleagues (and their cultural studies descendants). Collectively organized violence, directed toward a concrete goal, could be progressive. Random and unorganized violence, whether against people or things, was indistinguishable from what Genovese termed "antisocial and nihilistic action."

THE COLLAPSE of the revolutionary hopes of the 1960s forced many radicals to reconsider their politics. For Genovese, however, the future still belonged to the left. In 1978, he and the historian Warren Susman co-founded the journal *Marxist Perspectives*. Whereas in the 1960s Genovese had seen Marxist academics as almost universally unsophisticated in their work, he and Susman now proclaimed in their editorial statement that "Marxism as an intellectual force has come of age in the United States." Somewhat surprising, at least to anyone who knew Genovese, the statement held that *MP* would not be a place "for political partisanship and factional polemics." The ambition that had always characterized Genovese's work was not absent, though. The statement described Marxism's task as "putting the world back together" and added, "We regard this struggle to reintegrate the world as an inescapable moral duty."

While that struggle may have failed, the journal did succeed in publishing some of the most interesting and sophisticated left-wing thinkers around, including Eric Foner, E. Ann Kaplan, Etienne Balibar, Alexander Saxton, and Michael Taussig. *MP*'s subject matter ranged widely, and, interestingly enough, the journal defined as "a principal concern" "the historic struggle for women's rights and the shaky response of the Left to it." Nearly each issue featured an article by a non-Marxist, sometimes conservative, writer, under the heading "From the Other Shore," and these pieces often presented intriguing reconsiderations of the Western philosophical tradition from the right.

Marxist Perspectives came to an abrupt end in 1980, after Genovese came down with what at the time appeared to be a serious heart condition. The journal's demise owed just as much, however, to the diminishing prospects for radical political change. In the late 1970s, Genovese and *Marxist Perspectives* had staked a great deal of hope on the success of Eurocommunism, the reform movement that had brought Communist parties in Italy, France, and elsewhere around to the view that parliamentary democracy was their best route to power. When the promise of electoral victory in Europe failed, the journal seemed increasingly irrelevant. "We always knew that in the long run, we didn't want to publish just another journal," he says now. "We wanted it to have a real impact. Once the Eurocommunist movement unraveled, and we looked at the situation at home, it didn't seem like there was any point in continuing."

Once again, however, Genovese did not lose faith in Marxism. In 1983, he and Elizabeth Fox-Genovese published *Fruits of Merchant Capital*, a volume of essays that the historian Peter Kolchin termed "more self-consciously Marxist than any other major work by recent American historians." And all through the Reagan years, Genovese believed that the Soviet Union might revive itself. Even today he says, "The real test would have come if Andropov had lived. He would have been a great leader."

Still, the collapse of *Marxist Perspectives* did usher in a new phase of Genovese's life. In the 1980s, Fox-Genovese became a national figure for her research on antebellum Southern women and for her stinging critiques of contemporary feminism and its "bourgeois individualism." In 1986, she began teaching at Emory University in Atlanta. Genovese followed four years later, taking up a position as Distinguished Scholar-in-Residence at Atlanta's University Center. For some time, Genovese had immersed himself in the traditions of southern conservatism and had been friendly with a number of southern intellectuals, including John Shelton Reed and M. E. Bradford. But it was only with his move to Georgia that the Brooklyn-born historian became an actual southerner.

AND A CATHOLIC. Today, at the age of sixty-six, after fifty years of atheism, Genovese is going to church again. His wife converted to Catholicism in 1995, and Genovese began accompanying her to Mass soon after. "I'm a proper, traditional husband, so I went," he says.

"And what surprised me was how comfortable I felt. How at home, I mean." He is reticent about the details of what has to be called, strangely enough, a conversion. But he does say that he finds atheism intellectually unconvincing, of all things.

Oddly enough, Genovese's conversion might give some comfort to his critics. Back in 1994, Mitchell Cohen wrote in *Dissent* that Genovese "seems to be en route from one belief system to another when a little agnosticism might be in order." At the time, Genovese took Cohen to task for this conclusion. "When I write on religion I always carefully identify myself as an atheist," he pointed out. "I wish [Cohen] would identify that other belief system."

In retrospect, it is apparent that Cohen saw Genovese more clearly than Genovese saw himself. It also seems clear that what Cohen was seeking from Genovese was precisely what he was not going to find— namely, an acceptance of uncertainty and the possibility of a pragmatic approach to existence. "I was never agnostic," Genovese says. "I was an atheist. And I was never agnostic in my politics, either."

"NEVER AGNOSTIC." To many of his critics, Genovese's career is largely a case study in the misadventures of an intolerant absolutist. And given the fierce rhetoric that he has hurled from both sides of the political spectrum, it's easy enough to see why. But in many respects, Genovese's conviction that there is an ultimate truth has made him more, and not less, tolerant of those he has disagreed with. After all, if the truth is an absolute, if it exists out *there*, then someone who attacks your politics is not attacking you personally so much as he or she is attacking the truth itself. Genovese's faith in an objective truth, then, has often led him to take his opponents seriously. Indeed, the more uncompromising their attacks—the more serious their own convictions—the better. Of the slaveholders he says: "I was immediately struck by how serious they were. I was also taken by their critique of capitalism. I realized they were serious people. They were not cream puffs." As for Mussolini, he "was a Marxist and he was a good one. He was not some college boy." Even Goebbels, he says, was "a remarkable man. I have a very deep grudging admiration for that son of a bitch. The Nazis took themselves seriously as socialists. They wanted a politically controlled and directed economy, and they were dead serious about it."

Genovese today speaks in similar terms of his old foes on the left, such as the Weathermen revolutionaries of the 1960s and the anti-Stalinist Shachtmanite socialists with whom he once clashed at Brooklyn College. Of the Shachtmanites he says, "They were very active and very tough. Boy, they were tough guys. I respected them. I thought they were crazy, but I respected them." We're sitting in upholstered recliners in his book-lined den when I ask him if he had been ready to kill the people he respected if the revolution had required it. He answers without hesitation: "Of course. We all understood that. It wasn't personal."

The firm distinction Genovese draws between the personal and the political may make little sense to those, such as Staughton Lynd, who have been on the receiving end of his often brutal attacks. But it's impossible to understand the trajectory of his life, and in particular the trajectory of his relationship to the academy, without understanding how important that distinction is to him. And it's impossible to grasp his vehement hostility to today's academic left without understanding how he believes its members have eroded that distinction in their behavior—to the point where, for Genovese as much as his opponents, the personal is now political and the political is personal. Oddly enough, he believes it's a mistake that previous generations of even the most ultrasectarian leftists did not make.

Much of Genovese's disdain for the academic left stems from his own experience with professional politics in the academy. It's an experience that includes his old clashes with the New Left; his tenure as president of the Organization of American Historians in 1978–1979, when, by his account, he was "denounced by the radical feminists"; and, perhaps most of all, the hostility that his wife has faced within the academy for half a decade now. In this regard, it seems telling that while discussing the death threats he's faced over the years doesn't make him particularly angry, discussing the recently settled harassment suit against his wife at Emory raises his temper. "The only personal attacks on me and my wife come from the radical left, which is why I hate those bastards," he says. "The John Birch Society never attacked me personally, but here we have a whole political movement [making personal attacks] as a matter of course, as a matter of policy, and systematically."

FOR GENOVESE, this state of affairs is a far cry from what he believes the university should be. In perhaps his most influential essay, "On Being a Socialist and a Historian" (1971), he offered a resounding defense of academic work against the charges of irrelevance and bourgeois luxury that were being levied against it by many on the left. He argued both that scholarship had political value and that socialists had to "insist upon the depoliticization of the universities and the professional organizations" and "make the cause of intellectual freedom and diversity their own."

Genovese's point was not that scholarship itself should be apolitical, and his own work was proof of that. Rather, his point was that what had to be preserved was the idea of the university as a place where people could pursue truth without fear of losing their jobs or their lives because of their work. The classroom, he has suggested, should be "an ideological war zone," where students can learn to "sustain [them]selves in combat." But in hiring and promoting scholars no ideological criteria should be applied. In many ways, Genovese's scorn for the academy stems from his belief that such criteria have become more and more common in recent years.

THE MOST REVEALING, and startling, picture Genovese has offered of what the ideal university should be is his 1991 essay on Hans Rosenberg, his economic history professor at Brooklyn College. (The piece is included in *The Southern Front*.) Rosenberg was a conservative who had a special hatred for Communists. And Genovese was still a member of the Party when he attended Rosenberg's class on the formation of the modern state with a number of fellow Communists and with a group of Shachtmanite socialists, as well as with students of a less ideological bent. The class sounds like everything one would want a college history class to be: demanding, instructive, ideologically contentious. "Taking a course with Rosenberg was a privilege," Genovese tells me. "Boy, he was tough. But you always knew he respected his students. He knew we were well prepared."

Rosenberg, Genovese writes, delighted in "denigrating Marx's scholarship." Though the professor based his assertions on evidence, he did not pretend to be apolitical: "He was as hard in his politics and ideology as we were." In fact, Genovese recalls that Rosenberg was so hard that sometimes he fudged a point rather than give in. "We knew if push came to shove he wasn't going to surrender anything to his Marxist opponents." So, after each class, one or two Party members were given the task of checking out each of Rosenberg's assertions, and much of the following class would be taken up with their challenges to what he had said. (Genovese speaks with pride of the time he faced the same situation with a group of black students who checked on each of his assertions in a course he taught at Yale.) At one point, Rosenberg refused to give Genovese a top grade for an exam that Rosenberg himself called "first-rate."

A more politicized classroom, it seems, could hardly exist. (One can only imagine how strange the whole experience must have been to the students who were neither Stalinists nor Shachtmanites.) And yet Genovese speaks of that class not merely with affection but with what has to be called love. None of it—not the dismissal of Marx as "crazy," not the willingness to play with facts to win an ideological point, not the unjustly low grade—troubles him. This is, in fact, what he wants the university to be like. Why? To be sure, part of Genovese's affection for the class must stem from the fact that it was Rosenberg who led him to the Old South as a worthy subject of research. But what he really seems to have liked about Rosenberg was that he was serious, that he was a "slave driver," that he "challenge[d] our every prejudice, feeling, and cherished ideal" without regard for any sensibilities he might be offending. It was a classroom defined by authority, deference, and mutual respect.

It seems safe to say, then, that much of what Genovese despises about today's academy has to do with his belief that standards have been relaxed and that professors are more worried about their students' feelings than about their intellects. And his dismissive attitude toward the academic preparation most students receive in high school—an attitude many professors share—only increases his scorn for the "radical left," which somehow finds itself held responsible for this state of affairs.

Finally, though, there may be something else going on here. In his numerous attacks on multiculturalism and political correctness, Genovese has accused the left, often justly, of placing ideology over scholarship in its rejection of conservative historians. But Genovese's own attacks on certain variants of black studies, feminism, and cultural theory, attacks that frequently take the form of a defense of "professional standards" and scholarly excellence, too often seem to depend more on his own political hostility to the goals of academics in these fields than on any real evidence of scholarly shortcomings. And the fact that much of cultural studies has set itself to questioning the very values Genovese holds most dearly—authority, toughness, and work—only serves to alienate him further.

"On Being a Socialist and a Historian" was predicated on the idea that even scholarship whose premises one disagreed with had to be taken seriously. But when Genovese offers a wholesale indictment of our campuses as "deranged," it becomes difficult to take his embrace of the disinterested consideration of interested work at face value. And a sentence such as "Those who demand that we hear the women's voices of the past, it seems, mean only the voices of women who would be members of NOW and NARAL in the present" might be more tolerable if he gave some indication of familiarity with the best and most sophisticated of the "radical feminist nonsense" he so despises. It's striking. Genovese's whole career has been built on the serious consideration of his ideological opponents, from the slaveholders to the consensus historians to Herbert Aptheker to southern conservatives. Everyone but today's academic left.

Had the narrative of his life played out differently, Genovese might have been more willing to show those on the so-called cultural left the tolerance that he has always shown to his opponents on the right. Few people, to be sure, have been more clear about the need to engage with those who, as he puts it, "defy our sensibility." In not meeting that challenge, Genovese threatens to give up the fight. And such a surrender would be, in many respects, an ironic conclusion to his career. After all, of Irving Kristol's lament "The culture war is over, and the Left has won it," he has just this to say: "I think that may be the only stupid thing I've ever heard Kristol say. You lose that struggle, you lose everything."

—December 1996

TESTAMENTS BETRAYED
Yugoslavian Intellectuals and the Road to War

LAURA SECOR

MUCH HAS CHANGED since Gerson Sher traveled to Yugoslavia to research his dissertation amid the political and intellectual ferment of the late 1960s. For one thing, the idiosyncratic country that captured his imagination no longer exists. Nor does Praxis, the group of Marxist humanist philosophers Sher studied. But this is not the only reason he responds warily to a request for an interview: "I am appalled," he says, "that you should be interested in Praxis at this time."

Why? After all, according to the Harvard political theorist Seyla Benhabib, "the name Praxis has a distinguished history. It was used by dissidents against Stalinism and identified with the project of democratic socialism." Sher's dissertation, published in 1977 as *Praxis: Marxist Criticism and Dissent in Socialist Yugoslavia*, explored what seemed a promising strain of humanist thought emerging from the University of Zagreb and the University of Belgrade. In the 1960s and 1970s, a glittering roster of Western intellectuals attended the Praxis group's yearly retreats on the Adriatic island of Korčula: Jürgen Habermas, A. J. Ayer, Norman Birnbaum, Lucien Goldmann, and Herbert Marcuse were just a few of those who gathered around the Yugoslav group and served on the editorial board of its eponymous journal. Strange, then, that today the term "Praxis" and the names of some of its leaders are just as often associated with the notoriously antihumanist rhetoric of Serbian nationalism and the murderous politics of Slobodan Milošević.

History, the Praxists urged, "is made neither by objective forces nor dialectical laws; it is made instead by people, who act to transform their world within the limits of historical possibilities." So wrote Sher in 1977. In the precarious decade to follow, the Praxis philosophers would indeed transform their world. But the way they did so was not, at that time, imaginable to academics in the West. Who could have known that one of the Praxis philosophers would later become vice president of Milošević's party—and its chief ideologue during the Bosnian war? Or that another member, once a passionate critic of nationalism, would sign a 1996 petition calling for The Hague to drop war-crimes charges against the brutal Bosnian Serb leader Radovan Karadžić, whom the petition dubbed "the true leader of all Serbs"?

Not all of the Praxists followed their leaders down the dark road of Serbian nationalism. The Croatian members cleaved to their humanist principles through the bloodiest years of the Yugoslav wars. And in Serbia, some of the most courageous and lonely expressions of dissent have come from former Praxists and their students.

The fault lines along which not only Praxis but the Yugoslav nation would later splinter were invisible to the group's foreign admirers back in the 1960s. After all, to progressives abroad, Tito's Yugoslavia stood for something uniquely inspiring: not only was it less authoritarian than the Eastern-bloc countries, but Tito had adopted a uniquely ambitious program of worker self-management that promised to help Yugoslavia realize the most utopian Marxist project any country had yet attempted. To the extent the Praxis group spoke of nationalism, it was to oppose it as an atavistic threat to the universalistic principles of humanism and Marxism. The region's grim history and simmering internal rivalries were the last thing on anyone's mind.

Norman Birnbaum, now a law professor at Georgetown University, explains, "When we went to Yugoslavia at that time, we did think the nationality question had been solved. It was the Titoist truce, or illusion, or parenthesis." The Croatian-born historian Branka Magaš puts it differently. The Western leftists who took up with Praxis as late as the 1980s and early 1990s, she says, "never really saw Yugoslavia. They saw self-management. They only saw the country through the lens of what interested them."

LOOKING BACK ON YUGOSLAVIA during the Tito years, writes Tim Judah in *The Serbs: History, Myth, and the Destruction of Yugoslavia*, one "cannot fail to be struck by just how inconsequential some of the great debates of the past have turned out to be." Indeed, it might seem today that Marxist humanism and self-management were just a couple of blind alleys off the highway to Sarajevo. But when Praxis coalesced around these concerns in the 1960s, they looked for all the world like the yellow brick road to a utopia where democracy would at last nourish socialism. It was time for the Communist bureaucracies that had ossified in Eastern Europe to give way, the Marxist humanists argued, and let a dynamic, participatory socialism flower.

At its inception, the philosophical journal *Praxis* was merely the successor to *Pogledi*, a political journal issued from Croatia's capital, Zagreb, in the 1950s. *Pogledi* was a casualty of state interference: it lasted only three years. Chief among the defunct journal's contributors had been the University of Zagreb sociologist Rudi Supek, who participated in the French Resistance as an émigré during World War II and later led an underground prisoners' organization when he was interned at Buchenwald; and the University of Zagreb philosopher Gajo Petrović, a Serb from Croatia who gravitated toward the early Marx, existentialism, and Heidegger. Birnbaum remembers, "Supek and Petrović were impressive for their moral rigor, their utter disdain of careerism. They were people you loved to be around." From the ashes of *Pogledi*, Supek, Petrović, and their colleagues went on to start their summer school on Korčula in 1963 and a new journal, *Praxis*, in 1964. The group that formed around these ventures consisted of a close-knit circle of friends and colleagues—some from Supek's and Petrović's departments at the University of Zagreb and another eight from the philosophy department at the University of Belgrade.

The philosophers published their new journal in a Serbo-Croat Yugoslav edition and in a multilingual international edition. And its editorial collective adopted an agenda that was more unified than anything *Pogledi* had ever set forth: the Praxis group advocated freedom of speech and of the press, and they believed that Stalinist authoritarianism had to be redressed in practice and rooted out of Marxist theory itself. To this end, they prescribed a return to Marx's romantic early writings, particularly the *Economic and Philosophical Manuscripts* of 1844. Marx's more influential later work would emphasize the iron laws of historical determinism. But the 1844 *Manuscripts* waxed lyrical about the creative potential of human activity, through which man might realize his "species being."

This orientation was hardly a Yugoslav invention. If anything, the Praxists took their cue from neighboring Hungary, where Georg Lukács had amassed a following of like-minded dissidents. Like Lukács, the Praxists were captivated by the early Marx's theory of alienation. In an ordinary capitalist or a Stalinist socialist society, man was alienated from himself by the commodification of his labor and by the overweening power of a small, privileged class and its institutions. A utopian Marxist society, the Praxists imagined, would overcome that alienation; it would unleash human creativity—or "praxis" —by doing away with the ruling class through self-management. The workers would directly control not only their workplaces but also social and cultural institutions—even local political parties and governing bodies. The state, given enough time, would of its own accord "wither away," just as Marx had predicted.

Yugoslavia, despite Tito's bold initiatives, fell far short of this ideal. In Yugoslavia's hybrid economy, the much-touted self-managing enterprises were exposed to market pressures on the one hand and capricious state control on the other. Regional oligarchies took root: in the end, local power brokers manipulated and ignored workers' councils in much the way managers do everywhere. But the Praxists saw these problems as evidence that self-management had not gone far enough. They were at once self-management's most passionate exponents abroad and the Yugoslav system's fiercest internal critics.

That Tito tolerated Praxis at all is remarkable. Virtually no other Communist country, with the possible exception of Hungary, allowed as much vocal dissent as Yugoslavia did in Tito's day. But there were limits to Tito's tolerance. At a philosophy faculty meeting in 1967, Ljubomir Tadić, a Praxis philosopher at the University of Belgrade, instigated a particularly perilous game of chicken with the authorities. In the anti-authoritarian spirit of Praxis, Tadić publicly criticized the constitutional provision that allowed Tito to remain in office for longer than his eight-year mandate. When the renegade professor came under government investigation, the faculty stood united behind him, and he was permitted to keep his job.

With the enthusiastic support of the Belgrade Praxists, student demonstrations convulsed the University of Belgrade in June 1968. The students protested their poor living conditions and demanded an end to authoritarianism, unemployment, and, for good measure, the Vietnam War. Local Serbian authorities urged Tito to send military troops onto the Belgrade campus. After all, it was that same summer that Soviet tanks would put an end to popular protests in Prague. But unlike his ham-fisted counterparts in Moscow, Tito deployed a feline cunning to dispense with his foes. In a televised appeal, he proclaimed himself deeply sympathetic to the activists' concerns. In fact, he said, it was only Yugoslavia's bureaucracy that stood in the way of the agenda he and the students shared. If the bureaucrats did not allow him to meet these students' demands, he declared, he would resign. Of course, the demands were not met, and Tito did not resign. In fact, only two weeks after he gave this speech, he urged the University of Belgrade to dismiss its Praxis philosophers on the grounds that they were "corrupting" students. The plight of those philosophers, known as the Belgrade 8, became a matter of international concern.

That summer was particularly memorable at Korčula. Richard Bernstein, now a political philosopher at the New School for Social Research, recalls, "Everybody who was a significant leftist, in the East or in the West, came to the 1968 meeting. All the leaders of the student movements in Germany, Eastern Europe, and the United States were there." But even as the editorial boards of *Praxis* and the *New*

Left Review sunned themselves on the beaches of Korčula, the Belgrade 8 held on to their jobs by a slender thread.

THROUGHOUT THIS PERIOD, the Yugoslav government was undergoing a subtle but significant shift. From the end of World War II until 1966, Tito's main challenge had been to consolidate his unwieldy multinational state. Even within his inner circle, debates raged over whether Yugoslavia's six constituent republics—Bosnia, Croatia, Macedonia, Montenegro, Serbia, and Slovenia—should be granted greater autonomy or tethered more firmly to a central authority. History had taught that in the Balkans one ignored these questions at one's peril: the short-lived first Yugoslavia (1918–1941) opted for a rigid centralism; the state was governed by a Serbian monarchy, and the country's military, culture, and politics were overwhelmingly dominated by Serbs. Throughout those years of oppression, Croatia smoldered with resentments—and during World War II, the latent animosities exploded. Under fascist leadership, Croatia pursued a genocidal campaign against Serbs as well as Jews. The savagery of the killings shocked even German SS officers stationed in the Balkans.

With this history in mind, Tito's regime walked a fine line between a strong central state, which was by and large favored by Serbs, and a loose confederation of republics, which was generally favored by Croats and Slovenes. Centralism prevailed in the early postwar years, but momentum started to build in the other direction in the mid-1960s. A new set of constitutional arrangements slowly took shape, offering greater autonomy to each republic. But this did not appease those who favored a looser confederation. A Croatian nationalist movements was born of the sentiment that the reforms of the late 1960s had not gone far enough. Among the activists' grievances was that Croatia, which was more industrialized and generally wealthier than Serbia, Montenegro, and Macedonia, carried more than its share of Yugoslavia's economic burden. Extremists advocated Croatian secession. Students, intellectuals, and even local Communist authorities gathered around a Croatian cultural society called Matica Hrvatska until Tito disbanded the group, purged its participants from political life, and arrested student leaders.

Watching the growing nationalist militancy of their fellow Croatian academics, the Zagreb Praxists were horrified. And for this very reason, Tito suddenly found these Praxists indispensable: after all, nationalism was a greater threat to the fragile nation than Marxist critique would ever be, and the members of the Zagreb group were outspoken and eloquent against the greater evil. So even while the Belgrade Praxists, who were associated with student unrest, appealed to the international community for protection, their Zagreb counterparts, who were associated with the fight against Croatian nationalism, continued their work in peace.

Against this backdrop, *Praxis* published a special issue on nationalism in 1968. It was the high tide of the journal's resistance to the politics of ethnic identity. In one essay, Ljubomir Tadić, himself a Bosnian Serb, argued that nationalism contradicted the very notion of universal humanity. In place of justice, the nationalist asserts the right of the strong to dominate the weak and the power of violence to resolve conflict. "One quickly forgets," Tadić wrote, "that Serbian and Croatian nationalisms . . . have remained militant, despotic ideologies that lack political and cultural creativity in all their forms." Where social justice and political liberty were in decline, Tadić theorized, nationalism would emerge ascendant. But socialist Yugoslavia had demonstrated "the superiority of proletarian class-consciousness over nationalist consciousness, [and] the advantage of democratic unity over imposed unity or forced disintegration."

Other contributors were equally impassioned. Danko Grlić, a Croat, vividly evoked the irrationality of nationalism. Once unleashed, he warned, it would be impervious to logic: "You do not reason or theorize about the nation; for the nation you only struggle and die; you love the nation as the flesh of your flesh, as the essence of your being, drinking it with your mother's milk; it is body and blood."

THE ALLEGIANCE OF PRAXIS to a united Yugoslavia seemed clear enough. But given the ever present threat of government censorship, there was little that Yugoslav intellectuals published in those years that was completely transparent. The Zagreb philosopher Žarko Puhovski, the youngest Praxist by about twenty years, says that the group's disputes over politics and ideology were often disguised as conversations about less controversial questions of aesthetics or ontology. "One kind of debate functioned as a replacement for other kinds of debate," he recalls.

This was particularly evident when Puhovski himself edited a special issue of *Praxis* in 1973. He received a submission from the well-known Serbian novelist Dobrica Ćosić. It was a short piece that argued that true socialism was not possible in an unenlightened society and that faith in the people—of which Ćosić claimed to have little—was the "last refuge for our historically defeated hopes." Which people and what hopes? The article did not specify. But Puhovski detected a disturbing nationalist message all the same. Nor was he impressed with the article's argument or its rigor: "I had the junior approach of believing that philosophy and sociology were specialized fields," he recounts with a touch of sarcasm. "I didn't think Ćosić's piece was up to the level. It was bad nationalist propaganda." He turned it down.

His elders chided him that he simply did not understand how important a figure Ćosić was. Ćosić was best known as the author of Yugoslavia's most celebrated Partisan war novel, *Far Away Is the Sun* (1950), in which a company of Partisan soldiers affirm their commitment to Yugoslavism and Communism by executing a Serbian nationalist in their midst. But Ćosić's colors had begun to change: in 1968, he had been expelled from the Central Committee for accusing the regime of fostering Albanian separatism in Kosovo. Even so, he would not be widely considered a nationalist writer until the late 1970s and early 1980s, when he published a series of novels that explicitly addressed Serbian history and grievances. At that time, he cut such a distinguished figure in Belgrade that he was frequently called the father of the Serbian nation.

As the 1973 issue of *Praxis* neared press time, Puhovski was on his own: the editorial board split 7 to 1 in Ćosić's favor.

THE APPEARANCE OF NATIONALIST TENSIONS within the Praxis group was a harbinger of tensions that would soon spread across the country. Years later, when war raged in Kosovo, American newspapers would plug 1989, the year Milošević revoked Kosovo's autonomy, as the beginning of the end of Yugoslavia. But many Serbs would say the country's fate was sealed as early as 1974. That was the year a controversial revision of the Yugoslav constitution went into effect, devolving broader powers than ever before to the six republics and granting full autonomy to two provinces within the republic of Serbia: Kosovo and Vojvodina. Since the Serbs were scattered across the republics—more than a million lived in Bosnia and at least 500,000 in Croatia—these constitutional reforms were to feed a growing sense of grievance among the Serbs.

In Belgrade, two strains of protest greeted the 1974 constitution. A student strike seized the university campus in the name of Marxist ideals: where, the students asked, were the pan-Yugoslav interests of the working class reflected in this new constitution? The students feared that the reform, with its emphasis on divisions among the republics, would weaken Yugoslavia's socialist unity by opening a Pandora's box of ethnic grievances and demands. As if to prove the students right, other critics of the constitution, including Dobrica Ćosić, protested that it unfairly disempowered the Serbs.

In subsequent years, Serbian nationalists would bitterly complain that Tito's policy had been "A weak Serbia is a strong Yugoslavia." But why shouldn't it have been? Of the country's six official nations, the Serbs were far and away the most populous, outnumbering the Croats two to one. If multinational Yugoslavia's culture and politics were to be governed by majority rule, the country would not survive: the non-Serb populations had strongly developed national identities and long, distinct histories of their own. Not only that, but they occupied more compact territories than did the Serbs. If they felt overly dominated, they could be tempted to secede. So Tito restrained the potentially overweening influence of the Serbs by dividing Yugoslavia into territorial units and constantly readjusting the internal balance of power.

Today, some critics blame the constitution of 1974 for the growth of nationalist movements in Croatia and Slovenia. More likely, it was a response to the nationalist movements that were already stirring. In any case, the most scathing criticism was leveled by the Serb nationalists: the new constitution rested on a double standard. If Yugoslavia's units of political participation were its ethnic groups, or "constituent nations," then the Serbs in Bosnia and Croatia, who were represented by Muslim and Croatian leadership, respectively, went unrepresented. But if the units were territorial, then why was Serbia the only republic whose territory included autonomous provinces over which it had little control?

The truth was very simple: in multinational Yugoslavia, Tito had deliberately redistributed power from the strong to the weak. And if his belief really was that a strong Yugoslavia required a weak Serbia, perhaps he was not mistaken. Much later, in 1989, when Milošević finally did enforce Serbian control of its provinces, Serbia emerged strong—and Yugoslavia fell to pieces. The terrible irony in all of this is that the geographically dispersed Serbs may have benefited more than anyone from the years of Serbia's weakness. Of all the Yugoslav nations, only the Serbs needed a unified Yugoslavia more than it needed them.

IF 1974 MARKED THE BEGINNING of Yugoslavia's national crisis, it also augured the end of the Praxis group's legal existence. Tito purged the Belgrade 8 from the university the following year. The six-year struggle between the state and the professors had simply exhausted itself. Not only were the Belgrade 8 suspended from teaching, but also the journal *Praxis* was banned. This time, the protests of American academics (including Noam Chomsky, Daniel Bell, and Stanley Hoffman) fell on deaf ears.

For more than a decade, the Belgrade 8—Mihailo Marković, Svetozar Stojanović, Ljubomir Tadić, Zagorka Golubović, Dragoljub Mičunović, Miladin Životić, Nebojša Popov, and Trivo Indjić—wandered the globe, accepting visiting professorships abroad and meeting secretly in Belgrade. Only Indjić accepted the government's offer of a low-profile post at an institute. The others insisted on nothing less than a full return to the University of Belgrade, which was not forthcoming. Marković, the group's best-known member abroad, took a part-time philosophy post at the University of Pennsylvania. Stojanović taught at Berkeley and at the University of Kansas. Meanwhile, in Zagreb, the situation was slightly less dire. "There were pressures," remembers Žarko Puhovski. "I couldn't publish for two years. But it was nothing remotely like the situation in Belgrade."

The rest of the 1970s and the early 1980s were disappointing years for the Belgrade 8. They organized what they called the Free University, which mostly consisted of seminars held in private homes, but they could not advertise these meetings, and they were constantly on guard for police interruption. At least one Free University session convened at the novelist Dobrica Čosić's house. Neither a Marxist nor a philosopher, Čosić was a personal friend and shadowy influence on the Praxis group, although never an actual member. In the 1980s, his ties to Praxis pulled tighter; but to what extent the Praxists already shared his incipient nationalism remains a mystery. Čosić collaborated with Tadić on two projects in the early 1980s: one, a proposed journal that would criticize bureaucracy and champion freedom of expression, was immediately suppressed by the government; the other, a petition against censorship laws, was also swiftly defeated. The government press denounced Čosić and his Praxis friends as "hardened nationalists and open advocates of a multi-party system," but the group continued to convene as a committee to promote freedom of expression.

Meanwhile, Yugoslavia had gone into a deep economic slump: foreign debt had skyrocketed to nineteen billion dollars, unemployment was up to 17.5 percent, inflation topped 120 percent, and the standard of living precipitously declined. The Yugoslav experiment no longer enjoyed the prestige in the West it once had. And Tito's death in 1980 left the rickety multinational structure leaderless and volatile.

In Kosovo, the Albanian majority, which was largely poor, uneducated, and powerless, had grown restive. The Albanians had never had the status of Yugoslavia's other "constituent nations": Tito's regime reasoned that because there was an Albanian homeland outside Yugoslavia, they should be considered a "national minority" instead. The Kosovars countered that fully 40 percent of the world's Albanian population resided in Yugoslavia. Demonstrations swept the province in 1981, demanding first and foremost that Kosovo be granted the status of a republic, including the right to secede. The movement reached a fever pitch: Serbs and Montenegrins claimed that they were attacked and threatened, Orthodox holy sites were allegedly desecrated, and some activists began to call for secession and union with Albania. Yugoslav police squelched the riots, imposing a state of martial law whose severity scandalized Croatian and Slovenian intellectuals. A great many Albanians languished as political prisoners in Kosovo's jails. Meanwhile the province's Serb minority felt increasingly scapegoated and threatened.

WITH PRAXIS DRIVEN UNDERGROUND, the Korčula summer school, needless to say, was long since over. But something new had begun: the Inter-University Center, in the majestic Croatian city of Dubrovnik, was an international institution that sponsored conferences and short courses run by intellectuals from all over the world. Because it was not managed by Yugoslavs, it was relatively free from government interference. Once again, prominent Western leftists crossed the Adriatic. One of the Praxists approached Jürgen Habermas about teaching a course in Dubrovnik as a way of reviving the spirit of Korčula. The revered German philosopher and heir to the Frankfurt School returned to Yugoslavia with Richard Bernstein to co-teach a course in 1979. The Praxis group, however dispirited, reconvened in Dubrovnik, where it encountered a new set of sympathetic leftists from the West. Seyla Benhabib remembers that she went to Dubrovnik in 1979 in order to get to know Bernstein and Habermas. That she also encountered the Praxis group was merely a happy accident. All she knew about the Praxists' activities at that time was that "they had been expelled and gone into the opposition."

It was in Dubrovnik that Habermas, Bernstein, and the German philosopher Albrecht Wellmer hatched a plan to revive the Praxis journal that had so interested them in the 1960s. To provide the disfranchised dissidents with a new, international forum for their work could only do the cause of democratic socialism good, the Western philosophers figured. Together with Marković and Stojanović, they launched *Praxis International* in 1981.

The new journal attempted to pick up where the old one had left off but with a less Yugoslav focus: it included many *Praxis*-style theoretical essays on Marxism, and, as the 1980s wore on, it covered Eastern European countries in transition. Produced mostly in the United States, the journal was far more eclectic than the first *Praxis* had been: contributions in the late 1980s and early 1990s addressed the political thought of Cornel West, the relationship between feminism and socialism, and other topics of general interest to left-leaning intellectuals.

By this time, Mihailo Marković had clearly become the Yugoslav group's leader, and he came to play a crucial role in the revived journal. A fluent English speaker, he was gregarious, cosmopolitan, and urbane. Both his anti-Stalinist and his antifascist credentials were impeccable: he had fought in Tito's Partisan army during World War II and prided himself on extending aid to Yugoslav Jews. In his philosophical work, Marković emphasized Marx's commitment to human dignity, freedom, and self-realization.

Bernstein and Marković became close friends over the course of their joint stewardship of the journal. David Crocker, a philosopher at the University of Maryland and the author of *Praxis and Democratic Socialism: The Critical Social Theory of Marković and Stojanović*, also came to consider Marković a personal friend. Only Andrew Arato, a professor of sociology at the New School, had an instinctive dislike for the elder Serb. Marković reminded him of an apparatchik. "He was clearly an authoritarian personality. I remember once he kept me outside in a snowstorm for forty minutes, trying to convince me that political parties were a bad thing," Arato says with a laugh. "He wouldn't let me in the restaurant—as if by the sheer force of his personality he would persuade me that democracy didn't need to work through parties." Other Belgrade Praxists, he says, were very much in Marković's thrall. "But when they were not together with Mihailo, one could talk to them about everything. They were more flexible and more Western."

Of the Zagreb Praxists, very few of the old-timers were enthusiastic about the Belgrade group's new publishing venture. Zagreb's elder statesmen, Rudi Supek and Gajo Petrović, attended the first meeting. Supek was amenable to the new journal; but Petrović felt strongly that the name *Praxis* should not be used. *Praxis*, Petrović argued, connoted a joint Belgrade-Zagreb publication, whose international component came at the Yugoslavs' invitation. This new journal, however, was to be published in English and dominated by Belgraders and Americans. It was international before it was Yugoslav, and for this reason, he insisted, it should have a new name and a new identity. Perhaps Petrović also sensed that his Belgrade colleagues had changed and that political consensus was a thing of the past. If he did, he did not say so.

Praxis International's American editors were not particularly perturbed that, with the exception of Supek, they had lost the Zagreb contingent. Says Benhabib, "The question of ethnicity was irrelevant. They were all Yugoslavs. To us outsiders, it wasn't even like asking, 'Are you Italian-American or Irish-American?' It was more like asking, 'Are you Bavarian or from Berlin?' "

YUGOSLAVIA'S SIX REPUBLICS and two autonomous provinces were already on a collision course by the mid-1980s, but even the most astute Western observers did not perceive what lay ahead. The most visible sign of trouble was in Kosovo, where martial law had only stoked the flames of ethnic strife. The Serb minority clamored for Belgrade's attention: In 1985, Kosovo's Serbs sent a petition to the central government, claiming that Serbs had been raped, murdered, and driven from their homes by the province's ethnic Albanians. Couldn't Belgrade do something?

To what extent Kosovo's Serbs were persecuted remains debatable. To be sure, they were outnumbered, and there is no reason to doubt that they faced threats, vandalism, harassment, and even the occasional act of criminal violence from an Albanian majority that deeply resented Slavic rule. But to Yugoslavs outside Serbia, complaints of anti-Serb discrimination in Kosovo were incomprehensible. After all, Serbs were hardly an oppressed group in the nation as a whole, whereas the Albanians formed something of an underclass.

So it was a surprise to many of the Belgrade Praxists' admirers when three key members of the group—Marković, Tadić, and Zagorka Golubović—signed a 1986 petition in support of the Kosovo Serbs. Ćosić also signed. It was not just that the petition painted a florid picture of Serbian suffering in the southern province. It was also that the signatories obliquely urged the government to revoke Kosovo's autonomous status—something Serbian nationalists had been pushing the parliament to do. After all, the petitioners reasoned, with its "unselfish" aid to the impoverished province, Serbia had amply demonstrated that it took the Albanians' interests to heart. Ominously, the petition's authors intoned: "Genocide [against Kosovo's Serbs] cannot be prevented by . . . [the] politics of gradual surrender of Kosovo . . . to Albania: the unsigned capitulation which leads to a politics of national treason."

When Branka Magaš, a historian who had emigrated from Yugoslavia in 1961, saw the petition, she was alarmed. She republished it, along with her own devastating critique, in the British journal *Labour Focus on Eastern Europe*. Magaš's essay was called "The End of an Era," and she signed it with an assumed name that disguised her Yugoslav background. "This unexpected, indeed astonishing, alignment of *Praxis* editors with nationalism," she wrote, "has aroused considerable dismay among their friends and sympathizers, for it delineates a complete break with the political and philosophical tradition represented by the journal."

According to Magaš, the editors of *Labour Focus* were skeptical. Mihailo Marković's reputation as a humanist preceded him. Could there be some mistake? The editors sent Magaš's piece to the Praxists for a response. Marković, Tadić, and Golubović were outraged. They had not abandoned their ideals, they wrote. They pointed out that they continued to publish *Praxis International*, a journal dedicated to democratic socialism, and that they served on Ćosić's committee for freedom of expression. They insisted that they spoke out against repression, no matter what the victims' ethnic background: "Are we nationalists because we also write on national issues (which are very acute in Yugoslavia now), or because we, being Serbs, also defend Serbian victims of repression?"

To Magaš, this exchange sent up a red flag. The rhetoric of Serbian victimhood, she noticed, was disturbingly similar to the rhetoric of a document that had recently been leaked to the Yugoslav press: the draft Memorandum of the influential Serbian Academy of Arts and Sciences. The Memorandum was what the *New York Times* reporter Roger Cohen has called "an incendiary catalog of Serbian resentments and ambitions." Its authors claimed that Serbs outside Serbia were in grave danger, that Yugoslavia was disintegrating, and that despite Serbia's superior contribution to the winning side in World War II, its people were divided and underrepresented in post-1974 Yugoslavia. Many analysts have described the seventy-four-page document as the catalyst for Milošević's rise to power: it provided the conceptual blueprint for a Greater Serbia.

Magaš later discovered that one of its authors was Mihailo Marković.

IN 1989, Benhabib took over the American editorship of *Praxis International*. At the time, she knew that conflict was brewing over Kosovo, but she did not yet understand its history or its dimensions. Her Praxis colleagues were little help. It was curious, she thought, that Svetozar Stojanović, her Yugoslav co-editor, never wrote about recent developments in his own country.

Virtually all of Praxis's Western collaborators remember Stojanović as the most ideologically flexible of the Belgrade group. While Marković cleaved to Marx's 1844 *Manuscripts*, Stojanović explored the possibility of a limited free market. He was the only Praxist seriously to investigate liberalism, and in a 1971 *Praxis* essay he had dared to criticize Tito as a "charismatic leader." Remembers Arato, "Stojanović was more talented than Marković, and Marković was the boss."

But when Benhabib brought up Kosovo in 1989, Stojanović seemed annoyed and stunned. "Why do you want to know about Kosovo?" he asked. Benhabib replied, "There is a conflict there, and we don't understand what that conflict is about." Said Stojanović, "Have we ever written about the Palestinian conflict in *Praxis*?" It was Benhabib's turn to be uncomfortable. "Sveta," she remembers saying, "what are you talking about?"

"Well, you know," he reasoned, "a lot of our editorial board members are Jewish. There are just some issues we don't touch."

But, Benhabib protested, *Praxis International* did not avoid the Palestinian conflict because some of its editors were Jewish. It did so because the Middle East did not fall within its purview. Questions of nationality in Marxist countries, on the other hand, were obviously germane. Stojanović relented. However, Benhabib notes, "when the article about Kosovo was written, Sveta, who was a moderate man, did not write it himself. It was Mihailo."

Publishing Marković's Kosovo article, Benhabib says now, is the one editorial decision she truly regrets. The piece, which appeared in 1990, begins in an eminently reasonable tone. Nationalists on both sides of this debate, Marković declared, have failed to listen to each other's arguments. It was time to evaluate the facts.

The Albanians, Marković calmly explained, are a backward, clannish people who have proven incapable of lifting themselves from poverty. The other Yugoslav republics have poured endless funds into Kosovo, but without results. The reason for this is both simple and sinister: Albanian nationalists have adopted a rapid birthrate as a demographic weapon against the Serbs. As a result of this scheme and of fiscal mismanagement by corrupt Albanian leaders, there are simply too many Kosovar mouths to feed. Compounding these economic problems is an ideological rift. The ethnic Albanians did not fight alongside the Yugoslav Partisans in World War II; for this reason, Marković lamented, the populace never accepted the socialist revolution, and, worse, it nurtures fascist tendencies left over from the Axis occupation.

But the most incredible piece of Marković's argument was yet to come. It might seem, Marković mused, that the Albanians are just a small, poor, oppressed minority. But the truth is that throughout history the Albanians have had great powers on their side, while Serbia has limped along on her own two feet. And just who were the Kosovo Albanians' powerful protectors? The Ottoman Empire, Austria-Hungary, Italy, the Vatican, Great Britain, the Comintern, the United States, Pan-Islamic fundamentalism, Albania, and a cabal of bureaucrats in the Yugoslav government.

Some extreme solutions might suggest themselves, Marković noted: violent police repression and compulsory family planning, for instance, or a partition and "exchange of population" that would leave the mineral-rich north of Kosovo to Serbia and the rest to Albania. But Marković drew back from these possibilities. He proposed instead that autonomy be maintained, that investment in the province be scaled back, and that family planning be instituted "in a gentle and psychologically acceptable way, and by the Albanians themselves, using primarily educational means."

In today's light, the article is chilling. Benhabib is most struck now by the passage about the Albanians' birthrate and their subsequent abject poverty. "This is cliché neofascist thinking, racist thinking about an oppressed group. You will find racists everywhere saying the same thing." But back in 1990, the alarm bells somehow failed to sound. Benhabib knew very little about Kosovo, and to find out more, she had asked Stojanović to commission a piece.

"Sometimes I felt like webs were being spun around me," Benhabib says now.

Not long after Marković's article appeared, Yugoslavia began its bloody disintegration. In 1991, Slovenia and then Croatia declared independence, touching off the Serbo-Croat war. Benhabib was in Frankfurt then, and people started approaching her about her colleague Marković, who by this time had become vice president and ideologue of Milošević's socialist party. "We'd run into individuals who would say, 'Are you aware of what you are doing?' " she recalls. But it was after Bosnia ignited in 1992 that Benhabib became really uncomfortable. "We were being instrumentalized for prestige and credit," she now believes. The last straw was an interview Marković gave *The New York Times* in August 1992: "I don't understand why there is so much opposition to cantonization," he told the reporter, regarding the partition of Bosnia. "The alternative is creation of a Muslim state in the heart of Europe. Perhaps the Americans want to support this. . . . But we find this very disturbing."

By 1993, Benhabib says, "we found that the situation had gotten too dirty, morally and politically." The only way out was to stop publishing the journal and to cut ties with Stojanović and Marković. *Praxis International* published its last issue, *The Rise and Fall of Yugoslavia: Stations of a European Tragedy*, in January 1994; it included Slovenian, Croatian, and Serbian perspectives on Yugoslavia's disintegration. Richard Bernstein's friendship with Marković was shattered by the Bosnian war. As for Benhabib, she has not kept in touch with Marković or Stojanović: since the breakup, she says, "I have an aversion to following their careers."

IF MIHAILO MARKOVIĆ was not who his Western friends and collaborators had thought he was, who was he? Did he jettison his humanist beliefs to cozy up to a new regime? Or had he been a wolf in sheep's clothing all along?

"Many people have read Marković as being a cynic and a betrayer of Praxis," says Bernstein. But in Marković's distorted vision, Bernstein suspects, "Serbia represented the progressive element of Yugoslav society"—the element bent on keeping Yugoslavia united and on preserving its socialist structure. Over time, he lost all perspective. "That's the tragedy of Mihailo Marković," says Bernstein. "Instead of seeing the dark and ugly side of Serbian nationalism, he committed himself to it."

The full measure of that commitment was apparent when Marković became the vice president of Milošević's party in 1991. David Crocker saw his old friend at a conference in Africa that year. Why, Crocker asked, had he joined the Serbian government? The philosopher's answer was simple: "I got involved in politics to save the Serbs in eastern Croatia." Otherwise, Marković claimed, "they will be slaughtered."

What on earth had made him think such a thing? But he was not alone. By 1992, the terms of political debate in Yugoslavia had undergone a dramatic shift. No longer was it a question of exactly how tightly the six republics and two autonomous provinces should be yoked to Belgrade's central authority. As Communism crumbled across the former Eastern bloc, the Yugoslavs began to revive their own pre-Communist paradigms. But in Yugoslavia, these paradigms were extreme and unworkable, drawing on the country's ugliest memories and worst fears: a Serb-dominated unitary state, which non-Serbs remembered bitterly from the first Yugoslavia; and the fratricidal killing fields of World War II, in which Serbs were overwhelmingly victimized. It seemed increasingly impossible for the country either to stay together in multinational form or to break apart without apocalyptic destruction.

Looking back now on the 1968 nationalism issue of *Praxis*, one sees the apparent antinationalist consensus start to take a more ambiguous shape. Both the Serbs and the Croats repudiated the then-ascendant Croatian nationalist movement and supported the continuance of a united Yugoslavia. For the Croats, this stance was explicitly opposed to that of Croatian nationalism. But for the Serbs, the position was compatible with both a principled antinationalism *and* their own national interest: after all, Yugoslavia was really the only viable option for keeping the Serbs in one state. This is to say not that Marković, Tadić, and the others were hoping to create a Greater Serbia back in 1968—but that they didn't need such a hope. Yugoslavia was perfectly comfortable. The Croats may have seriously grappled with the issues of ethnicity and nation in Yugoslavia in 1968. But the Serbs who blithely upheld Yugoslavism did so with all the arrogance, however well intentioned, of any majority.

Furthermore, whatever else the Praxists were, they were Marxists. In Croatia, to go on being a Marxist—or a Yugoslavist—placed one in opposition to the right-wing nationalist regime of Franjo Tudjman. And indeed, many of the Croatian Praxists have remained strong supporters of human rights: Žarko Puhovski, who is now vice president of Croatia's Helsinki Committee on Human Rights, has raised his voice courageously against the Croatian army's ethnic cleansing campaigns. And the economist Branko Horvat ran for president in 1992 on an antiwar, anti-authoritarian platform.

But for the Serb Praxists, the situation was different: to continue to support the country's socialist forces was to ally oneself with Milošević's government, and to oppose Milošević, it seemed, was to oppose what was left of Yugoslav Communism. "His world fell apart," Benhabib says of Marković. "Liberalism was unacceptable. He did not want free-market capitalism." Certainly, the new opposition parties, most of which were not only nationalist but also right-wing or royalist, would not be acceptable to a Communist of Marković's generation. He apparently decided that Milošević represented the future of Yugoslav socialism. After all, Milošević had inherited the Communist Party apparatus, and his governing socialist party was among the last ones standing in eastern Europe. Of course, Milošević had mixed that deadliest of cocktails: socialism and nationalism. Marković became one of the regime's most outspoken and unrepentant apologists. And then, in 1995, he was purged from power—the government, it seems, had come to see his nationalist views as too extreme.

OF THE BELGRADE 8, none disgraced himself as thoroughly as Marković, but there can be no question that nationalism captured the hearts and minds of many other Praxists. Consider the case of Svetozar Stojanović and his ally Dobrica Ćosić.

In his 1997 book, *The Fall of Yugoslavia: Why Communism Failed*,

Stojanović wrote that the revolution in his thinking occurred in 1990, when mass graves from Jasenovac, Croatia's World War II–era concentration camp, were disinterred for reburial. Stojanović found himself confronted by his children's anger: he had never talked to them about Jasenovac before. After all, such memories were suppressed during the Tito years. From that moment on, Stojanović declared, he decided that his political work should be dedicated to the memory of Jasenovac.

Stojanović's political career would rise in tandem with that of his close friend Ćosić. In 1992, Milošević appointed Ćosić to a figurehead presidency of the rump Yugoslavia, and Ćosić brought Stojanović in as his top adviser. Many observers inside and outside Yugoslavia hoped that the presence of such reputable, if openly nationalist, figures marked a change of political course. Instead, it bought Milošević a year of improved public relations abroad, while within the government the moderates' hands were tied.

In his book, Stojanović condemns the Milošević regime's criminal activity on nationalist grounds: if one shares in collective pride, he reasons, one must also share in collective shame. And he claims that Ćosić protested Milošević's deployment of brutal paramilitary formations in Croatia and Bosnia. At the same time, however, Stojanović and Ćosić did support Milošević's territorial aims. Yugoslavia could not be dismembered along the frontiers of its onetime republics, Stojanović and Ćosić argued. A "deeper map," they believed, lay submerged beneath the map of Tito's Yugoslavia; and this true map would account for the swaths of Croatian and Bosnian land that had been populated by Serbs for hundreds of years.

Ćosić and Stojanović were open to various solutions: Croatian independence might have been acceptable, Stojanović implies, if Croatia had been willing to guarantee substantial autonomy to its Serb-populated territories. In practice, critics would object, such solutions were untenable. There would be autonomy for the Serbs in Croatia; and within that autonomy, should there be autonomy for the Croats in Serbian Croatia? And what, then, of the Serbs in Croatian

Serbian Croatia? It is tempting to see this line of reasoning, which leads ineluctably to a *reductio ad infinitum*, as a sophistic device whose real purpose was to force Yugoslavia's reintegration on Serbian terms.

Ćosić's presidency lasted only a year, and when he was ousted in 1993, Stojanović left politics as well. Six years later, in the eerie silence following the Kosovo war, the Serbian Academy of Arts and Sciences reconvened to consider the Serbian national question. At the June 1999 meeting, Ćosić spoke at length of the ruin suffered by the Serb nation. "I appeal to Slobodan Milošević's patriotic consciousness and civic responsibility to resign in order for indispensable changes in Serbia and the federal state to begin," he concluded.

Marković took a harder line: "Our tragedy lies not in the fact that this or that person was head of the state. Our tragedy lies in the fact that the great powers have decided to destroy our country."

ALTHOUGH ONLY STOJANOVIĆ AND MARKOVIĆ served in the government, most of the Belgrade 8 have been politically active in the 1990s, and only a few have explicitly opposed the politics of Serbian nationalism. Ljubomir Tadić and Dragoljub Mičunović formed Serbia's first democratic opposition party, the DS, in 1990. Although its founders' ties to Praxis gave it the reputation of being the left wing of Serbia's movement for liberal democracy, the DS established strategic alliances with parties on its right, including royalists and hard-line nationalists. The party's leaders explained that these compromises allowed them to make a credible showing in parliamentary elections. But the conversion of Tadić, at least, to nationalism nevertheless seemed complete. He lent his uncritical support to the Bosnian Serbs, even meeting personally with their leader, Radovan Karadžić. With Marković, Tadić signed a 1996 petition urging The Hague to drop its charges against Karadžić, "the true leader of all Serbs." This was a remarkable act for a man who had written so eloquently in 1968 about nationalisms as "militant, despotic ideologies." Gerson Sher, who remembers Tadić's 1967 book, *Order and Freedom*, as a "masterpiece" of humanist thought, says ruefully, "Tadić is the greatest mystery of them all."

Mičunović, Tadic's colleague in the DS, maintained a more moderate reputation. He remained visible in public life until his former student Zoran Djindjić ousted him from the DS leadership in 1994. Djindjić, who also studied with Habermas and contributed to *Praxis International*, is today a presidential hopeful and favorite in the West. Mičunović now heads a pro-democracy nongovernmental organization. David Crocker, who saw him in 1998, recalls, "He seemed a man who had given up in despair. The opposition had fragmented, nothing had come of it, and Milošević was more powerful than ever."

It is typical of recent Serbian politics that those Praxists who sought power were the ones who differed least with the ruling regime. Other Belgrade Praxists kept a greater distance from politics but continued to agitate for a genuinely democratic future. It was a member of the Belgrade 8—Nebojša Popov—who co-founded one of Serbia's most principled and least popular parties, the Civic Alliance of Serbia, in 1991. Among its stated aims was "to overcome nationalist and class collectivism." As the little brother of the two largest opposition parties, the Civic Alliance joined the Zajedno coalition that led protests at the University of Belgrade in 1996 and 1997. In one of the more surreal scenes to emerge from 1990s Belgrade, Popov appeared on Nikola Pasić Square with a pot of beans in February 1997. He and his colleagues were cooking beans for "all those hungry for freedom, truth, and democracy." They pledged to continue "beaning" for 330 days or until Milošević was deposed.

Among Popov's allies are members of another Praxis offshoot: the Belgrade Circle, a small nongovernmental organization. Its president, Obrad Savić, was one of the students the Praxists led in the protests of 1968. Savić has been unsparing in his criticism of Marković and Tadić's turn to nationalism; in return, Tadić has denounced him as the founder of "anti-Serb mondialism."

Some of the same people who were once drawn to *Praxis* and *Praxis International*—Habermas, Richard Rorty, Chomsky—today publish in *The Belgrade Circle Journal*, whose special issue on human rights will be published as a book this month.

ULTIMATELY, IT IS THE STORY of one of the Belgrade Circle's founders, the Praxis philosopher Miladin Životić, that sheds the starkest light on the Yugoslav tragedy. The foreign intellectuals who were drawn to the Praxis vision of self-managing socialism back in its halcyon days did not take great notice of young Životić, whose attentions were devoted mostly to culture. By the 1980s, Životić and his students had formed a vanguard of post-structuralist scholarship in Belgrade, turning away from the Praxis fascination with Marxism in favor of Foucault and Derrida. Together with the aging dissident Milovan Djilas, Tito's onetime heir apparent, they founded the Belgrade Circle in 1992. According to Richard Bernstein, "There came a point when Marxism, even Marxist humanism, was old hat. It no longer spoke to the right issues. The Belgrade Circle allowed the younger generation to rebel against the stale clichés of the older generation."

But Životić and his followers made their real reputation as peace activists. During the war years, the Belgrade Circle expanded to include a motley array of workers, filmmakers, intellectuals, and artists. At its height, it had five hundred followers, who convened every Saturday for public events geared toward interethnic dialogue and peace.

In 1993, Životić traveled to besieged Sarajevo, slipping through Bosnian Serb lines to meet with the city's Muslim leadership. Back in Belgrade, he received a series of anonymous telephone calls from strangers who threatened to slit his throat. He spoke out in solidarity with Kosovo's Albanians, and when Muslims in Serbia's Sandjak region came under threat, he went to live with them in protest. Against ethnic cleansing he proclaimed, "If living together is impossible, then life itself is impossible as well."

Although he had been permitted to return to the University of Belgrade in 1987, Životić had become unhappy there by 1994. He told

The New York Times, "I could not stand to go to work. I had to listen to professors and students voice support and solidarity for these Bosnian fascists, Radovan Karadžić and Ratko Mladic, in the so-called Republic of Srpska. It is now worse than it was under Communism. The intellectual corruption is more pervasive and profound." A friend remembers that Životić "was physically destroyed by the time and the evil amid which he lived."

In 1997, Životić gave a talk in London about the anti-Milošević demonstrations that were then taking place at the University of Belgrade. He knew that the West had high hopes for the activists, but he also knew that their leaders were themselves nationalists. Branka Magaš was at this talk. "He was very disappointed with the Praxis people," she says. "He was a humanist."

Two weeks later, Životić was dead. "He was extremely tormented by what had happened," says Magaš. "He died of a broken heart, I think."

—September 1999

THE COLOR TEST
Does the Law Focus Too Much on Black Suspects—
or Too Little on Black Victims?
EYAL PRESS

EARLY LAST YEAR, roughly two hundred people crammed into a
third-floor conference room at the Open Society Institute in Manhattan to hear Professors David Cole and Randall Kennedy debate the issues of race, crime, and justice. The debate was timed to coincide
with the publication of Cole's book *No Equal Justice*, a searing indictment of the racial inequities in the legal system. What lent the occasion drama, however, was a less fortunate coincidence: three weeks
earlier, four New York City police officers fired forty-one bullets at an
unarmed West Africa immigrant, Amadou Diallo, while he was standing in the vestibule of his Bronx apartment building.

The killing of Diallo, and the escalating clamor over police misconduct, have made the role of race in the administration of criminal
justice one of America's most volatile social issues. Cities across the
country have watched crime drop dramatically in recent years—and
seen prison rolls rise just as dramatically. At the same time, practices
such as racial profiling and zero-tolerance policing have raised some
unsettling questions: Has the reduction in crime come at too great a
cost in liberty? And to what degree does race determine whose liberties are violated?

To a great degree, argues David Cole. "We are administering a
criminal justice system that is deeply unfair and that indeed depends

on being unfair," he declared at the start of the debate. According to Cole, however, the central issue is not, as many critics would have it, intentional discrimination. After all, most courts have, in recent decades, banned the explicit use of race in legal proceedings. Rather, there is a deeper and more insidious problem: "Constitutional rights are all formally equal on their surface, but their deep structure is to exploit inequality," said Cole, a soft-spoken man whose calm, measured voice is belied by the force of his arguments. Thus, although the Constitution bars the police from arresting people on the basis of race, he explained, the courts have vastly broadened the police's discretion to stop and arrest virtually anyone they please. Society has been willing to grant police such sweeping discretionary power, Cole argues in *No Equal Justice*—one of the most unsparing, and lavishly praised, books on the criminal justice system to appear in recent memory—only because the burdens fall almost exclusively on impoverished and minority communities.

But has cracking down on crime been uniformly damaging to these communities? Hardly, countered Cole's debating opponent, Randall Kennedy. "When we talk about inequality in the administration of criminal justice, many people think immediately—and often exclusively—of the black suspect, the black defendant, the black convict," said Kennedy. "There is one actor, however, that is often quite marginalized . . . and that was marginalized in Professor Cole's opening statement." He paused. "That actor is the black victim."

Historically, Kennedy observed, African-Americans have suffered as much or more from the *under*enforcement of the law—that is, the refusal of authorities to punish those who victimize blacks—as from its overenforcement. It's a point Kennedy stresses in his own critically acclaimed book, *Race, Crime, and the Law*, and one he believes should inform any assessment of recent efforts to clamp down on inner-city violence. Kennedy, who is African-American, points out that many people in the black community have long complained about inadequate police protection. "Police brutality is of course a terrible thing," he said in the debate with Cole, "but blacks at every income level are also more likely to be murdered, raped, burgled, assaulted." And because the vast majority of crime is intraracial—that is, either white on white or black on black—policies that disproportionately *burden* black offenders disproportionately *benefit* black victims, leading to a paradox. "If you put the question of black victimization at the center," Kennedy explained, "protecting minority communities from crime may mean putting more minority criminals in jail." The room fell silent.

Cole and Kennedy are longtime sparring partners who have debated these issues both in print and in person and who seem to relish their confrontations. Ironically, however, the two law professors are in many ways kindred spirits. Both share a deep belief that racial disparities remain far too common. Both are public intellectuals who write as frequently in popular as in academic venues, and their views have shaped not only the scholarly debate but also the decisions of courts and legislatures.

Where they differ is in weighing liberty against security to determine which actors, and which rights, are in greatest need of protection. To Cole, the fact that over one million African-Americans are today in prison (seven times the incarceration rate for whites), and that minorities are routinely stopped and arrested under dubious pretexts, shows that we have adopted a set of punitive policies that would never be accepted were they evenly administered. But as Kennedy sees it, our central concern should be the treatment not of minority suspects but of their victims. These differences have led Cole and Kennedy to quarrel over everything from the impact of the drug war to the legal standards courts should use to redress discrimination—and have produced a dialogue of unusual depth between two highly provocative scholars.

COLE AND KENNEDY have known each other since the early 1980s, when they were classmates at Yale Law School, where Cole says he spent three years thinking he would become anything but a law professor.

"Law was not my calling," Cole confessed as we sat down for lunch in a faculty lounge at the Georgetown Law Center, where he now teaches. As an undergraduate at Yale, says Cole, "Forget contracts—I took Keats and Shelley. I took a yearlong course on Freud and spent much of my time writing film and music criticism for the *Yale Daily News*. I was planning to be a writer or a critic, not a law professor."

After completing his undergraduate degree in literature, Cole also seriously considered taking a job in the financial world. "Back in high school I'd kind of gotten obsessed with the stock market," he recalls, chuckling. "I had this high-school friend who was an options trader in Chicago. He offered me a job, and I thought, 'Why not? I'll go do that and freelance on the side.' "

"If I'd have taken the job, I'd be a multi-multi-millionaire by now."

What changed Cole's life—and sparked his interest not only in the law but in issues of civil rights and equality—was a summer internship at the New York–based Center for Constitutional Rights, a progressive nonprofit that specializes in human-rights litigation. "That politicized me more than anything else," he said. "It was a very radical place. . . . I was one of the only white males there, and I started working on all these international human-rights cases."

After landing a paid job at CCR, Cole got to know the legendary William Kunstler, the wild-haired radical attorney with whom he worked on the famous 1990 Supreme Court flag-burning case, *United States* v. *Eichman*. Though Kunstler insisted on arguing the case, it was Cole, who had not yet turned thirty, who wrote the briefs that convinced the Court to overturn the 1989 Flag Protection Act. His work on this case earned him a laudatory profile in the *New York Times*'s At the Bar column and prompted an opposing lawyer from the solicitor general's office to comment that Cole's brief was the best he'd ever read.

With his curly brown hair, boyish face, and casual attire, Cole still does not look the part of the typical law professor. He is tall and slender, with the long arms and lanky frame of a swimmer (a sport he lettered in as an undergraduate), and he has a distinctly humble manner. You would never know, from meeting him, that Cole is not only a prolific scholar, having published two books and dozens of prominent law review articles, but also one of the nation's preeminent civil-rights attorneys. During the past decade, he has litigated a dizzying array of high-profile cases, from *Finley* v. *National Endowment for the Arts*, where he defended the four artists accused of violating the NEA's "decency" standard, to *Massachusetts* v. *Secretary of Health and Human Services*, where he helped strike down a regulation prohibiting federally funded clinics from counseling women about abortion, to *American-Arab Anti-discrimination Committee* v. *Reno*, one of numerous cases where Cole has defended Arab immigrants against controversial antiterrorism laws that curtail civil liberties. Somehow, Cole also manages to write a column for *Legal Times*, serve as the legal-affairs correspondent for *The Nation*, and speak regularly on National Public Radio. After lunch, as we approached his fourth-floor office, a narrow alcove submerged in a sea of documents from the various cases he was litigating, I asked Cole how he is able to keep everything together. "I don't spend much time filing," he quipped.

IF COLE'S SCHEDULE was fast-paced before, it became a veritable whirlwind with the publication of *No Equal Justice*. "There was a long stretch—a good two months after the book came out—where I was doing at least one radio show a *day* on the book," he says. "It was just unbelievable."

It was, however, hardly surprising. *No Equal Justice* appeared in February 1999, the month of the Diallo shooting and two months before the start of the Abner Louima trial, a case involving a Haitian man who was brutally beaten and sodomized with a toilet plunger by two New York City police officers. Around the same time, the New Jersey attorney general's office released a report acknowledging that state troopers engaged in racial profiling, a problem that has surfaced in Maryland, Florida, and numerous other states. A few months later, Columbia University's Center for Violence Research & Prevention, in conjunction with the New York attorney general, published a study showing that over a fifteen-month period in New York City, blacks were 2.1 times more likely (and Hispanics 1.7 times more likely) to be stopped and frisked than whites—even when controlling for higher crime rates in minority neighborhoods.

The flood of bad news proved perversely beneficial to Cole. "When my book came out," he explained, "New York was being touted everywhere as the great crime miracle. Broken windows"—the theory that arresting petty criminals for low-level quality-of-life infractions would have a large deterrent effect on serious crime—"had supposedly solved the crime problem. Now I think the common perception is that the New York approach has come at a tremendous cost in terms of rights."

"Similarly with racial profiling," added Cole. "Five years ago, I don't think anybody outside the black community was conscious of the phenomenon of 'driving while black.' Today the latest polls are finding that 80 percent of Americans believe racial profiling is wrong, and around 60 percent believe it is widespread. . . . There has been a tremendous sea change in a relatively short period of time."

What there has not been, Cole believes, is an understanding of how racial inequality is structurally ingrained in the legal system. "The root of the problem," wrote Brent Staples in a March 12 *New York Times* Op-Ed, "is the tendency of white police officers—and white Americans generally—to associate blackness with criminality in the absence of any substantiating evidence." It's a common assessment, yet a misguided one, Cole believes. The real root of the problem, he argues, is less the prejudice of police officers than a series of little-noted Supreme Court rulings that have eviscerated the Fourth Amendment (which protects citizens from unreasonable search and seizure) and empowered the police to arrest people without any objective, individualized basis for suspicion.

In *Whren* v. *United States* (1996), for example, Cole notes that the Supreme Court granted officers the right to use any traffic violation as a pretext for stopping a driver even if they have no intention of enforcing a traffic law. In a 1991 decision, the Court ruled that the police may search passengers' bags in so-called bus sweeps without establishing any individualized basis for suspicion. In an earlier ruling, *Terry* v.

Ohio (1968), the Court determined that officers may stop people on the basis of "reasonable suspicion," a doctrine significantly vaguer than the "probable cause" standard previously demanded.

~~None of these decisions allows the police to arrest someone on the~~ basis of his or her race, Cole notes. What they do is grant law enforcement so much discretion that cops can stop virtually anyone for any reason, thus inviting racial profiling. Reviewing federal court cases involving drug stops at airports, Cole found that courts accepted the following justifications: suspect walked quickly through airport; suspect walked slowly through airport; suspect carried no luggage; suspect carried brand-new luggage; suspect traveled alone; suspect traveled with a companion. In over 90 percent of these cases, the suspect also happened to be black or Hispanic.

To Cole, that such patterns do not *appear* racially motivated makes them all the more insidious. Societies, he notes in *No Equal Justice*, aim to balance two competing interests in devising crime policy—liberty and security. Liberals and conservatives might disagree on where to draw the line, "but both sides agree, at least in principle, that the line should be drawn in the same place for everyone." America, however, has mediated the tension between liberty and security "not by picking one point on the continuum, but in effect by picking two points—one for the more privileged and educated, the other for the poor and less educated," writes Cole.

All of which leads Cole to conclude that in order to address inequality, we need to go much further than simply eliminating open, intentional racism. "I take issue with those, like Professor Randall Kennedy, who argue that as long as we can rid the system of *explicit* or *intentional* considerations of race, we will have solved the problem," he writes. To reduce the problem to such instances "is to ignore the lion's share of inequality that pervades the criminal justice system today."

IN FACT, as Cole is well aware, Randall Kennedy is a staunch critic of racial profiling. In *Race, Crime, and the Law*, Kennedy argues that although it may be "reasonable" for police officers to be more suspicious of minorities (due to higher rates of some forms of criminal conduct), such suspicion is incompatible with the ideal of creating a color-blind society. Kennedy's criticism of racial profiling focuses on those cases where courts have sanctioned the *explicit* use of race as one of many factors justifying heightened suspicion. In *United States* v. *Martinez-Fuerte*, for example, the Supreme Court held that the Border Patrol can lawfully consider Mexican ancestry in deciding which vehicles to search for illegal aliens. To Cole, such rulings are hardly the central problem. To Kennedy, however, concentrating on *purposeful* discrimination is important. He reasons that in the absence of discriminatory intent, assessing whether a law is actually harmful to minorities is far more complicated than liberal critics commonly assume.

"A racial disparity is not necessarily indicative of a racial discrimination," insists Kennedy in a crucial passage in *Race, Crime, and the Law*. He continues:

> Some critics attack as racist urban curfews that regulate youngsters on the grounds that such curfews will disproportionately fall upon minority youngsters. But are black communities *hurt* by curfews which limit the late-night activities of minors or *helped* insofar as some of their residents feel more secure because of the curfews? Some critics attack as racist police crackdowns on violent gangs because such actions will disproportionately affect black members of gangs. But are black communities *hurt* by police crackdowns on violent gangs or *helped* by the destabilization of gangs that terrorize those who live in their midst?

What Kennedy is doing, of course, is placing the treatment of minority *victims* at the center of the concern for equality. "It's something that's always been there but that people really haven't looked at," he told me in his spacious book-lined office at Harvard Law School, where he has taught since 1984. "Look at the history of the NAACP," said Kennedy, who wears large plastic-frame glasses and has a lively, animated manner. "The first thing the NAACP was concerned with, for its first twenty years, was lynching. Here was a practice where black people literally lacked the equal *protection* of the law." In the most haunting chapter of *Race, Crime, and the Law*, Kennedy chronicles the chilling litany of cases in which white judges and juries have exonerated those who raped, robbed, or murdered African-Americans. "Goodness gracious, anybody hurt?" reads the chapter's epigraph, from *Huckleberry Finn*. "No'm, killed a nigger."

It's not that Kennedy doesn't think minority suspects, too, have suffered from discrimination at the hands of white authorities. He recalls that while growing up in Washington, D.C., he would travel with his family to visit relatives in South Carolina, and his father would get pulled over for no apparent reason. "He was a black man with out-of-state plates in a nice car," explained Kennedy. "That was enough." Kennedy later interned at the NAACP Legal Defense Fund, an experience that politicized him in much the way that Cole's internship politicized him, and went on to clerk for the Supreme Court justice Thurgood Marshall.

"It was a great experience," says Kennedy of the clerkship. "Growing up, my father used to tell me about going to see Marshall argue one of the very last white primary cases, in South Carolina. In those days, if a problem arose in the black community, people would say, 'Hold on, Thurgood's comin'.' And he would." On the last day of his clerkship, Kennedy says, he brought his parents in to meet their hero. "My father told Marshall about seeing him argue that case. . . . It was very moving."

Given these experiences, it's hardly surprising that Kennedy, who serves on the editorial boards of both *The American Prospect* and *The Nation*, classifies himself as politically progressive. "I'm clearly on the liberal end of things." In fact, however, Kennedy's views are eclectic. He is above all a skeptic and provocateur who seems to delight in challenging the ideological assumptions of both the left and the right—and in courting controversy. In the *Harvard Law Review* back in 1989, he scathingly criticized several leading exponents of critical race theory, including Richard Delgado, Derrick Bell, and Mari Matsuda, for reinforcing dubious notions of racial distinctiveness. "Although promoted in the name of an insurgent, liberatory, intellectual endeavor," charged Kennedy, such scholarship tends to replicate "deeply traditional ideas about the naturalness, essentiality, and inescapability of race." His fiercest objection was to the critical race theorists' notion that ideas and sensibilities could be categorized on the basis of race (that is, that there is such a thing as "a black perspective"), a notion that ignored "the reality of intra-racial disputes."

His critique provoked an uproar, including articles in *The New York Times* and *The Nation*. Angry ripostes followed from Matsuda, Bell, and Delgado, who accused Kennedy of publishing the piece "for the purposes of justifying the current politico-legal system" and of turning a blind eye to the "flagrant exclusion" of minority scholars from positions of power. A year later, Kennedy launched the short-lived *Reconstruction*, a journal on African-American politics and culture that quickly established a reputation for bucking conventional wisdom, featuring articles by authors such as Stephen Carter, Glenn Loury, and . . . David Cole.

"I think Randy doesn't like to be pigeonholed, which leads him to take positions that will surprise people," says Cole, who contributed an essay to *Reconstruction* criticizing hate laws (on civil libertarian grounds). "It's part of his philosophy of color blindness: he wants to be seen as a scholar, not as a black scholar who is expected to take a certain position because of his identity."

Kennedy concurs: "There have been a number of times in my career where people have said, 'Don't say that, because you're black and what you say will lend credibility to a bad idea.' I understand that, but I don't shy away from writing what I think."

Which is why he has not refrained from drawing attention to the problem of black victimization. For all the outrage provoked by incidents like the Rodney King beating, Kennedy finds it disturbing that all too many critics, particularly those who view their mission as "advancing the interests of blacks," pay so little attention to the startling disparities in victimization rates. "Black teenagers are nine times more likely to be murdered than their white counterparts," he writes in *Race, Crime, and the Law*, and the overall murder rate for black males today is double the rate of combat deaths for American servicemen during World War II. Kennedy concludes that "blacks (and other people of color) suffer more from the criminal acts of their racial 'brothers' and 'sisters' than they do from the racist misconduct of white police officers."

It's a view that has provoked heated objections, particularly from other African-American scholars. Reviewing the book in the journal *New Politics*, New York University professor Derrick Bell complained that Kennedy's emphasis on black-on-black crime "causes him to lose sight of how horribly invidious the problem of racism is." Writing in the *Harvard Law Review*, Paul Butler, a former student of Kennedy's who comes under harsh attack in *Race, Crime, and the Law* for advocating black jury nullification, portrayed Kennedy (whom he mockingly dubbed "Respectable Randall") as an Uncle Tom who believes racism "only encumbers the bad blacks who commit crime and not the good Negroes who constitute the majority."

To Kennedy, who took pains to xerox and share these reviews with me, such assessments may be unpleasant but seem only to confirm his sense that what he is saying is important. "At the center of all discussions about racial justice and criminal law," he concludes, "should be recognition that black Americans are in dire need of protection against criminality."

THIS PREMISE UNDERLIES one of Kennedy's most controversial arguments: namely, that the different punishments for trafficking crack versus powder cocaine (a person convicted of selling five grams of crack receives the same punishment as a person convicted of distributing *five hundred* grams of powder cocaine) are not, as critics commonly allege, the product of racism. In *No Equal Justice*, Cole points to statistics indicating that 93 percent of those convicted of crimes involving crack were black and 45 percent of those convicted of crimes involving powder cocaine were white, a seemingly clear sign that maintaining the 100:1 disparity exacerbates racial inequality.

Not so, argues Kennedy. "To the extent that the enhanced punishment for crack offenses falls upon blacks," he writes in *Race, Crime, and the Law*, "it falls not upon blacks as a class but only upon a distinct subset of the black population—those in violation of the crack law." Kennedy advanced this argument in a highly controversial 1994 article in the *Harvard Law Review*, in which he assailed a Minnesota Supreme Court ruling that had invalidated the crack/cocaine distinction on the grounds that it "appears to impose a substantially disproportionate burden" on blacks. Nonsense, charged Kennedy. "It is a 'burden' on those who are convicted of engaging in this conduct," he countered. Law enforcement is a "public good" that "benefits the great mass of law-abiding people."

"One of the reasons I wrote about that," Kennedy told me, "is that I was reading through all these articles on the crack/cocaine distinction, and nobody—nobody—was talking about the history of congressional attitudes about crack. So I decided to look it up." He leaned forward. "Well, it so happens that the first person to draw attention to the dangers of crack was Charles Rangel," an African-American liberal Democrat who represents Harlem in the House, "and there were a substantial number of other black representatives who started saying, 'Hey, let's crack down on crack,' because they felt it wasn't being taken seriously." In other words, it was not racism but a concern about crack's devastating impact on inner-city neighborhoods that drove the legislation. Such concerns, Kennedy notes, are hardly rare in the black community: a 1993 Gallup poll, for example, found that 82 percent of blacks believed the courts in their areas did not treat criminals harshly enough, 75 percent favored putting more police on the streets, and 68 percent advocated building more prisons so that longer sentences could be given to criminals.

"The crack law may be wrong," says Kennedy (in which case Congress should change it), "but that is very different from saying it is racist" (in which case it should be viewed as unconstitutional). In his

Harvard Law Review article, Kennedy concludes that the presence "of a racially discriminatory purpose distinguishes those laws that are specifically *racial*, and therefore presumptively illegitimate, from those that merely give rise to racially disparate consequences that disadvantage some African Americans while benefiting others."

Soon after it appeared, Kennedy's article was cited in a Washington, D.C., court of appeals ruling that rejected a constitutional challenge to the crack/cocaine distinction.

It also provoked a lengthy rebuttal from David Cole. Writing in the *Georgetown Law Journal*, Cole argued that although Kennedy's effort to distinguish between the crack law's impact on law-violating and law-abiding blacks was understandable, "much of the world does not make that distinction." The drug war, Cole pointed out, was a major factor behind disproportionate minority arrests and harassment, actions that affect all members of the black community. Charles Rangel and other minority representatives in Congress, Cole added, had originally proposed placing crack on a par with cocaine, not creating a 100:1 disparity, and congressional black and Hispanic caucuses have since proposed overturning the law, in part because the disparities in the drug war have become so glaring: African-Americans, Cole noted, constitute "14% of all drug users" but "35% of all drug arrests, 55% of all drug convictions, and 74% of all sentences for drug offenses."

In addition, Cole charged, by arguing that only laws that are explicitly racist should be subject to review under the equal protection clause (the so-called intent doctrine espoused by the current Supreme Court), Kennedy would exempt from scrutiny the vast majority of modern discrimination, which is subtle, unconscious, and structural. Cole noted that Kennedy himself argued this point in a 1991 article on the controversial *McClesky* v. *Kemp* decision. Warren McClesky, a black man facing the death penalty for killing a white police officer, had challenged the death penalty's constitutionality by presenting evidence that defendants charged with killing whites were 4.3 times more likely to receive a death sentence than defendants charged with killing blacks. In a 5–4 decision, the Supreme Court ruled that while the statistics seemed to show disparate treatment, McClesky would have to show purposeful racial discrimination in his own case to raise constitutional concerns.

Kennedy has been an unsparing critic of the *McClesky* ruling, describing the Court as "haunted by anxiety over the consequences of acknowledging candidly the large influence of racial sentiment" underscored by the statistics. But if this is the case with the death penalty, why not with the drug war, where, Cole argues, racial selectivity is equally stark?

In his book, Kennedy differentiates between the death penalty and the drug war by suggesting that "death is different" because it is society's ultimate punishment. When we met, however, he seemed to have moderated his position somewhat. "I do have some qualms about what I wrote" in 1994, he confessed. Pointing to a Justice Department report released in April 2000 that found black youth *forty-eight times* more likely than whites to be sentenced to juvenile prison for drug offenses, Kennedy said, "If it's true that Congress would act differently if this were the impact on the white population, . . . then this is a policy of racial selectivity."

"But," he added, "I want to change the drug war because it is counterproductive or ineffective, not because it is racist. One of my criticisms of David and his allies is that they are using this very traditional approach—almost a sort of racial shaming tradition. I think he wants charges of racial discrimination to do political work, and I have real doubts about the efficacy of that. . . . I mean, people have tried making those charges for a long time now, and it hasn't really gotten very far."

"Furthermore," Kennedy added, "I get the sense that David thinks conservatives are sort of a lost cause, that they are barely worth talking to. Well, I think it's important to talk to conservatives. I think some conservatives, especially those who talk about limiting big government, should be concerned with the unaccountable behavior of the police. . . . But I think we need to reach out to conservatives who embrace the goal of building safe communities."

"He has a point," says Cole, acknowledging that his work focuses far more on the costs of law enforcement than on the costs of crime. Cole, however, insists that *No Equal Justice* does address the issue of community safety, albeit from a different angle. Citing the social psychologist Tom Tyler, who has conducted studies showing that the people most likely to obey the law are those who believe in its moral legitimacy, Cole argues that a system based on double standards paradoxically "fuels racial enmity and encourages crime" by making the targets of discriminatory practices less inclined to play by the rules. Gallup polls, Cole notes, indicate that three-fourths of African-Americans believe the criminal justice system is racially biased and a majority view the police as corrupt. "In the long run, I think we all lose from this approach," says Cole, who points to cities like Boston and San Diego, which have sharply lowered crime in recent years not by stopping and arresting massive numbers of minority citizens but by implementing community policing strategies, such as sit-down meetings with gang members and counseling and mentoring programs for youths. "One of my main points is that we have lots of choices in how we respond to crime. Boston and San Diego have decreased crime *and* civilian complaints about police misconduct."

Ultimately, Cole's book will not likely appeal to those who view punishment and incarceration as the best mechanisms for enhancing security. Interestingly, though, Cole admits that some people might answer his call for equality by arguing that criminal justice should be more punitive across the board. In Minnesota, he notes, when the Supreme Court invalidated the crack/cocaine distinction, the legislature responded not by liberalizing the crack law but by increasing the penalty for powder—an approach Cole deems overly punitive but still preferable to the existing double standard.

Still, Cole maintains that over time the "get tough" approach to crime would lose much of its appeal were the costs borne more equally. "At current trends," he notes, "one in four black male babies born today will spend at least a year or more of his life in prison. . . . We are the world leader in freedom but also the world leader in prisons. . . . This would not be accepted if it were one in four *white* babies."

IT'S WITHIN THIS CONTEXT that Cole finds fault with Kennedy's emphasis on security. "I don't think Randy has this intent, but his work unfortunately lends legitimacy to people who are advocating harsher and harsher policies that ultimately redound to the detriment of the black community," he says. In a recent article in the *Georgetown Law Journal*, Cole links this aspect of Kennedy's work to what he calls "the new discretion scholarship." During the past two decades, Cole notes, a growing number of scholars, building on the "broken windows" theory, have embraced the notion that in order to control crime in inner-city neighborhoods, courts need to broaden the police's discretion even further.

Dan Kahan and Tracey Meares, at Yale and the University of Chicago, respectively, champion aggressive order-maintenance policing under open-ended statutes, arguing that such policies, if well regulated, are far from racist and in fact benefit the law-abiding members of inner-city communities. In their articles, Kahan and Meares often cite Kennedy's emphasis on minority victimization to bolster their case. They have also echoed his arguments in a brief submitted before the Illinois Supreme Court in 1997 that endorsed a controversial anti-gang loitering ordinance; the law allowed the Chicago police to arrest people and remove them from the streets even if they were not engaged in criminal conduct. (The ordinance was recently overturned by the Supreme Court and has since been amended.)

To the consternation of Kahan and Meares, Kennedy signed on to a brief *opposing* the Chicago anti-gang ordinance. "I was definitely surprised and a little disappointed by that," says Kahan. "I mean, he's the person who inspired this whole new conception of how criminal law and policing and race relate to each other."

Kennedy, who is largely sympathetic to quality-of-life policing initiatives ("I think laws against littering and spitting and jumping through turnstiles do make people feel they can use the streets"), says he can understand Kahan's disappointment. "A good number of people wrote and e-mailed me to say, 'Gee, I read your book, I thought you'd be on the other side,' " he says. But Kennedy stands by his position. "Do the police have to have discretion—of course they do. The question is, Do they need that authority *augmented*? I think, to the contrary, we need to make sure they are doing what they're supposed to do." Kahan and Meares, he adds, "seem to think political power has changed so much that racial minorities don't have to worry about the police as armies of occupation. I think they are much too sanguine on that."

It's a little difficult to square all this with Kennedy's insistence that what minority communities most need is more law enforcement. ("There is a real tension here," he concedes.) Then again, perhaps his views have evolved somewhat in the course of recent events—and in the course of his dialogue with Cole. "He helps rope me in if I'm straying off too much," Kennedy explains, "and I get the sense that perhaps I've moderated his line on certain issues. For example, he does say explicitly in his book that we should also be concerned about the victims of crime. I would have liked to see him push that a little more, but I was happy to see that." He pauses. "Overall, it's been a very fruitful exchange."

—October 2000

MOO!
The Case for Animal Autobiography

JENNIFER SCHUESSLER

NOT LONG AGO, the distinguished Australian novelist Elizabeth Costello delivered a pair of rambling academic lectures on a "crime of stupefying proportions" going on unobserved all around her audience: the abuse and slaughter of animals. The range of reactions was predictable. A philosopher in the audience was heard muttering about "French irrationalism." A poet on the faculty sent a letter explaining his absence, saying that he objected to Costello's comparison of beef cattle with Jewish victims at Auschwitz. Others in the audience took issue with her use of anthropomorphism, her lack of historical perspective, and the way she spoke not as a scholar but as "a person whose sole claim to your attention is to have written stories about made-up people."

But Elizabeth Costello herself is a made-up person, the protagonist of the South African novelist J. M. Coetzee's own 1997–1998 Tanner Lectures, to be published in April as *The Lives of Animals*. For Coetzee, fiction may have been a slyly ambiguous way of raising a subject whose most passionate defenders are too often dismissed, in the words of the philosopher and *Animal Liberation* author Peter Singer, as "sentimental, emotional animal-lovers." After all, Costello herself asks in one of her fictional lectures, might literature succeed in advancing the cause of animal rights where philosophy has failed?

Last December, in a real-life twist on Coetzee's fable, a group of four literary scholars raised a similar question at the Modern Language Association conference in San Francisco. The venue was a panel on animal autobiography, sponsored by the newly formed Society for Animal Advocacy Through Literature. The society, founded by three professors from the University of Wisconsin with a strong background in animal-rights activism, aims to shake up the musty field of animal literary studies with an emphasis on texts that treat animals not as allegories of the human condition but as autonomous beings with their own experiences. As the panelist Marian Scholtmeijer, a professor at the University of North British Columbia and the author of *Animal Victims in Modern Fiction*, puts it, "We proceed from the idea that animals have not only been mistreated; they have also been misrepresented. Too many people are still stuck with animals as symbols of things other than what they are to themselves. That has become passé in modern times. Anyone who's still writing that way is writing bad literature."

The MLA panel is the latest manifestation of a small but growing wave of animal-centered literary study. Recent publications in the field include Randy Malamud's *Reading Zoos: Representations of Animals and Captivity*, Katharine M. Rogers's *The Cat and the Human Imagination: Feline Images From Bast to Garfield*, and the anthology *Animal Acts: Configuring the Human in Western History*, which contains essays on subjects ranging from Kafka's metamorphosed humans to Gary Larson's talking bugs.

But can *Far Side* cartoons really provide insight into the lives of animals? As the MLA panelists acknowledge, animals—the controversial sign-language pronouncements of Koko the gorilla aside—have so far been unable to write their own stories. But like Coetzee's Elizabeth Costello, the MLA panelists believe that imaginative writing can bridge the species gap in a way that science cannot. "Literature is freer than other disciplines to measure the Other's point of view," says Scholtmeijer. "It can also expand the number of people who have empathy—more people read fiction than animal-rights literature." As panel organizer Julie Ann Smith, of the University of Wisconsin at Whitewater, puts it, "Animals have something to tell humans about how to live in the world as physical beings in a more satisfying way."

In their papers, the MLA panelists focused on the same higher-order animals—apes, horses—that dominate Elizabeth Costello's lectures. Other species, it would seem, have a more serious P.R. problem. Anna Sewell's *Black Beauty* was called "the *Uncle Tom's Cabin* of the horse." But who will be the Harriet Beecher Stowe of the battery hen? (And will Francis Ford Coppola be interested in making the movie?)

In fact, some feminist critics have taken tentative steps toward the barnyard, seeing patriarchy at work in the elevation of noble wildlife over the dumb, domestic, "unnatural" breeders-in-overdrive of the farm. In *The Sexual Politics of Meat: A Feminist-Vegetarian Critical Theory*, Carol Adams used critical theory and literary analysis to draw parallels between cruelty to animals and violence against women. In "Thinking Like a Chicken: Farm Animals and the Feminine Connection," an essay in *Animals and Women*, Karen Davis, a poultry activist with a Ph.D., recounts how her essay "Clucking Like a Chicken," in which she turned herself into a human microphone held up to the beak of a hen, was rejected by the journal *Environmental Ethics* because it had "too much first person singular." The essay-within-an-essay reads like a brilliant parody of "deep ecology" godfather Aldo Leopold's exhortation to "think like a mountain"—except that Davis is dead serious about the need to hear "the music of the spheres in the cluck of a chicken" and the other noises drowned out by "the regal harmonies of the mountain and their ersatz echoes in the groves of academe."

The "animal autobiography" championed by the MLA panelists may pose a challenge to dominant approaches to ecology that emphasize nature as a whole and leave individual animals—except for us hairless bipeds—out of the picture. And while the SAAL has no official position on vegetarianism, its founding members—all vegans—don't rule out the possibility that literature can bring the horrors of the abattoir to an end. "Do you really believe, Mother, that poetry classes are going to close down the slaughterhouses?" Coetzee's

Elizabeth Costello is asked by her skeptical son. At the MLA panel, the real-life Marian Scholtmeijer concluded her paper with the answer that "the best animal autobiographies will convert us all to vegetarianism."

—*March 1999*

Dear Editors,

Having grown up on a chicken farm, I was interested to read Jennifer Schuessler's account of the poultry activist Karen Davis. Some of my earliest memories are of using cap pistols to round up birds for inoculation— and of my father's later wringing their necks.

A candidate for the Harriet Beecher Stowe of the battery hen is Edward Payson Evans (1831–1917). Born in New York State and educated at the University of Michigan and in Germany, Evans was a professor at Ann Arbor before retiring to Munich, where he and his wife wrote a remarkable corpus in history, law, and literature. In a magisterial work, The Criminal Prosecution and Capital Punishment of Animals, *Evans elegantly synthesizes late-nineteenth-century scholarship regarding "the judicial prosecution of animals, resulting in their excommunication by the Church or their execution by the hangman."*

To the fowl point in question, Evans analyzes a 1474 incident in which the magistrates of Basel "sentenced a cock to be burned at the stake 'for the heinous and unnatural crime of laying an egg.'" The practice continued at least until 1730, when, according to Evans, a gallinaceous malefactor was executed in the Swiss Prättigau. At issue was the oeuf coquatri, *an active ingredient for witches' brew. When hatched, the egg produced the basilisk, "which would hide in the roof of the house and with its baneful breath and 'death-darting eye' destroy all the inmates." The dismissal of the supernatural phenomenon of cocks' eggs merited a 1710 contribution to the* Mémoires *of the Paris Academy of Sciences.*

Evans places these proceedings and many additional ones in the context of fin-de-siècle criminology, which scrutinized the notions of delinquency and culpability following the tenets of social Darwinism, eugenics, and class conflict. The Dictionary of American Biography *commends Evans for his breadth: "Few heads in his generation could have held more, or more diverse, information." Chickens may have their iconic liberator in one of America's most engaging scholars.*

LEWIS PYENSON
Professor of History and
Graduate Dean
University of Southwestern
Louisiana

A RETURN TO JAVA

Benedict Anderson Attempts to Reimagine Indonesia

SCOTT SHERMAN

IN 1972, Benedict O'Gorman Anderson, a Southeast Asia specialist at Cornell University, was banned from Indonesia, where he had done his dissertation fieldwork in the early 1960s. In 1999, he returned to Jakarta for the first time in twenty-seven years to deliver what *The Times Literary Supplement* called an "eye-popping" lecture to an auditorium overflowing with power brokers and literati.

Much had changed in the intervening years. General Suharto, Indonesia's ruler since 1965, tumbled from power in 1998, a casualty of the Asian financial crisis. East Timor, after a prolonged and bloody independence struggle, broke free from Indonesian rule under the auspices of the United Nations. Fresh bursts of violence were erupting in the rebellious regions of Aceh and Irian Jaya, prompting fears that the vast Indonesian archipelago could splinter. And the entire nation was experiencing a period of democratic ferment, exemplified by the relaunch of the independent newsmagazine *Tempo*, which was banned under Suharto's New Order regime and which had invited Anderson to speak at a celebration marking its reappearance.

At a luxury hotel in downtown Jakarta, the sixty-two-year-old Anderson, wearing a light shirt and slacks to combat the stifling heat, faced a tense, expectant audience of three hundred generals, senior journalists, elderly professors, former students, and curiosity seekers. In fluent Indonesian, he lashed the political opposition for its timidity and historical amnesia—especially with regard to the massacres of 1965–1966, when the government brutally extirpated the Indonesian Communist Party (PKI) in what a Central Intelligence Agency report later declared "one of the worst mass murders of the twentieth century."

"I can only shake my head in disbelief," Anderson said coolly from the platform, "at the way that the 'opposition' demands that Suharto and his family be called to account for stealing so much money—perhaps they think of it as 'our' money?—and largely turns a blind eye to crimes a thousand times worse: systematic, planned murder on a scale never before seen in the history of the archipelago.

"We can see that the entire 'opposition' today," Anderson continued, "is not, fundamentally, a real opposition to the Dry-Rot Order"—a reference to Suharto's New Order but also an elaborate wordplay in Indonesian—"and that the Indonesia they wish to rebuild will, consequently, still have a mountain of skeletons buried in its cellars."

Anderson's lecture was not merely an eloquent harangue. It was also an emotional plea for a unitary Indonesia. "The modern world," he proclaimed, "has shown us sufficient examples of nations that have broken up because too many of their citizens have had shriveled hearts and dwarfish minds—to say nothing of excessive lust for domination over their fellows." Invoking the names of distinguished patriots who fought for Indonesian independence in the twilight of Dutch colonial rule, Anderson concluded: "I believe in, and hope for, a real revival of the common project which was initiated almost a hundred years ago," a project that "demands self-sacrifice, not the sacrificing of others."

It was a stormy homecoming for a man accustomed to controversy. Television stations and newspapers clamored for interviews, and *Tempo* reprinted Anderson's remarks for its middle-class readership. Since the speech, Anderson's visibility in Indonesia has soared: he contributes pungent essays, with titles like "Suharto's Gulag," to the Indonesian press; his books, proscribed by the New Order, are appearing in fresh editions; and a new generation is excavating the work of a scholar whose aura always had much to do with his status as persona non grata.

In the United States, Anderson is best known for his classic 1983 book, *Imagined Communities*, an innovative and celebratory essay on nationalism. With Indonesia at a crossroads, beset by political uncertainty and insurgent separatism, his speech in Jakarta was a calculated attempt to put the ideas of *Imagined Communities* into concrete practice—to affirm the "grand idea" of Indonesia and to urge Indonesians to "to participate voluntarily, enthusiastically, equally, and without fear in the common project of Indonesian nationalism." But the project can only succeed, Anderson insisted, if its participants resist militarism and ethnic chauvinism and if the Indonesian government accepts some degree of regional autonomy and federalization. The time has come, in other words, for Indonesian politicians and intellectuals to reimagine their community, without burying its past.

For Anderson, the stakes are high. Indonesia is much more than an academic specialty: he says he often thinks in Indonesian rather than in English, and he speaks the language constantly in his home. He writes about the country with considerable intimacy. The 1965–1966 slaughter came as a stunning blow to him. He once wrote that it "felt like discovering that a loved one is a murderer." And it left him with a haunting emotional question: "How still to love a murderer?" It's a question that has animated Anderson's work, and his life, for thirty-five years.

IN NOVEMBER 1956, while a student at Cambridge University, Anderson noticed a cluster of dark-skinned students, Pakistani or Indian, demonstrating against Prime Minister Anthony Eden's decision to invade Suez. Suddenly, out of nowhere, a band of upper-class English students singing "God Save the Queen" assaulted the crowd. "The scene seemed incomprehensible, and I feebly tried to get the educated louts to stop," Anderson has written. "My spectacles were smacked off my face, and so, by chance, I joined the column of the assaulted." Shortly thereafter he left Cambridge for Cornell to begin a forty-year career studying Indonesia.

The confrontation at Cambridge, his first direct encounter with nationalism, aroused his interest in Asia. But the connections were already there: His grandfather had been a cryptographer for the British imperial army in South Asia. Anderson's father, James, spent almost three decades crisscrossing China as an employee of the Chinese Maritime Customs, a Western-dominated consortium whose main purpose was tax collection. Benedict was born in Kunming in 1936, but Japanese encroachment, and the coming war, brought the family to California in 1942. In 1945, the family relocated to Ireland, where Benedict spent much of his youth. James Anderson, who died in 1946, was of mixed Anglo and Anglo-Irish origins; indeed, the O'Gorman side of the family had been active in Irish nationalist politics ever since the United Irishmen's rebellion of 1798. "Because of all this," Anderson says, "though I was educated in England from the age of eleven, it was difficult to imagine myself English."

Anderson's detour into Indonesian studies was largely accidental. At loose ends after graduating from Cambridge, he received a letter from a high-school classmate who was studying politics at Cornell. The department needed a teaching assistant—might Anderson be interested? Before arriving in Ithaca in 1958, Anderson learned that Cornell had America's largest and most distinguished Southeast Asian studies program. It was headed by George Kahin, whose 1952 book, *Nationalism and Revolution in Indonesia*, had established him as the country's foremost authority on Indonesia. Hounded during the McCarthy years, Kahin was nonetheless one of the first scholars, in the early 1960s, to oppose the Vietnam War. From him Anderson learned "the inseparability of politics and scholarship."

Another formative influence at Cornell was Claire Holt. Descended from a wealthy Jewish family in Latvia, she had been a dancer and dance journalist in Paris before arriving in Java in the 1930s. Holt had no academic credentials, but because she possessed encyclopedic knowledge of Indonesian language and culture, Kahin brought her to Cornell in the 1950s to teach. It was Holt who introduced Anderson to the contours and complexity of "traditional Javanese culture"— magic, bandit legends, gamelan music—that greatly influenced his early work. Notably, in his pathbreaking 1972 essay, "The Idea of

Power in Javanese Culture," Anderson compared the Western tendency to perceive power as embedded in social relationships with the Javanese tendency to locate power externally, as a force to be harnessed through means such as magic, sexual prowess, and masking.

Under the guidance of Holt and Kahin, Anderson went to Jakarta in 1961 to research his dissertation, which was published in 1972 as *Java in a Time of Revolution*. The early 1960s marked the twilight of President Sukarno's "Guided Democracy"—which Anderson later described as "populist-authoritarian, conservative-radical"—and for an indefatigable graduate student, it was a blissful time to be in Indonesia. Foreigners were scarce; the political elite was remarkably accessible. The presidential palace regularly hosted shadow plays—elaborate puppet shows set to gamelan music—and President Sukarno himself was often there, surrounded by a plethora of diplomats, students, and onlookers. Anderson recalls: "One could stretch out on a flea-infested mat along with everyone else, get one's plate of cold rice and curry and a glass of warm tea, and watch the whole night through."

When Anderson wasn't studying Indonesian and Javanese, he was plundering the archives for documents on the Indonesian revolution of 1945–1949; wandering through the old royal palaces of Java, most of which were decrepit but still accessible; and taking motorcycle excursions through the small villages of the interior. He even took up the *gendér*, a two-handed Javanese instrument consisting of bronze plates suspended over bamboo tubes of different lengths, which he studied under the direction of one of Java's most distinguished musicians. (Anderson has been equally industrious with regard to languages: he would eventually learn to speak Indonesian, Javanese, Tagalog, and Thai, and to read Spanish, Dutch, German, Russian, and French.)

But storm clouds were gathering throughout the early 1960s. Runaway inflation and a burgeoning U.S. presence in Vietnam contributed to an increasingly volatile political atmosphere. At its center, Sukarno, the mercurial left-wing nationalist, was engaged in a delicate balancing act between the PKI—the third-largest Communist party outside the socialist bloc, with three million members—and the powerful military. The PKI, with its parliamentary orientation, resembled the Italian Communist Party more than the Russian, but its growing strength, particularly in rural areas, made the military jittery. Anderson claims today that his feelings about the PKI at that time were mixed: he admired its incorruptibility, its nationalism, and its opposition to the Vietnam War. "Would it be so bad if the PKI came to power?" he mused in a letter to fellow Indonesianist Daniel Lev. But he also had his doubts: why, he wondered, did PKI rallies feature anti-Western songs composed under the brutally repressive—and anti-Communist—Japanese occupation regime of 1942–1945? In any case, darkness was approaching, and Anderson returned to Ithaca in 1964 with a strong sense that "the Indonesia I had known and loved was gone forever."

ANDERSON'S FOREBODING proved prescient. October 1, 1965, witnessed what appeared to be a coup d'état by disgruntled military officers in Jakarta and the surrounding provinces. Six government generals were murdered, their bodies tossed down a well. President Sukarno was briefly detained, then released. Government military forces led by Major General Suharto quickly regained control of the situation and blamed the coup attempt on the PKI. Sukarno was essentially relieved of his presidential duties; a broken man, he died in 1970.

A stream of propaganda—to the effect that the generals had had their eyes gouged out and their genitals mutilated by female PKI cadres—saturated the media. Two weeks later, what Anderson refers to as "the catastrophe" began: the military destroyed the PKI in a series of massacres that claimed somewhere between 600,000 and 1 million lives from October 1965 to January 1966. According to a declassified 1968 CIA study, *Indonesia—1965: The Coup That Backfired*, "In terms of the numbers killed, the anti-PKI massacres in Indonesia rank as one of the worst mass murders of the twentieth century, along with the Soviet purges of the 1930s, the Nazi mass murders during the Second World War, and the Maoist bloodbath of the early 1950s."

The Indonesian military insisted that the PKI was the sole *dalang* (puppet master) behind the coup, but Anderson and others in Ithaca were skeptical. So in January 1966, Anderson and two colleagues, Ruth McVey and Frederick Bunnell, produced their own account of the coup attempt. The team relied on a vast cache of provincial Indonesian newspapers owned by the Library of Congress but stored at Cornell, as well as classified Foreign Broadcast Information Service documents also stored at Cornell. The result of their research was a 162-page report that soon became internationally known as the Cornell Paper.

The Cornell Paper insisted that the coup attempt was not a Communist power grab but an "internal army affair" spearheaded by colonels from the province of Central Java. The authors admitted that some low-level PKI members participated but insisted that they were duped into it by the military. "The PKI had been doing very well by the peaceful road," the paper argued. "To undertake violence would have involved pitting itself against a vastly superior military force and might have thrown the President into alliance with the army"—a consequence that would have been "fatal to communist hopes."

Initially the authors quietly distributed the Cornell Paper to only a handful of academics. Since the massacres were still happening, Anderson and his co-authors remained anonymous, lest their work jeopardize the safety of friends and colleagues in Indonesia. But Cornell's Kahin sent a copy to William Bundy, assistant secretary of state for Far Eastern affairs, and arranged for McVey to talk with the syndicated columnist Joseph Kraft. The paper was soon transmitted, by an unknown source, to the military authorities in Jakarta, and Kraft devoted a column to the issue. Controversy erupted. In his 1969 book *The Communist Collapse in Indonesia*, the conservative journalist Arnold Brackman furiously assaulted the Cornell Paper: "Why did the Paper's authors rush to absolve the PKI and Sukarno in terms of scholarship when their motivation may have been ideological?" he fumed.

Anderson's name would not be attached to the Cornell Paper until 1971, but when he returned to Indonesia in 1967, he was already the object of suspicion. A U.S. embassy document from that year said Anderson was "regarded . . . as an outright Communist or at least a fellow-traveler." Still, Anderson was permitted to move freely within Indonesia, and in so doing, he discovered that certain leftists he knew in the early 1960s had vanished during the massacres. He was also allowed to attend the trial at which Sudisman, general secretary of the Indonesian Communist Party, was sentenced to death.

Of the PKI's top five leaders, Sudisman was the only one who was tried; the other four were summarily shot. Only two foreigners were continuously present in the courtroom: Anderson and Herbert Feith, an Australian colleague. The proceedings left a deep impression on both of them. Many PKI witnesses had broken under torture and were obsequious at the feet of the military judges. Amid the interminable parade of Communist witnesses, only two, Anderson recalls, talked back in the courtroom and refused to incriminate their comrades. One was an old woman who subsequently went mad; the other, says Anderson, "was this little Chinese kid who looked nineteen or twenty. Very calmly, and with great dignity, he gave his testimony. I was so impressed by it." Anderson pauses at the memory. "When you see all these top Communists groveling before the judge—*what gave that kid the courage to do this?*"

Sudisman, too, kept his composure when he addressed the court. Anderson recalls, "Sudisman was so dignified, so calm, and his speech was so great, that I felt a kind of moral obligation" to do something. "As Sudisman was leaving the courtroom for the last time," Anderson remembers, "he looked at me and Herb. He didn't say anything, but I had such a strong feeling that he was thinking: 'You have to help us. Probably you two are the only ones I can trust to make sure that what I said will survive.' It was like an appeal from a dying man." Anderson answered that appeal in 1975, when he translated Sudisman's speech into English from a smuggled copy of the court transcript. A radical printing collective in Australia published it as a twenty-eight-page orange pamphlet titled "Analysis of Responsibility," with an admiring introduction by Anderson.

And yet the deeper Anderson immersed himself in Indonesia's internal turmoil, the closer the end of his time there drew. After the Cornell Paper was officially published as "A Preliminary Analysis of the October 1, 1965, Coup in Indonesia" in 1971, Anderson still managed to visit Indonesia in early 1972. But once there, he found himself under attack in the Jakarta press. The weekly magazine *Chas*, which reportedly had connections to the intelligence services, published a front-page article under the headline CORNELL SCHOLARS: USEFUL IDIOTS. Shortly thereafter, Anderson was questioned by the police and ordered to remain in the capital. Meanwhile, *Chas* kept up the barrage with cover headlines like PRO-PKI POLITICAL GUERRILLAS EXPLOIT ACADEMIC WORK! THE CORNELL PAPER PROVED TO FALSIFY HISTORY!

In April 1972, Anderson was expelled from the country. On his return to Ithaca, he learned indirectly that he would be blacklisted from Indonesia until he publicly repudiated the Cornell Paper. It was the beginning of an exile that would endure for the better part of three decades.

HOW HAS THE CORNELL PAPER stood the test of time? In the absence of documentary evidence from archives in Washington, London, and, most important, Jakarta, it is impossible to confirm or disprove its arguments. Still, in academic circles, the document has anchored a long-standing scholarly feud about the still-murky origins of the 1965 coup. And in Indonesia itself, the Cornell Paper never lost its popularity: the document circulated like samizdat among activists and intellectuals throughout the New Order period.

In the official army version, PKI agents manipulated dissident army officers into taking action against the military hierarchy. Some prominent scholars have reached a similar conclusion. In his 1978 book, *The Army and Politics in Indonesia*, Harold Crouch, who teaches at the Australian National University, surveyed the various theories of the coup attempt and concluded that PKI leaders did indeed spearhead an uprising in collaboration with left-leaning military officers. "I do agree with Harold Crouch, and so do most PKI people I have talked to," Herbert Feith of the University of Melbourne comments by e-mail. But other scholars remain skeptical. Anderson's old friend Daniel Lev, who is retired from the University of Washington, accepts "the possibility" of high-level PKI involvement but insists that without new archival material "the Cornell Paper, even now, is still the most basic analysis of what happened."

For his part, Anderson still defends the main thrust of the Cornell Paper—that an intramilitary dispute triggered the coup attempt—and he still gets emotional about the liquidation of the PKI. But after decades of reflection, he has arrived at a clear-eyed perspective on the missteps of Indonesia's Communists. In the years leading up to 1965, he notes ruefully, the PKI was almost completely unarmed, but it embraced the rhetoric of Maoism. "That was a huge mistake," Anderson declares. "It created fear and anxiety about the Communist Party. It wasn't a guerrilla army. That's why they were massacred; they were all out in the open."

Some Indonesia scholars believe that the CIA had links to Suharto at the time of the coup attempt. But Anderson still places the burden for the bloodbath squarely on the shoulders of the military in general and Suharto in particular. "What was missing from the Cornell Paper," he says, "was the sense that the whole thing was manipulated from the top by Suharto, which I think is probably what really happened." If General Suharto was, in fact, the puppet master, what was his intention? Anderson replies: "The destruction of the Communist Party and the removal of Sukarno."

UNABLE TO RETURN TO INDONESIA, Anderson spent 1974 in Bangkok. "It was a wonderful time to be there," he recalls. A heady interlude between dictatorships allowed Thai radicalism to flower. But the good times ground to a halt in 1976, when the military overthrew the civilian regime and publicly shot and hanged student radicals in downtown Bangkok. Some young activists eventually found their way to Cornell, where, under Anderson's supervision, they sifted through the wreckage of Thai radicalism in a series of melancholy, innovative dissertations.

Throughout this period, Indonesia was never far from Anderson's mind. He became America's leading critic of the Suharto government in the 1970s, testifying frequently before Congress against U.S. military aid to what he called a "corrupt, dictatorial and aggressive military regime." In 1980, Anderson took direct aim at the U.S. foreign-policy elite, including the ambassador to Indonesia, Edward Masters: "In my judgment," Anderson said, "the Kissinger-Holbrooke-Oakley-Masters group has deliberately sacrificed the welfare of the East Timorese people, and even contributed directly to the catastrophe that has taken place on that island."

Not all of Anderson's colleagues shared his dark view of the Indonesian government. "Ben was never able to accept Suharto or his New Order, in part because the new regime represented the triumph of the worst anti-egalitarian forces in the society," says William Liddle, an Indonesia expert at Ohio State University who, like Anderson, writes regularly for the Indonesian-language press, albeit from a different political perspective. Liddle's early writings on the New Order were critical of Suharto from a liberal democratic perspective. "But starting in the late 1970s," he explains, "I increasingly saw the New Order's economic policies as laying the foundation for long-term democratization through an expanded middle class, a more educated population, and a lessened role for religion, especially fundamentalist religion, in political life. My views are rooted in the modernization theory of the 1950s in which I was trained—and confirmed, I believe, by the subsequent experiences of countries like South Korea, Taiwan, and Thailand. Ben's roots are more Marxian."

Anderson's long absence from Indonesia left him open to the charge that he had fallen out of touch with the country's politics. Nonetheless, observes Feith, his long-standing intimacy with the language and culture rendered him a force to be reckoned with. "Anderson is certainly a central figure among Indonesianists," Feith remarks, "outshining everyone else at least in his generation, with the possible exceptions of Clifford Geertz and Ruth McVey."

FREEVILLE, NEW YORK, sits eight miles east of Ithaca. Anderson lives in a spacious old farmhouse surrounded by rolling hills, grazing cattle, and a barn topped by a Javanese-style weather vane. A young Indonesian friend, along with his wife and two small children, occupies a cottage on the property; Anderson dines with them almost every night, and they look after the place when he's away. In nice weather, Anderson likes to shuffle around his garden, shears in hand. He cultivates the flowers he knew in Ireland as a boy: yellow irises, fuchsias, poppies, mock oranges, lupines. Directly across the street are another forty acres he also owns: some years ago, the old man who lived there sold the land to him at a cut rate, with the request that it be shielded from commercial encroachment.

On a breezy summer morning, Anderson's kitchen overflows with unruly stacks of books, journals, Asian newspapers, and doctoral theses. A portrait of the youthful Sukarno adorns one wall, a doleful relic in light of his ultimate fate. "Indonesia was really like another home for me," Anderson says. "Being kicked out was very painful." In the years after his banishment, he frequently discussed his work with his brother Perry, a distinguished historian and the author of the sweeping survey *Lineages of the Absolutist State*, among other books. Perry urged him to adopt a comparative perspective beyond Indonesia, and his stay in Thailand allowed him to do that. "Being in Thailand forced me to think all the time about if I had to write about Thailand and Indonesia in one space, how would I do it?" Anderson says. In that sense, his banishment from Indonesia was not entirely without benefit. "Probably I wouldn't have done *Imagined Communities* if Suharto hadn't given me this tremendous helping hand," he says with a sly grin.

The roots of *Imagined Communities* lie in what Anderson, in the late 1970s, saw as "a fundamental transformation in the history of Marxism and Marxist movements": the wars between Vietnam, Cambodia, and China in 1978–1979. Far from presenting a unified front against Western imperialism and capitalism, those regimes—whose "independence and revolutionary credentials are undeniable," Anderson noted—were engaged in undisguised fratricide. And so Anderson undertook a full-scale study of nationalism, a force whose power and complexity were not explained by the Marxist theory in which he'd been schooled. As Anderson notes, even one of nationalism's strongest scholarly proponents, the British Marxist Tom Nairn, writes that " '[n]ationalism' is the pathology of modern developmental history, as inescapable as 'neurosis' in the individual . . . with . . . a similar built-in capacity for descent into dementia."

For Anderson, nationalism was neither a pathology nor a fixed, immutable force. Rather, he wrote, "it is an imagined political community . . . because the members of even the smallest nation will never know most of their fellow-members, meet them, or even hear of them, yet in the minds of each lives the image of their communion." For centuries, the world was organized into empires governed by supposed divine right. Within them, liturgical languages, spoken only by the elite, were the medium of culture and of communion with the sacred. Nationalism emerged as speakers of vernacular languages came to reject this organization of society, discovering instead their horizontal ties with one another and conceiving of themselves as citizens rather than as subjects. Nothing was so crucial to this transformation as the rise of what Anderson calls print capitalism: the publishing industry, which produced books, newspapers, and other media in vernacular tongues. Through these media, readers could imagine that they belonged to a shared community.

Such observations flowed naturally from Anderson's work on Indonesia's independence struggle of the 1940s: he saw how a skilled nationalist intelligentsia, based in Jakarta, had summoned not only a nation called Indonesia but also a new language, Indonesian, which became the language of resistance to Dutch colonial rule. Indeed, anticolonialism provided a crucial context for Anderson. Rejecting the view that nationalism first emerged in western Europe, he argued that it originated in early-nineteenth-century Latin America and was then adopted by the European nation-states.

One of the most striking aspects of *Imagined Communities* is Anderson's upbeat view of nationalism. "It is useful to remind ourselves," he wrote, "that nations inspire love, and often profoundly self-sacrificing love." He rejected the identification of nationalism with racism, arguing that "from the start the nation was conceived in language, not in blood," and that its boundaries are potentially plastic. "Nationalism thinks in terms of historical destinies," he wrote, whereas racism "dreams of eternal contaminations." In a recent interview in the *Kyoto Journal*, Anderson argues that "in the U.S., if people didn't believe in America, they'd be shooting each other out of pickup trucks in five minutes flat. [Nationalism is] a kind of glue that makes people, on the whole, obey the law and respect each other, in very large communities. We're talking about hundreds of millions of people. It's hard to think of anything else on the horizon that can enforce that kind of everyday decent behavior."

Of course, in the name of the nation, people also exclude, persecute, and even kill those considered outsiders to the national community. But to Anderson, such virulence is best seen as a perversion of a basically positive force. Nationalism, he remarks, "can be exploited and abused by people who have other things mainly on their minds, like imperialism, monopolies, police states, racism, and so on." Still, in his recent collection, *The Spectre of Comparisons: Nationalism, Southeast Asia, and the World*, Anderson concedes: "My long attachment to, and interest in, anticolonial nationalism had occluded from my vision its menacing potentialities once it got married to the state."

Translated into twenty-one languages and bearing a title that has become common coin across academic disciplines, *Imagined Communities* is cited in virtually every contemporary work on nationalism. For the foremost scholars in that field, Anderson's is a work to be revered and contested—sometimes simultaneously. Anthony D. Smith, a professor of ethnicity and nationalism at the London School of Economics, cautions that Anderson draws too sharp a distinction between religious and national communities; many modern nationalisms, Smith points out, are religiously based. But it is Liah Greenfeld of Boston University who, in a forthcoming essay for *Critical Review*, takes sharpest aim at *Imagined Communities*. Anderson, she writes, "did not ask why suddenly large-scale communities were imagined as *nations*—rather than as classes or churches, for instance, which was more in line with earlier imaginations." Like other critics, Greenfeld questions Anderson's assertion that Latin America was the birthplace of nationalism, pointing to "the substantial recent historical scholarship discussing its earlier presence . . . in . . . Britain and France." She concludes, "One can go on and on listing the instances in which 'the spectre of comparisons' *fails* to haunt Anderson: the amount of available empirical counterevidence—to his general argument as well as specific statements—is staggering."

Nonetheless, with *Imagined Communities*, Anderson had laid the cornerstone for a new discipline. And as Feith observes, with more than a little admiration, "What is distinctive about Anderson's scholarship is not judiciousness; it is adventurousness and originality."

SUHARTO FINALLY FELL from power in May 1998. At last, Anderson could return to Indonesia. But when he did so, it was without fanfare, in part because he thought he might be turned away.

That had happened before. In 1981, Anderson received a visa from the Indonesian embassy in Washington. But when he arrived at the airport in Jakarta, he was detained and quickly expelled. It was, he believes, a malicious trick by the Suharto regime, because the intelligence officials laughed at him as they put him back on the plane. "When the plane took off for Bangkok," Anderson recalls, "I suddenly felt this agonizing pain all over my body. It was so bad that for most of the flight I had to lie on the floor of the cabin, to the astonishment of the passengers and stewardesses. I knew that nothing was really wrong with me; this was the way my disappointment and anger vented itself on my body. That was a lesson to me."

So, in December 1998, when he returned to Indonesia for the first time in twenty-six years, he avoided Jakarta entirely and spent ten quiet days in the provinces with old friends. "I wanted to make sure I was on solid emotional ground," he explains. He was, and a few weeks later he accepted the invitation to speak at the *Tempo* celebrations in the capital.

Anderson's speech was a call not only to unearth the skeletons of 1965–1966 but to preserve a nation that, comprising seventeen thousand islands, forms one of the world's largest "imagined communities." In a veiled reference to Indonesia's dominant ethnic group, the Javanese, Anderson cautioned that one should beware of "those who talk a lot about 'our splendid ancestors' "; after all, nationalism is properly a "common project for the present and the future." He thundered, "I see too many Indonesians still inclined to think of Indonesia as 'an inheritance,' not as a challenge nor as a common project." The breakaway efforts in Aceh and Irian Jaya, he reminded the audience, have little to do with ancient hatreds and much to do with neo-colonialism, corruption, and brutality emanating from Jakarta. The proper response to separatist movements, therefore, is genuine and full autonomy within a federal structure, along the lines of Brazil or India—something the Indonesian military has long resisted.

"I am sure there will be people in Jakarta who will shout, knee-jerk fashion, that a federal Indonesia was/is a Dutch colonial project—despite the fact that the Dutch have had no significant role in Indonesia for close to half a century," he stated. "Others will say federalism is a foreign-inspired scheme to dismember the unitary republic. Who are the foreigners who would have any interest in this dismemberment in the present post–cold war world? I can think of none." He continued: "I have no doubt that if these changes occur quickly and genuinely, separatist movements will lose their steam . . . and the Acehnese and Irianese will once again be invited seriously back into the common project and the deep horizontal comradeship from which they should never have been excluded."

The speech ended with a rumination on the notion of shame—without which, Anderson argued, the "common project" will be severely diminished: "I think that no one can be a true nationalist who is incapable of feeling ashamed if her state or government commits crimes, including those against her fellow citizens." He used his adopted country as an example. "During the Vietnam war," said Anderson, "a good part of the popular opposition came from just this good sense of shame among the American citizenry that 'their government' was responsible for the violent deaths of three million people in Indochina. . . . So they went to work in protest, not merely as advocates of universal human rights, but as Americans who loved the common American project. This kind of political shame is very good and always needed." He concluded: "If this sense of shame can develop healthily in Indonesia, Indonesians will have the courage to face the horrors of the Dry-Rot era, not as 'someone else's doing,' but as a common burden."

The speech was an ambitious effort to bury the legacy of General Suharto (whose party, Golkar, is still a dominant political force) and to reaffirm the ideals of the doomed president Sukarno: internationalism, nationalism, democracy, and social welfare. (Anderson is ambivalent about Sukarno's daughter, Megawati, who recently took over the presidency after a protracted constitutional struggle, but he has a wait-and-see attitude: "I'm not optimistic, but I don't think there's any point in saying, too loudly or too often, that she's bound to be hopeless.")

Anderson's remarks elicited a wide range of commentary. Indonesia's foremost novelist, Pramoedya Ananta Toer—who was imprisoned for fourteen years during the New Order and is now a perennial candidate for the Nobel Prize in literature—expressed pleasure with the speech. But others were less enthusiastic. "It was full of Andersonian originality and disturbing challenges to the Indonesians in the audience, most of whom had prospered during the New Order," says Harold Crouch, who was present at the speech. "But I felt that some of his comments were a bit gratuitous, with a touch of self-righteousness. It is a lot easier for foreigners living abroad to take the moral high ground, while his audience had to make a living for themselves and their families during the thirty-odd years of the New Order." Says Crouch: "Not everyone is willing to be a martyr."

ANDERSON JUST RETIRED from Cornell, but his schedule remains frenetic. A collection he edited, *Violence and the State in Suharto's Indonesia*, has just appeared, and his calendar is packed with speaking engagements and writing deadlines. These days, however, he spends much of his time in Thailand, which he uses as a springboard for periodic visits to Indonesia. He's not in perfect health, and he relishes the tranquillity of Bangkok, where he owns an apartment in a lower-middle-class neighborhood, one filled with "small-business people, schoolteachers, mistresses of policemen, this sort of thing." His high visibility in Indonesia makes it difficult for him to be productive there. "Indonesia is emotionally very stressful, even now, for me," he explains. "I hate to see how miserable everything is. I can't imagine how I could possibly get any peace or quiet there. The bliss of Thailand is that I'm largely invisible."

On his trips to Indonesia, he still endeavors to unravel the mysteries of 1965–1966. Lately he's been interviewing ex-prisoners who served in the Indonesian air force, whose role in the coup attempt has always been contested. He has also been conducting interviews with PKI veterans, most of whom served long prison sentences and are now old men. They are a suspicious bunch, leery of foreigners, but they have heard of Anderson, and they respect him and therefore submit to his questions. "I'm interested in their life histories," Anderson explains. "I ask them: What do you think it meant to be a Communist? What regrets do you have? How do you look back on all this? It's a kind of history of the left. I'm not going to write that history, but at least the material will be on the record."

His Indonesia is full of ghosts. In 1999, he attended a meeting of an organization called Pakorba, which stands for "Association of Victims of the New Order." The gathering was held in central Jakarta, in a nondescript building owned by the Ministry of Manpower. Anderson recalls: "It was an incredibly overwhelming experience. It was packed with elderly men and women. Everyone turned to look: Who is this white guy? I just took my seat. Clearly some people in the audience recognized me; a buzz went around the room." People started to come up to him. " 'Are you Ben Anderson?' Finally I was pushed onto the stage to say a few words." Many others spoke as well. "It was very emotional because these people got up and, as if they were in a Quaker meeting, talked about their lives and experiences. Toward the end, something absolutely astounding happened."

He was approached by a handsome, dignified Chinese man, who looked to be about fifty and who said: "I want to thank you for what you wrote about me." Anderson had no idea who he was. "You wrote about me after the Sudisman trial," the man answered. Before him, Anderson suddenly realized, was the Chinese kid who talked back to the judge in 1967. Anderson was dumbfounded: "*You were . . .*" "Yeah, that's me," the man replied.

They spent a day together, and Anderson listened to the man's story. He explains, "Many of the Communists, when they were trying to escape the sweeps on them, fled into the Chinese ghettos, partly because the Chinese are much more closemouthed than the Indonesians are, partly because these ghettos are accustomed to a certain level of clandestinity. And this kid, who was a radical kid, was somehow recruited by Sudisman to be his personal courier in terms of contacting other people who were hiding underground. Sudisman was the last surviving top Communist who hadn't been executed or murdered by the regime."

In the period leading up to the trial, the man explained to Anderson, he was tortured in prison. Before his testimony, he was instructed by his interrogators to follow their directives in the courtroom, or else pay a high price afterward. But he defied them and spoke his mind before the judge.

"The strange thing," Anderson says, "is that when he came out of the courtroom, two of the guards clapped him on the shoulder. A strange part of the culture of these guys is that when they see courage, even if you're an enemy, they respect it. After that he wasn't tortured anymore, though he spent years and years in prison."

Remembering their encounter at the Pakorba meeting, Anderson pauses. "It was like somebody came out of a grave," he recalls with astonishment. "I never thought this guy was alive." Anderson is extremely reserved, but he confesses in a soft voice, almost a whisper: "We looked at each other and just jumped into each other's arms. I just felt like crying."

—October 2001

PART IV

Scientific Subjects

OH MY DARWIN!

Who's the Fittest Evolutionary Thinker of Them All?

JAMES SCHWARTZ

AS THE FEATURED SPEAKER at the twentieth annual Darwin festival at Salem State College in Salem, Massachusetts, Harvard professor Stephen Jay Gould is lecturing to a packed auditorium—not only professional biologists and students but also retirees and blue-collar workers. It is the birthday of both Abraham Lincoln and Charles Darwin (who happened to be born in the same year as well as on the same day), and Gould is talking about American history. Stocky and clean-shaven, with a plump baby face and thick graying hair, he wears a tie in honor of the occasion but no jacket. He is unfolding bit by bit what he calls his Back to the Future theory of history, his belief that hundreds of chance occurrences got us where we are today. If Robert E. Lee's second in command hadn't misunderstood his orders, Gould suggests, the South might have won the Battle of Gettysburg, and then the war, and we might still be a divided country. He's building up to his central theme: that history is unpredictable and serendipitous, that human existence arose by chance, and that life, intelligent or otherwise, is devoid of any special significance in the larger scheme of things.

Toward the end of his rhythmic, free-form lecture, Gould pauses in mid-sentence. He has noticed that one person in the crowd of nearly a thousand is quietly leaving through a back exit. "Don't you want to hear the last ten minutes?" he cries out in obvious distress. "I don't mean to be arrogant about my status, but most of these folks you have all the time. Me you only got for a little while."

Such pugnacity is hardly surprising to Gould's numerous admirers and critics. For years, he has been an aggressive voice of reason in the argument against creationism and other varieties of pseudoscience. But Gould, who seems to thrive on controversy, is also entangled in a battle with a school of fierce anti-creationists called evolutionary psychologists, who believe that human nature is largely mapped out in our genes. Most recently the Massachusetts Institute of Technology psychology professor Steven Pinker has been responsible for generating public interest in evolutionary psychology (EP). Not only does Pinker have a gift for the clear expression of complicated ideas, but, with his good looks and stylish clothes, he knows how to get media attention. His first book, *The Language Instinct*, was an engaging discussion of the nature of language and its evolution. In 1997, Pinker's *How the Mind Works* appeared to great fanfare and quickly became a national best-seller.

The disagreement between Pinker and Gould is the latest variation on the old nature-versus-nurture debate that has been raging for centuries. The most recent skirmishes date back to the 1970s, when sociobiology, a new discipline dedicated to explaining social behavior in biological terms, was catapulted into the limelight. Gould became a leading early critic of sociobiology, penning eloquent disquisitions on the ability of humans—not their genes—to determine their own fate. But in the 1980s, molecular biologists began identifying more and more genes involved in human diseases and behavior. Sociobiology once again gripped the public imagination, but this time under the name evolutionary psychology—sociobiology with a relentless focus on human psychology.

The argument between evolutionary psychologists and their critics centers on elemental mysteries of human nature. It is about the sort of tough questions that kids ask—Why are some people bad? Why do some breeds of dogs kill squirrels, and can they be taught not to?—as well as some more adult concerns: Are older men genetically programmed to abandon their longtime wives and take up with younger women? To what extent is intelligence, sexual preference, or the capacity to nurture mapped out in our genes? How deeply entrenched are the hatred and distrust of warring ethnic groups throughout the world?

THERE IS A CERTAIN POETRY in the fact that Gould's office is located in Harvard's venerable Museum of Comparative Zoology, founded in 1859 by Louis Agassiz, its first director and Harvard's last creationist. The walls of Gould's office bear the names of the animal classes, the letters visible in faded black paint dating from the days when the room was still an exhibition hall. The office itself is the size of a basketball court, filled with crowded bookshelves and tables piled high with the great diversity of the world Gould celebrates in his writing. This is the perfect Gould habitat, sprawling and packed with stuff.

A brilliant essayist and lecturer, Gould is the most popular science writer in America, which is remarkable because he engages serious ideas and draws from a rich store of knowledge of literature and history. In addition to writing half a dozen books, Gould has published nine collections of the essays he's been writing for *Natural History* over the last twenty-five years. He thinks of himself as a scientist in the tradition of Galileo, who was unusual in his time for writing in Italian, the language of the people, rather than Latin, which was then the norm for serious scientific discourse. He is still troubled by the fact that his friend the late astronomer Carl Sagan was denied entrance to the National Academy of Sciences. "Scientists will say, 'He was a popular writer *but* also a good scientist,' " Gould complains. "The *but* has to be changed to an *and*."

Gould himself has been the object of a fair amount of sniping over the quality of his science. His theory of punctuated equilibrium—the idea that sudden rapid changes in evolutionary history are followed by long periods of relative stability—has a limited following among his colleagues. Gould proposed his theory—sometimes called jerky evolution—as an alternative to the classical theory of slow, continuous evolution. A Gould antagonist, Richard Dawkins, the English evolutionary biologist responsible for the term "selfish gene," has been known to refer to the theory of punctuated evolution as "evolution by jerks." In his most recent book, *Unweaving the Rainbow*, Dawkins characterizes Gould as a guy who's been "seduced by bad poetry."

WHEREAS GOULD PREFERS to see human behavior as a complex and unpredictable interaction of culture and a highly pliable set of genetic potentials, EPists have little patience with such a wishy-washy notion. They prefer to break down human psychology into a set of "complex adaptations," *specific traits exquisitely suited to perform their functions*, in the often repeated mantra. To EPists, it is a given that everything complicated and interesting about animals, and humans in particular—ranging from the way we find mates, to the working of the eye, to the ability to detect cheaters in social interactions—is the result of the long, slow incremental process of Darwinian natural selection.

"You can't have a parent without an eye and an offspring with one," Pinker explains to me. "It's all gradual and Darwinian." We are sitting at the dining room table in his newly renovated condo a few blocks north of Harvard Square. The apartment, like Pinker's understated dark dress shirt and black jeans, is up-to-the-minute and impeccable. Every counter and surface is shiny and clear; there's not a stray magazine or envelope in sight. It's the kind of home that makes you suspect that there must be a back room where all the mess is stored.

The eye is the classic example of a complex adaptation. As Pinker explains it, an animal picks up a random mutation for a clearer lens, which makes it better able to avoid predators and find mates than animals with less clear lenses. This individual will give rise to offspring with better eyes, and over the course of generations animals with clearer lenses will take over the population. At some point down the line, one of these animals may acquire another random mutation, this time for a rounder eyeball, which enables the eye better to focus images. In this way, mutation by mutation, over hundreds of generations, the multiple components of a complex function are acquired.

For Gould, it is Pinker's insistence on natural selection as the only valid scientific explanation for the origin of complex animal behaviors that is so galling. Although Gould acknowledges the importance of natural selection, he believes that the EPists have failed to appreciate other principles of evolutionary change such as random genetic drift, catastrophic events, and the constraints of basic laws of form. Furthermore, he contends, by identifying a genetic origin for many complex human behaviors, the EPists would have us believe that human behaviors are far more entrenched and immutable than they really are. Whereas Pinker argues that all of our complex mental functioning has been crafted over thousands of generations by natural selection to achieve a particular end, Gould believes that human attributes as basic as language may be accidental.

IT WAS A BRITISH GRADUATE STUDENT named Bill Hamilton who in the early 1960s had the insight that leads directly to Pinker's view of the human mind. Believing he'd forfeited his chance for a Ph.D. from London University by pursuing his heretical approach to the study of altruism, Hamilton sat for hours in train stations and public gardens to relieve the loneliness of his student rooms. While he sat, he mulled over a startling new idea, which he later named the theory of inclusive fitness.

Today, Hamilton is a tall, white-haired man of sixty-three, a Royal Society professor at Oxford widely considered the most influential evolutionary thinker since Darwin. "I had the feeling that I might be a crank," recalls Hamilton of his student days. He describes three experiences that influenced his thinking. When a schoolboy, he recognized that he felt a greater sense of obligation to his brothers and sister than to his school friends. Also, his mother kept bees, and he'd seen how the sister worker bees often sacrificed their lives for the good of the colony. Last he had been deeply dissatisfied with the lectures on evolution he received as an undergraduate at Cambridge University, where it seemed to him that his professors did not give Darwin's mechanism of natural selection its proper due.

Hamilton realized he could explain the puzzling phenomenon of sister bees sacrificing themselves for the good of the hive by shifting the perspective from the survival of an animal's offspring to the dissemination of its genes. Thanks to a peculiar system of sex assignment, a female bee shares more genes with her sisters than with her direct descendants. If the goal is to make the greatest number of copies of her genes, a female bee is better off helping her mother make more sisters than she is producing her own offspring. In 1964, Hamilton pointed this out in a seminal two-part paper titled "The Genetical Evolution of Social Behavior." More generally, his gene's-eye point of view made it clear that the traditional Darwinian concern with an organism's investment in its children was too limited. Post-Hamilton, sacrifice for siblings and more distant relatives as well as one's own children made sense. In 1976, Dawkins popularized this idea in an enormously influential book, *The Selfish Gene*.

But if it hadn't been for the Harvard entomologist E. O. Wilson, Hamilton's theory would very likely never have come to Dawkin's attention. Wilson seized on the idea and prodded his reluctant peers to recognize its significance. At sixty-nine, Wilson still has the lean, angular build of a marathon runner. Though he has an almost courtly conversational style and retains the aura of a Southern gentleman, he has a relentlessly driven, competitive nature that has resulted in an extraordinarily productive career. There are many folktales surrounding Wilson that illustrate one or another of the qualities that have made him successful, including the story of his reaction to Hamilton's 1964 paper. In one widely circulated version, Wilson is sent a copy of the paper to review, skims it, and, believing it to be the ravings of another manic graduate student, tosses it in the trash. Hours later, in the middle of the night, he realizes he's made a terrible mistake, bolts out of bed, and rushes back to the lab to retrieve the paper before the janitors empty the trash.

"That's a great story," Wilson says, laughing, "but it's not true." The truth, he insists, is that he read the paper on a long train ride from Boston to Miami (he's a reluctant flier). Hamilton's idea struck him as improbable and too simple, and it didn't seem to lend itself to broad applications. But when Wilson couldn't find a logical flaw in the paper, he grew angry. He, not Hamilton, was the world authority on social insects, and certainly no one else was going to explain the behavior of insect societies. Yet the more he thought about it, the more he became convinced that the theory was fundamentally correct. By the time he reached Miami, he had been converted. "I would never throw out an article like that," he explains. "At the very worst, I'd file it for future reference."

With Hamilton's ideas in mind, Wilson went on to formulate the basic tenets of sociobiology. In 1975, he published a beautifully illustrated overview of his theory titled *Sociobiology: The New Synthesis*. If he had confined himself to animals other than ourselves, as he'd originally intended, his life would have been more peaceful. But in a characteristically ambitious finale, he tacked on a chapter extending his theory to humans. Our species is genetically programmed to be warlike and territorial, he wrote, and males will typically dominate females in human social hierarchies. He hypothesized the existence of genes for spitefulness and homosexuality, genes for conformity that make humans easy to indoctrinate, and genes that make us favor kin and be wary of strangers. In a section on hunter-gatherer societies, Wilson cataloged the behavior patterns of various members. He found that, just as in ant colonies, different members of the groups played different roles. There were individuals of higher status, leaders and outstanding specialists, for example, who generally established themselves by their mid-thirties. These elites, he wrote, do more than their share of work and dominate the group's sluggish, unproductive members.

Inside the academic anthill, there was no doubt as to which kind of ant Wilson was. Already while a graduate student, he'd sensed he had a special destiny, as another Wilson tale suggests: He and a fellow graduate student are driving back to Harvard after attending a meeting at which all the greatest minds in evolutionary biology had gathered. Wilson's friend is awestruck at having been in the presence of such greatness. After driving along in silence for a while, Wilson turns to him and says, "It shouldn't be very hard to get to the top of that heap."

In Cambridge, the reaction to Wilson's book was intensely negative. Fifteen local scientists, including Gould and Richard Lewontin, a universally admired population geneticist, formed the Sociobiology Study Group. Together, Lewontin, who had been brought up by a French-Canadian nanny on Manhattan's Upper West Side, and Gould, the Queens-born son of a Marxist court stenographer, led the opposition. With his ease with mathematics and a powerful analytic mind, Lewontin brought rigor and salience to the critique of sociobiology. For months, the small group of allies plotted against sociobiology in Lewontin's office. At his own desk one floor above, Wilson had no idea what was brewing just below his feet. In November 1975, the Sociobiology Study Group published a letter in *The New York Review of Books*.

The letter, signed by all fifteen members of the study group, stated its objections in no uncertain terms. Sociobiology, it asserted, is part of a tradition of biological determinism that has "provided an important basis for the enactment of sterilization laws and restrictive immigration laws by the United States . . . and also for the eugenics policies which led to the establishment of gas chambers in Nazi Germany." The invocation of Nazism was clearly intended to cause alarm. Less widely appreciated, however, was that there had been a pseudoscientific crusade in the early part of this century to improve the American gene pool. Laws passed in more than thirty states led to the sterilization of tens of thousands of people judged mentally feeble or morally inferior, and immigration from nations deemed of inferior genetic stock was restricted. Gould and Lewontin's letter sounded a warning bell: supposedly objective science had been used—and could be again—to justify dubious politics and prejudices.

Wilson was not one to take the Sociobiology Study Group attack lying down. After licking his wounds for several weeks, he began a counteroffensive. Since both Lewontin and Gould were widely known for their radical politics, he devoted himself to the study of Marxist economic theory so as better to understand the "enemy in the field." In December 1975, his rebuttal appeared as a letter in the *NYRB*. In it, he accused the authors of intentionally distorting his meanings in order to make a case against him. In March of the following year, Wilson wrote a more detailed reply to his detractors in *BioScience*, a professional journal. In that article, he refers to a statement by a Harvard professor characterizing Wilson as a "privileged member of Western industrial society whose book attempts to preserve the status quo." Wilson points out that, as a Harvard professor, the author of the statement enjoyed identical privileges.

Today, Wilson recalls those days with a wry chuckle. "Gould and Lewontin going on in Marxist tones—we're talking about a bygone era, in an intellectual as well as a political sense. Sometimes we wondered, 'Who did Lewontin think he was, writing those letters from his Vermont dacha?' " The Vermont dacha is a reference to Lewontin's cabin in southern Vermont, where he has long spent as much time as possible, talking crops and weather with local farmers and acting the part of crusty old New England codger.

In 1978, Wilson was a featured speaker at the symposium on sociobiology held by the American Association for the Advancement of Science in Washington, D.C. Gould was scheduled to speak at the same session. Wilson, who had fractured his ankle jogging, had decided to deliver his speech from his seat onstage rather than make his way to the lectern. A few minutes after he had begun to talk, a group of protesters from the International Committee Against Racism stormed the stage. One dumped a pitcher of water over his head while the others chanted, "Wilson, you're all wet!" A few minutes later, the protesters withdrew, and the audience broke out in a spontaneous standing ovation for the injured, dripping Wilson. Gould took the microphone and quoted Lenin on the inappropriate use of violence. Later he explained that the attack on Wilson had been an "infantile disorder" of socialism.

Did Gould and Lewontin's attacks push Wilson further down the path toward human sociobiology? "Their attacks and other criticisms, coming particularly from the New Left saying that this was bad science and that I was racist and capitalist, were one of the major stimuli for me to move ahead," Wilson says. "Otherwise I might have delayed a considerable period of time before I wrote a book aimed at a broad audience." In 1978, he brought out *On Human Nature*, a broad defense of sociobiological theory. "Not just to answer them," he says, "but perhaps in part to respond to what I considered scurrilous and unfounded criticism." A few years later, Wilson began to move in new directions, becoming a tireless and influential crusader for the cause of biodiversity, the movement devoted to the preservation of the diversity of animal and plant species.

AN INCONSPICUOUS DIRECTORY in the dim lobby of the Museum of Comparative Zoology Laboratories informs you that Lewontin's office is on the third floor and Wilson's is on the fourth. It's a long, slow elevator ride up. A veteran of the sociobiology wars recalls unwittingly stepping into the elevator with Wilson and Lewontin in the late 1970s, shortly after Wilson had published a new monograph on ants. The tension was nearly unbearable as the elevator inched its way to the third floor. No one uttered a word. As the doors opened and Lewontin got out, he turned to Wilson and said, "I'm glad that you're doing real science again."

A central hall with laboratories on either side leads from the elevator to the Lewontin lab common room. In it, there's a vast rectangular wooden table covered with old copies of the *NYRB* and scientific journals. Mounted to the wall, a magnificent moose head has watched over generations of students. A minute after the appointed hour, Lewontin appears and ushers me into his office. Lean and fit, with a round face and a full head of dark hair, he looks much younger than his seventy years. Though he's one of Harvard's most eminent faculty members, there's no sign of his special status—no couches, Oriental rugs, honorary degrees, or art—not a luxury or frill of any kind.

Why is it, I ask, that he objects to the Wilson-Pinker view of major human behaviors as adaptations crafted by natural selection? "Instead of talking about adaptations," Lewontin replies, "we should say organisms do the things they can do: fish gotta swim and birds gotta fly.

"We'd be better off flying," he continues, though he, like Wilson, is afraid of flying in airplanes. "It would increase our fitness, we'd be better able to flee from predators. But if we flap our arms, we don't get any lift." He stands up and starts flapping his arms to illustrate. "Even if I picked up a pair of Ping-Pong paddles, it wouldn't help." He's walking around the room now, madly flapping his arms and still not getting any lift. "Until you're doing something, you're not doing it," Lewontin says by way of summary, "and natural selection can't help. What natural selection does is to make more efficient what the organism is already doing."

Lewontin's argument is that natural selection alone can't explain the origin of flight or of any complicated new function. Unless a little bit of change gives an animal a little bit of an advantage, the change won't be selected for, and obviously a little bit of a wing doesn't do any good. Darwin was well aware of the problem and devoted considerable thought to it. "An organ originally constructed for one purpose . . . may be converted to one for a wholly different purpose," he wrote in *The Origin of Species*. This principle of functional shift makes it impossible to presume that any complex adaptation was crafted by natural selection, argue Gould and Lewontin. In particular, it doesn't make sense to say that a specific human behavior was selected for its current function when its original function may have been entirely different. Gould later proposed the term "exaptation" (to be distinguished from "adaptation") for features arising along these circuitous pathways. This is the first line of defense against Wilson-Pinker sociobiological thinking.

But Gould and Lewontin went further. In 1979, they wrote a paper for a British conference on adaptation and natural selection titled "The Spandrels of San Marco," in which they argued that many aspects of the design of animals are purely accidental. The paper has acquired legendary status. There even exists a collection of essays using the techniques of postmodern literary criticism to analyze the spandrels paper as scientific rhetoric.

Gould and Lewontin cleverly chose an example from the history of architecture to illustrate their point. Spandrels are unintended by-products of an architectural design. At the medieval cathedral of San Marco in Venice, the spandrels are four triangular spaces inadvertently created when the church's dome was mounted on four rounded arches. In the case of the cathedral, Lewontin and Gould argued, it would be easy to infer that the lavishly decorated spandrel is the heart of the architect's design. By analogy, "adaptationists," as Lewontin and Gould dub sociobiologically inclined biologists, mistake a by-product of an adaptation for a genuine adaptation. The origin of a complex adaptation is impossible to know, and any such attempt to invent hypotheses is, according to Lewontin and Gould, unscientific speculation. Critics of sociobiology label these hypothetical scenarios "Just So Stories," after Rudyard Kipling's children's book in which fanciful explanations are offered for adaptations such as the elephant's trunk.

Lewontin added another important piece to the case in his 1984 book, *Not in Our Genes*. Even if it were possible to understand an individual in terms of his genes and environment, he argued, we still would not understand group behavior. The whole could not, even in principle, be reduced to the sum of its parts.

For a period in the early 1980s, it seemed Gould and Lewontin's views had gained the upper hand. But it was precisely at this time that the revolution in molecular biology spun into high gear. With the development of new techniques for the sequencing and manipulation of DNA, it became easier and easier to identify and clone genes. Suddenly genes were being identified for just about everything. In *Drosophila melanogaster*, the common fruit fly and beloved laboratory organism of generations of geneticists, genes were found that affected sexual behavior, the pace of the internal clock, learning, and memory. Not only that, but many virtually identical genes were found in humans, whose evolutionary line diverged from insects' more than half a billion years ago. Simultaneously, molecular biologists started identifying the genes that play roles in human disorders, such as Alzheimer's, Huntington's, and Parkinson's diseases. As the decade progressed, the flood of DNA information led to the formation of a generously funded Human Genome Project to sequence the entire three billion base pairs of human chromosomal DNA.

Now Gould and Lewontin were on the defensive. They had always argued that it was bad science to break up an animal into individual traits or behaviors in order to claim that they are determined by particular, selectable genes. In the early days, the Sociobiology Study Group had criticized the idea that there were genes for specific and variable forms of human behavior, including spite, aggression, xenophobia, conformity, and homosexuality. Later, Gould expanded the argument to include even body parts. "Hundreds of genes contribute to the building of most body parts and their action is channeled through a kaleidoscopic series of environmental influences," he wrote in a *Natural History* essay.

Yet by the early 1990s, gene-based explanations for human behavior were on the rise. The stage was set for the reemergence of sociobiology under the new name evolutionary psychology. In 1992, the husband-wife psychologist-anthropologist team of Leda Cosmides and John Tooby laid down the manifesto for the new discipline of EP in their introduction to an edited volume of original papers titled *The Adapted Mind*. EP was essentially an extension of Wilson's program applied exclusively to humans, with a few amendments to quell the leftist critique. Proponents of EP are quick to emphasize that human nature was crafted by natural selection to solve the problems of life on the African savanna 1.8 million years ago and that traits that may have been advantageous then, like xenophobia and aggression, may not confer a selective advantage in the modern world. Hoping to avoid the criticisms that were leveled against the first sociobiologists, the new generation insists it is most interested in understanding the evolution of universal features of the human species, not in the particular genes that make one person different from another, such as genes for IQ or homosexuality.

In 1997, an especially acrimonious debate over EP broke out when

Gould took on the new school of sociobiologists in a long two-part article in the *NYRB*. Describing his foes as "Darwinian fundamentalists," he addressed himself to what he saw as the essential weakness of the adaptationist approach: "The human brain must be bursting with spandrels that are essential to human nature and vital to our self-understanding but that arose as nonadaptations, and are therefore outside the compass of evolutionary psychology, or any other ultra-Darwinian theory."

No wallflower when it comes to protecting his turf, Steven Pinker leaped to defend his science. "The ideas of EP are not as stupid as Gould makes them out to be," he wrote in a letter to the *NYRB* published later that year. "Indeed, they are nothing like what Gould makes them out to be." It doesn't matter, Pinker argued, whether a complex adaptation originated as an exaptation or a spandrel; if it later serves a useful function for the organism, it must have been acted on by natural selection to serve that function. "That there is a particular school of adaptationism is a rhetorical device," Pinker told me. "The school is just about everybody," he asserted, referring to the legions of scientists who study animal behavior using the sociobiological paradigm. "Gould and Lewontin have influence over social scientists and literary types who read *The New York Review of Books* and *Natural History*; they didn't like the direction sociobiology was going. Marxists don't want there to be an innate human nature, particularly not one that smacks of selfishness, greed, and aggression. They always say that a person's science can't be divorced from his politics, but they never apply this argument to themselves."

In the case of Lewontin, at any rate, this charge is often made. "There's almost no scientific subject on which he's positive," says Bill Hamilton. "I can't understand how such a good mind can be so negative about science per se. The politics always comes first. He doesn't admit it, but that's the case." Writing in his autobiography, *Naturalist*, Wilson says that Lewontin "was stage-cast for the role of contrarian. He possessed a deep ambivalence that kept both friend and foe off balance." Before the book's publication in 1994, Wilson sent

Lewontin a copy of the manuscript, asking for his comments. After a long period of silence, Wilson had his assistant hunt Lewontin down. A few days later, the manuscript was returned unopened with a letter attached to it. "Dear Ed," Lewontin wrote, "Given that our disagreements are so fundamental and broad and given the wide-spread misapprehension that they are personal rather than scientific, you can always say with complete honesty that you gave me the opportunity to comment on your manuscript and I declined. Autobiography is not a genre I am tempted either to read or to write. In order to get through life we all create elaborate fictions about ourselves, but I have always felt that these were better left to the hours between waking and sleeping."

Gould, who has always been somewhat more interested than Lewontin in finding common ground with his opponents, has recently shown some openness to EP ideas about the differences between the sexual attitudes of males and females. In the EP view, males are likely to be promiscuous because it is advantageous to spread their sperm far and wide. Females, on the other hand, are programmed to be more selective: their eggs are more precious than male sperm, and they are strapped into months of gestation and suckling after conception. In his *NYRB* attack on EP, Gould goes so far as to call this line of reasoning the "most promising" EP has to offer, and he admits that it "probably does underlie some different and broadly general emotional propensities of human males and females." However, he cautions the EPists against pushing this theory too far and suffering the fate of Freudians, who "elevated a limited guide into a rigid creed that became more of an untestable and unchangeable religion than a science."

Lewontin, who married his high-school sweetheart and can to this day be seen walking hand in hand across Harvard Yard with her, takes a much harder line. "I'm a man, and I don't go around screwing young girls," he says. "I'm human, and so I have to be explained."

One can almost see Lewontin hiking through the Vermont woods shaking his head in despair at the loss of Comrade Gould. There had been no more articulate spokesman in the battle against bourgeois decadence.

MEANWHILE, Pinker, busy promoting his latest book, *Words and Rules: The Ingredients of Language*, marches forward. In a recent appearance in London, Pinker and Dawkins held a public forum titled "Is Science Killing the Soul?," which was attended by twenty-three hundred people and sold out weeks in advance. Pinker spoke of the fiction of the unified self. "It's only an illusion that there's a president in the Oval Office of the brain who oversees the activity of everything," he said, in what undoubtedly struck many as a particularly apt metaphor.

The notion that there is no unified self is fundamental to EP. If the brain is a collection of computers, each one of which performs a highly specialized function, then it makes sense to invoke natural selection acting over millions of years to account for the existence of those computers.

This view of the mind broken up into an array of independently evolved modules is disquieting to many. As the Rutgers philosopher Jerry Fodor, the author of a forthcoming book titled *The Mind Doesn't Work That Way*, puts it, "If there is a community of computers in my head, there had also better be somebody who is in charge, and, by God, it had better be me." If one does not believe that human intelligence is the sum of an array of computers, then one must postulate the existence of some more general cognitive ability that gives us the capacity for complex thought. And this general ability, Fodor believes, may be the result of a small but crucial evolutionary shift that distinguished our brains from the brains of other primates.

Like Fodor, Lewontin and Gould argue that the EPists have it wrong: language, consciousness, and most of our distinctively human mental capacities are side effects of the fact that our brain grew big for other reasons. Furthermore, they caution, these reasons cannot be reconstructed. Our extraordinary human abilities are epiphenomena of "all those loose connections with nothing to do," explains Lewontin. As an example of a nonadaptive trait he offers the uniquely human ability to use recursion in language, that is, to make sentences of the form: "I say that Noam Chomsky says, when people say . . ." Though chimps can be taught to compose simple sentences of the form "I want" or "I see" on a computer, they cannot be taught to use recursion.

Does Lewontin have a theory about the origin of this unique linguistic ability of humans? "You could invent a story," he explains with distaste. "You could say it was an advantage to early human beings in being able to say, 'I saw Joe doing that,' but that's just yak!"

Pinker insists that our ability to use language has evolved because language offered a selective advantage. "Being articulate is highly valued in all cultures," he says. "Tribal chiefs are high in verbal skills and have more offspring."

It is symbolically fitting that Gould and Lewontin were teaching their undergraduate course on evolution for the last time this spring while a few hundred yards down the road Pinker and a recently tenured Harvard animal behaviorist named Mark Hauser were giving a popular graduate seminar on evolutionary psychology.

The point of Pinker and Hauser's course is to trace the origins of human thought. There is no doubt that we can learn a lot about human language from studying apes and birds, Hauser told me after the seminar one afternoon. The way birds learn their songs is strikingly similar to the way humans learn language.

In his characteristically acerbic way, Lewontin dismisses this idea. It is simply impossible to say how novel abilities like human language arose. He jibes: "One way to get around the problem that language is a novelty is to define it in such a way that doesn't make it a novelty. You'll say bird twitter is language." In a 1998 article titled "The Evolution of Cognition: Questions We Will Never Answer," Lewontin wrote, "It might be interesting to know how cognition (whatever that is) arose and spread and changed, but we cannot know. Tough luck."

This spring, Lewontin will publish a collection of his essays with the appropriately contrarian title *It Ain't Necessarily So.*

EVEN IF GOD were to descend on Cambridge and part the waters of the Charles River at Lewontin's feet, it would still be unthinkable to imagine the skeptical biologist embracing religion. Gould, on the other hand, has recently been evincing a new sympathy for the realm of the unscientific. In his most recent book, *Rocks of Ages: Science and Religion in the Fullness of Life,* he not only sets out terms for a peaceful coexistence with the obdurate religious believers among us but seems to offer another defense against the sociobiological threat. His thesis is that it makes perfect sense to see science and religion as distinct and complementary forms of human endeavor: science addresses the "factual character of the natural world"; religion is concerned with spiritual meaning and morality.

This dualism stands in stark contrast to the views of Wilson, Dawkins, and Pinker, who categorically deny the existence of a soul or spirit. Indeed, from the outset, it was Wilson's goal to deny the existence of an independent moral realm. In *On Human Nature* he says, "Human behavior . . . is the circuitous technique by which human genetic material has and will be kept intact. Morality has no other demonstrable ultimate function." *Consilience,* Wilson's latest and most ambitious statement to date, takes an even more radical position, arguing that "there is intrinsically only one class of explanation." He goes on to make the bold assertion that "all tangible phenomena, from the birth of stars to the workings of social institutions, are based on material processes that are ultimately reducible, however long and tortuous the sequences, to the laws of physics."

Gould insists that it is not possible to reduce ethics to sociobiology or to unify knowledge by subsuming one theory in another. Even if human traits like xenophobia and aggression were in the end shown to be the result of adaptations in the Pleistocene era, Gould contends, science alone will not suffice as an explanatory system. The man who largely made his name insisting on the purposelessness of life has found a place in his heart for religion. But that's not to say Gould has turned into any kind of crypto-creationist. No matter who turns out to be right in the end, he and his adaptationist foes can at least agree with Darwin that "whilst this planet has gone cycling on according to the fixed law of gravity, from so simple a beginning endless forms most beautiful and most wonderful have been, and are being, evolved."

—November 1999

DREAM ON
Does Sleep Make Any Sense?
JIM HOLT

MODERN PHILOSOPHY IS FOUNDED in dreams—doubly so, in fact. It was a series of peculiar dream episodes, one of them involving a melon, that convinced the young René Descartes that his vocation was to establish a new philosophy. And it was through his "dream argument" (as it came to be called) that Descartes, in the first of his *Meditations*, began to make his way to a position of universal doubt—the necessary prelude, as he saw it, to the reconstruction of human knowledge on a secure foundation. Descartes noted that I might think "I am seated by the fire, attired in a dressing-gown . . . when in fact I am lying undressed in bed."

This Cartesian question—How can I be sure I am not always dreaming?—had earlier occurred to Plato and Cicero. It is one of the now-classic philosophical problems about dreams. The other classic problem—Can I be immoral in dreams?—was raised by Saint Augustine, who was perplexed that he continued to fornicate in his dreams even after he had renounced such wickedness in his waking life.

Contemporary philosophers have tended to focus on a third question: Do dreams amount to experiences that occur during sleep? This is largely the consequence of Norman Malcolm's book *Dreaming*, which appeared in 1959. Malcolm, a friend and disciple of Wittgenstein's, made the Wittgensteinian-sounding argument that the notion of remembering a dream is nonsensical, since there is no conceivable way of checking the alleged memory. Therefore, Malcolm concluded, dreams are not experiences had while sleeping but merely the propensity to tell weird stories upon awakening.

These are the questions that philosophers have asked about dreams. The ordinary person has rather different concerns. Why do I dream? he wants to know. What is dreaming for? Do my dreams mean anything?

A speculative answer to these latter questions was proposed by Freud, who held that dreams offered the disguised fulfillment of repressed wishes and that the function of dreaming was to keep our sleep from being disturbed by these troublesome desires. But the first empirical breakthrough in dream science came well after Freud, in 1953. That was when Nathaniel Kleitman—the father of sleep research, who died this past August at the age of 104—discovered REM (rapid eye movement) sleep. For periods totaling about two hours each night, Kleitman found, sleepers make jerky eye movements under their closed eyelids; if they are awakened during these periods, they recall having dreams, whereas if they are awakened during non-REM periods, they do not.

Since the discovery of REM sleep, new evidence has shown that we also dream during much of our non-REM sleep. Non-REM dreams tend to be repetitive and thought-like, with little imagery—obsessively returning to the suspicion that you left your Filofax somewhere, for example. If non-REM dreams are like neuroses, REM dreams, with their wild conceits and bizarrely stitched-together plots, are more akin to psychoses. Between these two states, there may not be a single moment of our sleep when we are actually dreamless.

It is hard to resist the notion that any activity that occupies as much of our lives as dreaming does must have some sort of evolutionary rationale. (Do other species dream? Some of them certainly do have sleep cycles like ours. The elephant, curiously, sleeps standing up during non-REM periods and then lies down for REM sleep.)

At the moment, there are two prominent—and conflicting—neurobiological theories that attribute adaptive value to dreaming. The Harvard sleep researcher Allan Hobson has hypothesized that the function of dreaming is to fix recent experiences in long-term memory; in other words, we dream about things worth remembering. Francis Crick and Graeme Michison, by contrast, see dreams as a sort of "brainwashing" process in which overlapping memories are eliminated; that is to say, we dream about things worth forgetting.

The most persuasive evolutionary take on dreaming, however, comes from Owen Flanagan, a philosopher at Duke who also holds a professorship there in the department of neurobiology. In his fascinating new book, *Dreaming Souls*, Flanagan submits that while sleep is certainly an evolutionary adaptation, and consciousness probably is, too, consciousness *during* sleep is merely a nonadaptive by-product of the two. "Dreams are the spandrels of sleep," he declares, invoking an evolutionary figure of speech popularized by Stephen Jay Gould and Richard Lewontin.

On the night shift, the brain renews itself by stockpiling fresh supplies of neurotransmitters for the next day. Flanagan believes that pulses from the brain stem, which are designed to get this restorative work going, activate stored images and thoughts more or less at random. The partly shut-down cerebral cortex, designed to process sensory experience by the light of day, then performs the same function with this chaotic input during sleep. The dreams that result, Flanagan argues, are neither dazzlingly poetic, as Nietzsche claimed, nor deeply meaningful and in need of elaborate interpretation, as Freud thought.

Trying not to be too deflationary, Flanagan maintains that dreams nonetheless have some self-expressive value, for the random thoughts activated are *our* thoughts and the narrative structures are imposed by *our* minds. Perhaps. Yet as we learn more about the neurobiology of dreaming, it gets harder to disagree with the advice of W. H. Auden:

> Should dreams haunt you,
>   heed them not,
> for all, both sweet and horrid,
> are jokes in dubious taste,
> too jejune to have truck with.

—November 1999

LITTLE BIG MAN
Are We As Old As We Are Tall?
JIM HOLT

IS LIFE ABSURD? Many people believe so, and the reasons they give often have to do with space and time. Compared with the vast universe, we are but infinitesimal specks, they say, and the human life span constitutes the merest blip on the cosmic timescale.

Others fail to see how our spatiotemporal dimensions alone could make life absurd. The philosopher Thomas Nagel, for one, has argued that if life is absurd given our present size and longevity, it would be no less absurd if we lived for millions of years or if we were big enough to fill the cosmos.

The issue of life's absurdity is moot, I suppose, but there is an interesting question lurking in the background: Which, from the point of view of the universe, is more contemptible—our minuteness or our brevity? Cosmically speaking, do we last a long time for our size or a short time? Or, put the other way, are we big or small for our life span?

The best way to go about answering this question is to look for a fundamental unit of space and of time that would render the two dimensions comparable. Here is where contemporary physics comes in handy. In trying to blend the theories that describe the very large (Einstein's general relativity) and the very small (quantum mechanics), physicists have found that neither space nor time is continuous on the tiniest scales. Each appears to be made up of discrete units—

geometric atoms, as it were. The shortest length that has any meaning is the Planck length, which is about 10^{-35} meters. The shortest possible tick of an imaginary clock (sometimes called a chronon) is the Planck time, about 10^{-43} seconds. (This is the time it takes light to cross a distance equal to the Planck length.)

Now, suppose we construct two cosmic scales, one for size and one for longevity. The size scale will extend from the smallest possible size, the Planck length, to the largest possible size, the radius of the observable universe. The longevity scale will extend from the briefest possible life span, the Planck time, to the longest possible life span, the age of the universe.

Where do we rank on these two scales? On the cosmic size scale, humans, at a meter or two in length, are more or less in the middle. Roughly speaking, the observable universe dwarfs us the way we dwarf the Planck length. On the longevity scale, by contrast, we are very close to the top. The number of Planck times that make up a human lifetime is very, very much more than the number of human lifetimes that make up the age of the universe. "People talk about the ephemeral nature of existence," the physicist Roger Penrose has commented, "but [on such a scale] it can be seen that we are not ephemeral at all—we live more or less as long as the Universe itself!"

Certainly, then, we humans have little reason to feel angst about our temporal finitude. *Sub specie aeternitatis*, we endure for an awfully long time. But our extreme puniness certainly gives us cause for cosmic embarrassment.

Or does it? In Voltaire's philosophical tale *Micromégas*, a giant from the star Sirius visits the planet Earth, where, with the aid of a magnifying instrument, he eventually detects a ship full of humans in the Baltic Sea. He is at first amazed to discover that these "invisible insects," created in the "abyss of the infinitely small," seem to possess souls. Then he wonders whether their diminutiveness might not indeed be a mark of superiority. "O intelligent atoms," he addresses them, "you must doubtless enjoy very pure pleasures on your globe, for having so little body and seeming to be all spirit, you must pass your lives in love and in thought, which is the true life of spirits."

In response, the microscopic humans begin spouting philosophical inanities from Aristotle, Descartes, and Aquinas, at which the giant is overcome with Homeric laughter.

Would we humans be less absurd if we were bigger? Probably not, but we would surely be less sound. Consider a sixty-foot-tall man. (The example comes from the biologist J. B. S. Haldane's beautiful 1927 essay "On Being the Right Size.") This giant man would be not only ten times as high as an ordinary human but also ten times as wide and thick. His total weight would therefore be a thousand times greater. Unfortunately, the cross section of his bones would only be greater by a factor of a hundred, so every square inch of his bone structure would have to support ten times the weight borne by a square inch of human bone. But the human thighbone breaks under about ten times the human weight. Consequently, when the sixty-foot man takes a step, he breaks a thigh.

If we humans are, from the cosmic perspective, absurdly tiny for our life span, perhaps we can derive some consolation from our impressive complexity of form. That is what John Donne did in his *Devotions Upon Emergent Occasions*. "Man consists of more pieces, more parts, than the world," he observed. "And if those pieces were extended and stretched out in man as they are in the world, man would be the giant and the world the dwarf."

—February 2000

BONOBOS IN PARADISE
A Primate's Progress
HELEN EPSTEIN

IN THE HUMID, swampy forests south of the Congo River in central
Africa, in an area as big as Italy but almost as remote as the Arctic, an
orgy has been going on for thousands of years. This is the territory of
the bonobo apes—black hairy creatures nearly as tall as men and three
times as strong. In gangs of up to a hundred, they travel through the
jungle, build nests, sleep in the trees, and have sex every two hours or
even more often. Bonobos look like chimpanzees, and until the late
1920s naturalists did not distinguish between the two species. Now we
know that chimps and bonobos occupy different territories, that they
differ physically, and that the bonobo way of life is so different from
that of the chimp that the two species seem to have evolved in separate worlds.

Bonobos have thinner limbs and wider faces than chimps. The hair
on their heads is longer, often with a middle parting, like that of the
creatures in the *Planet of the Apes* movies of the 1960s and 1970s. Like
many primates, they groom each other, picking bugs and snarls from
the fur of their fellow bonobos. In fact, they are such avid groomers
that sometimes one will have all its hair pulled out. This creates an
odd impression. Looking at photographs of bald bonobos, I think of
E.T., of Gandhi, of the elderly Dwight Eisenhower.

The really surprising thing about bonobos, however, is their society. For decades, primatologists have known that the world of the chimpanzee can be a brutal one. In the 1970s, Jane Goodall and other primatologists witnessed murder, infanticide, rape, and even a form of organized warfare among chimpanzees, and these events seemed to confirm what all the bloody centuries of human history had suggested. Not long before Adolf Hitler came to power, Sigmund Freud wrote, "We cannot, it is true, easily foresee what new paths the development of civilization could take; but one thing we can expect, and that is that [aggression,] this indestructible feature of human nature, will follow it there." After World War II, Konrad Lorenz and Robert Ardrey looked back on fifty years of dead bodies and cities in ruins and sought to attach biological, evolutionary roots to Freud's ideas. Birds, fish, and other animals fill up their niches and then turn on each other, and human beings do the same, they wrote. The chimpanzees that primatologists observed in the following decades showed us the likely evolutionary source of our self-destructive ways. Life was an inevitable struggle over resources, which in human culture escalated into crime and war.

Still, human beings do cooperate and form complex societies, and this behavior also needed to be explained. During the 1960s, Sherwood Washburn and his colleagues at the University of California at Berkeley argued that although human males had a natural instinct to compete with one another, they formed cooperative relationships when something important was at stake, such as big game that could only be brought down by several men at once. In Washburn's view, human evolution was driven by a combination of male aggression, cooperative hunting, and meat eating. Male hunting groups formed the seed corn of human societies.

The ideas of Lorenz, Ardrey, and Washburn have become increasingly controversial in recent years. Feminists in particular have argued that the so-called Man the Hunter hypothesis fails to account for the important roles women played in early human societies. Then, in the 1970s, new research emerged from several sites in Congo, where the bonobos live. These findings seemed to deal the greatest blow yet to the Man the Hunter scheme and to the idea of the inevitability of animal aggression. Under a vast tree canopy, in one of the world's most deeply troubled and unstable nations, a few intrepid teams of primatologists had been watching these strange, rare apes for two decades or so, and they found a sort of feminist paradise.

Murder, rape, and infanticide have never been observed among bonobos. Bonobo society displays features unheard of in chimps and other apes and rare even in the most enlightened human societies. Female bonobos, though smaller than males and often burdened with infants, form gangs that control aggressive males. Females have priority at feeding sites and sometimes initiate sexual acts. Bonobos have sexual relations almost constantly, from the age of one year, and much of this activity is homosexual. Male rank among bonobos often depends on females. For example, the son of a high-ranking female is more likely to hold high rank himself. The bonobo findings, says the Emory University primatologist Frans de Waal, "seem to be very inconvenient for the Man the Hunter scheme. They have thrown nearly half a century of thinking about animal behavior and human evolution off the track."

The distinctions between chimp and bonobo society have been widely reported, and both primatologists and nonprimatologists have weighed in with their preferences. For some, bonobo society provides a vision of what the world could be like if women ran it: bonobos inhabit a world where women's sexuality is a tool of diplomacy, an unthreatening way of dealing with conflict. In the erotic-literature section of my local library, I found an essay by the Cornell University anthropologist Meredith Small, who suggests that bonobos might even be our moral ancestors. Perhaps early human beings used "sex on a daily basis to make alliances, trade goods and favors, establish friendships and keep the peace," she writes. "Bonobos suggest that our idealization of private, monogamous sexual behavior might be a relatively recent deviation from our evolutionary heritage."

For the novelist Alice Walker, the bonobo is the mascot of sexual freedom and women's empowerment. Here is the dedication in her recent book, *By the Light of My Father's Smile*:

Our
  insouciant
  fun-loving
  nonreading
relatives
  the delightful cousins
Bonobo.

May Life be thanked
  for them.

The psychiatrist Ann-Louise Silver found bonobos useful for analyzing erotic dreams. She had been reading an article in *The New York
Times* that mentioned de Waal's bonobo research when, she writes, "I
began seeing the clinical implications of de Waal's work. Perhaps we
humans have a 'programmed' tendency to respond sexually to situa-
tions of competition and danger."

For de Waal, bonobo behavior "may provide a foundation for what
in humans we call 'sympathy' and 'empathy.' " In de Waal's coffee-
table book *Bonobo: The Forgotten Ape*, he writes:

> Who could have imagined a close relative of ours in which female al-
> liances intimidate males, sexual behavior is as rich as ours, different
> groups do not fight but mingle, mothers take on a central role, and
> the greatest intellectual achievement is not tool use but sensitivity to
> others?

It is likely that the bonobo has received more media attention in
recent years than any other ape. Does the bonobo deserve this? Why
has no one written a poem, or a coffee-table book for that matter,
about the gibbon, the diminutive ape of southeastern Asia that forms
monogamous relationships, sings duets with its mate in the forest,
and settles in circumscribed areas, which it defends against encroachment by other gibbons? After all, the gibbon's lifestyle, with its version of the nuclear family and private property, bears many intriguing
similarities to our own.

If anyone were to write a poem about the gibbon, it might well be

Richard Lowry, the young editor of the conservative biweekly *The National Review*. In the right-wing newsletter *Imprimis*, an indignant Lowry disparagingly associated the bonobo with the feminist, multicultural left:

> Among . . . "Bonobos," there is no observable violent behavior. . . . They live in a matriarchal society in which the females lord it over the passive and easily manipulated males; free love reigns since the "Bonobos" are not loyal to their mates and will have sex at the slightest instigation; the females are bisexual; and all . . . [bonobos] male and female are vegetarians.
>
> Review this list carefully, and you are bound to conclude that it is a perfect description of the ideal liberal society. In fact it is probably a pretty good description of life at, say, Brown University.

WHO ARE THE BONOBOS? Are they really who we think they are? And how much does our opinion of ourselves influence our view of them? Observers of foreign cultures can sometimes be fooled. The early observations of chimpanzees carried out by Goodall and by Adriaan Kortlandt suggested that these animals were peaceful, gentle creatures, too, before further research proved otherwise. Early in the twentieth century, the anthropologist Margaret Mead arrived on the South Pacific island of Samoa to study adolescence among the natives. She witnessed a culture much like that of the bonobos. The Samoans were peace loving and sexually free. There was little jealousy or repression, and adolescence was a time of happiness and blossoming sexuality. Mead argued that sexual repression and adolescent angst were inventions of Western civilization and were not inevitable in human society. Decades later, it was discovered that Samoan society is just as conflicted about adolescent sexuality as Western society is, perhaps even more so: Mead's informants had been teasing her. Could the bonobos be fooling their observers, too? Some of the world's most eminent primate researchers are locked in battle over the true nature of the bonobo—and over how much these distant relatives have to tell us about ourselves.

Craig Stanford of the University of Southern California is skeptical of the grand claims his colleagues have made on the bonobo's behalf. In his book *The Hunting Apes*, Stanford puts forth an updated version of the Man the Hunter hypothesis: meat captured by primate males, he writes, becomes a kind of symbolic currency with which troop members can manipulate one another. Wild bonobos rarely eat meat; nevertheless, when Stanford hears field reports that male bonobos defer to females at feeding sites, he interprets it as a strategic maneuver akin to bribery. Just as a human male may hope that offering chocolates and opening car doors will get him somewhere, a male bonobo surrendering his patch of shoots in the forest to a female may expect sexual privileges later on. What looks like female power is an illusion.

"It's real female dominance," counters de Waal, and the key to it, he argues, is female cooperation. Female bonding is much more common among bonobos than it is among chimps. Sometimes female coalitions gang up on males, even when there is no food around. De Waal further cites the work of his former colleague Amy Parish (she is now at USC), who notes that there are more than forty recorded cases of male bonobos sustaining serious injuries at the hands of females. "There is great reluctance among primatologists to admit that female dominance in bonobos exists," says de Waal. This reluctance is especially marked, he says, among male primatologists. He told me his female colleagues, including Parish, Meredith Small, and the University of Michigan psychologist Barbara Smuts, are far more receptive to the idea that real female dominance exists among bonobos than his male colleagues are.

As Stanford sees it, however, the notion that females dominate bonobo society is simply not supported by sufficient evidence. According to Stanford, animals in the wild behave differently from their better-observed brethren in zoos. "When you compare wild chimps with wild bonobos, many of the differences between the two species disappear," he told me on the phone, and so he has written in the pages of *Current Anthropology* and other journals. The structure of bonobo communities in zoos is unnaturally constrained. For example, in the wild, bonobo troops are large and dynamic. Seventy-five or more individuals may gather and then split off into smaller groups. A zoo colony, on the other hand, might consist of perhaps seven animals living together for a very long time. "If one of them happens to have a strong personality, that can change the social dynamics quite a lot," Stanford argues, and this may lead to premature generalizations about female dominance and aggression among bonobos in general.

Zoo living may also influence bonobo sexual behavior. When captive bonobos are compared with wild chimpanzees, the bonobos have sex far more often. But when wild bonobos and wild chimps are compared, says Stanford, the two species appear to copulate with a similar frequency. Therefore, he concludes, the hypersexuality of zoo bonobos may only be a consequence of the stress and boredom of living in captivity.

Yet, as de Waal notes, Stanford did not include homosexual encounters in his calculations. If he had, he would have found that bonobos scored many more sexual encounters than chimps, even in the wild. "Even greater than the reluctance to recognize female dominance is the reluctance to acknowledge the overwhelming role of sex in bonobo society," he explains. Again, this reluctance is most marked, says de Waal, who is Dutch, among Anglo-Saxon male primatologists. "The English-speaking world, with its Victorian heritage, is exceptionally squeamish about sex," he maintains. "U.S. investigators often try to downplay it. Some say bonobo sex is not real sex, it's something else; others ignore it altogether. But if this were happening with humans, we would know what to call it. It fits all the Paula Jones definitions."

In fact, some primatologists perceive similarities between human and bonobo sexuality. In *Bonobo: The Forgotten Ape*, de Waal describes bonobos having sex when they arrive at feeding sites and when they encounter rival bonobo groups in the forest. Such events might engender rivalry and even violence among chimps, we are told, but bonobos seem to have reached a higher, more evolved, perhaps more human, social plane. Human beings do not (usually) have big orgies before dinner parties or when two groups of strangers meet. However, human sexuality, like that of the bonobo, does have a social function other than reproduction.

Stanford does not believe that such comparisons go very far. He concedes that "bonobos do engage in a richer array of sexual activities than chimps do." But, he adds, "the problem is we still don't know enough about what bonobos do in the wild. There have probably been twenty times more man-hours put into watching chimps than bonobos. If you want to portray the bonobos as the sexy apes from Venus, it helps if you don't know much about them."

AT A RESEARCH STATION on the rural edge of Atlanta, Sue Savage-Rumbaugh of Georgia State University has spent the past twenty years getting to know a male bonobo named Kanzi, who is widely regarded as the world's most literate ape. Savage-Rumbaugh is primarily interested in language research, and she and Kanzi communicate using a keyboard, either an electronic one or a laminated card printed with about five hundred symbols representing simple things such as foods, objects, and feelings. She claims that actively training a bonobo to use the symbols doesn't work. Kanzi's adoptive mother, Matata, for example, failed miserably when Savage-Rumbaugh tried to teach her to communicate with the keyboard. But Kanzi, who was then a toddler, learned to use it easily, just by hanging around the playroom during his mother's lessons. "They learn better by observation, in the same way a child does. There is no difference," she insisted to me, "between the ways a child and a bonobo learn language."

Judging from Savage-Rumbaugh's research with Kanzi and a small number of other bonobos, one must say that these apes are outstandingly adept at getting messages across to human beings. Still, language and cognition experts such as Steven Pinker and Stephen Budiansky remain generally skeptical of scientists' attempts to communicate with apes. In *The Language Instinct*, Pinker argues that human language is as unique in nature as the elephant's trunk and Kanzi's exploits are no more convincing than the circus tricks that trained chimps perform.

Many animals, especially chimps, will do extraordinary things, such as ride bicycles and pour cups of tea, in order to obtain a food reward. Is Kanzi expressing a real affinity for language, or is he merely exceptionally shrewd? Kanzi can respond to spoken questions, which is impressive for an ape, but he rarely initiates exchanges, and when he does, the subject is invariably food. Conversing with Kanzi is very unlike conversing with a child, who asks questions about everything she sees just for the sake of asking, without anticipation of reward.

I wanted to see for myself whether I could perceive any kinship across the 2 percent of DNA that separates human beings from bonobos, so I arranged to visit Savage-Rumbaugh at Georgia State University's Language Research Center, where she works. She seemed oddly defensive. She had canceled our meeting at the last minute and only reluctantly agreed to see me one evening during my trip. Unfortunately, Kanzi and the other bonobos had fallen asleep by then. "I will not wake them up!" she said firmly. I hadn't asked her to.

During our interview, she suggested I come by the following morning so I could see the animals when they were awake. When she arrived to pick me up at the gates of the compound where she works, she pulled out one of the symbol keyboards she uses to communicate with Kanzi and the other bonobos. "We . . . speak . . . with . . . keyboard," she said, pointing to the relevant symbols on the laminated card as she spoke. The card had several hundred icons on it, and the abstract symbols did not resemble the things they are supposed to represent, nor were they in any order I could make sense of. Nevertheless, Savage-Rumbaugh insisted that she and I communicate by pointing at the symbols in silence, which I found vexing.

Savage-Rumbaugh allowed me to sit and watch the bonobos from a distance but would not let me go near them or attempt to communicate with them. Nevertheless, they were fascinating creatures. Photographs do not convey how spirited and agile bonobos are. Although they resemble pitch-black potbellied, hairy wrestlers, they move as gracefully as shadows. I sat on a plastic chair on the grass and watched Kanzi and his cage mates, an adult female with no hair and a heart condition, another adult female, and a toddler. Savage-Rumbaugh had brought the bonobos some bananas, and as she pushed them through the bars there was much commotion inside. The baby swung back and forth across the ceiling of the cage, clutching a banana in her foot. The hairless female ate slowly by herself, next to the bars, staring out at me. Kanzi sat on a rubber ball, as if on a small stool, and ate one banana after another. When all the bananas had been eaten and there were only peels strewn on the ground, Savage-Rumbaugh asked, "Do you want some more bananas?" Kanzi looked at her and squealed.

Savage-Rumbaugh disappeared into a laboratory building, and then returned a few minutes later carrying nothing. "I'm sorry, Kanzi, there are no more bananas," she said. Kanzi stared straight ahead. "Would you like some oranges?" This time Kanzi let out an even louder squeal. And then I saw what all the fuss was about. As de Waal had told me, "The first thing that strikes you about bonobos is the sex." With an unmistakable erection, Kanzi lumbered up behind the bald female and rubbed his torso rapidly against her back. The whole episode lasted only a few seconds, but indeed there it was. What did it mean? Was he attracted to his scrawny, ailing cage mate? Perhaps it was just an expression of simple joy from an ape who knew oranges were coming.

Whatever Kanzi was doing, it resembled only the most eccentric human behavior. Bonobo sexuality may be striking in its variety and frequency, but to say that these animals use sex the way human beings do seemed to me to be stretching the point. Savage-Rumbaugh agreed that in order to interpret what Kanzi was up to, we need to know what sex means to him and his species.

MORE AND MORE, people look to apes, as in the past they looked to God, to understand human behavior, impulses, and desires. In the nineteenth century, skeptics of evolution warned that this might happen. Human aggression, love, altruism, and everything we think and feel can all be explained, we are told, by genes selected long ago in our African ape-man past. After all, we share 98 percent of our genes with chimps and bonobos, and only some five million years of evolution distinguish us from them.

Three million years ago, our own ancestors were australopith-ecines, hairy ape-men with big teeth, jaws, and snouts who scavenged and hunted, had small brains, walked upright, but also spent time in the trees. Christopher Wills in *Children of Prometheus: The Accelerating Pace of Human Evolution* describes how, since that time, human beings have spread over the entire earth; they have built automobiles, computers, cities, and nations; they have invented written language and used it to compose literature and encyclopedias and laws. They have expressed themselves through music, sculpture, painting, and dance. Wills argues that human evolution continues at a fast pace, particularly in response to environmental and social changes that people themselves have created. What have the bonobos been doing in the meantime? On the face of it, their routine has changed very little.

Nevertheless, Savage-Rumbaugh believes their world might be just as complex as ours, but in ways we can't yet perceive. "We consider ourselves unique only because we have not observed enough or understood what is going on with other species," she contends. In her quest to understand the bonobo, Savage-Rumbaugh considers Kanzi more a colleague than a research subject. When anthropologists study another human culture, they use a key informant, someone from that culture who can describe its customs, beliefs, and the reasons for certain actions. "One day," says Savage-Rumbaugh, "we may be able to use Kanzi as a key informant for studies of bonobo culture."

The more we learn about bonobos, the more sophisticated we find their world, says Savage-Rumbaugh. "They mark travel routes," she told me; "they practice primitive agriculture."

Agriculture?

"Kanzi likes to plant things and watch them grow, and wild bonobos will knock over a bolingo tree so that the fruits will ripen sooner, and then come back two weeks later to harvest them. I've seen bonobos plan for the future and have discussions about the past." They also, according to Savage-Rumbaugh, exhibit empathy. She says that the bonobos she works with sometimes know when she is sad and will groom and brush her hair to cheer her up. And, she has written, they make sensitive sexual partners:

> Slow motion study of videotaped copulatory bouts [between bonobos] indicated that, in many cases, the speed and intensity of thrusting was visibly altered or terminated as a function of changes in the facial expression or vocalizations of one of the participants. . . . On numerous occasions, either the male or female was observed to terminate thrusting when the partner could not be engaged in eye contact or otherwise indicated disinterest by yawning, self-grooming, etc.

A few years ago, Savage-Rumbaugh visited Congo and observed wild bonobos at a research station called Wamba, run by a team of primatologists from Kyoto University. At one point, she found herself surrounded by a crowd of bonobos. The group consisted of about five to ten subgroups, which she followed for several days. "One subgroup might move off into the forest, with a lot of drumming and hooting, and then another one would go off in another direction," she recalled. "Eventually all the subgroups would disperse, and then meet up later in the evening. How did they coordinate all this complex moving and regrouping?" She then noticed that whichever subgroup she was watching was always the last to move off. She could only conclude that these bonobos were observing her, just as she was watching them.

IT IS CERTAINLY TEMPTING to view the good bonobo and the bad chimp as two competing candidates for humanity's progenitor. But increasingly, observers are recognizing how similar bonobos and chimps are to each other—and how difficult it is to generalize about the habits of either species.

According to USC's Amy Parish, chimp females sometimes form alliances and gang up on males, just as bonobo females do. There is increasing evidence that some groups of bonobos eat meat. Bonobos can also be violent, as a U.S. zookeeper recently discovered when the bonobo in his care, who had been sulking for days, came up behind him and bit off his finger. Groups of chimpanzees often make tools, which they use for fishing or for sopping up water from places that are hard to reach, but different groups living in different environments make different types of tools. Bonobos were once thought never to make tools, but Kanzi has on several occasions fashioned a stone knife in order to retrieve food from a box secured with rope.

Richard Wrangham of Harvard University points out that primate behavior is affected by local environments, which provide varying kinds and amounts of foods. Chimpanzees live north of the Congo River and often share their forests with gorillas, with whom they must compete for the most digestible fruits and plants. For this reason, females must disperse and forage by themselves, and so they never have the opportunity to form coalitions. There are no gorillas in the forests south of the Congo River where the bonobos live, and their food is more abundant, which permits bonobos to move through the forest in larger groups. This, in turn, gives females an opportunity to form coalitions and to assume greater power within the group.

Primate cultures, though various and fascinating, have probably remained more or less fixed for thousands or perhaps millions of years, changing only in time with the local ecology. They have not spontaneously developed and changed over generations the way human cultures have. Human societies evolve in response both to environmental changes and to what people learn from each other. In *The Cultural Origins of Human Cognition*, Michael Tomasello, co-director of the Max Planck Institute for Evolutionary Anthropology, argues that what makes human beings unique is that they are so good at learning from one another and that they create new, original things with what they learn. What this means is that chimps and bonobos may really be different sides of the same ancient coin and that the ape in us, or whatever is left of her beneath the grand complexity of modern human culture, may be both bonobo and chimp, sexy and aggressive, civil and rapacious, a serene vegetarian and a watchful carnivore, a peace-loving feminist and a macho brute.

Bonobos and chimps have a great deal to tell us about how our ancestors may have lived five million years ago, how the first tools were made, and how different ecological circumstances may have enabled different types of social groups to form and to survive. However, if we think of these creatures as nothing more than primitive versions of ourselves, we may never know how and why they behave the way they do.

We may never know in any case. Fieldwork has already been cut back because of the Congo war, and those researchers who venture into the forest are taking considerable risks. There are many precious minerals underground where the bonobos live. Field-workers who bring expensive equipment into the forest are often accused of looking for diamonds to steal.

If those who study the bonobo are endangered, so too is the bonobo itself. There are about ten thousand bonobos left in the world, and they could easily be wiped out in five years. Even when the Congo war eventually ends, loggers threaten to clear the bonobos' habitat. In a way, it's a miracle that the bonobos have survived this long.

—October 2000

THE GOSSIP INSTINCT
Did Schmoozing Precede Musing?

DANIEL ZALEWSKI

WHERE DID LANGUAGE COME FROM? Until recently it's a question that's left most experts speechless. The linguist Noam Chomsky, for all his elaborations on the hardwired nature of language, has long refused to speculate on precisely how we developed this gift for gab —leading some evolutionists to brand him a mystic. Other heavyweights, like the biologist Stephen Jay Gould, only go so far as to suggest that speech arose accidentally, a mere upshot of our big brains. This restraint can be frustrating, but it has an obvious explanation: airy-fairy speculations on the origins of language have been trotted out for hundreds of years, pinpointing everything from parrots to menstrual rituals as the precursor to chatter. Indeed, scholarly pique with such tomfoolery is long-standing: in 1866, the Linguistic Society of Paris forbade all papers on the topic.

But things changed in 1990, when MIT's Steven Pinker published a seminal paper arguing that natural selection could account just fine for language—much as it could for other one-time-only evolutionary tricks like an elephant's trunk. While many readers found his logic convincing, they noted that Pinker remained a bit vague on exactly which "selection pressures" (as they're known in the Darwin business) made language a necessary adaption. Why we evolved speech remains an open—if newly respectable—question.

Perhaps the most striking figure to dive into the post-Pinker fray is

Robin Dunbar, a University of Liverpool anthropologist and authority on gelada baboons. His theory is a doozy: Language, Dunbar suggests, evolved among hominids as a "cheap and ultraefficient form of grooming"—that mildly distasteful practice of leafing through a companion's fur for loose skin and tangled burrs. Furthermore, he says, "language evolved in order to allow us to gossip." Say what?

Here's the argument: grooming, explains Dunbar in *Grooming, Gossip, and the Evolution of Language*, is the basic way that primates maintain social cohesion. In fact, many chimps spend up to one-fifth of their waking hours picking away at each other—far more time than is needed for hygiene's sake. This overkill is, of course, precisely the point; these extended massage sessions are a sign of loyalty, a key to forming alliances within often volatile social groups.

But what does all this touchy-feely stuff have to do with language? As primates descended from jungle treetops to the savanna, they amassed in larger groups for protection. (Baboons, for example, form extended families of around fifty.) Dunbar theorizes that the challenge of keeping track of the primate pecking order—who was grooming whom, and so on—led to a massive increase in brain size, a necessary precursor for language. At the same time, as small groups grew into mobs, internal conflicts and petty squabbles erupted, requiring ever-more-elaborate grooming rituals to keep the peace. This raised a conundrum: how, Dunbar wondered, could a hominid spend *more* than one-fifth of his day grooming and still have time for necessities like hunting and mating? As Dunbar sees it, language erupted onto the scene to solve this problem, allowing "a kind of vocal grooming" to replace the hands-on approach. After all, you can stroke only one friend at a time, but you can verbally massage a crowd.

Dunbar's argument actually rests on some vanguard theories regarding hominid evolution. Traditionally, anthropologists have suggested that ecological exigencies—the need to coordinate hunting efforts or determine if fruits were poisonous—provided the selection pressure for hominid brain expansion. But in 1988, the British psychologists Richard Byrne and Andrew Whiten laid out the "Machiavellian intelligence hypothesis" as a different way to explain the upswing in intelligence. The theory says that primates' immersion in the social whirl caused them to develop a singular ability to *predict* how others would react, encouraging chimps to manipulate and flatter their friends—tricks requiring heavy brainpower.

The Princeton primatologist Alison Jolly thinks that the data in Dunbar's book linking primate brain size with group size lend concrete support to this theory. "His central insight, that language evolved primarily for social ends, is dead-on," she says. "Linguists don't see this, but those of us out in the field know that what's singular about primates is their social savvy."

So what are the implications of Dunbar's theory, other than to imbue expressions like "you scratch my back, I'll scratch yours" with sociobiological sex appeal? As Dunbar sees it, his proposal suggests that language evolved not as deep thoughts but as gossip: schmoozing came first, musing second. In many ways, this position isn't new. The anthropologist Bronislaw Malinowski always maintained that language primarily "oil[ed] social wheels," and he disparaged the "false conception of language as a means of transfusing ideas from the head of the speaker to that of the listener." In this vein, Dunbar likes to think that his theory will help dismantle "the standard linguistics view that language evolved exclusively for solving problems and exchanging information."

As one might expect, Dunbar's difficult-to-falsify speculations have proved a bit much for linguists—even the evolution-minded Pinker. "It sounds like a classic Just So Story, doesn't it?" he says. "Saying that language evolved so we can gossip is like saying that eyes, with all their complex visual circuitry, evolved so we can flirt. I'm sorry, but the grammatical machinery must be there for a reason—in my view, for making complex propositions like *the wildebeest is on the other side of the lake.*" And the University of Hawaii linguist Derek Bickerton, who advances the controversial idea that the circuitry for language was established in a single "catastrophic" mutation, dismissed the theory in *Nature*, saying Dunbar had committed the Fallacy of Most Frequent Use: "By this reasoning, computers were invented to play video games or surf the Net."

"Linguists don't understand how I can write a book on this subject without a lengthy discussion of grammar," says Dunbar with a shrug. "But that's not the point. I'm not studying *how* language is structured so much as I'm investigating what selection pressures led to its development. I see my story as quite complementary to Pinker's."

Whether it's right or wrong, Dunbar's theory has certainly got linguists chatting. Four years after his argument was first propounded in *Behavioral and Brain Sciences*, a leading cognitive-science journal, it continues to spark new commentaries and rebuttals. (The most recent set of responses appeared this past September.) The publication of Dunbar's book will likely only provoke more nit-picking from his peers—but then again, he rather seems to enjoy it. In fact, his book contains a rapturous description of what it feels like to be groomed. "To be groomed by a monkey," he writes, "is to experience primordial emotions: the initial frisson of uncertainty . . . the gradual surrender to another's avid fingers flickering expertly across bare skin, the . . . nibbling of flesh as hands of discovery move in surprise from one freckle to another newly discovered mole." Ugh. Perhaps this is one mystery that was better left unexplored.

—*March 1997*

THE LOOKING-GLASS WAR
Why Don't We See Ourselves Upside Down in the Mirror?

JIM HOLT

THE OTHER DAY as I was wandering down an old tenement block on New York's Lower East Side, I chanced upon an odd little shop. It sold only one item: mirrors that do not reverse left and right, or True Mirrors, as the store calls them. There was one in the shopwindow. Looking at my reflection in it, I was appalled by how crooked my facial features seemed, how lopsided my smile was, how ridiculous my hair looked parted on the wrong side of my head. Then I realized that the image I was confronting was the real me, the one the world sees. The image of myself I am used to, the one I see when I look into an ordinary mirror, is actually that of an incongruous counterpart whose left and right are the reverse of mine.

There is nothing very strange about the fact that ordinary mirrors reverse left and right, is there? "Left" and "right" are labels for the two horizontal directions parallel to the mirror. The two vertical directions parallel to the mirror are "up" and "down." But the optics and geometry of reflection are precisely the same for all dimensions parallel to the mirror. So why does a mirror treat the horizontal and vertical axes differently? Why does it reverse left and right but not up and down?

This question might seem foolish at first. "When I wave my right hand, my mirror counterpart waves his left hand," you say. "When I wiggle my head, I should scarcely expect my counterpart to wiggle his feet." True enough, but you might plausibly expect your counterpart to appear upside down, with his feet directly opposite your head—just as his left hand is directly opposite your right hand.

Foolish or not, the issue has been vexing philosophers for at least half a century now. As far as I can tell, it first arose in the early 1950s, as a sort of sidebar to discussions of Immanuel Kant's theory of spatial relations. In his 1964 book *The Ambidextrous Universe*, the science popularizer Martin Gardner stirred things up by arguing that the puzzle has a false premise. A mirror does not really reverse left and right at all, he claimed; instead, it reverses front and back along an axis perpendicular to the mirror. In his view, we merely "find it convenient" to call our image left/right reversed because we happen to be bilaterally symmetric. In 1970, the philosopher Jonathan Bennett published an article endorsing Gardner's supposed resolution of what by now had become the "mildly famous mirror problem."

But the sense of closure was premature. In 1974, the MIT philosopher Ned Block wrote a long, diagram-filled piece for the *Journal of Philosophy* in which he contended that the question "Why does a mirror reverse right/left but not up/down?" has at least four different interpretations. Block claimed that the four interpretations had been clumsily conflated by Gardner and Bennett; he also insisted that in two of the four, a mirror really does reverse left and right. Three years later, in an equally lengthy article that appeared in *The Philosophical Review*, an English philosopher named Don Locke declared that Block was only "half right." Mirrors actually reverse left and right in *every* relevant sense, he argued.

Reading these papers, and others that have appeared since, one comes to feel that the mirror problem defies philosophical reflection. People can't seem to agree on the most basic facts. For example: Stand sideways to a mirror, shoulder to shoulder with your image. Your left/right axis is now perpendicular to the mirror's surface. Gardner and Bennett say that in this case and this case alone, a mirror really does reverse left and right. Block and Locke say that in this case and this case alone, left and right are the *same* direction for you and your mirror image. (Having just dashed into the dressing room to try this,

I *think* I'm in the Block-Locke camp. My right arm and my mirror counterpart's right arm both pointed east; on the other hand, he was wearing his watch on his right wrist, whereas I wear mine on my left.)

The key to the mirror puzzle would seem to lie in some subtle disanalogy between left/right and up/down. Both of these pairs of directions are relative to the orientation of the body (unlike, say, east/west and skyward/earthward). But as any child will attest, left/right is much harder to master than up/down. The human body displays no gross asymmetries between its two sides. (There is, of course, the heart, but that is hidden.) So "left" and "right" have to be defined in terms of "front" and "head": your left hand is the one that is to the west when you stand on the ground and face north. This would remain true even if a surgeon cut off your two hands and sewed them onto the opposite arms.

Left/right is thus logically parasitic on front/back, whereas up/down is not. And a mirror, everyone agrees, reverses front and back. That must be why it also reverses left and right—if indeed it does, which to this day remains unclear.

Fatigued by the debate? Then visit the little shop I discovered (www.truemirror.com) and get yourself a True Mirror. But don't try shaving in front of the thing—your face will be a bloody mess.

—November 2000

PART V

Philosophical Investigations

OUT OF BODY, OUT OF MIND
How I May or May Not Have Solved the Mind-Body Problem and Nearly Ruined My Life

COLIN MCGINN

UNIVERSITIES ARE DEDICATED to the pursuit of knowledge. Not just its pursuit—its capture. That is why they exist. But what if there are questions whose answers simply cannot be known, if what interests academics the most can be known the least?

Take our own nature as conscious beings—something of a unique fascination to us all. We want to know, among other things, how our consciousness levers itself out of the body. We want, that is, to solve the mind-body problem, the deep metaphysical question about how mind and matter meet. But what if there is something about us that makes it impossible for us to solve this ancient conundrum? What if our cognitive structure lacks the resources to provide the requisite theory? That would be distressing news for the knowledge-manufacturing industry. And the bringer of the news might expect the opprobrium that traditionally greets the unwelcome messenger: Don't *say* that.

I became a proponent of mystery one dark night in Oxford seven years ago. At about two in the morning—and I don't know, maybe the moon was full—I was seized with the terrible conviction that our cognitive apparatus simply does not fit the mind-body problem. The reason the problem is a problem is not that consciousness is intrinsically outré (ontologically anomalous, as we analytic philosophers like to say); rather, the human intellect has been biologically set up to deal with other sorts of questions, and this one happens not to lie within its given modus operandi. We seem pretty good at answering questions about material objects in space, and also at handling the terms of ordinary psychology, but nature has not prepared us to answer the question about how mind and body come together. To a Martian, with a different innate cognitive structure, the problem might look easy, while elementary mechanics might prove terminally baffling. It is all a question of whether the appropriate intellectual equipment happens to have been installed in one's head. Problems only seem profound when we lack the mental gear with which to crack them. The profundity of the mind-body problem is thus neither a mark of objective miracle nor a misconception in the formulation of the problem. It is just the perimeter of our conceptual anatomy making itself felt.

But one can have some odd thoughts in the dead of night, and maybe I was succumbing to small-hours delirium. I rose and wrote down some notes, the better to conduct a sober morning perusal. And lo! the thought still clung to me the next day. I had an acceptable explanation of the theoretical intractability of consciousness. Our modes of concept formation, which operate from a base in perception and introspection, cannot bridge the chasm that separates the mind from the brain: they are tied to the mental and physical terms *of* the relation, not to the relation itself. This solves the metaphysical problem in a way, because now we are under no pressure to think that the world contains something heavy with intrinsic impossibility: from the fact that *we* cannot make sense of something it does not follow that *it* makes no sense. We know that consciousness exists and that it is robustly natural, though we cannot in principle produce the theory that would make its nature manifest. There is thus nothing mysterious about the existence of the mystery.

I began expounding this position in conversations and seminars, often causing a marked widening of the eyes. At that time I was Wilde Reader in Mental Philosophy at Oxford, and some waywardness was assumed to come with the title. (Brian Farrell, who had held the post for thirty years before me, reported that his newly acquired mother-in-law had said to him, "So you're the Mental Reader in Wilde Philosophy, are you?") I boldly announced to anyone who would listen that I had finally dismantled the mind-body problem. Sir Peter Strawson, Waynflete Professor of Metaphysical Philosophy (a position of considerable seriousness), once retorted, good-naturedly, "But I thought *I'd* done that."

A year after my sleepless night, I managed to write a paper on the topic called "Can We Solve the Mind-Body Problem?," which I submitted to the *Journal of Philosophy*, one of the leading American journals in the field. Hitherto they had accepted every paper I had ever sent them, but this one was rejected without explanation. Eventually it found its way into the British journal *Mind* in 1989. I now sometimes feel as if it were the only paper I had ever written, so identified have I become with its content. And it is obviously perceived as some sort of provocation. "Oh, so *you're* the guy who thinks it's all a mystery," people begin, eyes aflame. "Well, just listen to *my* solution."

I then wrote some other papers expanding on the position, which were to come out as a collection, *The Problem of Consciousness*, in 1991. Soon afterward, Owen Flanagan of Duke University dubbed Thomas Nagel and me the "New Mysterians," an allusion to a defunct 1960s rock band called Question Mark and the Mysterians. In a famous 1974 paper, "What Is It Like to Be a Bat?," Nagel argued that consciousness constitutes a serious obstacle in the way of materialism—though he has never in fact embraced the insolubility thesis that I defend. Noam Chomsky should also have been brought under this ironic honorific, since he has for years held the view that the human cognitive system divides the class of intelligible questions into the mere problems and the insuperable mysteries; indeed the term "mystery" in its present use is a legacy from him. I have derived much low-fat nourishment from Chomsky's writings on this subject, and discussions with him have been important to my own development of the basic viewpoint. The modular conception of mind, with linguistic competence as one module among others, is integral to my picture of cognitive limitation.

The label "mysterian" is potentially misleading, however: none of us regards his conviction of the limits of human understanding as in any way mystical or romantic. On the contrary, the view is motivated by a ruthlessly naturalistic perspective on the human intellect. As Chomsky often observes, the human mind is just a collection of specific finite organs, as biologically natural as the organs of the body. There are therefore limits to our knowledge in the way that there are limits to our motor abilities.

THE REVIEWS OF MY BOOK WERE, as one politely says, mixed. They tended toward the edgy and distancing. The two extremes were represented by the philosophy professors Jerry Fodor, my colleague at Rutgers, and Daniel Dennett, author of *Consciousness Explained*. Fodor sympathized with my position, though he dissented from some applications I make of it. Dennett began his review by declaring that he was embarrassed to be in the same profession as me and went on to suggest that I belong to a sinister cadre of "New Jersey Nihilists" intent on destroying cognitive science as we know it. ("New Jersey" because I moved from Oxford to Rutgers in 1990—though this move had nothing to do with my views about the dark roots of consciousness.) My fellow Garden State nihilists were said to include Chomsky, Fodor, and Nagel—all fearfully dangerous chaps. The label lacked factual accuracy: Chomsky was and still is at MIT, Nagel at NYU; Fodor formulated his notion of "epistemic boundedness" while at MIT; and I had my idea at Oxford. Moreover, there is nothing nihilistic about the position, any more than it is nihilistic to suggest that human beings cannot learn every possible language by means of their innate human language module. Sometimes pessimism is just the rational upshot of realism, not an urge to tear down the good and the beautiful. My response to all this ad hominem labeling was to suspect the operation of what might be called Tufts's Syndrome (Dennett is a professor at Tufts)—a condition characterized by the patient's hysterical hostility to anyone who questions his grandiose ambitions. But here I ruefully begin to play a game I deplore.

In general, the reactions I have received, other than those I have outlined above, have fallen into three main categories. One grudgingly admits the logical possibility of my thesis's being correct but insists that there is absolutely no reason to take it seriously: the solution may be just around the corner; we should get on with our researches undaunted by the fear that our intelligence might be the wrong shape for the mind-body problem. Another sort of reaction is brutally pragmatic: we should proceed as if the deep problems are soluble, despite all the evidence to the contrary, so that we can continue to receive funding for our work and keep up our motivation. Put less cynically: since the value of a theory of consciousness would be very high, and since there is at least a nonzero probability of the problem's solubility, it is rational to keep aiming for a solution in the hope that fate will smile upon us.

A third response is to associate my view with religious tenets, either favorably or unfavorably. Thus I have had people congratulate me on finding a place for God in our soulless contemporary worldview—my position being thought to imply that the supernatural soul is alive and well and living in New Brunswick. Then there are the secular scientific types who think they have found the chink in the otherwise hard glaze of my official atheism. Next, they insinuate, I will be extolling pan-psychism, ESP, or the spirit world.

Perhaps the most unexpected response came from a woman attending a conference I participated in with Dennett and the mathematician and philosopher Roger Penrose at Dartmouth in April. The conference dealt with consciousness, computers, quantum physics, and similar abstract topics, though it was intended for the general public. I was expounding my usual position, putting special emphasis on the point that while consciousness is a nonspatial phenomenon, human thought is fundamentally governed by spatial modes of representing the world, so that our ways of thinking tend to force consciousness onto a Procrustean bed of broadly Euclidean design. The woman, who seemed oddly agitated, objected, saying that while it might well be true that the male mind could not solve the problems raised by these areas, the *female* mind would be much better at handling them. I explained that my position was that the problem goes much deeper than that, applying to the human cognitive system as such. After all, I noted, it is not as if when asked about the mind-body problem or the puzzles of quantum theory women come right out with the correct solution. She retorted that I was not entitled to make this claim, since there were no female philosophers or physicists at the conference to ask.

The least common reaction is the one that seems to me the most obvious: that my diagnosis of this particular philosophical problem is simply too facile, too convenient. But, I must reply, most of the great dead philosophers have been as pessimistic as I am about solving the core philosophical problems. What is new about my position is not the unsolvability thesis as such but the particular explanation I give of it. I suspect the reason for the opposition is, in part, that my cognitive pessimism collides with the kind of indelible optimism characteristic of modern (especially American) culture. Instead of can-do and leave-it-to-me, I am preaching don't-try and it's-never-going-to-work. I deny, in effect, the perfectibility of man, epistemologically speaking.

I RECENTLY PUBLISHED A BOOK, *Problems in Philosophy: The Limits of Inquiry*, that sets out these general views in a systematic and explicitly metaphilosophical way. In addition to writing about consciousness, I discuss free will, the self, meaning, mathematics, knowledge—extending my treatment of consciousness to these other topics. Cognitive closure, I argue, turns out to be rather pervasive. I also suggest that while human reason is not equipped to solve the problems in question, there may be other epistemic systems that can do better. Thus the genetic code arguably contains precisely the information about our mental makeup that we cannot acquire by the exercise of our rational faculties, since the genes have to encode the information necessary to organisms with consciousness, free will, and so on. I can hear the howls of protest now: "It's bad enough to downgrade human reason by drawing boundaries around it, but now you are suggesting that DNA molecules are better philosophers than we are!" Well, yes, that is my suggestion, put crudely. Human reason is an adventitious biological organ whose job description plainly does not include solving every problem about the natural world, whereas genes have the biological task of engineering organisms from the ground up, so they had better have access to the information needed to perform this feat.

I once gave a talk on this to some biologists, and they construed my argument as a reason to back the Human Genome Project. I pointed out, however, that it was a consequence of my view that, whatever valuable philosophical information the genes might contain, it was not going to be translatable into human language. Our conceptual scheme does not, according to my argument, coincide with the informational resources of the genes. This is not to say that we are "stupider" than the genes, since plainly we can do many things with our minds that they cannot do. The upshot of these reflections is, rather, that the concept of intelligence needs to be understood much more subtly than we are anthropocentrically inclined to think.

Earlier this year, *Scientific American* ran an article on whether science can explain consciousness. There is a rather eerie photograph of me, seated on a Gothic rocking chair with a curling dead twig seeming to grow out of my skull. Some say I resemble the film actor Anthony Hopkins in the role of Hannibal Lecter. I certainly look severe. I would have preferred one of the shots taken of my cat and me pretending to play chess together, the point being that chess is to the cat mind what consciousness is to the human mind—out of cognitive reach. The caption beneath the picture describes me as a "Hard-Core Mysterian," which is, I suppose, pretty much what I look like. If I'd been asked, I'd have preferred to be called a commonsense noumenalist, following Kant's use of the term "noumenal" to denote that region of reality that is incognizable by us. But by now I realize that once in the public realm one's identity is apt to become detached from one's own conception of it. From now on, a hard-core mysterian is what I am condemned to be—a guru of ignorance, a high priest of mental lack.

By chance, a man from Con Edison came to read my gas meter

with that very issue of *Scientific American* stuffed into his back pocket. I indicated the picture of me, to his intense amazement. I awaited hushed inquiries. He confided that he was particularly interested in the article on wasps that lay their eggs in the bodies of live grubs and that he hadn't gotten around to the consciousness article yet. I had to agree that wasp child rearing was indeed an interesting subject. The next time he came, he made no mention of the article in which I had figured. Clearly, grubs and wasps were a far more fascinating subject than consciousness.

WHAT DIFFERENCE has being a mysterian made in my life? From an internal point of view, it has released me from the uncomfortable sensation that philosophical problems have always stimulated in me—the feeling that reality is inherently preposterous, ill formed, bizarre. Now I believe that the eeriness of consciousness and allied enigmas is just a projection of my limited intellect interacting with the phenomena—it is not a feature of the phenomena themselves. I also feel less intellectually embarrassed in the face of problems than I used to, as if I really *ought* to be able to do better. It is not that I have been given the right tools but lack the necessary skills; rather, nature has given me a toolbox with other jobs in mind. A happy side benefit is that I feel no temptation to deny the existence of things that are terminally puzzling. I can now, for example, see my way clear to believing in free will again after twenty-five years of denying its very possibility—on the grounds that neither the random nor the determined could accommodate it. Free will is, indeed, I still think, a phenomenon about which we can form no intelligible theory, but, given the idea of cognitive closure, it does not follow that it is unreal. We can be free without being able to understand the conditions of the possibility of freedom.

On the other hand, it is disappointing to arrive at the conclusion that the problems that have always most interested me are not humanly solvable. I would, truth to tell, dearly love to see these problems grandly resolved in some new large-scale theory of the cosmos—

as Newton, Einstein, and Darwin resolved their daunting problems. I don't really *want* to stop trying to solve the mind-body problem, futile as the effort now appears to me to be. As Wittgenstein remarked, grappling with philosophical conundrums is something that we human beings cannot easily shake off, even when our metaphilosophy assures us of their unanswerability. As a consolation, though, I have a reason now to work more on ethics, which looks to be an area in which the human intellect can get some real purchase. Ethics is an area of mere difficulty rather than blank mystery.

My mysterian identity does have its downside. I work in a university and assert that the central aim of universities will remain thwarted. This is not a very popular line to take. It discourages the students. It casts something of a pall over the proceedings. People no doubt think I am a traitor to the noble cause of knowledge. But let me observe that knowledge of our limits is, after all, one sort of knowledge, and quite an interesting sort. Psychologists study perceptual and memory limits: why can we not study the limits of theoretical reason? And whoever said that the human mind, at this transient evolutionary moment, has been so constructed as to be able to deliver the answer to any question about that vast intricate world we live in? It is amazing that we know as much as we do, but we should be wary of epistemic greed. There is a lot to be said for species modesty.

—November 1994

WHAT'S SO FUNNY?
Making Sense of Humor
JIM HOLT

ISAAC NEWTON IS REPORTED to have laughed precisely once in his life—when a friend asked him what use he saw in Euclid's *Elements*. Joseph Stalin, too, seems to have been somewhat agelastic. "Seldom did anyone see Stalin laugh," Marshal Zhukov reports in his reminiscences. "When he did, it was more like a chuckle." Other famous agelasts include William Gladstone and Ruth Bader Ginsburg. Did Jesus laugh? That was a core question of Umberto Eco's *The Name of the Rose*. Because I was unable to finish the novel, I'm not sure what the answer is; in any event, I do not recall many guffaws in the Gospels. ("The total absence of humour from the Bible," Alfred North Whitehead once observed, "is one of the most singular things in all literature.")

Rabelais declared, "Man is the laughing animal." Are we to infer, then, that Newton, Stalin, and the rest were somehow inhuman? Not necessarily. Rabelais was only echoing Aristotle, who in his *Parts of Animals* asserted not that all humans are laughers but that "all laughers are humans." Some have contested even the latter claim. Thomas Mann and Isak Dinesen, for example, both insisted that their pet pooches were capable of a kind of inward laughter (though this would be hard to verify). What is certain is that purely spiritual entities—angels, gods—have no place on the laugher curve. That is because, whatever else it is, laughter is *physical*. You need to have a body to do it.

It is the sheer physicality of laughter that has made it so mysterious to philosophers and scientists. "Those who know why the kind of joy that kindles laughter should draw the zygomatic muscles back toward the ears are very knowing indeed," Voltaire wrote. Actually, the laughter reflex involves the contraction of some fifteen facial muscles, along with the simultaneous stimulation of the muscles of inspiration and those of expiration. Oddly, all these contortions prove very healthy for *homo ridens*: robust laughter triples the amount of oxygen in the blood, reduces stress hormones, and bolsters the immune system by heightening T-cell activity.

To understand the nature of laughter, theorists have traditionally looked not to its effects but to its causes: the comic, the risible, the humorous. The easiest way to define the humorous is as that which elicits laughter. This, however, makes "humor causes laughter" a barren tautology. The proposition becomes useful only when humor is characterized independently of laughter.

There are three moldy old theories that purport to do this. The superiority theory—propounded in various forms by Plato, Hobbes, and Bergson—locates the essence of humor in the "sudden glory" (Hobbes) we feel when, say, we see Bill Gates smashed in the face with a custard pie. The incongruity theory—held by Pascal, Kant, and Schopenhauer—says that humor arises when the seemly and logical abruptly dissolves into the low and absurd. "Do you believe in clubs for small children?" W. C. Fields is asked. "Only when kindness fails," he replies.

These theories do not address, however, why feelings of superiority or incongruity should call forth a bout of cackling and chest heaving. An advantage of the relief theory—proposed by Freud—is that it at least tries to explain the causal link between humor and laughter. In this view, the laughable (ideally, a naughty joke) liberates the laugher from inhibitions about forbidden thoughts and feelings. The result is a discharge of nervous energy that distracts the inner censor from what is going on.

If none of these theories has ever been tested experimentally, the reason is simple: it is impossible to produce laughter under laboratory conditions. It is not, however, difficult to go out into the world and see what makes people laugh. Yet for all the centuries of speculation about laughter, no one had bothered to do this until Robert Provine came along. A psychologist who teaches at the University of Maryland's Baltimore County campus, Provine sent assistants to college campuses and shopping malls to eavesdrop on conversations and see what triggered volleys of laughter.

The results were dispiriting. The domain of the risible turned out to consist largely of such howlers as "Got to go now!," "What's that supposed to mean?," and "It must be nice." Only 10 percent of the laugh lines could be rated humorous even by the most charitable standards ("You don't have to drink—just buy us drinks"). These findings, along with the well-known contagiousness of laughter (which in its extreme form has caused epidemics of hysterical giggling among convent girls in Africa), have led evolutionary psychologists like MIT's Steven Pinker to conjecture that the primary Darwinian function of laughter is to serve as a social glue.

Could there really be a common denominator to a phenomenon that encompasses so many varieties? Diabolical laughter, laughter as a joyous awareness of our finitude, as an escape from gravity into levity, as a tool of mockery.

Perhaps the most delightful form of laughter, for the crafty don at least, is the *risus sophisticus*. According to *The Oxford Companion to Philosophy*, this is an ancient rhetorical counterploy identified by Gorgias of Leontini as "destroying one's adversaries' seriousness by laughter and their laughter by seriousness." Such tricks are "characteristically employed," the *Companion* adds, "by an aged philosopher commenting upon a paper of unfollowable complexity by a young postdoctoral Fellow."

—April 1998

WHOSE IDEA IS IT, ANYWAY?
A Philosophers' Feud
JIM HOLT

"IMAGINE THE FOLLOWING blatantly fictional situation. . . . Suppose that Gödel was not in fact the author of [Gödel's incompleteness theorem]. A man named 'Schmidt,' whose body was found in Vienna under mysterious circumstances many years ago, actually did the work in question. His friend Gödel somehow got hold of the manuscript and it was thereafter attributed to Gödel. . . . So, since the man who discovered the incompleteness of arithmetic is in fact Schmidt, we, when we talk about 'Gödel,' are in fact always referring to Schmidt. But it seems to me that we are not. We simply are not. . . .

"It may seem to many of you that this is a very odd example."

These words were spoken by Saul Kripke to an audience at Princeton University on January 22, 1970. Kripke, then a twenty-nine-year-old member of the Rockefeller University philosophy faculty, was in the midst of the second of three lectures that he was delivering without written text, or even notes. The lectures, which were tape-recorded and eventually published in 1980 under the title *Naming and Necessity*, proved to be an epoch-making event in the history of contemporary philosophy. "They stood analytic philosophy on its ear," Richard Rorty wrote in the *London Review of Books*. "Everybody was either furious, or exhilarated, or thoroughly perplexed." Kripke's lectures gave rise to what came to be called the New Theory of Reference, revolutionizing the way philosophers of language thought about issues of meaning and truth. They engendered hundreds of journal articles and dissertations about "possible worlds," "rigid designators," and "a posteriori necessity." They led to a far-reaching revival of the Aristotelian doctrine of essences. And they helped make their author, already something of a cult figure among logicians, into the very model of a modern philosophical genius—a stature *The New York Times* certified in 1977 by putting Kripke's glowering visage on the cover of its Sunday magazine.

Now imagine, if you will, the following blatantly fictional situation. Suppose that Kripke was not in fact the author of the New Theory of Reference. A woman named "Marcus"—let's call her Ruth Barcan Marcus for greater verisimilitude—whose warm body can still be seen tracing out mysterious trajectories through the campus of Yale University, actually did the work in question. The young Kripke went to a talk she gave in 1962 containing the key ideas; almost a decade later, he presented a greatly elaborated version of them without crediting Marcus. Thereafter they were attributed to Kripke. So, since the person who discovered the New Theory of Reference is in fact Marcus, we, when we talk about "Kripke," are in fact always referring to Marcus. Or are we?

This may seem to many of you a very odd story. Nevertheless, it is precisely the story that a philosopher by the name of Quentin Smith dared to tell a largish audience last winter at an American Philosophical Association conference in Boston. Only, for Smith, a professor at Western Michigan University, the story was not blatantly fictional. It was true.

When Quentin Smith spoke to the Boston audience, it was something like a philosophical version of David and Goliath—an upstart forty-three-year-old professor from a minor midwestern university attempting to rewrite intellectual history and take on the reputation of the man whom Robert Nozick has called "the one genius of our profession." The philosophical world first got wind of Smith's charges in the fall of 1994, when the paper he was to present at the upcoming APA conference—titled "Marcus, Kripke, and the Origin of the New

Theory of Reference"—was listed among the planned proceedings. Before long, philosophy bulletin boards on the Internet were festooned with messages to the effect that someone was going to accuse the great Saul Kripke of plagiarism—a quite reasonable inference, given the inflammatory way the abstract for Smith's paper was worded.

The colloquium itself took place on December 28 at the Marriott hotel in Boston's Copley Place. It was not an altogether edifying spectacle. Ruth Barcan Marcus, whom Smith would be championing, did not attend. Nor did Kripke. Nor, for that matter, did most of his Princeton colleagues (their absence was interpreted by some philosophers as a token of their solidarity with Kripke, by others as a conspicuous failure to show support for him). Yet a contingent of Princeton graduate students did make their presence felt, heckling Smith ("Marcus put you up to this, didn't she?" one hostile auditor was heard to yell) and pointedly striding out of the room as he detailed the "historical misunderstanding" that led to Kripke getting credit for ideas that, he claimed, were properly Marcus's. "From the point of view of the history of philosophy," Smith declared, "correcting this misunderstanding is no less important than correcting the misunderstanding in a hypothetical situation where virtually all philosophers attributed the origin of [Plato's] Theory of Forms to Plotinus."

Smith's startling claims did not go unanswered. The chosen respondent was Scott Soames, a young philosopher of language at Princeton whom some in the audience seemed to regard as a sort of philosophical hit man dispatched by Kripke's department. (In fact, he had been approached with the request to serve as commentator by the APA program committee after a couple of other philosophers declined the job.) "My task today is an unusual and not very pleasant one," Soames began, going on to rebuke Smith for his "shameful" insinuation that Kripke was guilty of intellectual theft. He heaped scorn on Smith's claim that Kripke learned the main doctrines of the New Theory of Reference from Marcus, misunderstood them initially, and, upon finally sorting them out in his mind, mistook them for his own—and that the rest of the philosophical profession was somehow duped in the bargain. "If there is any scandal here," Soames concluded, "it is that such a carelessly and incompetently made accusation should have been given such credence."

But that was not the end of it. Under APA rules, the colloquium speaker is allowed a reply after the commentator is finished. So Smith got up to deliver his rejoinder—which, at twenty-seven pages (not including footnotes), was nearly as long as his original paper and Soames's response combined. "I do not believe it is relevant or helpful to adopt the sort of language that Soames uses in his reply," he told the audience. "Philosophical disagreements are not solved by the disputants' labeling each other's work with a variety of negative and emotive epithets; they are solved by presenting sound arguments, and I shall confine myself to presenting arguments." A smattering of applause greeted this remark.

Some way into Smith's apparently endless review of textual and philosophical minutiae, the colloquium chair, Mark Richard of Tufts, tried to cut him off. Several members of the audience objected, clamoring that he be allowed to speak on. Richard acquiesced, but, in contravention of protocol, then permitted Soames a second rejoinder. ("I began to get the feeling he was acting under Soames's direction," Smith later recalled.) "If Marcus had these ideas before Kripke, how come no one said anything about it for more than twenty years?" Soames asked the audience rhetorically. "Maybe that's a question women philosophers should be asking the profession," piped up one person of gender present, causing a hush to fall briefly over the gathering.

Today, more than a year later, *l'affaire Kripke* is still alive. The colloquium papers—Smith's original, Soames's response, and Smith's counterresponse—have recently been published in the philosophy journal *Synthese*. And the two adversaries are currently busy refining their briefs in another pair of papers of even greater length—Smith's latest draft is almost seventy pages. Meanwhile, such philosophical eminences as Elizabeth Anscombe, Donald Davidson, and Thomas Nagel have signed a letter to the APA asserting that "a session at a national APA meeting is not the proper forum in which to level ethical accusations against a member of our profession, even if the charges were plausibly defended." The letter, which was published in the association's quarterly proceedings, goes on to demand that the APA issue a public apology to Kripke.

The philosophical profession, it seems, has divided into several camps defined not only by convictions about intellectual originality and propriety but also by a variety of strong feelings about Kripke the man. He is, after all, the sort of remote and brooding figure who inspires more awe than affection. His personal eccentricities have made him a subject of intense rumor-mongering. And even those who profess unstinting admiration for his intellectual achievements often complain that he has set himself up as the "policeman" of analytic philosophy, arrogantly punishing other philosophers for being derivative and stupid. And now, ironically, it is Officer Kripke himself who has come under a cloud.

Ruth Marcus declined to discuss the affair—though, to show that Smith was not "a voice in the wilderness," she did send me a dozen or so journal articles published by philosophers over the years crediting her with being an originator of the New Theory of Reference. By contrast, Kripke himself is quite open in ventilating his sense of hurt and exasperation. "Number one," he says, "what Smith is saying is not true, and, number two, even if it were true, the matter should have been handled more responsibly."

There *is* something exasperating about the matter. It is easy to tell when someone has borrowed the prose of another; one can simply look at the passages in question and see if they match, word by word. Ideas are rather trickier to identify. When a new one is discovered and put in clear, explicit form, intimations of it have a way of coming out of the woodwork of earlier texts. Was it there all along, or are we just, as it were, retrojecting? Did Oliver Heaviside really hit upon $E=mc^2$ before Einstein? Did Fermat adumbrate the fundamental theorem of calculus in advance of Newton? Can all of Freud's insights be found in *Hamlet*?

THE DAUNTING COMPLEXITY of the ideas at stake in the Kripke/ Marcus case does not make their genealogy any easier to determine. Although they mostly pertain to the philosophy of language, their deeper source is in modal logic, the formal study of the different modes of truth—necessity and possibility—that a statement can possess. First studied by Aristotle, fashionable among the medieval Schoolmen but largely neglected by their modern successors, modal logic enjoyed something of a renaissance earlier in this century, owing to the work of philosophers like C. I. Lewis and Rudolf Carnap.

In the 1940s, Ruth Barcan Marcus—then the unmarried graduate student Ruth C. Barcan—added new formal features to the apparatus of modal logic, greatly enlarging its philosophical implications. And, a decade later, the teenage prodigy Saul Kripke supplied it with something it had hitherto lacked: an interpretation, a semantics. Drawing on Leibniz's conceit that the actual world is only one in a vast collection of possible worlds—worlds where snow is green, worlds where McGovern beat Nixon—Kripke characterized a proposition as *necessarily* true if it holds in every possible world, and *possibly* true if it holds in some possible world. He then proved that modal logic was a formally "complete" system, an impressively deep result that he published in *The Journal of Symbolic Logic*, in 1959, at the tender age of eighteen.

Not long thereafter, in February 1962, Kripke attended a now-legendary session at the Harvard Faculty Club. The occasion was Ruth Marcus's delivery of a paper titled "Modalities and Intensional Languages." The milieu was not a particularly clement one for the speaker, since Harvard's philosophers tended to take a dim view of the whole notion of necessity and possibility. ("Like the one whose namesake I am," Ruth Marcus later recalled, "I stood in alien corn.") This was especially true of the commentator for the paper, Willard Van Orman Quine, who, as Marcus characterized it, seemed to believe that modern modal logic was "conceived in sin"—the sin of confusing the use of a word with its mention.

Although Marcus devoted the bulk of her talk to defending modal logic against Quine's animadversions, she also used the occasion to dilate upon some ideas in the philosophy of language that she had begun to develop while working on her Ph.D. thesis in the mid-1940s, ideas concerning the relationship between a proper name and the object to which it refers. Since the beginning of the century, the received theory of proper names, conventionally attributed to Gottlob Frege and Bertrand Russell, was that every such name had associated with it a cluster of descriptions; these constituted its meaning or sense. The referent of the name was the unique object that satisfied the descriptions. According to the Frege-Russell theory, the referent of the name "Aristotle" would be the unique thing satisfying such associated descriptions as "teacher of Alexander the Great," "author of the *Metaphysics*," and so on.

If proper names are indeed descriptions in disguise, then they ought to behave like descriptions in all logical contexts—including the context of modal logic. But, as Marcus observed, they simply do not. The statement "Aristotle is Aristotle," for example, is necessarily true, whereas "Aristotle is the author of the *Metaphysics*" is merely contingent, since it is possible to imagine circumstances in which the historical Aristotle became, say, a swineherd instead of a philosopher. Such intuitions suggested to Marcus that proper names are not attached to their objects through the intervention of descriptive senses. Rather, they refer directly to their bearers, like meaningless tags. To use the older idiom of John Stuart Mill, proper names have *denotation* but no *connotation*.

The foregoing is, perforce, little more than a caricature of Marcus's actual argument, which was almost rebarbative in its complexity and abstraction. It is little wonder that in the discussion that followed on that day in Cambridge, she, Quine, and the precocious undergraduate Kripke often appeared to be talking at cross-purposes. In retrospect, however, one thing is clear: Marcus's use of modal reasoning to undermine the traditional theory of the meaning of names was a step

toward the New Theory of Reference—a theory that emerged full-
blown from Kripke's Princeton lectures a decade later. But was Marcus's work more than that?

THIS IS THE QUESTION that Quentin Smith began to brood on in
the winter of 1990, when he received a letter from Marcus—with
whom he was not personally acquainted—informing him that an allusion he had made in a published paper to the "Kripke-Donnellan theory of proper names" was not strictly accurate given that she, too, had
had a role in launching the theory. (Keith Donnellan of UCLA is another philosopher involved in the elaboration of the New Theory of
Reference.) Smith is a boyish-looking, soft-spoken, and seemingly
diffident man. He began his career as a phenomenologist, but later
apostatized and became an analytic philosopher. Judging from his list
of publications, one can see that he is extraordinarily prolific and ver-
satile—his recent book *Language and Time* was pronounced a "masterpiece" by one reviewer, and his forthcoming works include *The
Question of Ethical and Religious Meanings* and the demurely titled *Explaining the Universe*. Yet until his appearance in Boston, he was a
little-known figure in his profession.

At the time he got the letter from Marcus, Smith was just starting
work on a book-length history of analytic philosophy. He went back
and read Marcus's "Modalities and Intensional Languages." He took a
look at some of her earlier papers. From 1990 to 1994, he struggled to
work out the intellectual relations between Marcus's work and
Kripke's. (After her Cambridge showdown with Quine et al., Marcus
had gone on to expand her contributions to philosophical logic and to
do highly influential work on the theory of belief and the nature of
moral dilemmas.) Smith began to correspond regularly with Marcus
but, he says, received no detailed commentary from her. Finally he
reached his conclusion: nearly all of the key ideas of the New Theory
of Reference—the very ideas with which Kripke had "stood philosophy on its ear"—were in fact due to Marcus.

That was the sensational claim that Smith unpacked before the APA conference a year ago, in a paper that, owing to what he called its "unusual nature," he was surprised the program committee accepted. After detailing six major ideas that, he maintained, had wrongly been credited to Kripke and others, he went on to suggest two reasons for the "wide misunderstanding" of the historical origins of the New Theory of Reference. The first was innocuous enough: despite Marcus's reputation as a pioneering figure in logic and the philosophy of language, the philosophical community had simply not paid enough attention to her early work. The second, though, was a bit unsettling: Kripke himself had failed to attribute the relevant ideas to her—and not out of malice, but out of obtuseness. Although he had been present at Marcus's seminal talk, the young Kripke did not really understand her ideas at the time—so, at least, Smith inferred from some of his remarks during the transcribed discussion. In the 1980 preface to *Naming and Necessity*, Kripke notes that most of the views presented therein "were formulated in about 1963–64." To Smith this suggested that Kripke only came to grasp Marcus's arguments a year or two after she made them—and that his newfound insight made it seem to him that the ideas were novel and his own. "I suspect that such instances occur fairly frequently in the history of thought and art," Smith concluded with artful blandness.

In defending Kripke against Smith's "scandalous" and "grotesquely inaccurate" brief, Scott Soames began by declaring his respect and affection for Ruth Marcus (he had been her colleague at Yale when he taught there in the late 1970s and more recently contributed to a Festschrift for her). His criticisms, he said, were aimed solely at Smith. While conceding that Marcus did deserve credit for anticipating some of the tenets of the New Theory of Reference, he insisted that this "in no way diminishes the seminal role of Saul Kripke." Moreover, he continued, some of the ideas that Smith attributed to Marcus—that proper names are not equivalent to descriptions, for instance—had already been formulated by other logicians, notably Frederick Fitch. This was a claim that Soames probably came to regret, for it allowed Smith to point out that Fitch was actually Marcus's *adviser* when she was writing her dissertation in 1943–1945, and in a paper Soames did not refer to, Fitch mentioned his indebtedness to his doctoral student for her insights.

Such palpable hits, though, are rare. For the most part, the ongoing dispute between Quentin Smith and Scott Soames over who is the real mother-father of the New Theory of Reference involves rather delicate philosophizing. Take the notion of rigidity. A "rigid designator" is a term that refers to the same individual in every possible world. ("Benjamin Franklin," for example, is a rigid designator, whereas "the inventor of bifocals" is not.) The phrase "rigid designator" was coined by Kripke—no one questions that. Smith, however, insists that Marcus was the one who discovered the concept (priority with words is easy, with concepts hard). Impossible! rejoins Soames: rigid designation presupposes the more general notion of the referent of a term in a possible world, and Marcus did not have a sufficiently rich semantic framework to support such a notion. Twofold error! Smith ripostes. Not only was Marcus in possession of a semantic framework as rich as Kripke's, but such a framework is not even needed to define the concept of rigid designation. All it really takes is the basic elements of modal logic and the subjunctive mood—which, Smith adds with a flourish, are precisely the means Kripke himself used to introduce rigid designation in *Naming and Necessity*.

That is about the simplest volley one can find between these two opponents (and Soames no doubt feels he still has another shot to take). Most of the issues of attribution turn on technical arguments of such subtlety that they make, say, the scholarly dispute over the corrected text of *Ulysses* that took place a decade ago look like junior-high forensics. Assemble a random jury of professional philosophers, and they probably wouldn't know what to think after listening to Smith and Soames argue their cases. And yet the allegation itself is so pointed, and so grave. If Smith is right, Kripke is diminished twice over. Not only is his reputation based on an achievement that actually belongs to another philosopher—a woman neglected by the largely male profession, no less—but he failed to realize this because he did not understand the theory at first. For a genius, the only accusation worse than intellectual theft is dimness.

HAPPILY, IT IS POSSIBLE to get some purchase on this debate without working through all the fine points of the Smith-Soames exchange. Life is, after all, short. The simplest way to begin is by asking: just what is the New Theory of Reference? As a philosophical movement, it can be viewed as a reaction against several earlier currents in twentieth-century analytic philosophy. By reviving the rich metaphysical notion of "possible worlds"—and taking seriously our intuitions about them—it cocks a snook at the logical positivists, who insisted that discourse is only meaningful when it can be tested against our experience of the actual world. By freely drawing on the exotic devices of modal logic, it rejects the more down-to-earth methods of the ordinary-language philosophers, who took their inspiration from the late work of Wittgenstein.

Yet where the New Theory of Reference really cuts against the traditional philosophical grain is in its anti-mentalism, its refusal to make semantics depend on the contents of the minds of language users. Meanings are not located inside the head, the theory says; they are out there in the world—the world described by science. This anti-mentalism is apparent in the claim that proper names refer to their objects directly, without the mediation of mental ideas or descriptions. But adherents of the theory don't stop there. They also argue that many common nouns—words like "gold," "tiger," and "heat"— work in the same way. Such "natural kind" terms have no definitions in the usual sense, the theory holds. What determines whether a given bit of stuff is gold, for example, is not that it is heavy, yellow, malleable, and metallic; these are merely its phenomenal properties, which might be different in another possible world. What makes it gold, rather, is its atomic structure—which, being the same in every possible world, constitutes its essence. Of course, it is a fairly recent scientific discovery that gold has the atomic number 79; before that, people talked about gold without having any concept in their heads that distinguished it from the other elements (and most people still do).

If it is not meanings in the heads of language users that connect terms like "Aristotle" and "gold" to their referents, what does do the trick? Causal chains, says the New Theory of Reference. The term is first applied to its object in an initial baptism—say, by an act of pointing—and is then causally passed on to others through various kinds of communicative acts: conversation, reading, and so on. Thus my present use of "Aristotle" is the latest link in a causal chain stretching backward in time (and eastward in space) to the Stagirite himself.

So the New Theory of Reference encompasses a slew of interrelated ideas. In an early collection of articles about the New Theory, *Naming, Necessity, and Natural Kinds* (1977), the editor Stephen Schwartz provides a dependable taxonomy. The "three main features" of the New Theory, he writes—each of which "directly challenges major tenets of traditional thinking about meaning and reference"— are the following: "Proper names are rigid [they refer to the same individuals in all possible worlds]; natural kind terms are like proper names in the way they refer; and reference depends on causal chains."

HOW MANY OF THESE three main features are due to Kripke? Smith himself allows that the second and the third, as presented by Kripke in his 1970 Princeton talks, are "genuinely new." The ideas whose provenance is being contested all fall under the first feature, the rigidity of proper names. So Soames seems to be right in asserting that while Ruth Marcus may have anticipated some of these ideas, this does not detract from Kripke's "seminal role" in the creation of the New Theory of Reference. Even philosophers who have had serious intellectual disagreements with Kripke tend to concur on this point. "Probably not one of these ideas is Kripke's alone, and he has never pretended otherwise," says the Rutgers philosopher Colin McGinn. "But Kripke was the first to put them in an attractive form so that non-logicians could see their significance, and to draw out implications others didn't notice."

Yet it is hard to deny that Quentin Smith has displayed considerable brilliance, not to mention nerve, in prosecuting his case that the prime mover behind the New Theory of Reference was Ruth Marcus, not Saul Kripke. Indeed, it sometimes seems that Smith is too clever by half, giving Marcus credit not only for the ideas she clearly had, in more or less inchoate form, but also for all the logical consequences he has been ingenious enough to tease out of them. Smith defends his effort as a legitimate inquiry into the history of contemporary philosophy, a dispassionate presentation of philosophical arguments aimed at clearing up the genealogy of an important theory. If this inquiry has created a heated controversy, there's a simple explanation: it's just that it concerns living, active philosophers.

Smith's critics disagree. They argue that it was wrong for him to air his charges in a public forum. After all, even if he didn't directly accuse Kripke of plagiarism, he did raise delicate questions of professional ethics and intimate questions about the inner workings of Kripke's mind. "It's hard for me to remember just what my state of mind was thirty years ago," Kripke himself responds when I bring up Smith's claim.

"Sure, Ruth said in her 1962 talk that proper names were not synonymous with descriptions," he says. "A subset of the ideas I later developed were present there in a sketchy way, but there was a real paucity of argumentation on natural language. Almost everything she was saying was already familiar to me at the time. I knew about Mill's theory of names and Russell's theory of logically proper names, and I hope that, having worked on the semantics of modal logic, I could have seen the consequences of such a position for modal logic myself. I certainly don't recall thinking, 'Wow, this is an interesting point of view, maybe I should elaborate on it,' and I doubt that any unconscious version of that thought took place."

Though Kripke chose not to respond to Smith in public, he did briefly consider taking legal action against the APA. And this past spring, he resigned from the organization. "I remember my wife [Princeton philosopher Margaret Gilbert] screaming when she happened to see the abstract of Smith's paper in the 1994 APA proceedings," says Kripke. "It really was worded in a libelous way. The program committee had to deal with hundreds of papers and didn't devote enough time or expertise to determining whether Smith's charges had any merit. A lawsuit has crossed my mind, but I'm reluctant to take that course because I'd have to sue the APA. And can you imagine a judge and jury trying to decide these technical matters in the philosophy of language?

"I don't think I've ever acted in bad faith," Kripke concludes. "I just try to contribute to the profession what I can. And if it keeps leading to all this backbiting, in the future I might not bother."

KRIPKE'S SELF-DEFENSE IS, in the eyes of many of his peers, a persuasive one. But it also leads them to ponder his controversial presence in the field. Is Saul Kripke an incomparable genius? A boy wonder who never fully made good? Kripke's career weighs heavily on his colleagues. And it's easy to see why.

Going back and rereading the few things Kripke has published— *Naming and Necessity*; his 1982 book, *Wittgenstein on Rules and Private Language*—one cannot help being struck by the amount of sheer pleasure they afford. For humor, lucidity, quirky inventiveness, exploratory open-mindedness, and brilliant originality, he is singularly readable among analytic philosophers. And there is his disarming candor. At one point in *Naming and Necessity*, he offhandedly remarks: "Actually sentences like 'Socrates is called "Socrates" ' are very interesting and one can spend, strange as it may seem, hours talking about their analysis. I actually did, once, do that. I won't do that, however, on this occasion. (See how high the seas of language can rise. And at the lowest points, too.)"

But Kripke is no stranger to controversy. His criticisms of colleagues can be fierce. And he himself received something of a mauling for his Wittgenstein book when the initial excitement over its appearance gave way to a backlash. Works by P. M. S. Hacker and Gordon Baker (*Skepticism, Rules, and Language*) and by Colin McGinn (*Wittgenstein on Meaning*) eventually convinced many philosophers that Kripke's interpretation was wrong. "For the first time," McGinn observes, "fallibility intruded into his life."

What's more, critics have charged Kripke with haughtily ignoring the progress that other philosophers have made on problems he's worked on. Jaakko Hintikka, a distinguished philosopher at Boston University and the editor of *Synthese*, says that he decided to print Smith's and Soames's papers because "they point to a pattern in Kripke's career—a pattern that has repeated itself over and over again. Another such case occurred in 1982, when Kripke published his interpretation of Wittgenstein's 'private language argument' without any acknowledgment of the very similar work that Robert Fogelin had already published on the subject six years earlier."

Hintikka is referring to Kripke's "skeptical solution" to a paradox about rule following raised by Wittgenstein. Fogelin, a philosopher who taught at Yale before moving to Dartmouth, had published his own interpretation of the Wittgenstein paradox in his *Wittgenstein* (1976). In the second edition of this book, Fogelin included a footnote that went on for six pages, pointing out the close parallelism between his treatment and Kripke's, arguing that nonetheless his own was more complete.

"I've no doubt that Kripke has acted in good faith," Hintikka continues. "He's not appropriating anyone else's ideas, at least consciously. He's not guilty of anything more serious than colossal naïveté and professional immaturity. The real blame in all this lies with the philosophical community—which, owing to its uncritical, romantic view of this prodigy, is far too quick to give him credit for new ideas while neglecting the contributions of others. Kripke probably got his results independently, but why should he get all the credit?"

OTHER PHILOSOPHERS AGREE that the "cult of genius" that has grown up around Saul Kripke may have done neither Kripke nor the profession much good. "Given the rather arid work most philosophers today do, they feel the profession needs a genius in the nineteenth-century romantic mold," comments Robert Solomon, a philosopher at the University of Texas, whose books include *About Love.* "Wittgenstein was the last genius figure we've had in our midst. He became the darling of Cambridge University, and all the students used to imitate his odd way of talking and his neurotic gestures. Now that he is gone, we need another one, and Kripke, with his own legendary eccentricities—some pleasant, some not—has been thrust into the role. He's so pampered and coddled and adored by those around him, you wonder whether he can tell the difference between right and wrong. He's like an idiot savant who needs to be protected."

Solomon also raises the question of gender. "Where are all the women philosophers?" he asks. "How many cases have there been in the last two millennia where a bright male became celebrated for developing ideas first discovered by a bright female?" (When I mention this point to Kripke, he replies with vexed amusement, his raspy voice leaping into the falsetto range: "I don't think that *Robert Fogelin* has ever claimed to be a woman.") Several reviewers of Marcus's volume of collected papers, *Modalities* (1993), have joined Smith in complaining that her early work in philosophical logic has been unjustly scanted and have hailed her as the originator of the direct-reference idea. Perhaps, though, it is natural that most philosophers should regard a theory built around the notion of a "rigid designator" as a male thing.

By now, a quarter of a century has passed since Saul Kripke galvanized the Anglo-American philosophical world with the New Theory of Reference—elements of which had been anticipated by Ruth Marcus a quarter of a century earlier still. The question that Smith raised is a significant one in the history of ideas. But does the New Theory of Reference remain a vital area of inquiry today? "Very much so," Scott Soames tells me. "The theses presented in *Naming and Necessity* have become enormously influential. They're still being extended into new areas of the philosophy of mind, like characterizing the role of belief and desire in the explanation of behavior." Others disagree. "In the late 1970s and the 1980s, the journals were full of articles about the philosophical aspects of modal logic and the implications for truth and reference," says Barry Loewer, a philosopher of mind at Rutgers. "Now you hardly ever see them." Robert Solomon takes a jaundiced view of the enterprise. "When people start fighting over who first got the ideas, the movement must be dead," he says. "The whole business about possible worlds and rigid designators and natural kinds is almost embarrassing in retrospect. It occupies a square millimeter in the square centimeter that constitutes a narrow conception of the philosophy of language, a tiny patch in the hectare that is philosophy." ("What does he know?" honks Kripke in response. "He's a *phenomenologist.*") Certainly, the philosophical outlook implicit in the New Theory of Reference could not be more unfashionable in the wider intellectual world at the moment. Imagine: regarding the external world as *real*, full of objects that have *essences*—essences that are disclosed not by poets or phenomenologists but by *scientists*!

IN THE PAST DECADE, not much has been heard from Kripke. As rumor, speculation, and controversy swirl around him within the philosophical world, he seems to be little known without. When I mention him to lit-crit people, political scientists, and academics/intellectuals of other nonphilosophical stripes, the usual response is something like: "Kripke? Yeah, I've heard of him. He's that guy who was on the cover of *The New York Times Magazine* ages ago." People who can discuss the philosophy of Richard Rorty in excruciating detail are unable to identify a single idea even vaguely associated with Kripke. The name carries little in the way of description; it has no "Fregean sense" for them. Will Kripke outlast his time? Will his name survive? The whole problem puts me in mind of a passage from *Naming and Necessity*: "Consider Richard Feynman, to whom many of us are able to refer. He is a leading contemporary physicist. Everyone *here* (I'm sure!) can state the contents of one of Feynman's theories so as to differentiate him from Gell-Mann. However, the man in the street, not possessing these abilities, may still use the name 'Feynman.' When asked he will say: well he's a physicist or something. He may not think that this picks out anyone uniquely. I still think he uses the name 'Feynman' as a name for Feynman."

Similarly, if the New Theory of Reference is true, the academic in the street can still use the name "Kripke" to refer to Kripke—even if all he can tell you is that "he's a philosopher or something." And if the New Theory of Reference is false? If names are equivalent to descriptions? In that case, when we talk about "Kripke," we are talking about "the inventor of the New Theory of Reference." And so we can be absolutely certain that Quentin Smith is mistaken, for it becomes a *necessary* truth that it's Kripke who originated the theory. Only in some possible world, "Kripke" might be Marcus.

—February 1996

HABEAS CORPUS

Jeremy Bentham Attends His 250th Birthday Party

EMILY EAKIN

INVENTOR, NEUROLOGIST, inveterate planner and schemer, the English political philosopher Jeremy Bentham (1748–1832) racked up any number of firsts during his lifetime. Strictly speaking, he was not the first person to embrace utilitarianism—the philosophy with which he is usually credited. But he coined the words "international" and "preprandial" and dreamed up the panopticon, the high-surveillance prison that Michel Foucault would later make famous as an expression of the sinister coercive power of the modern state.

Bentham also devised an interest-bearing currency (he called it "circulating annuities"), an underground icebox (the frigidarium), and a system for long-distance communication (the "conversation tube"), which, despite the limited technology of his day, neatly presaged the telephone. More than one hundred years before Brigitte Bardot was born, Bentham devoted an entire section of his model penal code to cruelty to animals. And according to Philip Schofield, a scholar at University College, London, Bentham may well have been the world's first jogger—an activity he referred to with characteristic exactitude as "circumgyration."

This winter Bentham may add another first to his list when he becomes the first human being to attend his 250th birthday party. Two dozen scholars are marking the occasion with a conference at the University of Texas. And thanks to a live video hookup connecting the revelers in Austin with the philosopher's residence in London, Bentham—what's left of him—will be at the party, too.

It sounds like a lurid publicity stunt, but it's nothing less than what the eccentric Brit intended. As a utilitarian, Bentham believed in promoting the greatest good for the greatest number with the least amount of pain. Accordingly, he left instructions in his will for the preservation of his corpse so that humankind might "reap some small benefit by my disease" and—more to the point—so that his followers might take inspiration from his continued presence in their midst. Today, Bentham's "Auto-Icon" (his skeleton minus the head, for which a more palatable wax replica has been substituted) resides fully dressed inside a glass box at University College.

What more efficient way to represent oneself to posterity than to serve as one's own memorial? (Was he also the first performance artist?) It probably never occurred to Bentham, however, that his final act might someday have more than one meaning. No longer just a poster boy for the movement—efficiency embodied—the Auto-Icon has become a particularly apt symbol of utilitarianism's ambiguous status today: a much-loved, much-despised theory that, depending on whom you ask, either has outlived its uses or is just now coming into its own. As the UC-Berkeley law school professor and conference participant David Lieberman puts it: "Utilitarianism has long been out of favor in academic jurisprudence and moral philosophy. But, paradoxically, it's more than ever before at the center of government decision making."

In the nineteenth century, utilitarianism was a driving political force. Bentham peddled his blueprint for a democratic constitution to countries all over the world—the Portuguese nearly adopted it—and his disciples briefly had their own party, the Philosophic Radicals, in the House of Commons. In this country, however, Bentham had less luck. When he wrote to the White House in 1811 to propose that the Americans try out his civil and penal codes, James Madison gave the Brit the cold shoulder. No doubt the utilitarian's scorn for both the doctrine of natural rights—good revolution, bad foundations, was

Bentham's take on the War of Independence—and the separation of powers struck the mastermind of *The Federalist Papers* as misplaced.

Now, however, Benthamism is back in style, albeit in a new, high-tech guise. Rational-choice theorists, number crunchers, cost-benefit analysts: these are the utilitarians of the 1990s. And though Bentham would hardly recognize his ideas in the policy wonks' computer algorithms, the goal is still very much the same—calculating utility preferences.

"Utilitarianism fits in very nicely with our highly technologized age," says Jean Bethke Elshtain, a professor of social and political ethics at the University of Chicago and a speaker at the Bentham conference. "Because we can quantify in such sophisticated ways, we assume we can apply econometrics to everything—family, work, love." David Lieberman agrees. "Bentham is the perfect icon for what modern society has become," he observes. "Aggressively materialistic, aggressively technocratic, aggressively hedonic."

But just because Benthamism is Us doesn't mean the professors necessarily approve. "Bentham's claim was that there was a first principle that should guide all public policy: the greatest happiness," says James Fishkin, a professor of political philosophy at UT who is directing the conference. "But now we see all kinds of problems with that notion: What about the interests of the few? The minority? The vulnerable? We want to tell him what he got right and what he got wrong."

To that end, Fishkin is asking some of his panelists to address their remarks directly to Bentham's video presence. And if the results of our informal survey are any indication, the skeleton may be in for a rough ride. Chicago's Elshtain, for example, will deliver a paper titled "Bentham Stuffed"—an allusion, she explains, not just to her subject's physical state but also to her sense of utilitarianism's "conceptual poverty" as a philosophy of human life. More sympathetic but still critical, the UT philosopher David Braybrooke will ponder "Bentham's Master Idea: Could It Have Turned Out More Happily?" "Bentham was his own worst enemy," Braybrooke argues. "His master idea was that social policy should be chosen according to statistical evidence of its impact. Unfortunately, as soon as he got this idea, he came up with the 'felicific calculus' of pleasure and pain. And this concept has driven out of sight other ways of collecting statistical evidence." Even UT's James Galbraith, one of the few economists planning to attend the conference, says he has serious reservations about utilitarian-inspired economic theory today. "The whole field of welfare economics is in dire straits," he says. "We can't escape the necessity of evaluating social conditions, but there must be ways forward that bypass the utilitarian approach."

Still, no matter how nasty things get, Bentham is expected to remain a perfect gentleman throughout the ordeal. And he will be richly rewarded for his stoicism. Fishkin is planning to surprise the birthday boy with an elaborately decorated cake—a meticulous replica of Bentham's beloved panopticon.

—March 1998

THE QUEST FOR UNCERTAINTY
Richard Rorty's Pragmatic Pilgrimage

JAMES RYERSON

THE TRANQUIL HIBISCUS-LINED eucalyptus grove in the UC–Santa Cruz arboretum is a nice spot for reflecting on philosophy's age-old questions. Fortunately for Richard Rorty, a nature lover with a distaste for those sorts of questions, it's also an excellent place for bird-watching. We have driven here on a bright California morning to do a bit of both. As we pass his binoculars back and forth, searching the grevilleas for hummingbirds, it's hard to believe that this shy, gentle-mannered sixty-nine-year-old Stanford professor is the same man whose ideas have been widely denounced for the past twenty years as cynical, nihilistic, and deeply irresponsible.

"I have even lost a friend in all of this," says Rorty of his fractious career as America's most famous living philosopher. "It was Carl Hempel, one of the best-loved figures in the profession and a model of moral character." Hempel, a teacher of Rorty's, had fled Hitler's Germany and symbolized all that was most inspiring about the scientific, social democratic, truth-seeking world of Anglo-American philosophy. "Hempel read my book *Philosophy and the Mirror of Nature* and wrote me a letter saying, in effect, 'You have betrayed everything I stood for.' And he really didn't like me after that. I'm still very sad about it."

Rorty points to a bird flying overhead. "That's a kestrel," he adds without a pause, in his doleful, sighing voice, "the smallest American falcon."

The charge of betrayal is one Rorty has learned to accept over the years. Like his idol John Dewey, whom he credits with breaking through "the crust of philosophical convention," he has pursued twin careers as disciplinary bad boy and high-minded public philosopher. He has set out to deflate the aspirations of his profession—he rejects the idea of truth as an accurate reflection of the world—while placing his own unorthodox philosophical views at the center of an ambitious vision of social and historical hope. In recent writings especially, he champions an unlikely brand of "postmodern bourgeois liberalism" that has largely infuriated postmodernists and liberals alike.

A lucid writer with a penchant for dropping the names of virtually all the major thinkers in the philosophical tradition, Rorty has a knack for making his radical rejection of truth and objectivity seem an easy and agreeable shift of one's current perspective. Harold Bloom is not alone in judging him "the most interesting philosopher in the world today." But the success of philosophy's preeminent anti-philosopher has not come easily. Seemingly everyone who is impressed with one facet of Rorty's work harbors severe reservations about another. Those who share his admiration for analytic philosophers like Donald Davidson, Wilfrid Sellars, and Willard Van Orman Quine are angered by his opinion that analytic philosophy does not exist "except in some such stylistic or sociological way." Political theorists are dismayed by his proposal that their work be replaced by "genres such as ethnography, the journalist's report, the comic book, the docudrama, and, especially, the novel." Fellow enthusiasts of Hans-Georg Gadamer, Jacques Derrida, and Martin Heidegger aren't comfortable seeing their favorite Continental thinkers discussed in the frank Anglo-American idiom in which Rorty was trained. And radical postmodernist fans of his assault on the idea of objective truth are disappointed to hear that his politics are "pretty much those of Hubert Humphrey."

In practice, this assortment of provocations adds up to one of the truly original personalities in academic life. A heavy-moving man with a snowy drift of hair and dark, impish eyebrows, Rorty embodies a rare blend of intellectual traits. The University of Chicago philosopher James Conant notes that "in certain ways he resembles a Parisian intellectual: he reads everything, he drops a lot of names, he's interested in very big questions." But as Rorty plods along the arboretum's dirt paths in his frumpy, oversized sweater, with binoculars resting on his thickset torso, he looks every bit the stereotype of the sober, diligent Anglo-Saxon scholar. He manages to combine genuine personal modesty with sweeping philosophical ambition, and calls on clear prose and sensible-sounding argument to unite a range of wildly adventuresome ideas. The result is exceedingly unusual in a specialized academic world: a "syncretist hack," in his own self-effacing words, who in style as well as substance melds the most impressive elements of two intellectual traditions.

But can the man who shattered philosophy's mirror of nature pick up the pieces? Over the past few years, Rorty has increasingly turned from the scholarly criticism of philosophy toward the public espousal of what he calls "social hope." In 1998, he left his longtime post at the University of Virginia and took a job at Stanford as professor of comparative literature—though he proposed the alternative title "transitory professor of trendy studies." That same year, he published a polemical work of intellectual history, *Achieving Our Country: Leftist Thought in Twentieth-Century America*, in which he encouraged a revival of national pride among the American left and disparaged cynical "cultural leftists" who rely on theoretical approaches to politics at the expense of practical, piecemeal reform. A year later, he published *Philosophy and Social Hope*, a paperback selection of his most accessible writings, marketably packaged with a cover image by the German film director Wim Wenders. Its title alludes to the Deweyan notion that in politics we should "substitute *hope* for the sort of knowledge which philosophers have usually tried to attain." By Rorty's lights, a "post-metaphysical culture," in which we forsake the rhetoric of the true nature of the world, will help promote a classless, casteless, and egalitarian society in the long run. "The inculcation of antilogocentrism in the young will contribute to the strength of democratic societies," he asserts.

Rorty's critics charge that his blithe disregard for the notion of objective truth threatens to undermine the public's moral and intellectual integrity. The conservative cultural critic Neal Kozody complains that "it is not enough for him that American students should be merely mindless; he would have them positively mobilized for mindlessness." Others see in Rorty a more promising example of intellectual conduct. In his 1987 book, *The Last Intellectuals*, Russell Jacoby bemoaned the disappearance of "public intellectuals." But in a new edition of his book, Jacoby refers to Rorty as an all-too-infrequent exception—a university scholar who "represents an effort to invigorate a public philosophy." The distinguished UC-Berkeley intellectual historian David Hollinger concurs: "Being a public intellectual is an easy thing to do badly, and Dick is one of the few people who can carry it off with integrity."

Yet no matter how attractive it might sound, Rorty's message of hope will not hold up if his attack on the last two thousand years of philosophy as misguided and socially useless fails to persuade. In the recently published *Rorty and His Critics*, Rorty goes head-to-head on this very matter with twelve of his most distinguished critics, including Jürgen Habermas, Donald Davidson, Hilary Putnam, Daniel Dennett, and Jacques Bouveresse. Despite Rorty's general disdain for the profession's ideals, the book suggests that his work has had a real impact on some important younger guns of the mainstream philosophical establishment. Still, the consensus among these friendly adversaries is that Rorty has gone too far with interesting ideas. "My own experience suggests that you can use Rorty as a great source on difficult thinkers like Heidegger or Sellars," says Dennett. "And if you multiply what he says by the number .673"—which Dennett playfully calls the "Rorty Factor"—"then you get the truth. Dick always exaggerates everything in the direction of the more radical."

Stauncher critics maintain that the Rorty Factor is considerably smaller. As the New York University philosopher Paul Boghossian remarks, Rorty faces the perilous task of rejecting the notion of objective truth while avoiding the charge that his own views are thus untrustworthy. "I just think he has never really pulled off the trick," Boghossian says. "I don't think that anybody has, but in particular I don't think that *he* has."

WHEN A YOUNGSTER, Rorty showed few signs of being an intellectual agitator in the making. "My parents were always telling me that it was about time I had a stage of adolescent revolt," he remembers. "They were worried I wasn't rebellious enough." James and Winifred Rorty set the bar high in that regard. Both were active members of New York City's anti-Stalinist, Trotskyist left—they had broken with the American Communist Party in 1932, a year after Richard was born. For years, James Rorty worked with the philosopher Sidney Hook on leftist causes like the anticapitalist, revolutionary American Workers Party; he later joined Hook in moving away from radicalism altogether. Winifred Rorty was the daughter of Walter Rauschenbusch, the legendary Social Gospel theologian, whom young Richard was raised to think of as "a sort of socialist hero." The Rortys typically spent half the year in rural Connecticut or New Jersey and the other half in Park Slope, Brooklyn, or the Chelsea Hotel in Manhattan. Surrounded by luminaries like A. Philip Randolph, Norman Thomas, Irving Howe, and Lionel and Diana Trilling, they epitomized the intellectually cosmopolitan lifestyle of the time, as depicted in books like Edmund Wilson's *Memoirs of Hecate County*.

Dragged in and out of various schools—and bullied at many of them—the timid, bookish Rorty was the sort of boy who sent opals as a gift to the Dalai Lama ("a fellow eight-year-old who had made good"), hunted in the mountains of northwest New Jersey for wild orchids, and worried that his love for those plants was incompatible with the Marxist criticism he had read of Walter Pater's aestheticism. At fifteen, he went off to the University of Chicago to get his bachelor's degree at the so-called Hutchins College, which permitted precocious students to enter in the middle of high school. There he studied a classical curriculum under scholars like Leo Strauss and Richard McKeon and alongside students like the future classicist and cultural scourge Allan Bloom.

Rorty decided to stay on at Chicago for a master's degree in philosophy, which was tantamount to a career choice. James Rorty was "rather surprised and dismayed" by the idea and asked his friend Hook to give his son advice. ("He wasn't encouraging," says Rorty of Hook. "He just said things like 'publish early and often.' ") In 1952, Rorty moved to Yale for his Ph.D., and by 1956 he had quickly finished a dissertation on the concept of potentiality—too quickly perhaps. "I was drafted into the army because I stupidly didn't delay my dissertation until past my twenty-sixth birthday," he explains. "I have no idea why I was that dumb." After a two-year military stint in which he worked in the computer section of the Signal Corps (he was awarded a programming medal for persuading his higher-ups to adopt the more efficient Polish system of logical notation), Rorty taught at Wellesley College for three years and then in 1961 landed a job at Princeton, which had one of the most distinguished philosophy programs in the country.

At Princeton, the search for the foundations of knowledge was conducted in the forbidding and highly technical terms of analytic philosophy. By rigorously analyzing the meanings of words and the objects they refer to, Rorty's new colleagues hoped to reveal the structure and accuracy of our statements about the world. "My first years at Princeton I was desperately trying to learn what was going on in analytic philosophy," he confesses. "Most of my colleagues had been at Harvard, and you had to know what they were talking about at Harvard in order to be with it."

After about two years of fumbling about, Rorty got into the swing of the analytic approach and began to make a name for himself with innovative work in the philosophy of mind. He was especially intrigued by the ideas of Sellars, Quine, and, later, Davidson. These were thinkers inclined to tackle problems by tearing down chunks of philosophy that they felt were misconceived and focusing their attention on what remained. Rorty's predicament was that his favorite thinkers were often tearing down different aspects of philosophy. While Sellars questioned whether our sense perceptions really afforded a privileged form of knowledge, Quine wondered whether logical truths could be distinguished from empirical findings. Over a number of years, Rorty began to stitch together these various innovative projects in a creative way, for he was able to see more commonality than difference in them. The only problem was that if neither sense perception nor logic offered us the prospect of utter certainty, then how could we determine the accuracy of our claims in representing the world?

By the early 1970s, Rorty had taken an even bolder turn: In part through his growing interest in the work of Derrida ("the cleverest man I'd read in years"), he was led to reread the work of Derrida's hero Heidegger. Reading Heidegger drew Rorty into the so-called hermeneutic tradition of Continental thought, which eschewed the project of breaking down language into its component parts in favor of an approach to knowledge more akin to literary interpretation than to scientific analysis. With a leg in the analytic and Continental traditions, Rorty was positioned to see similarities among Heidegger, Ludwig Wittgenstein, and Dewey, three very different philosophers who nonetheless all asked what he called a "therapeutic" philosophical question: How can we avoid, rather than solve, the philosophical problems that bedevil us?

Rorty explored these highly controversial ideas in his 1979 classic, *Philosophy and the Mirror of Nature*, in which he argued that there was no sense in trying to give a general account of truth. "Granted that 'true' is an absolute term," he wrote in a later essay, "its conditions of application will always be relative." That is, whatever we may hope to mean when we call a belief "true," we use the word only when we feel our belief is justified—and justification always raises the question "Justified to whom?" To critics who would argue that the *justification* of our claims may always be relative to a particular audience but that *truth* is not, because it consists of accuracy to the way the world really is, Rorty had a frustratingly simple response: there's no point in saying that truth has anything to do with the way the world really is.

In the spirit of the earlier pragmatist tradition, Rorty argued that the notions of "truth" and "accurate representation" are nothing but compliments we pay to sentences that we find useful in dealing with the world. To say that science is useful in predicting and controlling nature because it describes the true nature of the world is, in Rorty's view, a tautology, for we have no criteria for whether we have described "the true nature of the world" other than success in predicting and controlling nature. And once we see that science is deemed successful only when it helps us achieve certain goals, he explained, we will realize that other forms of inquiry can be considered equally successful at achieving different goals—without ever having to ask whether one form of inquiry better describes the way the world really is.

As for the charge that he was ignoring the fact that there is a world beyond the confines of our thought, Rorty conceded that the world does shove us around. "Yet," he asked, "what does being shoved around have to do" with making claims about the world, which we always do in the terms of our language? Any attempt to square linguistic statements with the world is to compare apples and oranges, to try to climb out of our own minds and language to see the world as it is in itself, and Rorty saw no profit in it. Indeed, following his own pragmatist criteria, he did not suggest that he was offering an alternative view of the world; rather, he proposed that his way of talking about things was useful. Instead of spending valuable time asking whether various types of inquiry—science, political thought, poetry, alchemy—are better or worse at capturing the truth, we should ask whether there are new ways of describing and redescribing the world that better serve our variety of goals, with the understanding that "hope of agreement is never lost so long as the conversation lasts."

Rorty's colleagues were not pleased, though they were hardly surprised. "My recollection is that for the first ten years at Princeton, I was one of the boys," remembers Rorty. "But for the second ten years, I was seen as increasingly contrarian or difficult." In addition to philosophical differences, there were personal complications: "I got divorced and remarried, and because my first wife was a philosopher and a friend of my colleagues', there were problems. It was not a friendly divorce, and I didn't handle it very well."

Rorty made it known that he was interested in a job elsewhere, preferably a university professorship, so he could avoid the issue of how he was supposed to fit in with a philosophy department. In the early 1980s, as *Philosophy and the Mirror of Nature* began to make waves throughout the academy, the University of Virginia made him the offer he wanted. "After years of thinking that what my colleagues were doing must be important," he recalls, "I began to think, maybe the analytic establishment is not the future of philosophy. Maybe it's just a bubble."

FOR ALL ITS AUDACITY, *Philosophy and the Mirror of Nature* couldn't have appeared at a more opportune moment, and its ideas couldn't have been espoused by a better-situated academic. At the time it was published, legions of scholars in the humanities were inspecting the discourses of the past and seeking a theoretical warrant for assessing those discourses in ways—historical, sociological, and political—that didn't presuppose a timeless, universal notion of truth. "If you wanted non-foundational-sounding stuff," Rorty concedes, "mine was as good as any."

Rorty's critics were quick to find something suspicious in his popularity with nonphilosophers. "One of the central morals of the book," says Paul Boghossian, who studied with Rorty at Princeton, "is that whatever there is that's still worth doing in philosophy is best done by literary critics rather than philosophers. This had tremendous, obvious appeal to those academics in the humanities who were already abandoning the study of literature narrowly conceived for much more general reflections on the relations between language, knowledge, truth, power, and society. Unfortunately, I don't think it's really possible to do good philosophy without a considerable amount of training in the subject."

Even some of Rorty's supporters have significant reservations about his views. The philosopher Daniel Dennett, who feels that Rorty's philosophy of mind is "just about perfect," nonetheless has qualms about Rorty's unwillingness to consider science a privileged form of inquiry and about his willingness to take seriously the philosophical views of thinkers like Derrida and Michel Foucault: "Dick Rorty has failed to discourage a lot of nonsense that I wish he had discouraged. It's an obligation of us in the field to grit our teeth and discourage the people who do the things that give philosophy a bad name. I don't think he does that enough."

Critics are also quick to pounce on some of Rorty's telltale stylistic quirks. Rorty's writings are littered with philosophical lists; for instance, many sentences will begin with a clause like "What Heidegger, Dewey, Cavell, Gadamer, Kuhn, Derrida, and Putnam are all saying is . . ." It's a technique that may allow nonphilosophers to feel they have a handle on an extraordinarily diverse range of thinkers, but to most philosophers the implied comparisons sound forced, if not downright inaccurate. "Almost everybody I know who figures in one of these lists invariably wants to get off," notes Conant, "even though it's extremely flattering to appear on these lists and Rorty has made some people quite famous."

Rorty sympathizes with those—like Thomas Kuhn, to take a prominent example—who have pleaded with him not to characterize their work in ways they find distorting or misleading. "It's a natural reaction," he says. "They think of themselves as having made a quite specific point, and with a wave of my hand I seem to subsume their specific point as part of some great cultural movement, or something like that. They think that it's a way of putting them in bad company and ignoring the really interesting thing they said, which my net is too gross to capture." Still, Rorty defends this tendency: "I don't see anything wrong with doing that. Regardless of how they feel about it, if you think there's a common denominator or a trend, then why not say so?"

EXPELLED FROM THE MAINSTREAM philosophical community, Rorty took up ranks with those outside the discipline who had embraced his work. Given the widespread interest in Continental philosophy, the University of Virginia needed more professors to teach the material. So, Rorty explains, "I just picked up the slack." Teaching literature students was a relatively painless transition for him. "Princeton's got the best philosophy students in the country, so I missed that. I had to teach in a way that didn't allude to Quine's criticism of the analytic-synthetic distinction," he muses. "But it didn't matter much. By that time, I wasn't teaching in a way that required students to keep up with philosophical journals."

His scholarly interests, too, grew increasingly alien to the work done in academic journals. Though he continued to publish in those journals, picking "the same highly professionalized nits" that he picked in *Philosophy and the Mirror of Nature*, Rorty moved on to themes of more general concern, such as how to think about morality, liberal democracy, and a private self in a world without the possibility of objective truth. He addressed these issues in his 1989 book, *Contingency, Irony, and Solidarity*.

In his adolescence, Rorty had admired William Butler Yeats's ideal of holding "reality and justice in a single vision." Indeed, the desire for an all-encompassing perspective on the world had driven his intellectual curiosity. "I desperately wanted to be a Platonist," he admits, "to become one with the One, to fuse myself with Christ or God or the Platonic form of the Good or something like that." In *Contingency*, Rorty rebuked that objective. Morality, he felt, was not the voice of some inner part of ourselves that we needed philosophical reflection to discover; rather, it was simply the practical effort to work with other members of a community to find some mutually acceptable code of self-protection. Art, by contrast, involved the individual's efforts at "self-creation."

As for the liberal tradition of political thought, Rorty agreed with "ironists" like Foucault that liberalism's supposedly timeless balance of rights and duties is a mere historical contingency; at the same time, he agreed with "liberals" like Habermas that liberal democracies are worth fighting passionately for. The absence of any universally valid notions of human rights or individual liberties was no reason to find fault with the well-functioning institution of liberal democracy itself. The sole factor responsible for keeping liberal democracy alive, Rorty argued, was the hatred of cruelty and a solidarity with those who suffer. He offered books like George Orwell's *1984* as examples of how writers can redescribe the world in ways that cultivate this sort of solidarity. When faced with opponents who don't share our worldview, Rorty explained, we cannot hope to refute them, but we can concretely elucidate our worldview in the hope that it will make their worldview look untenable. "There is no answer to a redescription," he pronounced, "save a re-re-redescription."

Alongside this talk of incremental redescription, a grander vision seemed to be taking shape. At stake was nothing less than the progression of Western culture into its next stage of maturity. The first stage of this maturation, in Rorty's eyes, was overcoming the pre-Enlightenment religious outlook, which required humans to appeal to something nonhuman and divine for moral guidance and truth when in fact they should have been seeking moral guidance among themselves. Many thinkers acknowledge the freedom that this aspect of the Enlightenment has brought. But Rorty regrets that few of them see a parallel between overcoming the dubious religious idea of a nonhuman divine Other and overcoming the dubious scientific idea of conforming our inquiry to the way the world really is.

Such metaphysical pretensions, Rorty believes, are the traces of unprofitable ways of talking about the world, and if philosophers can persuade people to stop talking as though our worldview describes things as they really are, they can make a substantive contribution to the de-divinizing of the world. Rather than assuming that our inquiry can cease when it hits the hard bedrock of truth, people, Rorty believes, must realize that the goals of inquiry continually evolve and are best met by an enduring commitment to experimentation, novelty, poetic creativity, and pluralism.

So are philosophers useless, or do they have a world-historical role to play in dispelling deep metaphysical superstitions? Rorty acknowledges this tension: "You're right. I wobble on that point." But he draws a distinction between the day-to-day irrelevance of worrying about truth and the epochal significance of learning to talk in ways that sidestep the ideal of certain knowledge. "Just because world-historical movements are happening doesn't mean you can apply that knowledge in everyday practice."

AS RORTY TURNED toward political and cultural questions, he had less and less patience with his postmodernist colleagues in the humanities. In particular, he disliked their politics. "I was surrounded by what seemed to me an idiot left in the literature departments," he explains, "people who claimed to be politically involved but who, as far as I could see, weren't." In *Achieving Our Country*, Rorty responded by excoriating what he described as a "spectatorial, disgusted, mocking left." He laid the charges of complacency and political impotence on academics who had permitted "cultural politics to supplant real politics." He lamented the disappearance of the "reformist left," Americans such as Eugene Debs and Franklin Roosevelt who, "between 1900 and 1964, struggled within the framework of constitutional democracy to protect the weak from the strong."

In *Rorty and His Critics*, Rorty comes as close as he ever has to an apology for throwing his philosophical weight behind literary scholars who used his work for suspect political ends. When he arrived at the University of Virginia to teach Continental philosophy, Rorty confesses, he "did not foresee what has actually happened: that the popularity of philosophy (under the sobriquet 'theory') in our literature departments was merely a transitional stage on the way to the development of what we in America are coming to call the Academic Left." These leftists, Rorty asserts, "have convinced themselves that by chanting various Derridean or Foucauldian slogans they are fighting for human freedom. . . . The political uselessness, relative illiteracy, and tiresomely self-congratulatory enthusiasm of this new Academic Left, together with its continual invocation of the names of Derrida and Foucault, have conspired to give these latter thinkers a bad name in the United States." He concludes: "I am, I must admit, chastened. But I am not ashamed. . . . There are other things to do with Foucault and Derrida than are currently being done with them by the School of Resentment, just as there are other things to be done with Nietzsche than to use him as the Nazis used him."

But has Rorty articulated a politics any more practical than that of the academic left he disdains? Though he has made specific proposals in *The Nation* in favor of campaign finance reform, universal health care, and the more equitable financing of primary and secondary education, many critics find his views too much those of a relatively uninformed outsider. At a City University of New York lecture on public intellectuals in May, the judge and libertarian economist Richard Posner attacked Rorty's conception of politics for its indifference to the workings of actual economic or socioeconomic policy. Rorty's political outlook, Posner charged, is "unworldly," "pessimistic," and "almost Spenglerian," with a whiff of "nostalgia for the militancy and class struggle of the old labor movement."

Meanwhile, leftists like the New School political philosopher Richard Bernstein have attacked Rorty for his complacent disregard of the more sinister overtones of his pro-American stance, calling his views on politics "little more than an ideological apologia for an old-fashioned version of Cold War liberalism dressed up in fashionable 'post-modern' discourse." Even the economist Robert Kuttner, a figure whom one might expect to be more sympathetic to Rorty's strain of redistributionist-minded liberalism, has attacked his call for eliminating Social Security benefits for the wealthier elderly. In *The American Prospect*, Kuttner called Rorty's *New York Times* Op-Ed piece in March on this topic "so politically innocent and self-defeating that one didn't know whether to laugh or to cry." Kuttner explains his irritation: "I was annoyed at the Social Security Op-Ed because I thought, and still think, that Rorty simply missed the logic of social solidarity: the greater security and equality for have-nots that is inherent in universal social programs. And this from a professed egalitarian."

IF RORTY HAS MET with mixed reactions in the public realm, he has, ironically, enjoyed a small revival in the philosophical world he left behind. Several of the most highly respected thinkers within contemporary Anglo-American philosophy—John McDowell, James Conant, and Rorty's former student Robert Brandom—have expressed their intellectual debt to Rorty. In the preface to his seminal 1994 book, *Mind and World*, McDowell acknowledged that he sketched out his initial ideas "during the winter of 1985–6, in an attempt to get under control my usual excited reaction to a reading—my third or fourth—of Richard Rorty's *Philosophy and the Mirror of Nature*." He added that it should be "obvious that Rorty's work is in any case central for the way I define my stance here."

As McDowell explains in his essay "Towards Rehabilitating Objectivity" in *Rorty and His Critics*, Rorty's greatest accomplishment has been to help us escape from the idea that we need philosophy to bridge the supposed gap between our knowledge and the world. ("It was largely from him," McDowell says, "that I learned to think like that.") But McDowell feels "a piece of mere sanity" is missing from Rorty's account. Like Rorty, McDowell emphasizes that we cannot get outside our particular perspectives or worldviews. But unlike Rorty, he does not conclude that this means we must give up our notions of truth and objectivity altogether. To preserve a distinction between a truth that consists of consensus and a truth that consists in getting things objectively right, McDowell argues, "is not to try to think from outside our practices; it is simply to take it seriously that we can really mean what we say from within those practices." Indeed, he asks, what would it mean to have a *worldview* if, à la Rorty, we avoid the idea that our statements are true in light of the way the *world* is in our *view* of it?

In an exceedingly rare statement of self-doubt, Rorty replies: "Sometimes McDowell almost persuades me that I should back off from my highly unpopular attempt to replace objectivity with solidarity. . . . Sometimes I think that I really must have the blind spot he diagnoses." But in the end, though he finds "about 90 percent of *Mind and World* very appealing indeed," Rorty cannot figure out why McDowell refers to consensus as "mere consensus." If one norm of inquiry, consensus, can fully capture the sense in which our knowledge is in touch with the world, then why does McDowell insist on the need to add a second, perhaps more commonsensical but metaphysically heavier, norm of inquiry—that of getting things right about the world? "Here again," says Rorty, "the question is whether we have a difference [between choosing one norm of inquiry or two] that could ever make a difference."

James Conant believes he can show Rorty the difference. In his essay in *Rorty and His Critics*, "Freedom, Cruelty, and Truth: Rorty Versus Orwell," Conant claims to demonstrate that Rorty's pragmatism cannot satisfy its own requirement of being useful—which, after all, is the only reason that Rorty adheres to it. In *Contingency, Irony, and Solidarity*, Rorty championed Orwell's *1984* as a model of how literature can create greater awareness of suffering. But Conant worries that Rorty himself offers the individual no resources with which to condemn a world of Orwellian thought control. In the totalitarian scenario of *1984*, the protagonist, Winston Smith, remembers having seen airplanes in his childhood, before the Party took power. And yet, since the Party took power, everyone but Winston has been brainwashed into believing that the Party invented the airplane. When Winston says "the Party did not invent the airplane," by Rorty's standards he does not make a knowledgeable statement, because he cannot bring about the consensus of his peers. Isn't this a case where McDowell would be right in suggesting that an appeal to a second, nonconsensus norm of inquiry makes a difference? "If Winston tries to do everything that Rorty thinks he can do," explains Conant, "then he'll quickly come to the conclusion: 'The Party invented the airplane.' But if he tries to do something that is left out of Rorty's theory of justification, which is to try to get it right, trusting his memories and so on, then he has reason to think that the Party didn't invent the airplane."

Rorty's response to Conant is straightforward and bleak: "The difference between myself and Conant is that he thinks that someone like Winston, trapped in such a society, can turn to the light of the facts. I think that there is nowhere for Winston to turn." For Rorty, the way to prevent a situation like this from coming about in the first place is not to reclaim the notion of objective truth but rather to promote what he calls "truthfulness"—namely, the freedom to say publicly what you believe, even when it is disadvantageous to do so. If we take care of making sure people can say what they believe, he argues, "truth" will take care of itself.

For Conant, though, it is unclear if Rorty can speak of truthfulness without having a notion of objective truth. Indeed, he points out that in *1984* part of the horror is that Winston's fellow citizens have been encouraged to cultivate a high degree of "doublethink"—that is, to believe they speak the truth even though they are not saying anything that is true. Conant believes that such doublethink satisfies—indeed, perversely resembles—Rorty's prescription of "truthfulness."

"Rorty's quite right that consensus is a necessary condition of justification," Conant says. But Conant feels there's room to balance that insight with the idea of truth as getting things right—all without succumbing to the traditional philosophical idea that getting things right involves capturing the world as it is apart from our view of it. "It's an overly restricted set of options that causes Rorty all his trouble," Conant concludes. "The right things to say in philosophy are much more delicate than that."

WHY IS RORTY—the advocate of pluralism, of not knowing things for sure, of openness and variety—not more comfortable with the balancing act that philosophers like McDowell and Conant want to pull off? For all the important mysteries about Rorty, his colleagues call attention to one seemingly insignificant aspect of his personality: his voice. Rorty's voice is, as Daniel Dennett notes, "sort of striking—these firebrand views delivered in the manner of Eeyore." When philosophers talk about Rorty, few can resist trying to imitate his distinctively somber delivery. Of Rorty's mode of presentation the British philosopher Jonathan Rée says: "There's a tremendous kind of melancholy about it. He tries to be a gay Nietzschean, but it's an effort for him." For Conant, hearing Rorty speak for the first time was something of a revelation. "It's easy to read his writings in a register of excitement and a heightened, breathless voice," he explains. "But the note that I heard when he was reading these sentences in his own cadences and rhythm was—for want of a better word—depression. I thought, this is the voice of a man who feels as if he's been let down or betrayed by philosophy." Jürgen Habermas concurs that Rorty's anti-philosophy "seems to spring from the melancholy of a disappointed metaphysician." And for Conant, this melancholy goes far in explaining the intransigence with which Rorty holds to his pluralistic philosophy of dialogue and playfulness. "It's as though he's been let down by philosophy once, and he's not going to let it happen again," Conant says.

BUT HOW ARE WE to square this vision of philosophical depression with the explicit role that hope plays in Rorty's philosophy? For David Hollinger, Rorty's somber intellectual mood is not one of depression but rather one of hope wisely tempered by experience. "I think Dick is rightly concerned about the legacy of naive optimism that Dewey is constantly being assaulted for," he says. "There's this idea that the children of the Enlightenment were smug and Panglossian; they felt they had renounced God and could go forth on a Promethean basis. In contrast to this, Rorty injects a sober realism about the evils of the world: Do you know about the Holocaust? Do you know about the atomic bomb? There is a feeling in Dick that this Enlightenment inheritance is basically right, if only we could be a little bit more chastened about it. Dick really does see himself in world-historical terms. And he is one of the few people who can do this without being pretentious about it."

Conant, though, insists that there remains a strong tension between Rorty's disenchanted philosophical views and the place that hope has in his public philosophy of late. "Part of the reason that the concept of hope plays such a central role," he says, "is that he's trying to give us hope without giving us a great many of the things that used to allow for the possibility of hope. So the concept of hope itself becomes important, and he wants to supply it, and so it has to go on the title page, because any of the things that might have brought us hope in their wake—truth, beauty, humanity—have been left out."

Rée, too, senses Rorty's apparent need to push forward with a positive vision and social message despite his disappointment with philosophy. "Rorty found his distinctive voice in the shock of a kind of bereavement," he says. "Long ago, truth must have been a god to him." But though Rée, as a Gadamer scholar, thinks Rorty's philosophical stance may be unimpeachable, he is not sure that humankind can master its own future the way Rorty seems to believe. "One possible picture of metaphysics," he explains, "is that it's rooted not in the studies we make as students but in the ways we try to make sense of ourselves starting from earliest infancy. Our notions may not withstand a Rortyan scrutiny—they may not be justified in any way. But nevertheless they're not arbitrary. We've grown to be the people we are because of them. It's more than a matter of will that we came by them, and it's more than a matter of will to change them."

Has Rorty really rejected his onetime ideal of holding reality and justice in a single vision? Or is he merely passing it off in another guise? After all, though he encourages pluralism and not knowing, he puts forth a view that settles many questions, and settles them once and for all. He suggests that the single measure for assessing all vocabularies is whether they are useful. Has he, contrary to his own intentions, simply created another kind of metavocabulary—a general way of assessing all ways of talking?

Achieving the proper sort of uncertainty may be hard to do, but it is critical to Rorty. When reflecting on his early days at Princeton, he begrudges the intellectual climate there. "Analytic philosophy was correlated with intellectual talent," he remembers. "Exposing the hidden assumptions and unclear terms in arguments: that was the only skill that was valued." Rorty confesses that he wasn't "good at it, wasn't sharp enough." But he regrets the inability of his sharper colleagues to second-guess their teachers or their own most basic assumptions. For Rorty, the most pernicious idea in that intellectual atmosphere was that technical clarity in problem solving was the chief intellectual virtue. "That's a recipe for scholasticism if I've ever heard it," he says, shaking his head disapprovingly. "What about imaginative virtues? If you don't allow people to be unclear, intellectual progress grinds to a halt. It's the vague people who are the pioneers."

—December 2000

HIGHER SUPERSTITIONS
The Case for Astrology

JIM HOLT

THE FUNDAMENTAL PROBLEM in the philosophy of science might be called the demarcation problem: What is it that distinguishes science from nonscience or pseudoscience? What, for example, makes evolutionary theory scientific and creationism pseudoscientific?

Philosophers of science have taken three broad approaches to this problem. One approach is to look for some criterion that demarcates science from pseudoscience—like Karl Popper's criterion of falsifiability, which says that a theory is scientific if it is open to experimental refutation. Let's call this approach *methodological positivism*.

A second approach is to argue that science is demarcated from pseudoscience not by its methodology but by a sociological criterion: the judgment of the "scientific community." This view, associated with figures like Thomas Kuhn, Michael Polanyi, and Robert K. Merton, might be called *elitist authoritarianism*.

Finally, one might deny the very possibility of demarcation, arguing that there is no rationale that privileges scientific over nonscientific beliefs. This view is often called *epistemological anarchism*.

The most impish of the epistemological anarchists was Paul Feyerabend (1924–1994), whose methodological motto was "anything goes." His good friend Imre Lakatos (1922–1974) took an opposing view—a blend, as he saw it, of Popper and Kuhn. Instead of asking whether a single theory was scientific or unscientific, Lakatos examined entire research programs, classifying them as "progressive" or "degenerating." He used the contrast to show how scientific consensus could be rational, not just a matter of mob psychology.

Feyerabend found this unpersuasive. "Neither Lakatos nor anybody else has shown that science is better than witchcraft and that science proceeds in a rational way," he wrote in "Theses on Anarchism." But Lakatos never gave up trying to convince his friend that his views were wrongheaded—and Feyerabend returned the favor. Their correspondence from 1968 to 1974 (when Lakatos died of a heart attack) has just been published as *For and Against Method*, edited by Matteo Motterlini.

The letters have their share of ribaldry. "I am *very* tired because my liver is acting up which is a pity, for my desire to lay the broads here (and there are some fine specimens walking around on campus) is considerably reduced," Feyerabend wrote from Berkeley. The friendly affection between the two philosophical antagonists is much in evidence. Lakatos, writing from the London School of Economics, often signed his letters "Love, Imre."

Philosophically, however, there is no detectable convergence of their positions over the six years of correspondence. That is not surprising, really, given how vexed the demarcation issue is. Take a seemingly easy case: astrology. We all think astrology is a pseudoscience (*pace* Feyerabend), but it is not easy to say why. The usual arguments are (1) astrology grew out of a magical worldview; (2) the planets are too far away for there to be any physical mechanism for their alleged influence on human character and fate; and (3) people believe in astrology only out of a desire for comforting explanations.

But the first argument is also true of chemistry, medicine, and cosmology. Nor is the second decisive, for there have been many scientific theories that have lacked physical foundations. When Isaac Newton proposed his theory of gravitation, for example, he could furnish no mechanism to account for how gravity's mysterious "action at a distance" was possible. As for the third argument, people often believe in good theories for illegitimate reasons.

Surely, though, astrology fails Popper's criterion of falsifiability?

This seems a promising line of argument, since horoscopes yield only vague tendencies, not sharp predictions.

Yet such tendencies, if they exist, ought to show up as statistical correlations for large populations. Indeed, attempts have been made to detect such correlations—notably in the 1960s by Michel Gauquelin, who surveyed the times of birth and subsequent careers of twenty-five thousand Frenchmen. Gauquelin found no significant relationship between careers and zodiac signs, which are determined by the position of the sun at the time of birth. But he did turn up associations between certain occupations of people and the positions of certain *planets* at the time of their birth. For instance, in accordance with the predictions of astrology, individuals born when Mars was at its zenith were more likely to become athletes, and those born when Saturn was rising were more likely to become scientists.

But if the scientific status of astrology cannot be impugned on Popperian grounds, perhaps it can be on Lakatosian ones. Some years after Lakatos's death, the philosopher Paul R. Thagard made a detailed case for astrology being a "dramatically unprogressive" research program, and hence pseudoscientific. Astrology has not added to its explanatory power since the time of Ptolemy, Thagard pointed out. It is riddled with anomalies, which the community of astrologers shows scant interest in clearing up. And it has been overtaken by alternative theories of personality and behavior, like Freudian psychology and genetics. (Not that the latter two aren't also vulnerable to the charge of being pseudoscientific.)

Lakatos himself clearly thought astrology was pseudoscience—as was much else. "The social sciences are on par with astrology, it is no use beating around the bush," he wrote to Feyerabend. ("Funny that I should be teaching at the London School of Economics!" he added.)

As for Feyerabend, the only definition of science he was finally prepared to tolerate was "what follows from a principle of *general hedonism*." And what about the truth? *"The truth, whatever it is, be damned. What we need is laughter."*

—September 1999

THE MYSTERY OF THE MILLIONAIRE METAPHYSICIAN

Or, The Quest for A. M. Monius

JAMES RYERSON

IN JUNE 2000, the philosopher Dean Zimmerman moved from the University of Notre Dame to Syracuse University with his wife and three kids, only to see their new house catch fire the day they moved in. Much of what they owned was destroyed. "We were out of the house for six months," he recalls. "It was a miserable experience."

The week after the fire, Zimmerman got a fortune cookie at a Chinese restaurant that brought encouraging news: "You will move to a wonderful new home within the year," it read. Zimmerman, a metaphysician with side interests in resurrection and divine eternity, was heartened by the prophecy. And when he returned to the restaurant three months later, his second fortune was equally promising: "A way out of a financial mess is discovered as if by magic!"

The next day Zimmerman received a letter from the A. M. Monius Institute. Printed on official-looking stationery and signed by the institute's director, Netzin Steklis, the letter offered Zimmerman a "generous" sum of money to review a sixty-page work of metaphysics titled "Coming to Understanding." As the letter explained, the institute "exists for the primary purpose of disseminating the work 'Coming to Understanding' and encouraging its critical review and improvement." For Zimmerman's philosophical services, the institute was prepared to pay him the astronomical fee of twelve thousand U.S. dollars.

Meanwhile, three thousand miles away in England, the University of Reading philosopher Jonathan Dancy returned from a short vacation to find his house in dire need of repairs. He also discovered a letter waiting for him. "I arrived home thinking that the roof has collapsed and I must do something about it," he remembers. "I wasn't sure how I was going to do it."

Dancy's letter from the A. M. Monius Institute made him the same remarkable offer that had been made to Zimmerman. "I thought, 'This is very weird,' " Dancy says. "At first, I thought they were offering me twelve *hundred* dollars." And the roof? "This was a godsend," he says, "as far as that goes."

Zimmerman and Dancy were not the only scholars who received lucrative offers—and ultimately payment—from the institute. Soon the roster had grown to include at least nine other philosophers: Ermanno Bencivenga of the University of California at Irvine; Jan Cover of Purdue University; John Hawthorne of Syracuse University; Trenton Merricks of the University of Virginia; Eugene Mills of Virginia Commonwealth University; Gideon Rosen of Princeton University; Michael Scriven of Claremont Graduate University; Theodore Sider of Syracuse University; and Ted Warfield of the University of Notre Dame.

The institute's letter claimed that a "very substantial sum" had been earmarked to help contribute to "the revival of traditional metaphysics." Given the number of philosophers involved, that sum was at least in the neighborhood of $125,000. Who could afford to spend that much money on philosophy? And of those who could, who would want to? No one had a clue.

The institute, for its part, was maddeningly secretive. Many of the philosophers spoke by telephone with Steklis, who refused to disclose any information about the author of the manuscript, the institute's funding, or her superiors. ("She made these mysterious references to 'the board,' " Zimmerman remembers.) As instructed, the philosophers downloaded "Coming to Understanding" from the institute's Web site, www.ammonius.com. Then, with a collective sense of puzzlement and excited disbelief, they awaited the arrival of their contracts in the mail.

To judge from both the reviewer's contract and "Coming to Understanding" itself, the institute meant business. For one thing, the manuscript, signed by one A. M. Monius, suggested the handiwork of a serious thinker—not a prankster. "It didn't seem like a joke," Zimmerman says. "It wasn't *that* funny. It was clearly the work of a fairly able writer—a smart person, one capable of making some gross philosophical errors while at the same time having some clever ideas." Theodore Sider was pleasantly surprised. "To tell you the truth," he says, "when I actually got into it, I enjoyed it." Dancy concurs: "There are enterprises you wouldn't want to be associated with. But I was much reassured by the work. It was better than many manuscripts I had referred for leading publishers. It was at least different."

The contract looked even more professional. Written in fluent legalese, it featured an eleven-point list of terms and conditions, including the requirement that the reviewer had published "an article (not merely a review) in *The Journal of Philosophy, The Philosophical Review, Mind, The Monist, Noûs,* and/or *The Review of Metaphysics.*" Reviewers were offered the choice of writing a "substantial critical review" or a "testimonial." A review meant a "reasoned criticism (whether favorable or unfavorable)" that offered "detailed positive suggestions" for improving the work; it had to be at least thirty pages long and "consistent with professional standards regarding reviews of this nature." Alternatively, for a two-page testimonial that would "praise 'Coming to Understanding' and highlight its merits and significance," the institute was willing to pay four thousand dollars.

Despite the institute's evident professionalism, its anonymity and mysteriousness made reviewers skittish—even after they had received countersigned contracts. "Some of us were wondering, What the hell? Is this for real?" says Jan Cover. Sider acknowledges that "it was a bit of a risk, because I had no idea who these people were." Dancy assumed that he had only a "one-in-ten chance" of getting paid and confesses that he is "still wary about the whole affair." Trenton Merricks shares that anxiety, noting that he had hoped A. M. Monius was "George Soros—and not some cult leader!"

For all the reviewers' reservations, their checks came through as promised. All their reviews, except for Gideon Rosen's, now appear on the institute's Web site, and all eleven reviewers have been paid in full. (Only Ted Warfield chose to write a testimonial.) "My hourly rate went way up," noted one reviewer, who wished not to be identified. Merricks, who received a three-thousand-dollar bonus for his review, laughs when he confesses that he spent the extra money on LASIK eye surgery. "It's so embarrassing," he says sheepishly. "I could never justify paying the money under normal circumstances. But with the bonus—bada bing!"

Eventually the excitement of actually having been paid began to die down. But curiosity about the institute and the identity of the author only continued to grow. "It is certainly the most bizarre philosophical undertaking in anyone's memory," Zimmerman contends. "It's unheard of. It's insane. You ordinarily get paid two hundred dollars by Oxford to review a six-hundred-page book." A few inquisitive reviewers snooped around and made some preliminary Web searches and telephone calls. But they turned up few leads.

Early this April, one reviewer contacted *Lingua Franca*, hoping to interest some "literary sleuths." I was assigned to the story. At one point in my research, the available evidence pointed to suspects as diverse (and as seemingly improbable) as the esteemed Princeton philosopher Mark Johnston, the film actress Sigourney Weaver, and a suspiciously named professor of religious studies at the University of Virginia, Anne Monius. None of those individuals, it turns out, is in any way responsible for the work or financial backing of the A. M. Monius Institute. But I have discovered who is. So here, for the first time, I recount the mad hunt for—and the unmasking of—the mysterious A. M. Monius.

MY INVESTIGATION BEGAN with the little information that the A. M. Monius Institute provided about itself. Dialing the telephone number on the institute's letterhead put me in contact with the institute's voice mail, which I called for several weeks without a reply. In addition, the letterhead listed a bricks-and-mortar address in Pennsylvania. On a map, it appeared to be located at the end of a small road just off Interstate 95, near the New Jersey–Pennsylvania border.

In a reverse-address directory, the institute matched three other telephone numbers, all under the name Jitendrah Shah. When I called one of these numbers, I reached a computer-sales business. I asked for Netzin Steklis and was assured that I had the wrong number. I called back several times, asking repeatedly for the A. M. Monius Institute until I provoked an irritated outburst: "Their number is 321-5809!" I asked the man how he had come to know the number so suddenly. "Why don't you ask them?" he barked back. "You want to buy a computer, you talk to me." Then he hung up.

Perhaps a more fruitful lead, I thought, was the institute's name. Antiquity boasted two Neoplatonist philosophers by the name Ammonius. Ammonius, son of Hermeas, produced commentaries on Aristotle's works, including *On Aristotle's Categories*. Since "Coming to Understanding" discusses *Aristotle's Categories* at some length, the son of Hermeas seemed a likely candidate for the institute's eponym. As for the other Ammonius—Ammonius Saccas, thought by some to have been the founder of Neoplatonism—he was a figure clouded in mystery, having sworn Plotinus and his other students to secrecy about his teachings. That sounded a bit like A. M. Monius, too. But it was all moot: of the few scholars who know much about either Ammonius, none had heard of a well-to-do dilettante with a passion for their object of study.

It was time to turn to Netzin Steklis, a woman with a name that seemed designed by God for clean and economical database searches. ("Netzin" is short for "Nenetzin," which means doll in Aztec; "Steklis" is a German name.) Having spoken with Steklis by telephone, most of the reviewers told me that they assumed she was simply an office assistant who carried out the daily chores of running the institute.

The truth was far stranger: Netzin Gerald-Steklis, when not performing grunt work for this enigmatic institute of metaphysics, is the director of the Scientific Information Resource Center for the Dian Fossey Gorilla Fund International. She is thirty-four years old and married to Horst Dieter Steklis, a distinguished anthropologist at Rutgers University twenty-one years her senior. They live in Arizona with their two children, though they travel often to Rwanda, where they conduct field research as primatologists. The Steklises immediately became suspects, though doubtful ones. Given their intense commitment to gorillas—reported in both *People* magazine and *The New York Times*—neither fit the part of a philosopher manqué musing on the unworldly abstractions of speculative metaphysics. They did not respond to telephone messages I left on their home answering machine.

As far as I could tell, Steklis's only connection to exorbitant wealth was through her affiliation with the Dian Fossey Gorilla Fund. The fund's board of trustees included a number of wealthy mavericks (and thus suspects), not least among them the intrepid alien-slaying actress Sigourney Weaver and the multibillionaire software guru Larry Ellison, chairman and CEO of the Oracle Corporation.

The final important piece of information available about the institute was its deed of incorporation, which yielded two names: Joseph H. Hennessy and Marc Sanders. A Web search produced Hennessy's name on a list of members of the Philadelphia Bar Association. By telephone, the bar association identified Hennessy as a partner in the Philadelphia office of the law firm Morgan, Lewis & Bockius.

Hennessy made a strong suspect: In addition to earning undergraduate and law degrees, he had master's and doctorate degrees in political thought from Notre Dame. As a lawyer, Hennessy presumably had some disposable income. (His company profile mentioned neither a wife nor kids.) But would A. M. Monius be that careless, leaving a relatively uncommon and easily traceable name on a public document? I decided to put Hennessy on the top shelf until I had more to go on.

Sanders was another story. He didn't seem to work at Hennessy's firm. But that fact wasn't much help, for his was a fairly common name. Searches on the Web and on Lexis-Nexis produced a list of matches all across the country: a mathematical consultant to a program for gifted youth, a realtor, a legal assistant, a high-school basketball coach, an Immigration and Naturalization Service agent, a contributor to a lay journal of Catholic thought called *Eutopia*, and many others. Worse, directory assistance seemed to cough up an "M. Sanders" in just about every town with a plausible connection to the institute. Even if I could identify and confront a potential suspect with that name, would I be prepared to call his bluff if he were to play dumb?

Reaching the end of my factual rope, I turned to a close reading of "Coming to Understanding" for possible clues.

"COMING TO UNDERSTANDING" is a remarkable document. As Ermanno Bencivenga observes in his review, in its sheer temerity the work resembles such philosophical landmarks as René Descartes's *Meditations*, Immanuel Kant's *Critique of Pure Reason*, and Arthur Schopenhauer's *The World as Will and Idea*. (Bencivenga describes it as "a self-standing piece of reflection which asks to be judged on its own merit.") With few citations and nary a footnote, the manuscript seeks to provide "a large-scale account of reality, its origin, purpose, and how it hangs together." The questions it engages are grand: Does reality have a purpose? Why are things intelligible at all?

As a work of metaphysics, "Coming to Understanding" picks up where science leaves off. The purview of science is the world of "contingent beings"—things that might not have existed, or might have been otherwise, such as you, me, electrons, mountains, and the law of gravity. Science strives to explain the nature, properties, and causes of these contingent beings, which as a whole make up our physical reality.

But science does not and cannot explain why there are contingent beings in the first place. That is a question for metaphysics: Why do contingent beings exist? Or, put plainly, why is there something rather than nothing?

"Coming to Understanding" aspires to answer this "antique, impassable" question, but first it must rule out three of its "more familiar competitors": theism, Spinozism, and the Many Worlds hypothesis. All of these positions, A. M. Monius feels, share the same basic flaw: instead of actually explaining the existence of contingent being, they wind up claiming that contingent being is not really *contingent* but *necessary*. Contingent being, so construed, is "an illusion and so not there to explain at all."

Theism, for instance, originally argued that contingent being is the result of a necessarily existing God who necessarily creates "the world as it actually is." Voilà: the explanation of contingent being. But as Baruch Spinoza pointed out in his *Ethics*, theism thereby shows that contingent being is necessary (for it could not have been otherwise). This conclusion was problematic for theism, which intended to distinguish God from physical reality. Spinoza, on the other hand, was willing to bite the heretical bullet, and he accepted the conclusion that God and nature were equivalent and equally necessary.

"Coming to Understanding" deems such a result unacceptable and declares that a satisfactory metaphysics must figure out a way to explain contingent being without explaining it away by necessitating it. The key, the work argues, is to realize that theists, in attempting to overcome Spinoza's challenge, produced an argument of "the right form" but with "the wrong content."

After Spinoza, theists realized that contingent being could remain contingent (and thus distinct from God) if it had been created to serve some *purpose*. (The fact that a hammer exists for some purpose makes its existence intelligible without making it necessary.) Theism concluded that God's purpose in creating contingent beings was that contingent beings would come to love God, a love that God recognized as a fundamental good. Contingent beings thus exist not *necessarily* but "because they should, i.e., because it is good that they do."

A. M. Monius believes that theism made subtle but important mistakes with this argument, and "Coming to Understanding" presumes to salvage the theistic explanation by correcting for its flaws through a series of intricate arguments. "Coming to Understanding" proposes replacing the theists' God with reality as a whole, or Being. It also advocates replacing God's personal intention (that contingent beings come to love God) with an impersonal, fundamental good (that contingent beings come to understand the form of Being). Having made these substitutions, A. M. Monius reaches the following conclusion: "Contingent being exists for the sake of the coming to understanding of the form of Being Itself by contingent being." In other words, "the central theme of the whole drama of reality" is that beings like you and me and A. M. Monius come to understand the purpose and structure of reality.

And as it happens, the purpose and structure of reality are precisely what A. M. Monius has on offer. In sophisticated detail, the last two-thirds of "Coming to Understanding" are devoted to a discussion of categories similar to Aristotle's, such as the Universal, the Particular, the Spatiotemporal, and the Cognizable. A. M. Monius believes that these categories demarcate the fundamental types of Being and—in light of their interrelations—suggest the purpose of contingent being.

GIVEN THIS GLIMPSE into the mind of A. M. Monius, what might an investigator infer about the author? First, consider the ambition and bravado with which A. M. Monius attempts to revamp metaphysics in a mere sixty pages. This is no meek, closeted egghead but rather a poised and confident builder of worlds. "Whoever wrote this," Dancy says with some admiration, "speaks with an authority that you have to earn, normally."

The overarching conclusion of "Coming to Understanding" also betrays a touch of egotism, for the argument is stunningly self-important in its implications: the meaning of life is, in effect, to come to understand the message of "Coming to Understanding." And yet there are signs of self-perspective as well: "Perhaps in this task mistakes will be made," A. M. Monius muses before exposing the structure of Being, "but at least it is the right task."

Many reviewers point out in addition that "Coming to Understanding" bears the telltale marks of an amateur's effort. Though many of the philosophers were genuinely impressed with features of

A. M. Monius's argument, they are not under the illusion that it is a great work of philosophy—or even, most reviewers felt, one that meets professional standards.

"It's what you would expect from an intelligent amateur," says Sider, "someone who does not have any training in speculative metaphysics but who is very smart." The argument, he adds, includes "a common pattern of non sequiturs that you get beaten out of you as a graduate student."

Bencivenga complains in his review that there is feeble hand waving at critical junctures in the argument. For instance, the impersonal purpose, or fundamental good, that A. M. Monius believes makes reality intelligible is "just a name for a mystery," Bencivenga explains, "which itself calls for a solution." A major problem that struck Sider was the manuscript's failure to address "the typical, atheistic, materialist response to this sort of argument." Namely, if everything must have an explanation, then everything—including the coming to understanding of Being—must have an explanation. Something is going to have to remain unexplained. So, Sider asks, "why not just be content with the mundane, materialist description of the world rather than bringing in God or Coming to Understanding or whatever you like?"

DESPITE THEIR CRITICISMS, most of the academic reviewers were predisposed to appreciate this sort of metaphysical speculation. Many of them first learned of the A. M. Monius Institute from Zimmerman, whom they know from an annual conference he founded called "Metaphysical Mayhem" (originally "Mighty Midwestern Metaphysical Mayhem"). "Zimmerman and Sider"—a fellow Mayhemite—"are probably the two best people in the world under the age of forty working primarily in metaphysics," says Ted Warfield.

The Mayhemites differ from their many peers who descend from the antimetaphysical tradition of logical positivism. As Zimmerman explains, the Mayhemites admire philosophers like Princeton's David Lewis and Saul Kripke, Notre Dame's Alvin Plantinga, and the late

Roderick Chisholm of Brown University, all of whom helped to revive metaphysics by arguing that a range of traditional philosophical topics—ontology, existence, essence, natural kinds—are in fact central to contemporary philosophical concerns about reference, meaning, necessity, and possibility. Some paper titles from past Mayhems provide a flavor of their arcane interests and humor: "The Varieties of Vagueness (Fewer Than You Think)"; "Impenitent Cartesianism"; and "The Homogeneous Stuff Objection to the Doctrine of Temporal Parts."

Jan Cover, a former mountain climber who speaks in the distinctive accent of the Anabaptist community in which he was raised, describes the Mayhemites as "a bunch of up-and-coming, some people say, 'stars,' who are just hard-nosed, analytic-style, logic-chopping, think-real-hard-and-do-kick-ass-old-fashioned-metaphysics types." Cover's enthusiasm is infectious. In his review of "Coming to Understanding," he claimed that one "would be hard-pressed to locate a richer, deeper contemporary approach to the most fundamental questions of metaphysics." He even went to the trouble of appending a list of typographic corrections—including suggestions for better ways of formatting the indentation of paragraphs.

AS I BECAME INCREASINGLY CONSUMED by the A. M. Monius Institute, I began to think of A. M. Monius in very much the same way that A. M. Monius thought of Being—as something that existed for the purpose of my coming to understand it. With the stakes this high, I felt I needed to bring in some bigger guns. Armed with my impressions of the manuscript as well as my tentative suspect list, I placed a call to the renowned literary detective Donald Foster.

Foster, a professor of English at Vassar College, is perhaps best known for using meticulous textual analysis to expose the journalist Joe Klein as "Anonymous," author of the political roman à clef *Primary Colors*. I sent Foster a copy of "Coming to Understanding" and a set of writing samples from suspects on my list. Foster agreed to see what he could do for me.

Given the limited information that I had provided, Foster was not able to identify the author of "Coming to Understanding." But with some confidence, he felt he could rule out a few of my suspects: "Though one can admire Sigourney Weaver's force and form when blasting space aliens," he wrote in a memo, "she's not a writer to take on the logical positivists." As for Larry Ellison? "My oracle says, 'No way,' " he said. "Same for Horst Dieter Steklis."

Foster suggested I look for a white male who had attended Notre Dame, though again he was merely going on instinct—not offering his professional opinion. "Another possibility," he added, "is that A. M. Monius may be a bright and ambitious, but somewhat shy, Rwandan gorilla."

I CONFESS: we were having some fun at A. M. Monius's expense. And who could blame us? It's not every day that you find yourself scripted into a Thomas Pynchon novel.

Still, all of the philosophers I spoke with made a point of emphasizing how much they admire the spirit behind A. M. Monius's attempt to help revive metaphysics. They applaud his intellectual commitment, not just his financial one. Zimmerman notes that modern philosophers have rarely had patrons in the way that thinkers like Gottfried Leibniz once did. And though it's true that Roderick Chisholm was for a short time supported financially by Dr. Albert C. Barnes, wealthy inventor of the medicine Argyrol, in few such cases does the apparent benefactor also serve, as A. M. Monius does, as the chief philosophical instigator and problem poser.

"Would that there were more nonprofessionals who got jazzed about philosophy!" Zimmerman exclaims. With palpable excitement, he ponders the possibility that the institute might back "slightly broader projects, like a research center"—or better yet, he adds in jest, "support the Mayhem!"

Certainly, there was something right about this conception of A. M. Monius. This was not your stereotypical amateur metaphysician, the kind who stumbles into rarefied speculation about the structure and purpose of the universe as part of a more general descent into paranoia and madness. The institute's philosophy was far too disciplined for that.

And yet there was some evidence—such as the belief that the institute had made a genuine methodological breakthrough in metaphysics —that the author of "Coming to Understanding" might not have a completely realistic outlook. After all the reviews were in, the institute's Web site began promoting a new round of lucrative research grants for the purpose of "directly improving central aspects" of "Coming to Understanding." The advertisement for these grants makes the rather strong boast that the "closest analogy to the upcoming program of the Institute is the widespread collaboration on specific problem-solving found in the bio-medical sciences, along with its pinnacle achievement of the mapping of the human genome."

As one reviewer groaned: "Oh, no—not more money to think about Monius."

THE DISCOVERY OF THE IDENTITY of A. M. Monius came about much faster—and with much more serendipity—than I had expected. When I spoke with Foster about the text of "Coming to Understanding," he told me of one intriguing clue that he had ferreted out. The term "kindmates," which A. M. Monius uses on page 7 of the manuscript, does not appear in the *Oxford English Dictionary*. As far as Foster could tell, the term appeared only in essays from the late 1980s by Mark Johnston, chair of the Princeton philosophy department.

Johnston made a poor candidate for the author; he is much too professional a philosopher. But perhaps he had been hired by A. M. Monius as a tutor? Or perhaps A. M. Monius had attended some of Johnston's seminars at Princeton? When I called Johnston, he admitted that he had been using "kindmates" for approximately fifteen years, but he hadn't thought "that it was original with me." He couldn't think of anyone he had taught who might fit the bill. But my suspect profile now included a likely Princeton connection.

Around this time, I finally made contact with Steklis at her home in Arizona. She was extremely courteous and apologized for having to "play this game with you." As expected, she could not divulge much information, though she did deny that her husband or the Dian Fossey Gorilla Fund was in any way involved, save for the connection to her. She also informed me that the funding behind the institute was "not drug money."

Having spoken with Steklis, I felt I could call Hennessy without setting off any alarm. Hennessy, too, could not have been kinder or less forthcoming. "You're going to have to tell me why you're talking to me," he explained politely, "because I'm a lawyer and I need to be careful whom I'm talking to because of client confidences." He was willing, however, to deny that he was A. M. Monius.

So I returned to Marc Sanders. Following up on Foster's "kind-mates" tip, I checked directory assistance in Princeton, which did in fact produce a listing for a Marc Sanders. Furthermore, a database search on "Marc Sanders" and "Princeton" turned up a red-hot clue. In the "Institutions" listings of the June 1978 issue of *Current Anthropology*, there was a peculiar announcement: "The Institutum Philosophiae Naturalis, located in Princeton, N.J., has been formed to encourage theoretical and epistemological inquiries in the physical, natural, and social sciences which, because of their unusual scope or method, cannot be adequately supported within the confines of a single scientific discipline or traditional funding source." The IPN owed "its conception and backing to its Executive Director, Marc Sanders, a Princeton-area businessman."

To my ear, the listing read like the promotional materials for the A. M. Monius Institute: both institutes existed to "encourage" a brand of far-ranging inquiry beyond the traditional boundaries of science; both bore ancient-sounding names; and IPN, like the A. M. Monius Institute, seemed to be able to draw academic heavyweights to its cause. Indeed, IPN's advisory board included some of the most famous names in postwar American intellectual life: the physicist Freeman Dyson, the paleontologist Stephen Jay Gould, the historian of science Thomas Kuhn, and the psychologist B. F. Skinner.

Sanders thus became my primary suspect. Even if he was not the actual author of "Coming to Understanding," I figured, he had to be financially involved. With no success in tracking down a sample of his writing, I decided to call his home in Princeton. When he picked up the telephone, I explained that I was writing an article about the A. M. Monius Institute, that I had already spoken with Steklis and Hennessy, and that I wanted to speak with him as well. He asked if I could call back the next day, and I agreed. An hour later I received an e-mail from him. Assuming that I had already figured him out, he confessed to being A. M. Monius.

AND THEN, just like that, it was over. But not before Sanders made an appeal to leave his anonymity intact. "Now that you have discovered that I am Ammonius," he wrote, "I know that you will think it your job to inform the world." He had chosen to remain anonymous, he explained, so that his "failure to become a professional philosopher" would not come to light and thus tempt professional philosophers to "simply dismiss the idea of reviewing my work out of hand because the work was known to be by a devoted amateur."

It was a sad note. Having read it, I found that the unveiling of the man behind the great tapestry of the A. M. Monius Institute reminded me of the scene at the end of *The Wizard of Oz* when the dog, Toto, pulls back the curtain to reveal that the Wizard is actually a small and timid-seeming character, with nothing like the presence of his imposing facade.

But wait one melodramatic second: Wasn't there also something odd about Sanders's plea? After all, the philosophers I had spoken with had assumed from the very beginning that "Coming to Understanding" was the work of an amateur. Not only did the draft itself suggest an amateur's hand, but the whole elaborate production of the institute was a bright, shining neon advertisement for the fact that this was not a professional philosopher working through professional channels.

No, quite obviously it was the *money* that had convinced the reviewers to write their reviews. If anything, the institute's anonymity had only made reviewers reluctant to participate. So I wrote Sanders back, suggesting that if his primary goal was, as he stated, to attract reviewers, then he should rest assured that my article would only broaden the range of philosophers who might be interested in contributing to his project.

His reply was revealing, for his message had changed. He explained that he no longer expected that he could genuinely interest the sort of professional academics who read *Lingua Franca*. Despite his deep admiration for the work of trained philosophers, he had come to form a poor impression of the insular, cliquish culture of their discipline. "I have found professional philosophers to be a proud, demanding bunch who protect their terrain with great contempt for outsiders," he wrote. "My past attempts to publish my work did not get beyond the first contact stage because I had 'no standing in the academy.' "

Even the exciting process of having "Coming to Understanding" reviewed on his institute's Web site had left him somewhat dejected. "Obviously, none of the philosophers who reviewed the work would have done so without the substantial honorarium each was paid," he conceded. But that, on its own, did not concern him: "I look on the sums involved as probably inadequate remuneration for serious philosophical engagement, which I have come to value more than anything else." What actually disappointed him was that many of the philosophers failed to take his work seriously *even after* they had been offered a charitable sum of money to do so. He noted that there were some "intellectually honest people"—he cited Jan Cover as an example— who "really engaged with the work" rather than merely "going through the motions" and thus "made the whole enterprise worthwhile." But by and large, his worst suspicions about the profession had been confirmed. Having said that, he refused to provide me with any further details.

BY CUTTING OFF CONTACT, Sanders had left me with some loose ends. What was his connection to Steklis? How had he made his fortune? How much philosophical education had he had? What kind of organization had the Institutum Philosophiae Naturalis been? I could have pushed harder on these questions, but my deadline was nearing, and my leads had run dry. (Steklis and Hennessy had been forbidden to speak with me further, and the two surviving Institutum board members that I knew of, Dyson and Gould, never responded to my queries.)

Or perhaps it was something else that kept the investigation from pressing on. It was perfectly true that there were enough tantalizing contradictions in what I knew about Marc Sanders to sustain further inquiry. Here was a man who wanted to participate in scholarly debate as just another philosopher but who had managed to participate in so eccentric a fashion that he had made himself unlike any other philosopher before him. He was an independent scholar who resented his professional counterparts enough that he showered them with money. And he sought to join in the post-positivist world of contemporary metaphysics while retaining the mystical ornaments and trappings of the majestic visionaries of past philosophy whom the positivists had so effectively mocked. All this was true of Sanders, and genuinely intriguing.

But the mystery of the A. M. Monius Institute had come to seem all too human in the aftermath of having solved it. One began to long for some sense of the enigma again, instead of the dreary realities of worldly motivation, embarrassment, and pride. As Socrates so eloquently reflects in Plato's *Phaedrus*—in a passage close to A. M. Monius's heart: The seeker of pure knowledge is "delighted at last to be seeing what is Real and watching what is True, and so feeds on all this and feels wonderful. . . . And when one has seen all things as they really are and feasted upon them, one sinks back inside heaven and goes home."

—July 2001

PART VI

Arts and Letters

BLACK LIKE ME

Conceptual Artist Adrian Piper Gets Under Your Skin

ADAM SHATZ

LAST SUMMER Adrian Piper, an artist known for her confrontational installations about race, came out to her friends at Kripalu, a yoga center in the Berkshires. Only she didn't tell them she was gay; she told them she was black. A fair-skinned woman with no discernably African features, Piper is often the only person in the room who knows this.

I happened to arrive at Kripalu the following morning to interview Piper. We were chatting in a lobby decorated with flyers for workshops on "celebrating anger" and "goddess chants" when a man came over to greet her. "What a surprise that was last night," he said warmly. "We had no idea you came from *that* culture." More than matching his effusiveness, she replied, "Yeah, well, I always tell people that this is the only place in the world where white people don't make racist comments when they think they're among themselves."

Piper, a woman of fifty with big eyes and a dancer's figure, turned to me and said, "I've been coming here since 1992. No one knew I was black because I never said it. It's not that people don't discuss race— they talk about their interracial relationships, they talk about crime and poverty and slavery. But they don't make racist remarks. So I've never had to come out. It's a real safe place for me."

It might seem odd that an artist so closely associated with racial politics would choose not to disclose her race to some of her longtime companions. But such a paradox is typical of the life and work of Adrian Piper. As an artist, she is an in-your-face political activist; in person, she is extremely private, even fearful. "My primary motivation as an artist," she told me, "is to create a context in which I feel comfortable, a context in which people like me feel safe." Viewers, on the other hand, tend to register only Piper's aggression, not her fear. Her art is designed to get under your skin—all the more so if your skin is white. Piper addresses art-world sophisticates as if their high-mindedness were an elaborate self-deception. "All of us, socialized into a racist society, are racists," she says matter-of-factly.

It is an assumption that may be especially painful, if not infuriating, to the kind of whites who might turn out for an exhibit by a black artist. But making such viewers squirm is one of Piper's aims. In *Aspects of the Liberal Dilemma* (1978), you walk into a square room and face a photograph of a group of black people staring into the eye of the camera. You are all alone. Suddenly the silence is filled by Piper's voice-over:

> It doesn't matter who these people are. They're parts of a piece of art. . . . You want to have an aesthetic experience: to be fulfilled, elevated, edified. . . . In looking at this picture, you carefully monitor any subliminal or undisciplined reactions you have to this image of assertive, aggressive, angry-looking blacks; they might be a part of the piece. How do the images in this picture relate to each other? How is the two-dimensionality of the picture plane treated? . . . Are these the right questions to ask about this work? . . . Are you being preached to? Again? . . . Why do you feel embarrassed if someone else in the room sees you staring at yourself like this? . . . What exactly is the aesthetic *content* of this work? What is it trying to tell you?

It's a blistering parody of how a believer in art for art's sake might respond. But if this monologue echoes your thoughts, you're bound to feel burned. Aestheticism, Piper seems to be telling you, is simply the last refuge of the liberal racist.

One of the first artists to inject identity politics into the arid geometries of 1960s conceptualism, Piper has tirelessly explored what it feels like to be on the receiving end of the racial gaze—what it feels like to be the target of racial stereotypes. Her work—which includes videos, performances, photographs, and drawings, in addition to installation pieces—has been shown at the Museum of Modern Art, the Whitney, the Kunsthalle Berne, and the Paris Biennale; and there are plans for a traveling retrospective next year. "I think art historians are finally acknowledging just how generative she has been," says the art critic Maurice Berger. "I don't see how you could *not* be influenced by Adrian's work if you're dealing with issues of race and representation." Piper's collected writings on art and aesthetic theory, *Out of Order, Out of Sight*, were published in two hefty volumes in 1996, and her autobiographical essay, "Passing for White, Passing for Black," published in *Transition* in 1992, is on its way to becoming a classic in the literature on racial passing, cited by literary critics, philosophers, and legal scholars. For better or worse, her life as a black woman who involuntarily passes for white has only added to the public's fascination with her.

As if that weren't enough, Piper is also a Harvard-trained philosopher with a tenured chair at Wellesley. This fall, as a fellow at the Getty Center in Los Angeles, she will be working on a massive study of Kant, a thinker she reveres despite his frankly racist views. ("Humanity is at its greatest perfection in the race of whites," he blithely proclaimed.) She works in a distinctly unglamorous, distinctly cautious branch of philosophy that is generally resistant to addressing the bold social questions raised by her artwork. In Piper's current project on Kant, tentatively titled *Rationality and the Structure of the Self,* she paints an adoring portrait of the German philosopher as a theorist of the supremacy of reason over instinct and desire. No one will mistake this sober work of philosophical argument for social criticism. Most of Piper's academic peers don't know that she is an artist, much less a maker of racially charged work, and she prefers to keep it that way.

PIPER'S ART IS DIFFICULT TO INTERPRET. Is her point that, because race is a cultural myth, we would do well to discard it? Or is it that, myth or not, race now corresponds to real and insurmountable differences? Is Piper a visionary of an America beyond the color line or a pessimist who thinks that beliefs about race have wrought irreparable damage? In fact, she is both, which makes her a telling symptom of America's racial confusion since the end of legal segregation. Ours is the era of *The Cosby Show* and the Simpson trial, of a rising black middle class and a rising black prison class, of elegant attacks on the idea of race in the academy and racially motivated attacks in the street. Angry and hopeful by turns, Piper's art lends itself to the agendas of both racial militancy and color-blind idealism, often at one and the same time.

That doubleness of perspective is also evident in Piper's critical writings about her work. Like the legal scholar Derrick Bell and the sociologist Andrew Hacker, Piper doubts that whites will ever share power with black people on an equal basis. Bleaker still, she views racism as a "visual" and "cognitive" pathology that is "deeply buried in the structure of the self." In a 1992 article in *The Yale Journal of Criticism*, Piper portrayed racism as a defensive, almost helpless "alarm reaction" by the self to individuals who "do not conform to one's preconceptions about how persons ought to look or behave." And according to Piper, black people are more jarringly "anomalous" to whites than Asian, Latino, or Arab immigrants. As she puts it, "The fact that African Americans did not choose to come here, did not feel they had anything to gain by coming here, makes their attitude, their carriage, their background, their history, their behavior, their assumptions completely different from those of any of these groups." In this extensive inventory of black otherness, Piper comes close to the grim arguments of Nathan Glazer's *We Are All Multiculturalists Now*, in which black Americans appear as the lone outsiders to the American Dream, irremediably beyond hope of genuine inclusion.

At the same time, she believes that we are innately equipped with the hardware to analyze and combat racism, namely reason. According to Piper, racism is not only a pathology; it is also a "cognitive error" that cries out for the kind of cognitive therapy that, she insists, art can best supply. When we look at works of art, she observes, we engage in an especially attentive kind of "cognitive discrimination," the making and sifting of fine-grained distinctions about visual data. When the normal process of cognitive discrimination breaks down, we see a person as a member of a race rather than as an individual. By administering a kind of racial shock treatment in her art, Piper tries to force viewers to reflect on what happens—and who gets hurt—when they fail to be as discriminating about people as they are about art. It is a passionate, direct appeal to her viewers' ability to see the error of their ways. (Pleasure seems almost beside the point in Piper's aesthetic program, which is mainly concerned with patterns of cognition.)

According to Piper, viewers ideally experience works like *Aspects of the Liberal Dilemma* in three stages: trauma, reflection, and rational illumination. First, the audience feels discomfort, irritation, resentment. (Protesting to Piper that you're not a racist is about as effective as telling a Freudian analyst you're not repressed; it's simply a symptom of denial.) Then they step back, examine their reactions, and ask why they feel the work—an installation that speaks to anyone who enters and therefore to no one in particular—is addressing *them*. Finally, they come to grips with their internalized racism, see it for the ludicrous, hurtful thing that it is, and perhaps leave the room with a commitment to change.

But Piper's art does not always work as she expects. In 1980, she mounted *Four Intruders Plus Alarm Systems*, an installation featuring photos of black men accompanied by recordings of voices engaged in rambling anti-black monologues. She imagined that she was giving her viewers a taste of their prejudices and a chance to examine them rationally. To her horror, though, several viewers thanked her for "expressing their views so eloquently." It's not clear, either, that Piper's art alters the behavior of sophisticated viewers who understand her satirical aims. There is a long and complicated history in the arts of white liberal audiences who, confronted by black rage, have flogged themselves in penitence, owned up to their racism . . . and done nothing. It could be that, despite her intentions, Piper ends up playing a kind of dominatrix to her white liberal admirers, providing them with the ultimate masochistic frisson.

THE ONLY CHILD of a real estate lawyer from West Virginia and a Jamaican woman who worked as a secretary at City College of New York, Adrian Margaret Smith Piper was born in 1948 in the Sugar Hill section of Harlem, a genteel enclave of black professionals. Among Daniel and Olive Piper's friends were some of Harlem's most distinguished citizens, including the Delaney sisters, Adam Clayton Powell, and Romare Beardon. Although they had little money—Daniel Piper's Harlem clients often paid him in cakes and mended shirts— her parents were determined to provide Adrian with an elite education. At the age of six, Adrian earned a scholarship to New Lincoln, a progressive private school. With piano lessons at home, art classes at MoMA, and summers spent upstate at a liberal, integrated camp, Piper came to acquire, she says, a sense of entitlement more common to privileged white males than to young black girls. Her parents never told her she should expect anything less from the world because she was "colored," a mild-mannered term then favored by some members of the black bourgeoisie. In fact, Piper told me, "My parents didn't even talk about race. They wanted to shelter me. They really believed that if I got all this education I would remain unscathed."

Still, from early on, Piper was acutely aware of being different. "Everyone in my neighborhood thought that my family and I were white," she recalls. "And particularly in the early 1960s, when Harlem was becoming more working-class, we were often treated very badly." On the way to school, neighborhood kids jeered at her, calling her "Paleface"—an experience that inspired one of her *Political Self-Portraits*, a 1978 work in which she typed an anguished recollection over a passport photograph. "It wasn't possible to say, 'Hey, stop harassing me, in fact I'm a sister.' It was very painful, and I had to deal with feelings of irrational anger at people who were acting out on me for reasons that had nothing to do with who I was."

Though many of the kids at New Lincoln were leftists and Piper helped run the school's chapter of the Student Nonviolent Coordinating Committee, she found herself treated as a racial curiosity. More than once, friends invited her to their homes and made their parents try to guess her racial identity. And then there was the fifth-grade instructor who asked Daniel and Olive Piper whether their daughter understood that she was colored.

She did, of course. But what exactly did it mean to be colored? Did it mean you weren't black or white but a little bit of both? Or neither? There were no simple answers in Piper's family, which was as haunted by color consciousness as the characters in a Harlem Renaissance novel. Daniel Piper, an extremely light-skinned man who had passed for white during World War II because he wanted to see combat, could easily have crossed the color line permanently but opted not to out of loyalty to his family. Many of his relatives had chosen to pass, severing their ties to the black Pipers so as not to provoke any suspicion among whites. When Adrian was an adolescent, her paternal aunt—who had made headlines for being the first black woman to attend Vassar College and Yale Medical School—married a white man, and the black Pipers never heard from her again.

Early on, Piper could sense that race was a painfully contradictory concept: at once cultural fiction and inescapable reality, alternately flexible and rigid, rarely predictable, and almost always traumatic. In her immediate family, passing constituted an unpardonable betrayal. Hence the bitterness of works like the video *Cornered* (1988), in which Piper lashes out at viewers who "feel that my letting people know I'm not white is making an unnecessary fuss [and] that the right and proper course of action for me to take is to pass for white." These early experiences probably explain why, despite her professed view that race is a fictional construct, she has clung to it as though it were the surpassing truth of her identity—and perhaps of yours as well. As she taunted viewers of *Cornered*: "If someone can look and sound like me and still be black, then no one is safely, unquestionably white. No one. The chances are quite good that you are in fact black."

When a teenager, though, Piper longed to be released from the burdens of identity. She found liberation in the streets, in LSD experimentation, and in art. The 1960s had, conveniently, arrived.

AT THE AGE OF FOURTEEN, Piper joined a Puerto Rican gang led by a gay performance artist who held séances and conjured spirits along upper Broadway. Three years later, she was living on her own, supporting herself through fashion modeling. She dropped acid, made psychedelic drawings, and took up yoga. In the evening, she made extra cash dancing in a leotard in elevated cages at nightclubs. Fearing for her sanity, Piper's parents had her briefly committed to Hillside, a mental institution in Queens.

Then, one day in 1967, Piper, now a student at New York City's School of Visual Arts, walked into the Dwan Gallery and left transformed. The exhibit she saw was Sol LeWitt's *46 Variations on Three Different Kinds of Cube*, a room of forty-six stacked cubes, some open, some closed, arranged in rows four feet high and lit so as to render visible each cube's contours. Piper's sense of wonder is still fresh when she evokes LeWitt's austere yet oddly sensual installation: "The cubes had such presence, such dignity; there was something so simple about them. And yet at the same time, there were such mysteries, because it was clear they were generated by a system, but you couldn't tell what the system was. It reminded me of hearing a Bach fugue without having studied the sheet music in advance. It was a very mind-expanding work. It was a concrete and physical demonstration of the beauty of mathematics and the rule of logic."

When the art critic Rosalind Krauss panned LeWitt's show in *Artforum*, Piper was so enraged she wrote the artist to console him; LeWitt, in turn, sent her two studies for the piece (which now hang in Piper's living room in Wellesley) and suggested they meet for a beer. Soon she was living in a loft in Little Italy above LeWitt, a quiet, avuncular man twice her age who became her mentor. While continuing to pay her rent by modeling, Piper published conceptual pieces in Vito Acconci's *o to 9* magazine and participated in group shows at the Paula Cooper and the Dwan Galleries. Her best work from this period—for example, *Utah-Manhattan Transfer* (1968), in which a New York City subway map lies on the Mormon heartland, creating a pixilated palimpsest—has the purity of form, the economy of means, and the flair for high pranks that distinguish her mature work.

Nowhere in these early abstract pieces is there any hint of concern with race or identity. The conceptualism of artists like Sol LeWitt was ardently formalist, almost completely devoid of reference to a world beyond the play of rectilinear shapes and phenomenological states. (To this day, Piper maintains that she is "a formalist, very, very deeply.") Though works like *46 Variations* may have contained a subtle parody of the madly rationalized world that the masters of the war in Vietnam had built, as social protest they were fairly inert. In its cultural profile, moreover, conceptualism was as "white" as its fiery contemporary the Black Arts Movement, led by Amiri Baraka and Larry Neal, was "black." "Most of us had no idea Adrian was black," says Lucy Lippard, a feminist art critic who has known Piper for years. "She didn't hide it. But I don't think I realized it until I met her parents at the loft on Hester Street."

When, I asked Piper, did she begin to identify herself publicly as a black woman? "I always did," she insisted. "Some things are so basic that it just doesn't occur to you to mention them." Even so, it is striking that in her metacriticism—the reflections on her own practice collected in *Out of Order, Out of Sight*—Piper moves from a virtual silence about her racial identity to loquacious self-assertion in the mid-1970s.

"What most affected me was the struggle for open admissions at City College," says Piper, who enrolled there as a philosophy major in 1970. "Black students were shutting down the campus. I was physically in this situation where I was trying to take notes in my philosophy classes and people would stride in and say, 'This class is over. We're having a rally. Now!' " Piper didn't join them on the barricades, however. "I was your basic apolitical philosophy nerd," she says. Though she exaggerates her political innocence—she was active in both feminist and antiwar groups—it's clear that the events at

City College shook her profoundly. The spectacle of black defiance, of protesters disrupting the seminar, represented something new to Piper, something strikingly "anomalous," to borrow her preferred term.

Amid the tumult at City College, Piper began to wonder whether the kind of quiet, cerebral art she had been making was not a useless passion. "I was being confronted by urgent political struggles, and I was doing this very rarefied and elitist work. I was feeling impatient to get past that scrim of obfuscation between me and the external world," she explains. Like many women artists in the 1970s, she solved her dilemma by doing away with the medium of the art object and making herself the medium instead. She would now confront her viewers directly.

In one of her unannounced performances from the series *Catalysis* (1970–1972), Piper roamed the streets wearing clothes she had soaked in vinegar, eggs, milk, and cod-liver oil, a stunningly attractive (and stunningly malodorous) vagabond. "No one could have smelled anything like this before! It had to be anomalous," she explains. On the subway, men in suits fondled her: "They thought I was engaged in some kind of sexual provocation—you know, the whipped-cream-and-honey school of sexual arousal! So that was very disconcerting. It was really amazing to me that I could be constructed that way." In these audacious experiments, Piper was honing her talent for making herself, as she would later put it, a "cognitive anomaly," an object of fascination, bewilderment, and fear.

Piper used the same strategy in her *Mythic Being* series and addressed race explicitly for the first time. Ironically, she did so by disguising herself as a man. From 1972 to 1975, the Mythic Being, with "his" Afro, penciled mustache, and dark shades, was Piper's alter ego. Upon entering Harvard as a graduate student in philosophy in the fall of 1974, she began introducing unsuspecting Cambridge pedestrians to the Mythic Being. In one performance, she sat on a street corner leering lasciviously at white women; in another, she staged a fake mugging. "People reacted to me as though I were a black male, and that's incredibly unpleasant," she says. "White women would clutch their purses and go into neighboring cars in the subway—the usual bag of tricks. But nobody ever blew my cover."

It's remarkable that no one did. Piper is frail, almost waiflike. In the surviving documents of the *Mythic Being* series, she suggests a female Charlie Chaplin clumsily trying to emulate black street macho. But the absurdity of Piper's charade was lost on her viewers, a failure of perception that she considers symptomatic of racism. In her view, the whites who recoiled from the Mythic Being were not practicing cognitive discrimination. Their reactions were dramatic proof of what Piper calls the "Great Gap"—"the gap between what's actually there and the mediating effects of associations and stereotypes." *The Mythic Being* established the Great Gap as Piper's signature subject and obsession. Moreover, it helped her to "free myself from my past" and to define herself, without reluctance or fear, as a black woman artist. After this, she no longer needed a masquerade.

Piper maintains that she was marginalized by the art world for embracing her black identity: "People just stopped showing up in my life. It was almost a stampede. I became persona non grata." Of course, it would not be surprising if some of Piper's white art friends felt alienated, befuddled, or enraged by her new aesthetic; nor would it come as a shock if some revealed themselves as racists. But the truth is that there was a mutual parting of ways. Piper was living in Cambridge and making fewer trips to New York. She was becoming enraptured by Kant at the very moment that French critics of the Enlightenment like Derrida, Foucault, and Baudrillard were seducing her artist peers.

Not that Piper much cared. At Harvard, she found supportive mentors in the philosophers Raymond Firth and John Rawls (who had published his *Theory of Justice* to great acclaim three years earlier), and she was determined to pursue an academic career. At the same time, she was the lone black woman in the department, and there were stressful encounters of the racist kind. Not long after she arrived, an esteemed philosopher came up to her and quipped, "Miss Piper, you're about as black as I am." (In her *Transition* essay, Piper says this incident "destroyed my illusion that these privileged surroundings were benevolent and safe.")

Piper says she encountered more racism at the University of Michigan, where she got a job in 1979. The department had hired her thinking she was white, and when they found out that she was not, Piper remembers, "their attitude just changed 180 degrees. They got real evil. These guys were so unsympathetic that if I wrote an article and mentioned Descartes's cogito, they'd start pounding me about where he says that in the text and why haven't you provided a footnote. But they made me work at a level of analysis and precision that I would never have had to otherwise. It was a great victory to be denied tenure. Everybody there knew what was going on." (A source at the University of Michigan declined to comment on her case.)

Fortunately, Piper was able to secure a tenured position at Georgetown, where she taught for several years, but the Michigan experience left her dejected. To make matters worse, Piper's father died, and her four-year-old marriage to a neuropsychologist she had met in Ann Arbor collapsed. And she was experiencing recurring bouts of chronic fatigue syndrome.

Astonishingly, at the same time, Piper was enjoying the most productive phase of her career as an artist. Far from New York City, she was making acerbic works of art that combined intellectual rigor, racial straight talk, and conceptual elegance. And though her purpose was always to confront and enlighten viewers about race and perception, she approached her audience from a multiplicity of angles and through an array of media.

In installations like *Aspects of the Liberal Dilemma* and *Four Intruders Plus Alarm Systems*, Piper made some of her sharpest, toughest statements about the stereotyping of black men. The latter work unfolded in a classical conceptual chamber, a black cylindrical room excluding all external light. Inside were four boxes containing enlarged silk-screen photographs of black men (the "four intruders") staring directly at the viewer, their eyes lit from behind. "The effect," as she wrote in her notes, was deliberately "ominous and claustrophobic." In case you felt this wasn't art, in case you felt assaulted by it, in case some of your best friends were black, in case you thought black anger was cool, in case you didn't feel threatened by black men but still

didn't want your daughter to marry one, in case you felt unfairly accused of racism—in case you felt any of these things, Piper provided
four headphone sets (the "alarm systems"), each playing a first-person
monologue that might have just read your mind. If you stayed inside
this racial comedy of horrors long enough to examine the "intruders,"
you would have observed that their expressions were not threatening.
But Piper didn't spell this out, intent as she was on illustrating the
Great Gap. And so a number of white viewers and critics looked at
these four black men, saw that they weren't smiling, and perceived
them as "angry."

The viewers may have been guilty of poor cognitive discrimination, but they were picking up on something. There was an almost
corrosive rage in the works from this period—particularly in the extraordinary series of pieces, beginning with *Political Self-Portraits* and
culminating in *Cornered*, in which Piper explored the difficulties of
being a black person whom others mistake for white. You might think
a white appearance protected her from the worst of white racism, but
Piper claims the opposite was true. "Because someone who is visibly
black sounds the alarm to white people to be on their best behavior,
they never find out what it's like when white people do not have that
warning signal, do not have the cue of a black skin to tell them there
are certain things they had better not say," Piper told me. "They assume that white people behave in their absence the way white people
behave in their presence, and that's just not true!"

In 1986, Piper began passing out a "calling card" at dinner and
cocktail parties to whites who, imagining themselves in all-white company, had made remarks that Piper considered racist. The card read:

Dear Friend,

I am black.

I am sure you did not realize this when you made/laughed at/agreed
with that racist remark. In the past, I have attempted to alert white
people to my racial identity in advance. Unfortunately, this invariably causes them to react to me as pushy, manipulative, or socially
inappropriate. Therefore, my policy is to assume that white people

do not make these remarks, even when they believe there are no black people present, and to distribute this card when they do.

I regret any discomfort my presence is causing you, just as I am sure you regret the discomfort your racism is causing me.

Sincerely yours,
Adrian Margaret Smith Piper

Zap! The card uniformly stunned its recipients into silence. "No one who got this card ever initiated dialogue with me," she says. She seems genuinely surprised. Here, once again, Piper believed that shock tactics could force her interlocutors into rational reflection on their own racism.

IN THE LATE 1980S, the New York art world rediscovered Adrian Piper. Amid the sordid dramas of contemporary racial politics, from the killings in Bensonhurst to the Willie Horton ad campaign, Piper's installations about black men and "vanilla nightmares" looked eerily prescient. Multimedia work about identity was flooding galleries and museums, and much of it was indebted to Piper. Her early experiments with masquerade could be seen in Cindy Sherman's coy self-portraiture, while her bracing use of language seemed to prefigure the guerrilla montages of Barbara Kruger. And Piper was especially pleased by the rise of a group of gifted young black artists, notably the painter Glenn Ligon and the photographers Lorna Simpson and Carrie Mae Weems, who explored issues of identity in a more poetic, searching vein.

In 1987, New York City's Alternative Museum held a twenty-year retrospective of Piper's work. The next year, the John Weber Gallery began to represent her and in the fall of 1990 mounted an exhibit of her recent work. Reviewing the show in *The New York Times*, Michael Brenson proclaimed, "If the fall season in New York can be said to belong to one artist, that artist is Adrian Piper." The following year, Piper's installation *What It's Like, What It Is*, a cousin of *Four Intrud-*

ers, was included in MoMA's *Dislocationary Art* show alongside works by Bruce Nauman, Chris Burden, and Louise Bourgeois.

Not all the attention was favorable, however. There were, for example, accusations of racial hectoring from some quarters of the art world. In *Women Artists News*, Barbara Barr railed against Piper's work as "about as racist as anything you can expect to hear these days. It's just the other side of the coin—a grandiosity (and fatalism) about being 'black.' " But the most hostile attack came from a prominent art critic with philosophical training who claimed to respect Piper as an artist and thinker. In a 1987 essay titled "Adrian Piper: Self-Healing Through Meta-Art" published in *Art Criticism*, Donald Kuspit attempted to psychoanalyze not only the work but its maker. While praising Piper's "extraordinary power of articulation," Kuspit portrayed her as a controlling narcissist, "an actress who wants, almost hysterically, every condition for her performance to be just right, including its interpretive aftermath." In Piper's work, wrote Kuspit, "ambiguity and anxiety are resolved through aggression but the aggression is a vicious circle that leads back to them. Piper cannot escape the labyrinth of her spoiled self."

It was a brutal case history, and its subject was furious. In an open letter to Kuspit published in the zine *Real Life Magazine*, Piper dissected his rhetoric, corrected his spelling errors, and offered a damning caricature of Kuspit as a captive of his own *ressentiment*. In the drawing she made to accompany her reply, Piper declared war without mercy on the critic/aggressor. She depicted Kuspit as a beetle, crying in terror as he is sprayed by a can of insecticide labeled "Meta-Art."

It was a powerful, point-by-point rebuttal, but Piper's shock at being psychoanalyzed may reveal a streak of naïveté. For years, she had collapsed the boundary between her work and her identity; it was only a matter of time before a critic took the liberty of wandering speculatively from one to the other.

RECENTLY PIPER HAS TAKEN a hiatus from the art world, devoting herself to philosophy. She has not made a new work since 1995. She spends much of her free time in the house on Cape Cod that she inherited from her parents and plans to move there permanently after her Getty residency. She lives alone. She tries to fast once a week. Though intellectually gregarious, she is reserved, even fretful, when discussing her personal life. On a good day, she wakes up at 4:30, practices yoga from 5:30 to 8:00, meditates, works for a couple of hours on her manuscript on Kant, has brunch, works some more, and crashes into bed by 9:30 p.m. It is a schedule that leaves little time for a social life. "Adrian is a bit wary of interacting with the world," says one friend. "It is a privilege just to have a phone number or a fax number of her whereabouts. There are always shields or intermediaries." In her own life, Piper's solution to racism has been to insulate herself from unpleasant experiences. It's an understandable choice not to suffer, but it's also, ironically, just the kind of escape she forbids viewers of her art.

Sitting in her Cape Cod backyard in a pair of slacks and a Kant T-shirt, Piper gives the impression of someone who has renounced the outside world for cerebral pursuits. Her study of Kant is as remote as possible from the vanilla nightmares and alarm systems that disrupt her art. "In my heart of hearts, I'm not a very political person," she says. "If I were not forced to fight in order to survive, I'd spend all my time reading, listening to music, and doing yoga." One of the glories of philosophical work, she told me, is that "you leave behind your immediate environment or memories of past environments."

In her manuscript, one thousand pages thick and growing, Piper argues against the Humean claim that we are driven by desire and instinct and that we only use our reason in order to satisfy these unruly impulses. In Piper's view, Kant was right to stress the power of reason not only to trump desire but to define rational ends. It's a surprising argument coming from an artist who has relentlessly paid tribute to the power of irrational forces over the human mind. It's also something of a leap of faith. Kant, she explained to me, must be right, because if he were not, "racism would not be amenable to rational reflection or analysis." I suggested that there might be insuperable conflict between the rational optimism of her philosophy and the racial pessimism of her artwork. She replied, "Not really. I feel our capacity, the human capacity, is infinite. We're a great mystery. I believe we have the capacity to get through this. The problem is we don't have the will.

"I address my work to people who know that any event can be the subject of reflection. And coming up against my work, having it press all those deeply conditioned buttons, that can be a subject of reflection. I know there are people who are ready for that kind of experience. They're not in the majority, but I know they are there."

—November 1998

SHELL GAME
T. S. Eliot's Crustacean Problem

IN "THE LOVE SONG OF J. ALFRED PRUFROCK," the young T. S. Eliot famously wrote: "I should have been a pair of ragged claws/Scuttling across the floors of silent seas." But do these claws belong to a lobster or a crab? Or neither?

This spring, a long-overdue literary debate on this question finally took place. In his recent, heavily annotated edition of Eliot juvenilia, *Inventions of the March Hare*, the Boston University English professor Christopher Ricks opted for the crab reading. But Richard Poirier begged to differ. Reviewing Ricks's volume in *The New Republic*, the eminent literary critic (and New England native) noted that "crabs are endowed only with rudimentary claws, when they have them at all," and concluded that "these are most likely the claws specifically of a Maine lobster." He also took issue with the relevance and chronology of Ricks's annotations.

Ricks was not about to let Poirier's challenge go unanswered. "Like many other people," he replied in a letter to *TNR*, "I find 'scuttling' to be particularly evocative of a crab—lobsters don't much go in for scuttling." More pointedly, he accused Poirier of "willingly ignoring or distorting the plain evidence that plenty of readers before me here have seen a crab in their mind's eye."

Clearly, the matter needs further clarification. Accordingly,

Lingua Franca asked a number of critics and scholars for their thoughts.

LOUIS MENAND, *professor of English at the CUNY Graduate Center*: "Definitely lobster. The correct association is with the following sentence in the chapter on Gérard de Nerval in Arthur Symons's *The Symbolist Movement in Literature*, Eliot's introduction to the French poets: 'One day, he was found in the Palais-Royal, leading a lobster at the end of a blue ribbon (because, he said, it does not bark, and knows the secrets of the sea).' (This was too bizarre even for the French: Nerval was promptly institutionalized.)

"The famous black melancholy of Nerval was one of the moods Eliot clearly set out to reproduce in his poem, for he ends it with an extended riff on a line from Nerval's sonnet 'El Desdichado': 'J'ai rêvé dans la grotte où nage la sirène.' (Eliot appropriated another line outright from the same poem ten years later for the cadenza in *The Waste Land*: 'Le Prince d'Aquitaine à la tour abolie.') The romantic identification in Symons's anecdote of the poet with the lobster—the creature from another element being paraded unhappily about on a leash—must have been too delicious for Eliot not to try to work into his poem.

"Crab claws are too prehensile anyway for the sexual misery 'Prufrock' means to evoke and not nearly funny enough. Lobster claws (and note that Eliot names only claws: do not synecdochize him too quickly!) are a witty variation on Tennyson's super-eroticized hands in *In Memoriam*: swollen with longing but clumsy and vaguely mutant, desiring but undesired. Why would we want to give all these associations up for an everyday trope like a crab?"

CLAUDE RAWSON, *professor of English at Yale University*: "I think it's almost certain that Eliot was thinking of a crab. After all, the poem invokes Prince Hamlet, who once spun a crab metaphor of his own:

'For you yourself, sir, should be as old as I am—if, like a crab, you could go backward.' Furthermore, the crab is so much a twentieth-century image of self-disgust: it's the animal in Sartre's *La Nausée* and a kind of emotional lingua franca for a certain sense of horror and self-abasement. If you look at the twentieth-century imagination, crabs are what comes to mind."

MARJORIE PERLOFF, *professor of English at Stanford University*: "I've always thought it was a crab: I think there Ricks is right. This debate is a symptom of the fight over Eliot between the British and the Americans. I'm usually on the American side, because the British have a strange way of neglecting the American. But lobsters don't scuttle across the floors of silent seas do they? I'm very bad on crustaceans."

NICHOLAS JENKINS, *assistant professor of English at Harvard University*: "It's always good to see poetry inspiring passion, even if the passion here seems as much for the academic equivalent of arm wrestling or distance spitting as literary hermeneutics. In other circumstances, I feel sure that these two wonderful and athletic readers would clasp hands and agree that poetic language doesn't really operate at this literalistic level and that the fascination of these lines by Eliot has to do with the linguistic energies contained in words like 'ragged' and 'scuttling,' with the question of why 'across' here is infinitely richer than 'on' or 'over' would have been, with the relation of 'claws' to Prufrock's evident sexual obsession with fingers, sleeves, and arms and to Eliot's own lifelong obsession with drowning and the unknowable nature of the undersea world. In some ways, it's extremely important for the reader to be capable, in Keats's phrase, of 'being in uncertainties . . . without reaching after fact,' of *not* getting distracted, of *not* bothering with what mysterious submarine creature it is exactly or even to think that one can, or ought, to say, Is it a crab? Or a lobster? I'd call that a red herring."

HELEN VENDLER, *University Professor at Harvard University*: "It isn't either. You're not supposed to envision an animal, you're supposed to envision a scuttle. Poets don't give you more than you need to use to understand the feeling they want to convey."

—September 1997

INFIDELITY

Milan Kundera Is on the Outs With His Translators.
But Who's Betraying Whom?

CALEB CRAIN

IN *THE BOOK OF LAUGHTER AND FORGETTING*, the Czech-born novelist Milan Kundera neatly epitomized what makes translation impossible. His specimen was the Czech word *lítost*. On the one hand, he writes, *lítost* means too much: "It designates a feeling as infinite as an open accordion, a feeling that is the synthesis of many others: grief, sympathy, remorse, and an indefinable longing." No word in any other language casts a semantic penumbra with the same range and chiaroscuro. But on the other hand, *lítost* means too little. "Under certain circumstances," Kundera explains, *lítost* "can have a very narrow meaning, a meaning as definite, precise, and sharp as a well-honed cutting edge." And no word in any other language leaves a semantic footprint exactly the same size and shape.

Among his fans, Kundera's discussion of *lítost* is famous. However, if you buy *The Book of Laughter and Forgetting* today, you won't find the two sentences just quoted. They've been excised. They were in the Czech original and in the English translation by UCLA professor Michael Henry Heim that appeared in 1980. But in the recent translation by Aaron Asher, published in 1996, the sentences do not appear. Nor are they in the current French edition, which is the basis of Asher's work. And you won't find any Czech edition of *The Book of Laughter and Forgetting* in print at all.

"To cross out what one has written is a highly creative act," Kundera once told an interviewer. No doubt Kundera himself deleted the lines about *litost*, perhaps because he no longer stands by them. For a decade and a half, Kundera has crusaded against unfaithful translations, and in the course of that campaign his own generalizations about untranslatability may have begun to sound too much like a sloppy translator's excuse. "He began to be obsessed," explains Asher, Kundera's longtime American editor and new French-to-English translator. "Maybe that's too strong a word; maybe I shouldn't use it; but there are good obsessions."

The crusade has been effective, but at a cost. In America, Kundera's most famous novels have been reappearing in brand-new translations, which follow his Czech originals more closely in vocabulary, syntax, and even punctuation. But oddly enough, these new versions—all authorized by Kundera—are translated from the French rather than directly from Czech. They sometimes read awkwardly; in the circuitous journey from Czech to French to English, flavor and details have been lost, and mistakes have been introduced. Furthermore, while retranslating his novels, Kundera has also been rewriting them—sometimes tailoring them to his audience. As Allison Stanger, a political science professor at Middlebury College, noted in an open letter to Kundera in the *New England Review*, "Your Czech audience now reads one version of [*The Joke*] while your French- and English-language audiences read quite another."

Every author has the right to be finicky, even ornery, about his masterpieces. But a perfect translation may be a contradiction in terms. Is Kundera damaging his books and reputation for the sake of an unreachable ideal? Between Kundera and his translators, the air is thick with feelings of betrayal. *Litost*, roughly speaking, is the Czech word for "regret," and Kundera seems to be learning the hard way that you can't have translation without it.

MILAN KUNDERA rose to the world's attention hand in hand with the news of his homeland's political hard luck. Westerners sympathetic to the Prague Spring—the brief thaw in totalitarian Communism crushed in 1968—read Kundera all the more sympathetically because of it. The novelist seemed to be the world representative of "Czech Fate," to borrow the title of a fatalistic essay he wrote shortly after the Russians invaded his country. That essay infuriated a young dissident named Václav Havel, and time proved Havel right: Kundera's moody pessimism made for bad politics. But it made for good novels. In the 1980s, *The Book of Laughter and Forgetting* and *The Unbearable Lightness of Being* became international best-sellers thanks to the dark gifts that, in Kundera's opinion, the Czechs' political destiny had bestowed on them—a melancholy thoughtfulness, a taste for existential paradox, and a talent for sexual libertinage.

But despite the push that political history gave him, Kundera has always stoutly defended his novels from politics per se. During the Cold War, he evenhandedly loathed both his Communist censors and the Westerners who saw him as a dissident. "Spare me your Stalinism, please," he snapped in 1980 at a TV panelist who suggested that his first novel was a critique of Soviet totalitarianism, "*The Joke* is a love story."

If nothing else, Kundera's experience of Communism taught him that literary stubbornness pays off. In December 1965, Kundera had submitted to his Prague publisher the manuscript of *The Joke*. In the novel, a young man mails his girlfriend a postcard containing ironic praise of Trotsky; failing to appreciate the young man's sense of humor, the Stalinist authorities who intercept the postcard ruin his life.

Throughout the following year, censors summoned Kundera to their offices to request changes in the novel. As Kundera steadfastly refused, the censors became meeker and meeker, until finally their objections vanished altogether. In 1967, *The Joke* was published untouched, just as Kundera wanted it. Three editions quickly sold out—120,000 copies, in a country of only fifteen million people. Kundera launched his career as a novelist with a triumph over editorial meddling.

That triumph was short-lived. In August 1968, Russian military force ended the Czech experiment in "socialism with a human face."

Paradoxically, however, the capitalist West was the first to insult the integrity of Kundera's novels. In 1969, while still in Prague, Kundera received the British edition of *The Joke*. Chapters had been shortened, shuffled, and deleted altogether. "I was appalled," Kundera later remembered. In a scorching letter to *The Times Literary Supplement*, he denounced his British publisher for having "merely considered my text as a free basis for bizarre inventions of manipulators."

Soon after, as Moscow directed the "normalization" of Czech culture, Kundera lost his job teaching at a film school, and his books were pulled from libraries and stores in Czechoslovakia. It would be a decade before Kundera was at liberty, economically as well as politically, to take his translations personally in hand. But the seeds had been sown: Kundera had won an early victory over editorial tampering and witnessed outrageous infidelities in the translation of his first novel. When at last Kundera was able to examine his translations closely, he would not be inclined to compromise.

IN 1975, Kundera left his homeland and took up residence in France, where he has lived ever since. Four years later, a shock revived Kundera's anxiety about translation. During an interview for the Italian newspaper *Corriere della Sera*, Alain Finkielkraut asked Kundera why his recent novels had moved away from the "florid and baroque" style of *The Joke*.

Kundera had no idea what Finkielkraut was talking about. In Czech, Kundera has always been distinguished by his tempered, almost neutral prose style—a difficult achievement in that language. Thanks to the Counter-Reformation, the gap between spoken and written Czech is wider than in most other languages. In 1621, the Czech-speaking nobles, largely Protestant, were decimated; the Catholic Church labeled almost all books in Czech heretical; and for two centuries, Czech survived as a language spoken mostly by peasants and the urban lower class. Rip van Winkle slept for only one generation; written Czech slept for six or seven. When it was self-consciously resuscitated, in the early nineteenth century, it sounded a bit medieval, and that formality has not yet mellowed. Writers like Jaroslav Hašek, Bohumil Hrabal, and Josef Škvorecký have taken literary advantage of the contrast between written and spoken Czech by reveling in dialect and slang. Kundera, however, has eschewed low and high for a careful middle path. His style is relaxed but always correct, somewhat like a medical manual for home use.

The night after his interview with Finkielkraut, Kundera read Marcel Aymonin's French translation of *The Joke* for the first time. On top of Kundera's deliberately restrained prose, Aymonin had layered *un beau style*, the way decadents used to drill jewels into living turtles' shells for ornament. Where Kundera had written "The sky was blue," Aymonin had translated "Under a sky of periwinkle, October hoisted its showy shield." Kundera was furious. "Rage seized me," he later recalled. Spurred by that rage, Kundera revised the French translation, with the help of the author Claude Courtot. A more faithful French edition appeared in 1980. The rage also triggered a cascade of retranslations of *The Joke* in other languages—English (1982), Spanish (1984), Italian and Portuguese (1986), German (1987), and Dutch (1988)—as Kundera took advantage of his growing prestige to switch to more attentive publishers.

In the United States, meanwhile, Kundera seemed to be having better luck. The first American to translate a book of his was Peter Kussi. (I studied Czech with Kussi at Columbia.) Kundera himself had solicited Kussi's help, through Antonín Liehm, a mutual friend who had edited the journal *Literární Noviny* during the Prague Spring. Kussi's 1974 translation of Kundera's novel *Life Is Elsewhere* was nominated for a National Book Award.

Pleased with Kussi's work, Kundera requested that Kussi also translate his *Farewell Waltz*, which appeared under the title *The Farewell Party* in 1976. And in the late 1970s, Kussi translated a couple of new short stories by Kundera. At the time, no one—not even Kundera—realized the stories would eventually fit together into the novel *The Book of Laughter and Forgetting*. Kussi's version of "The Cap of Clementis" appeared in *The New Yorker* in May 1979. Shortly thereafter, Knopf refused to allow Kussi to continue as Kundera's translator. "This parting I ascribe to the machinations of editors," Kussi says today. Kundera himself has written that Knopf's "reasons [were] obscure to me" and that at the time Kussi "had all my confidence." One gets the impression there was confusion on all sides but no hard feelings between translator and author.

Luckily for Kundera, Knopf replaced Kussi with a translator just as devoted and skillful, UCLA's Michael Henry Heim. Years earlier, Heim had translated for a scholarly journal a chapter from *The Joke* that had been gutted from the British translation. Kundera was "deeply touched by this noble gesture of solidarity with mistreated, humiliated literature," and at first he thought as highly of his new translator as he had of Kussi. In Heim's 1980 translation, *The Book of Laughter and Forgetting* was a literary and commercial success. Heim's clean, fluent style appeared to be the perfect vehicle for Kundera's sparely told, interlocking stories of sexual and political disillusionment.

The concord would not last. By this point, a new figure had entered the story—a high-profile American editor named Aaron Asher. Perhaps Kundera would eventually have fallen out with Heim in any case. But, as Kundera's editor, Asher was closely involved with their earliest disagreements. "He is the mystery man," the Smith College professor Maria Němcová Banerjee says when Asher's name comes up. Asher commissioned Banerjee to write *Terminal Paradox*, her study of Kundera's novels, and he has done good turns for many of the other figures in the Kundera saga as well. But over the years, while Kundera has become more reclusive—he stopped talking to journalists in 1985—Asher has become more and more the author's intimate.

Asher's privileged access has aroused curiosity and suspicion, as has his metamorphosis from Kundera's editor into his translator. He has become something of a lightning rod for anger about Kundera's highhandedness. "I'm behind the eight ball," says Asher. He insists his goal throughout has been to ensure more faithful translations for Kundera, and he is unhappy about "having to defend something that needs no defense." To dispel some of the mystery surrounding his relationship with Kundera, Asher offers his own account.

Since the early 1970s, Asher had been hearing about Kundera from Philip Roth, whose books Asher edited. Another Asher author, Carlos Fuentes, finally introduced him to Kundera in 1979. Kundera was eager for an American publisher who would accommodate his scrupulous attention to translations, and Asher soon lured him to Harper & Row. Heim was asked to continue as Kundera's translator. "I admired Heim's translation of *The Book of Laughter and Forgetting*," Asher says now. He commissioned from Heim a brand-new translation of *The Joke*, as well as translations of a new manuscript (*The Unbearable Lightness of Being*) and an older play (*Jacques and His Master*). As Asher himself admits, these commissions would turn out to be something of an irony in light of later events.

Trouble started in the mid-1980s, when Kundera began to look over Heim's working translation of *The Unbearable Lightness of Being*. "Kundera's English had gotten good enough for him to express doubts to me," Asher says. According to Asher, Kundera flagged passages that struck him as problematic and asked for Asher's opinion. Revising the translation was "very difficult," Asher remembers, in part because fax machines were not yet common. But editor and author worked over the proofs for months—Kundera writing in French, Asher replying in English. "What irksome months they were!" Kundera told an interviewer shortly afterward.

It was Asher's first experience working so closely with Kundera's prose—a collaboration that would soon deepen. Nonetheless, Asher insists, the result "wasn't a retranslation by any means. *The Unbearable Lightness of Being* is Heim's translation; it has his signature on it."

Heim recalls the process of revising *The Unbearable Lightness of Being* somewhat differently. "I had quite an exchange of letters with Kundera," Heim explains, "but as the correspondence was in Czech, Asher was out of the loop." According to Heim, the back-and-forth between translator and author was "perfectly amiable." Some points Heim conceded, and on others he stood his ground.

At least publicly, there was as yet no sign of a rift.

EVEN KUNDERA has wondered: "An undue obsession with translations? I can't say." In his own defense, he has pointed out that for nearly two decades Czechs formed only a hundredth or a thousandth of his readership. "My books lived their lives as translations; as translations they were read, criticized, judged, accepted or rejected. I was unable not to care about translation."

Attentive, however, is not the same as implacable. In Kundera's case, an exile's natural concern has been aggravated by a philosophy of translation that is unusually hard-line.

Traditionally, the translator has been caught, like the runner in a game of pickle, between fidelity and license. Neither base is safe. If he is strictly faithful to the original text's linguistic structure, the result may be choppy, if not incomprehensible. But if he freely recasts the original text's structure in order to convey its meaning clearly, he risks losing the linguistic details that make it distinctive as a work of literature. As one Italian proverb puts it, "The pretty ones are never faithful, and the faithful ones are never pretty."

In "The Task of the Translator," Walter Benjamin famously resolves this conundrum with an extreme choice: fidelity, at the expense of elegance and meaning. Choppiness is good, Benjamin asserts, because it indicates that the translator has not smoothed away the details that distinguish the original from the target language—and from the pure language they both aspire to become. Benjamin's theory of translation soars beautifully into the empyrean, but it's not entirely practical. Though he advocates "a literal rendering of the syntax" of the original, Benjamin acknowledges that his strategy is "a direct threat to comprehensibility."

Nonetheless, Kundera has adopted something like Benjamin's radical fidelity (shorn, however, of the Romantic notion of "pure language"). "O ye translators, do not sodonymize us!" he writes in an essay that excoriates French translators of Kafka for showing off their synonymicons. Like Benjamin, Kundera eggs his translators even to solecism. "For a translator, the supreme authority should be the *author's personal style*," Kundera writes in *Testaments Betrayed* (1993). "But most translators obey another authority: that of the *conventional version* of 'good French' (or good German, good English, etc.)." It exasperates Kundera to hear a translation praised for its "flow." He cherishes even the idiosyncrasies of his punctuation and has boasted that he "once left a publisher for the sole reason that he tried to change my semicolons to periods."

In less polemical moments, Kundera has conceded that no translation can be absolutely faithful. He insists, however, that a translator unafraid of odd-sounding language will not only render the author's style and thinking more accurately but also enrich the target language.

This rigid fealty is not the norm—at least not according to translators and scholars of translation. "To be too close to the original, as Kundera wants his translators to be, undermines the English poetics of the text and works against, rather than in favor of, the translation," says the University of British Columbia's Peter Petro, who edited *Critical Essays on Milan Kundera* and is himself a Slovak-English translator. In the opinion of Robert Wechsler, whose publishing house, Catbird Press, has exposed American readers to lesser-known Czech authors such as Vladimír Páral and Jáchym Topol, Kundera "should be seen as an extremist."

IN 1988, Daniel Day-Lewis and Juliette Binoche starred in Philip Kaufman's movie version of *The Unbearable Lightness of Being*. "Not my film," Kundera grumbled in *Le Nouvel Observateur*, complaining of the "doleful monotony of film orgasms." But the movie pushed Kundera's international reputation to its peak. That year, Kundera finished his seventh book of fiction, *Immortality*—the last he would write in Czech—and, thanks to his movie-enhanced clout, he was in a position to dictate terms. Returning to his earlier translator was one priority. "He wanted Kussi," recalls Asher, who had moved from Harper & Row to Grove Press. For the first time in his translation career, Kussi was well paid—"very well paid," he admits. To ensure that the translation met Kundera's standards, author and translator agreed that as soon as Kussi had finished his draft, he would bring it to Paris for consultation. Once the two men agreed on a final version, "that would pretty much be it," says Kussi.

"But that *wasn't* it," Kussi continues. "I found myself in a very, very unpleasant situation." Changes began to appear in the manuscript after Kundera had signed off on it, and Kussi could not figure out who was responsible. Concerned, he wrote repeatedly to Kundera but received no answer. He fought to restore as much of his translation as he could, but many changes appeared in the final, printed version without his approval or any word from Kundera. Despite this confusion, Kundera's novel and Kussi's translation jointly won a prize from the British newspaper *The Independent* in 1991.

Kussi's frustrations were minor compared with the blow that Kundera was about to deal Heim. In 1990, Asher returned to Harper & Row, which had been rechristened HarperCollins, and began acquiring the paperback rights to all of Kundera's earlier novels. When Asher suggested a paperback rerelease of Heim's earlier translation of *The Joke*, Kundera hesitated. In 1982, Kundera had trusted Heim's work—in fact, he had praised it as "the first valid and authentic version of a book that tells of rape and has itself so often been violated"—but now he was "gripped by suspicion." Sure enough, upon scrutiny Heim's translation struck Kundera as "not my text." Where he disapproved of Heim's rendering, Kundera laboriously patched in turns of phrase from the earlier, reviled British translation or inserted his own "word-for-word translations either in English or in French." Asher collated Kundera's changes to create a brand-new edition—the fifth in English—released under Aaron Asher's personal imprint at HarperCollins in 1992.

"I offered to send Heim the revised version," Asher says today. "Most of it is still Heim's." Trust, however, had broken down. Heim refused to allow his name on the book. "I had not been consulted about the changes," Heim writes by e-mail, "and therefore could not lend my name to them." The book was published without any translator listed at all.

There was, however, an author's note. It told the story of an author

betrayed by his translators over and over again. With a touch of melodrama, Kundera portrayed Heim as having earned Kundera's trust
only because he was the most slippery kind of traitor: the kind who
means well. "I was all the more unhappy," Kundera wrote, "because I
did not believe that it was a matter of incompetence on the translator's part, or of carelessness or ill will: no; in good conscience he
produced the kind of translation that one might call *translation-
adaptation*. Is this the current, normal practice? It's possible. But unacceptable. Unacceptable to me."

As a personal attack on a translator admitted to be working in
good faith, Kundera's note was virtually unprecedented. Heim is
probably one of the few translators whose reputation could have survived it. His work has been recognized by the American Literary
Translators Association; his translations of Danilo Kiš and Bohumil
Hrabal have been widely acclaimed; and he is currently at work on a
new Günter Grass novel, *My Century*, due out this fall. When Heim is
asked today about his quarrel with Kundera, he warns that it is "not
my favorite topic." He answers a reporter's questions about dates and
facts, but politely declines to elaborate. "I stand by the work I did," he
says. Last December, at a San Francisco Slavicists' conference where
translations of Kundera were discussed, Heim said only that he was
happy to have had the opportunity to translate the best of Kundera's
novels.

In private, however, Heim has admitted that he was upset. "Heim
said to me, 'I don't really want to talk about it; I was hurt,' " says
Banerjee, who for her part has "always liked Heim's translations." The
tight-knit world of translators is not happy about how Heim was
treated. "I am with Michael Heim on this," says Petro. "An author
can say whatever he wants, but he is rarely so strong in the target language as to be the judge himself. One has to have a respect for the
translator, after all." Wechsler thinks Kundera has been "sort of a
bully." Kussi calls it "questionable or outright wrongheaded" of Kundera to "attack his translators in public."

"He's consistently been raising his translators to the sky, then becoming disillusioned with them," notes Kussi, whose experience par-

allels Heim's. Over the years, he recalls, "Kundera had treated me very well." Kussi had been the author's guest in Paris and on Belle-Ile, off the Brittany coast, and when Kussi wanted to write an essay on the author, Kundera had cooperated. Kundera and Kussi had worked happily together updating Kussi's version of *Life Is Elsewhere*; in the preface of the resulting 1986 edition, Kundera had dubbed Kussi "a true artist among translators." "I benefited on balance," Kussi readily admits. But the late changes to his translation of *Immortality* had upset Kussi, and in the mid-1990s it nonplussed him to receive a cool, businesslike letter from Kundera, asking if he would be willing to revise *Farewell Waltz*. "It was almost as if he was hoping I would say no," Kussi says. He did not revise his old translation. As it happens, Kundera found a way—a highly unusual way—to manage without him.

IN HIS 1986 BOOK *The Art of the Novel*, Kundera recalls with horror meeting a translator who knew no Czech. When asked how he had translated Kundera's first novel, the man took a picture of Kundera out of his wallet and replied, "With my heart." As Kundera wryly observes, "Of course, it turned out to be much simpler: He had worked from the French rewrite."

But nowadays Kundera is demanding that his novels be translated from the French rewrite rather than from the Czech original. How did it come to this?

Part of the answer lies in Kundera's growing pride in his identity as a French citizen. The Communists stripped him of his Czech citizenship in 1979, and he was "moved and filled with gratitude" by France's gift of citizenship two years later. In 1984, his French improved by nearly a decade of living in France, Kundera began "the detailed revision of all my French translations." In the end, the revisions would cost him more than two years and "as much energy as the writing of two new books." But at long last, in 1987, he triumphantly instructed Gallimard to print at the back of each revised French volume a notice declaring that the new translations had "the same authenticity value as the Czech text" ("la même valeur d'authenticité que le texte tchèque"). In the mid-1980s, furthermore, Kundera began writing his nonfiction in French rather than Czech. Not Kundera's books but Kundera himself seemed to be undergoing translation. And why not? At the time, the Iron Curtain looked permanent.

In the early 1990s, HarperCollins proposed paperback reissues of four of Kundera's Czech-written books. Suspicious of the old English translations, proud of his French editions, and estranged from both of his longtime Czech-to-English translators, the author considered an unorthodox alternative: instead of correcting the old translations, why not commission brand-new translations from the French? "He asked me to take a look," says Asher, "and asked some other people to take a look. The upshot was that, yes, according to his principles, if not everybody else's, these books would be closer to what he had originally written if they were retranslated." Asher's wife, Linda, had been elegantly and accurately translating Kundera's French nonfiction since 1984, but she was busy with Kundera's essay collection *Testaments Betrayed*. According to Asher, an impatient Kundera asked him, "Why don't you do it? Your French is good enough. You know exactly what I need." Asher, who had recently left HarperCollins to go freelance, accepted.

Today, the Ashers together hold the Kundera franchise. In addition to revising *The Joke*, Aaron has retranslated from the French *The Book of Laughter and Forgetting* (1996), *Farewell Waltz* (1998), and *Life Is Elsewhere* (due out in 2000). A revised, but not retranslated, *Laughable Loves* will appear this fall. In addition to translating Kundera's essay collections *The Art of the Novel* and *Testaments Betrayed*, Linda has translated Kundera's new novels, *Slowness* (1996) and *Identity* (1998), both of which Kundera composed in French.

AS EVERY TRANSLATOR KNOWS, it is easy to pick apart a translation. It is easy to find an awkward passage that never finished its journey through translatorese and into English, or a knotty passage that was furtively omitted, or a plain old-fashioned mistake. With that caveat in mind, one might still consider the question looming over this debate: Are the new translations of Kundera better?

The answer depends, in part, on what you are looking for. Asher stresses that a difference in philosophy is at the heart of Kundera's break with his American translators. "Heim and Kussi are very good translators," he says, but "they've allowed themselves some latitude. They didn't do bad translations; their intentions weren't wicked. But a translator is comparable to a performer, a pianist, not the composer. If a translator thinks he's a composer, he should get out of the concert hall."

"There are some passages in these translations that sound foreign," Asher admits of his own work. "I like the foreignness." Under a theory of translation like Kundera's, even stilted prose may be an asset.

Michelle Woods, a graduate student at Trinity College, Dublin, has studied the different editions of *The Joke*. In her opinion, the style of the 1992 Asher-Kundera edition conforms, for good or ill, to Kundera's rigorous translation philosophy; to Woods, the new *Joke* sounds "less familiar, less idiomatic" than Heim's 1982 version. My own impression is that, with a few exceptions, the difference between the two is not dramatic. Paradoxically, the 1992 *Joke* may be an improvement because its improvements are so modest: it is largely Heim's text, with intermittent fixes.

Aaron Asher's translations of Kundera from the French, however, are something else entirely. As Benjamin wrote, "Translations . . . prove to be untranslatable not because of any inherent difficulty, but because of the looseness with which meaning attaches to them." Kundera has admired Leoš Janáček's attempt to capture the nuances of speech with musical notation, and he has appreciated Hemingway's delicate ear for the rhythms of dialogue. Since Kundera knows that such subtle achievements are fragile, it is hard to understand why he imagines that his own style can survive a double translation. Like the children's game of telephone, the process amplifies garbling.

Asher's fidelity to the punctuation and arrangement of clauses in the original Czech is uncanny, given that he does not know that language; and at times, it is ingenious, attesting to Kundera's close involvement and Asher's hard labor. Furthermore, to Asher's credit, there are a number of spots in the new *Book of Laughter and Forgetting* where he has corrected Heim's literary "improvements." For example, Asher succeeds in restoring an unusual simile ("all the years of her marriage landed on her like a heavy sack") that Heim had flattened into a cliché ("like a ton of bricks"). Kussi is a more cautious translator than Heim. Asher, however, does restore a maple that had turned into an alder in Kussi's *Farewell Waltz*.

But my own sense is that the flaws in the French-to-English retranslations far outweigh their merits. Take Asher and Kundera's disregard for "flow." It may be principled, but at times it's a serious impediment to the reader. "Why don't I go (and never will go) and inform on him?" Olga wonders to her own and the reader's bafflement in Asher's *Farewell Waltz*. Or, earlier in that book: "Olga thought him ridiculously theatrical, and she was delighted to see him go and that, finally, she would soon be alone with Jakub." These sentences may be faithful to Kundera's syntax, but they are hostile to the reader.

Furthermore, as an inexperienced translator, Aaron Asher makes outright mistakes. He needlessly creates verb-tense chaos by translating "Voici deux mois qu'ils avaient fait connaissance" as "It is two months since they met." Kussi's "They had met two months earlier" does the trick just fine. In *The Book of Laughter and Forgetting*, when a Communist dictator writes a letter to the musician Karel Gott (renamed Karel Klos in the new edition), Asher mistranslates the dictator's reassuring "nous ne vous en voulons pas" as "we want nothing from you." In fact, the sentence contains a common French idiom meaning "we are not angry with you."

With misplaced loyalty, Asher has also reproduced awkward turns of phrase that were only translator's expedients in French and never appeared in the original Czech. For example, in Asher's *Farewell Waltz*, Růžena complains of her lover Klíma that after their one-night stand "he had shown no sign of life." That's a doggedly faithful rendering of the French "il n'avait pas donné signe de vie"; in English, the expression usually describes the comatose rather than the merely inattentive. The Czech text does not justify the blunder: "se neohlasil ani slůvkem" (literally, "he did not announce himself by even a small word"). Similarly, in Asher's *Book of Laughter and Forgetting*, Edwige tells her lover, "I'm making pee," because in French that's what one does—*on fait pipi*. In English and in Czech, however, urination takes place as a verb, and Heim's "I'm in here peeing" is much closer to the efficient Czech *čurám*.

In other spots, Asher has introduced non sequiturs because he has separately translated two sentences with word-for-word fidelity but failed to take into account that, within their new English context, the sentences must accommodate each other. "I wonder . . . which of your distant ancestors had a big nose," a father muses to his wife in Asher's *Farewell Waltz* while staring at their toddler son, and then adds, "Isn't that right?" In Kussi's version, the father asks, "Who knows? Maybe one of your distant ancestors sported a long schnozzle," and continues, more logically, "Isn't that possible?"

At the end of the day, I also miss Heim's and Kussi's greater command of literary style. "Everyone gave way to disheartenment" is no more accurate than Kussi's "Everyone suddenly felt very let down," but it is much less felicitous. Heim's *Book of Laughter and Forgetting* compares the lonely, isolated Tamina to a walled-in "patch of grass," which is poignant. But Asher describes her as "a bit of lawn," which sounds like something that needs to be mowed. A man described in Kussi's English as a "courier of disaster" becomes in Asher's a "mailman of misfortune."

In *Testaments Betrayed*, Kundera discussed Stravinsky's attempt late in life to make authorized recordings of himself playing and conducting his own music. The attempt is somewhat analogous to Kundera's intervention in his own translations, and in Kundera's case, as in Stravinsky's, "this wish to take on the role of performer himself often provoked an irritated response." A few irritated translators may be a small price to pay for artistic integrity. And in fact the translators in question have already dusted themselves off and moved on. But Kundera's tight control is not serving his work. Like a jealous husband trying to enforce his wife's love, Kundera faces an unpleasant realization: commanding obedience may not bring his texts any closer to him.

—October 1999

Contributors

TED ANTON is the author of *Eros, Magic, and the Murder of Professor Culianu* and *Bold Science: Seven Scientists Who Are Changing Our World*. He is a professor of English at DePaul University. "The Killing of Professor Culianu" was nominated for a National Magazine Award in reporting in 1993.

ROBERT S. BOYNTON directs the graduate magazine program in New York University's Department of Journalism. His writings have appeared in *The New Yorker, The Atlantic Monthly, The New York Times Magazine, The Nation,* and other publications.

CALEB CRAIN is the author of *American Sympathy: Men, Friendship, and Literature in the New Nation*. He was a senior editor and contributing writer for *Lingua Franca*. His writings have also appeared in *The New York Times Book Review, The New Republic, The Nation,* and other publications.

EMILY EAKIN is a culture reporter for *The New York Times*. She was a senior editor and deputy editor of *Lingua Franca* from 1996 to 1999.

HELEN EPSTEIN has written on medicine and science for *The New York Review of Books, Granta, New Scientist,* and other publications. Her *New York Review of Books* essay on AIDS in South Africa appears in *The Best American Science Writing 2001*.

HILLARY FREY is the assistant literary editor of *The Nation*. She was the managing editor of *Lingua Franca* in 1999 and 2000. Her writings have appeared in *The Nation, The New York Times, The Village Voice, In These Times,* and other publications.

CONTRIBUTORS

JACK HITT is a contributing writer at *The New York Times Magazine* and *Harper's*, and a former contributing editor of *Lingua Franca*.

JIM HOLT contributed the Hypotheses column to *Lingua Franca* from 1997 to 2001. He writes on mathematics, science, and philosophy for *The Wall Street Journal*, *The New York Review of Books*, and other publications.

G. KINDROW is the pseudonym of a professor at a large midwestern university.

FRANK LENTRICCHIA teaches literature at Duke University. He is the author most recently of a novel, *Lucchesi and the Whale*.

LARISSA MACFARQUHAR is a staff writer at *The New Yorker*. She was a senior editor of *Lingua Franca* from 1993 to 1994.

COLIN MCGINN is a professor of philosophy at Rutgers University. He is the author of *The Making of a Philosopher: My Journey Through Twentieth-Century Philosophy* and many other books.

SCOTT MCLEMEE is a reporter for *The Chronicle of Higher Education* and the editor of *C. L. R. James on the "Negro Question."* He is a former contributing editor of *Lingua Franca*. His writings have also appeared in *The New York Times*, *Newsday*, and other publications.

DANIEL MENDELSOHN is a lecturer in classics at Princeton University and a regular contributor to *The New York Review of Books* and many other publications. He is the author of *The Elusive Embrace: Desire and the Riddle of Identity* and of *Gender and the City in Euripides' Political Plays*. He is currently at work on a book about Archimedes for the Science Lives series and on a new translation of the complete works of C. P. Cavafy, to be published by Knopf in 2003.

JAMES MILLER is a professor of political science and director of liberal studies at the New School University and the editor of *Daedalus*. His books include *"Democracy Is in the Streets," The Passion of Michel Foucault*, and, most recently, *Flowers in the Dustbin: The Rise of Rock and Roll, 1947–1977*.

EMILY NUSSBAUM is a writer based in New York and a former editor of *Nerve*. She was a contributing editor of *Lingua Franca*. She is a contributor to *The New York Times Magazine* and other publications.

RICK PERLSTEIN is the author of *Before the Storm: Barry Goldwater and the Unmaking of the American Consensus*. He was an assistant editor and associate editor of *Lingua Franca*.

EYAL PRESS is at work on a book about the struggle over abortion in Buffalo, New York. He is a former contributing editor of *Lingua Franca* and regular contributor to *The Nation, The American Prospect, The New York Times Magazine*, and other publications.

JAMES RYERSON is a senior editor of *Legal Affairs*. He was previously a senior editor of *Lingua Franca* and editor of *Feed*. His writing has appeared in *The New York Times Book Review, The Washington Post Book World*, and other publications.

MICHAEL SCHUDSON is a professor of communication and an adjunct professor of sociology at the University of California, San Diego. He is the author of *The Good Citizen* and many other books. A different version of "Paper Tigers" appeared in *From Sociology to Cultural Studies*, edited by Elizabeth Long.

JENNIFER SCHUESSLER is an assistant editor of *The New York Review of Books*. Her writings have appeared in *The New York Times, The Washington Post, The American Scholar*, and other publications.

JAMES SCHWARTZ is a writer based in Brookline, Massachusetts. His article "Death of an Altruist," which appeared in the July/August 2000 issue of *Lingua Franca*, was chosen for inclusion in *The Best American Science Writing 2001*. He is currently at work on a book about the development of the modern theory of heredity.

LAURA SECOR is the deputy editor of *The American Prospect*, and former senior editor and managing editor of *Lingua Franca*. Her writing has appeared in *The New York Times, Los Angeles Times, The Nation, Dissent*, and other publications.

RUTH SHALIT is a New York–based writer and former associate editor at *The New Republic*. Her work has recently appeared in *The Wall Street Journal*, *Details*, and *Salon.com*.

ADAM SHATZ writes about culture and politics for *The New York Times* and other publications. He was a contributing editor of *Lingua Franca*.

CHRISTOPHER SHEA is a Washington, D.C.–based writer. He is a former contributing writer of *Lingua Franca* and former reporter for *The Chronicle of Higher Education*. His work has appeared in *The Washington Post Magazine*, *Preservation*, and other publications.

SCOTT SHERMAN is a contributing editor to the *Columbia Journalism Review*. He is a former contributing writer to *Lingua Franca*. He has contributed to *The Nation*, *Los Angeles Times*, and *Dissent*.

ALAN SOKAL is professor of physics at New York University. He is co-author with Roberto Fernandez and Jurg Frohlich of *Random Walks, Critical Phenomena, and Triviality in Quantum Field Theory*, and co-author with Jean Bricmont of *Fashionable Nonsense: Postmodern Intellectuals' Abuse of Science*.

JAMES SUROWIECKI is a staff writer at *The New Yorker*. His writing has appeared in *The New York Times Magazine*, *Wired*, *Fortune*, and other publications.

MARGARET TALBOT is a senior fellow at the New America Foundation. She is a contributing writer to *The New York Times Magazine*, a contributing editor to *The New Republic*, and the recipient of a Whiting Writer's Award in 1999. She was the editor and co-editor of *Lingua Franca* from 1991 to 1993.

MICHAEL S. WARDELL is the pseudonym of an assistant professor at a large midwestern university.

DANIEL ZALEWSKI is a story editor at *The New York Times Magazine*. He was associate editor and senior editor of *Lingua Franca* from 1994 to 1998.

Acknowledgments

THIS BOOK showcases the work of many authors; it owes its existence to an even larger cast of colleagues and friends. *Lingua Franca* itself is the product of Jeffrey Kittay's imagination and even audacity—I hope *Quick Studies* embodies his commitment to editorial excellence and intellectual illumination. Chris Calhoun and Lorin Stein had the wit to see that assembling this collection made good sense and the agility to bring it into existence with great ease. Lorin also improved the manuscript at every turn with his meticulous taste. For several years, Alissa Levin brought her visual intelligence to bear upon all aspects of *Lingua Franca*'s layout and design; it is both fitting and gratifying that she designed this book as well.

At *Lingua Franca*, I had the good fortune to work with a number of remarkable people. Anne Kinard, Carol E. Abrams, Patty Rosati, and especially Robin Hutson labored tirelessly to raise the magazine's external profile and internal morale. My predecessor Judith Shulevitz gave *Lingua Franca* much of its seriousness and vivacity. During my own time at the magazine, I was blessed with the company of exceptionally talented editors; indeed, those editors conceived and edited many of the pieces in this book. Among them were Inigo Thomas and Rick Perlstein; Daniel Zalewski, Emily Eakin, and A. O. Scott; Laura Secor, James Ryerson, Andrew Hearst, and Kate Julian. Ingrid Sterner untangled the writing, and Erika Wren uncovered the illustrations. Matthew Price and Jim Holt were of frequent assistance.

A number of others provided guidance and support as the book proceeded. I am thankful to John Plotz for his spontaneous generosity and wise counsel; so too to Liberty Aldrich, Jonathan Bolton, Lisa Hamilton, Ivan Kreilkamp, Alex Ross, and Andrew Weiss. My mother, Brenda Star, and my brother, Anthony Star, were characteristically discerning and kind.

I am grateful to Caleb Crain for his friendship, shrewd insights into the introduction, and scholarly knowledge of the *Lingua Franca* archives, and to Hillary Frey for all that, and much more.

Alexander Star

Index